Reinventing Democratic Socialism
for People Prosperity

Robert Corfe is an industrial publicist and political
scientist who has been active in politics and research for
many years. As a freelance journalist he has written
articles for a number of papers and magazines in this
country and abroad, and is the author of many socio-
economic booklets. After a long career in senior
management in industry, in 1987 he founded the
Campaign For Industry, a body committed to promoting
UK-based productivity but inevitably critical of the City
institutions. His many years of residence in Continental
Europe has given him a unique perspective of Britain's
industrial and political problems. He is currently setting
up the Socialist Business Values Association.

Reinventing Democratic Socialism

for People Prosperity

Robert Corfe

Arena Books

First published in 2000 by Arena Books
third impression 2001

Arena Books
6 Southgate Green
Bury St. Edmunds
1P33 2BL

ISBN 0-9538460-0-8

British Library Cataloguing in Publication Data.
A catalogue record for this book is available from
the British Library.

Dewey classification: 320.5'315

Printed & bound by Rowland Typesetting Ltd.,
Bury St. Edmunds, 1P32 6NU.

Cover design
by Jon Baxter

Typeset in
Times New Roman

Acknowledgements

This book has developed out of a paper, entitled, *Socialist Business Values: Myth or Reality*, originally presented to the Labour Finance and Industry Group, which was arranged for private circulation to its membership in 1999. Chapters 11-15 were first published in booklet form in January 1994 by Collindist Publications under the title, *Socialising Productive Capitalism*. A shortened version of Chapter 16 first appeared in the July 1993 issue of the *Certified Accountant*. Chapters 17-21 first appeared in the March-July/August 1993 issues of *Management Accounting*. Chapters 16-23 subsequently appeared in booklet form in February 1994, under the title, *The Crisis of Anglo-Saxon Capitalism*, with an introduction by Sir Peter Parker, published by Collindist Publications. Chapters 24-33 were first published in booklet form in November 1990 by Collindist Publications under the title, *Action For Prosperity*. Chapters 34-43 were first published in booklet form in April 1990 by Collindist Publications under the title, *The Priorities of Politics*. Information on Britain's imbalance of payments in tangibles in Appendix B, has been extracted from tables in the May 1999 issue of *Export Times*, and thanks are extended to the publishers for permission to reproduce same.

**

Preface

It is not known if Socialism still exists in any real sense. The Labour party is in government, and parties of the left are winning power throughout the industrialised world, and further afield. There is only one adjective describing the beliefs of those adhering to the Labour party, and indeed, to most movements of the left, and that is *Socialism*, but it is a word which is used with increasing circumspection by politicians responsible for its promotion.

The non-principled pragmatism of the Labour party, and other movements of the left elsewhere in the world, can be easily understood. It simply developed out of electoral necessity in achieving power. Old-style Socialism, with regard to both its image and content, had lost its appeal. This was a consequence of the transformation of society over the past sixty years, and the changing sociology of work. The doctrines of Socialism had been stymied by progress. It was unable to keep abreast of unanticipated changes, and its famous dialectic was unable to understand - let alone explain - the immense socio-economic developments of the present era.

Parliamentary movements of the left have everywhere reached a watershed, and at the moment of writing, there is no knowing as to their future. Politicians and statesmen are reliant on opinion polls in assessing the day-to-day mood of an electorate that has become more volatile and cynical than at any time in living memory. Political leadership is no longer a matter of maintaining established principles, but rather of spin-doctoring or clever public relations. But these are only interim measures until new concepts are devised in the light of change, so that issues may be comprehended and resolved for a better tomorrow.

In the present age it is the fickleness of negative voting which puts political parties in and out of power, but this is an unsatisfactory basis for the electioneering chances of a movement in reforming politics. This is because reforming movements are organs of change, and change can only be appealed to through positive patterns of thought. Conservatism, on the other hand, means preserving the status quo, and so the mentality of negative voting is more aligned to opposition to change. The Labour party is not merely discomfited by the lack of a New Socialist philosophy, but greatly endangered by its absence. The changing mood of the electorate is always fast, and always unexpected, and often inexplicable, and great giants are brought crashing down before they understand the cause.

The vulnerability of the Labour party stems from the following: it is wrought with internal dissent between Old and New Labour, it lacks any kind of theoretical base for promoting its beliefs; it is cynically perceived as an efficient electioneering machine bereft of principles; and it is supported by an electorate which made a choice between several unattractive alternatives. It is therefore subject to defeat through the slightest mood swing or whim of the electorate, precipitated through accident, unexpected event, or design.

The Labour party therefore needs to construct a sound theoretical base for conviction politics, in attracting and securing a substantial loyal following for a long-term future. This book has been written to fulfil such a function. And economic principles and ideas on the nature of capitalism must lie at the core of New Socialism, just as they were at the core of the Old. It is a long time since the nature of capitalism was debated by Labour party activists.

But the New Socialism will be very different from the Old. And so will its mood and anger. The cloth-capped proletariat and their collective values have gone forever - or form too small a minority to fight the great battles which lie ahead. The Socialism of the future will be fought by the classless middle-middle majority, and so the struggle will need to be tempered to the character of a constituency very different from that of the past.

As this book reveals, the issues to be fought for and against in the future, need be no less intense than the battles of the past, but they will be different. As the weapons of the Old Socialism are cast aside, a new language or terminology needs to be invented in forging the weapons for tomorrow. All this is to be achieved in updating thought and concepts to meet the new realities which have raced ahead of our ability to keep ahead of change.

Integrity must be put back into the nature of political struggle. People are tired and cynical of spin-doctoring and short-term pragmatism. They yearn again for meaningful principles and a sense of political direction, and for the ring of truth and intelligence in underlying ideas. In that way only lies a better future, and in that way lies the true path of democratic Socialism. In any event, New Labour cannot hope to thrive as a healthy organism until it has adopted a sound philosophy for a new epoch.

Robert Corfe
July 2000

CONTENTS

CONTENTS

CHAPTER 38
The Moral Bankruptcy of Our Financial System

CHAPTER 39
Social Prosperity Only Achievable Through Autonomy

CHAPTER 40
The True Foundations For Disinterested Politics

CHAPTER 41
The Underlying Grounds of Conflict In The Contemporary World

CONTENTS

CHAPTER 42
The Meaning of New Socialism

CHAPTER 43
Freedom Within The Integrated Community

PART VI
CONCLUSIONS

CHAPTER 44
The Responsible Society

***

PART I

Socialism In An Age of Change

"The globalisation of poverty in the late 20th century is unprecedented in world history. This poverty is not, however, the consequence of a 'scarcity' of human and material resources. Rather it is the result of a system of global oversupply predicated on unemployment and the worldwide minimisation of labour costs."

Michel Chossudovsky, *The Globalisation of Poverty*, Zed Books, 1998, p. 26.

The Socialism of tomorrow will entail a complete revaluation of values. This is necessitated by the transformation of society, for the supporters of New Socialism will be the classless middle-middle majority, and their ideals and view of the world is quite different from that of the proletariat of an earlier age. Socialism has always been concerned with majority interests, and so its sights need to be readjusted in appealing to a majority which differs from that of a generation ago.

At the same time Socialism must be concerned with that minority at the base of society. The ethics of Socialism are still concerned with justice as fairness, and with egalitarian values, and so New Socialism must embrace an ethos which is disinterested as regards social origins or other differences in the community.

But there is another and more significant factor for a changed value system for Socialism. It is argued in this book that the time has arrived for employees to take over the part-ownership and management of their employing enterprises in a direct or real sense. A first impression might convey that this amounts to Old Socialism of the far left. Far from it ! Co-determination and employee ownership arrangements, in both this country and abroad, have already brought educated knowledge workers in certain sectors of industry closer to the status of owners in a real sense. The eminent American guru of industrial management, Peter Drucker, has even gone so far as to maintain that, "the knowledge worker is both the true 'capitalist' in the knowledge society and dependent on his job. Collectively, the knowledge workers, the employed middle-class of today's society, own the means of production through pension funds, investment trusts, and so on."[1] The purpose of New Socialism must be to advance this process in the interests of both employees and the community in promoting greater efficiency.

If this is to be the course of the future, it can now be seen that New Socialism must identify and promote a set of Socialist business values, and this introduces an entirely new aspect into the nature of Socialism. In preparing such theoretical changes, and embodying them into the core system of Socialism, the following ten chapters comprising Part I of the book, are given over to considering the sociology of Socialism in a variety of situations. This is a necessary exercise before embarking on the economic principles of New Socialism; analysing the nature of contemporary capitalism; and describing the new terminology for the struggle which lies ahead.

There is much analysis and descriptive material in the following ten chapters which may seem far removed from ordinary political discussion, but in envisaging such changes as we have in reinventing democratic Socialism, there is the need to broaden the discussion across continents and time scales in considering the underlying wants of humanity. It is necessary to transcend the hum-drum issues of day-to-day policies, as discussed in Parliament or town halls, if sound and long-term principles are to emerge and strengthen the New Socialism for tomorrow.

---

[1] Peter F. Drucker, *The Age of Discontinuity,* Heinemann, 1969, p. 259.

CHAPTER 1
How Internationalism Serves The Self-Interest of Peoples

"The much-touted efficiency of the world trade system is a grotesque myth."

Richard Douthwaite, *Short Circuit*, Resurgence, 1996, p. 34.

1 - Socialism should be people-oriented rather than nation-oriented   2 - Interdependence of peoples greater today than ever before   3 - International ills of globalisation, malformed economic growth, and unfair lending terms   4 - Benign and malign modes of international investment   5 - Mainstream parties not ideologically geared to confronting international issues   6 - Injustice as the cause of instability and war

1   It is tempting to embark on a review of political first principles from the narrow viewpoint of a particular society. This is because the more immediate or daunting problems of any age are seen with greater intensity from such a perspective. It is a temptation which needs to be resisted, for such an approach too easily leads to a false impression of primary underlying socio-economic problems threatening the well-being and peace of all peoples.

The crisis of Socialism, both as embodying a set of principles and as a workable system of government, now necessitates its consideration from the radical aspect of first principles. Immense and unanticipated changes in society, economic structures, and the sociology of work, have cast doubt and confusion on every tenet of Socialist belief. Any meaningful discussion of Socialism needs therefore to begin with a consideration of humankind in general rather than of humankind in particular.

Out of necessity the true spirit of Socialism has always been international. This is because Socialism is not concerned with promoting the powerful vested interests of ruling financial elites, usually expressed in the ruthlessness of nation states or transnational corporations, but rather in the welfare of people themselves, irrespective of status, class, nationality, race, cultural background, religion, gender, etc. Socialism recognises the need for equality of opportunity and the principle of egalitarianism in achieving this welfare of people at large.

But because of the geographical division of humanity, Socialist movements are obliged to organise nationally, and furthermore, because they wish to address immediate problems within specific areas, they are bound to develop differing characteristics according to the varying conditions in which they struggle for a greater measure of justice.

1-2

But no such differing directions of development should lead to any diminution in the belief that the ultimate purpose of Socialism is the welfare and needs for equal rights of peoples everywhere on the globe. This is because the ethics of Socialism should be based on the Rawlsian hypothetical contract theory of the original position of equality. This entails that justice should be understood as fairness as if we were thrust into the world ignorant of the most socially significant facts about ourselves, e.g., class, race, social standing, etc. Only under such an assumed Veil of Ignorance can sufficient intellectual objectivity be achieved in conceiving the ideally just society.

Socialism which loses sight of its essential international ethos, or degenerates into nationalism in an exclusive or aggressive sense, contradicts its true purpose, sometimes transforming itself, in both thought and deed, into a directly opposing ideology. Such a situation was witnessed with the rise of different forms of fascism in the 1930s. This does not mean, of course, that true Socialists or Socialist movements in times of danger or war, may not be patriots of the first order, and neither does it mean that Socialists need not cherish or take pride in the cultural traditions or land of their environment. Such loyalty or love should be taken as a natural reflection of healthy integration into the community as a whole.

2   The significance of the international dimension of politics, irrespective of belief systems, is of greater importance today than at any period in previous history. It is a cliché to state we are part of a global village, but the interdependence of the world has now reached frightening proportions. The forces for good or evil, effecting the planet, may be triggered by events or conditions almost anywhere in the world. There are too many adverse factors, of which we are already fully aware, well beyond the reach of national, transnational, or other politically influential bodies. The response of political pundits and well-meaning nation states in the face of these factors is at best an outpouring of benevolent platitudes, unaccompanied by action, and at worst and usually - turning a blind eye under the fatalistic conclusion that nothing can be done.

Perhaps the greatest long-term threats to the welfare of peoples everywhere may be seen to stem from the following three tendencies: firstly, globalisation; secondly, the deterioration of the environment due to the destruction of the rainforests, and the release of noxious gases by industry, the internal combustion engine, and domestic fuel consumption; and thirdly, the promotion of economic growth accepted as a good in itself. The concept of growth, as understood by the economics establishment, is accepted as unquestioned dogma across the entire political spectrum, but a more critical approach to the current world situation would reveal the falsity of this doctrine. Not only has it led to waste on a massive scale, but to excessive abundance and scarcity,

1-3

the rape of the environment, and most significantly, to the economic polarisation of peoples, leading inevitably to disease, poverty and famine. In the words of Hans-Peter Martin and Harald Schumann, "in a global pincer movement, the new International of capital is turning whole countries and social orders upside down."[2]

The above three factors are interrelated, and all are promoted by the big corporations which in quoting the words of Theodore Roosevelt in another context, "stalk the world quietly with a big stick." Globalisation entails the untrammelled pursuit of financial market forces, not only unaccountable to national or democratic authority but even unaccountable to itself in the sense of its self-destroying tendency. It would be a false notion to perceive transnational organisations in the benevolent light of transferring jobs from the richer more industrialised countries to poorer areas of the world in a Robin Hood-like fashion. Likewise, the distant hope cherished by some Socialists that globalisation might work out all right in the end, in equalising industrial conditions throughout the world is again an optimistic picture stemming from a false understanding of the mechanics of this particular type of capitalism. In the words of David Korten, "as economic globalisation progresses, we find growing islands of great wealth in poor countries and growing seas of poverty in rich countries. The North and South distinction is now most meaningfully used to acknowledge the reality of a world divided by class lines more than by geography."[3]

3   The owners and controllers of globalisation are the impersonal anonymous financial forces of the international markets which work without planning or forethought , as millions of currency is transferred at the push of a button from one region of the world to another. The unchanging universal principle is the maximisation of investors' profits and the consequent depression of workers' wages. The criticism of profit in this context is not that investors place their capital in a particular productive enterprise in an identifiable location, for this would a blessed situation in recognising the proper and essential function of profit. The criticism is aimed at purely speculative financial activity divorced entirely from the productive and job-creating process of specific industrial plants.

Globalisation does not even necessarily advance innovative technology, for well-paid jobs in fully automated plants are often relocated from richer countries to poorer regions where intensive labour methods in slave-like conditions are judged to be more

---

[2] Hans-Peter Martin & Harald Schumann, *The Global Trap*, Zed Books, 1997, p. 7.

[3] David C. Korten, *When Corporations Rule The World*, Earthscan, 1996, p. 114.

1-3

profitable. In such instances the benefits of scientific progress - not to mention the advance of employees' rights and conditions - are put into reverse gear. Everywhere there is insecurity, and always the needs of long-term planning in maximising market share for the benefit of the community is sacrificed for the short-term demands of shareholders.

Meanwhile, the argument for economic growth (as interpreted by the economics establishment) is pursued as the self-fulfilling purpose of economic activity, even though it leads to untold waste; the despoliation of natural resources; and even to the contradiction of its stated purpose: viz., to the self-destruction of the economy itself. These ills we term malformed economic growth. The expansion of world trade, for example, is lauded as a major beneficiary to the peoples of the world in creating jobs and fulfilling consumer dreams. But to comprehend expansion in this light is clearly a nonsense. The criss-crossing of merchandise half way across the world to destinations where it is already grown, manufactured, or otherwise produced in sufficient quantity, is financially beneficial to traders and their investors, but often leads to hunger or starvation in the exporting countries; to job losses in the importing countries; to inflated costs of the merchandise itself; and to huge and unnecessary wastage of energy resources - in addition to pollution - in transportion by sea, air, truck and rail.

International bank lending or investment by the developed countries to the Third world and former East bloc European states, seen from the standpoint of promoting growth, has proved a disaster from every perspective, and most notably, because in the words of Michel Chossudovsky, the irony persists that "the solution to the debt crisis becomes the cause of further indebtedness."[4] Whilst the East bloc countries often lacked a financial and commercial legal framework for responsible management, with the result that business activity fell under the control of competing criminal networks incapable of promoting productive activity; Third world countries were seduced into establishing unsuitable industries in advance of their capabilities and existing infrastructures.

This led, inevitably, to a multitude of ills: widespread unemployment and desperate poverty due to the demise of traditional industries or agricultural patterns of production; the despoliation of virgin land and forest, utilised as new farmland; the eviction of self-sufficient farmers to join the unemployed proletariat and shanty towns of the great cities, as their land was taken over for exporting high value cash crops,

---

[4] Michel Chossudovsky, *The Globalisation of Poverty*, Zed Books, 1998, p. 68.

1-4

only financially beneficial to the great landlords; the exhaustion of scarce water resources by large scale industry, leading to drought conditions in the domestic sphere; widespread pollution and contamination, in addition to appalling working conditions due to the lack of Western-style safety regulations; and finally, corruption and bribery on a massive scale by ruthless dictators and inept and under-funded bureaucracies. In noting the financial power of the great corporations, it should be borne in mind that the "transnationals either directly or indirectly command 80% of the land around the world that is cultivated for export crops such as bananas, tobacco and cotton."[5]

4 All these ills of lending and investment may be traceable to the single aim of maximising profits within the short term by the industrialised nations. This amounts therefore to a criticism of the International Monetary Fund and the World Trade Organisation, originally established in an aura of best intentions by the Bretton Woods Agreement in 1944 towards the end of the Second World War. The factor that doomed these political bodies from the start as instruments of altruism is that in matters of detail - in the "small print" - they were dominated by powerful (usually American) business interests with a programme fully formulated and understood from the viewpoint of their vested interests.

These institutions were therefore never in any real sense purely benevolent bodies for regenerating a war-torn or impoverished world. Had they been more altruistic or far-seeing in their approach in regenerating Third world economies, they would have sought an alternative development strategy. For example, they would have invested in intermediate technologies, in ensuring the fuller employment of the populations they sought to assist, but as this would have resulted in a lower or more sluggish return on investment, they avoided such a course. A serious investment in intermediate technology would have contributed to the material welfare of entire populations - particularly of the poor - and by a gradual process, the peoples of such countries would have achieved a broader education base and so eventually a sounder foundation for democratic government and self-determination.

What happened instead with the top-down establishment of advanced industries and the building of expensive infrastructures, as dams and road systems, was the cruel division of these societies into a widening divide of rich and poor, and all the ills which follow from this. Hence more than fifty years after the establishment of the Bretton Woods institutions, we see the greater part of the world, particularly central and south

---

[5] Joshua Karliner, *The Corporate Planet*, Sierra Club Books, San Francisco, 1997, p. 17.

1-5

America and most of Africa, reduced to a state of economic if not political chaos, their peoples living on the breadline of existence. Wars, civil strife, and terrorism reaching occasionally to the heart of the industrialised West has followed in the wake of these conditions. The General Agreement on Tariffs & Trade is another political organisation which has to be mentioned in the context of undermining world economic stability. In the words of Korten, "the global economic integration being implemented through GATT is advancing conditions that are at odds with the most basic principles of market economies and is putting in place an economic system that is designed to self-destruct - at an enormous cost to human societies."[6]

Of even greater concern to the peace and stability of the world is perhaps the ineptitude of the great financial institutions of the West to assist the East bloc countries in joining the democratic brotherhood of the industrialised North after the collapse of the Berlin Wall. I remember shuddering with apprehension when the first abrasive representatives of Western banks made their initial visits to the East bloc countries. The greed on the faces of these uncouth men as they proudly presented the name cards of their banks was an intimation of misfortune to come. Quick profits were their sole intention !

They neither understood nor cared to understand these strange and very different societies in which they sought to develop business. Very soon they were inadvertently in league with gangsters, as huge amounts of capital flowed eastwards, much of it to be lost in the byzantine intrigues of mafia bosses in complex trading deals, but little finding its way into productive job-creating activity. Selfishness, corruption, and banditry accompanied by the ruthless assassination of anyone with the moral integrity to oppose, either intentionally or unintentionally, the interests of the mafia gangs, soon reduced the Commonwealth of Independent States into a condition of economic and political anarchy. In the words of Robert Skidelsky, "an estimated 40% of the turnover of goods and services is now controlled by organised crime; an estimated 100,000 criminals are organised in 3,000 to 4,000 gangs: the Russian murder rate is estimated at ten times that of the United States."[7]

5   The economic aspect of difficulties of the East bloc peoples, however, was only of secondary concern to those in the West and elsewhere. Of more concern was the breakdown of the industrial infrastructure and responsible management, and the

---

[6] David C. Korten, op. Cit., p. 80.

[7] Robert Skidelsky, *The World AfterCommunism*, Macmillan, 1995, p. 184.

1-5

resulting dangers posed by decrepit nuclear plants and rotting arsenals of weaponry throughout the old Soviet Union. These environmental dangers fell into two categories: outdated and unreliable nuclear power plants constructed on the Chernobyl pattern; and rusting dumps of bombs and ammunition situated in locations from Murmansk in the West, to several miles outside Vladivostock in the far east of Asia. Much of this weaponry was dumped in the sea (this accelerating its deterioration) under the supervision of demoralised armed forces paid months in arrears, many of whom sacrificed their health and eventually their lives in manhandling radioactive as well as other highly toxic material. The stupidity of compounding one life-threatening danger with another would be laughable if it was not for the international seriousness in threatening the health and lives of peoples throughout the planet.

All these factors are common knowledge amongst informed people in the industrial West, and all are the source of constant anxiety. But in the mainstream political sphere, amongst leading parliamentary groups, they are issues on which no clear guidance is given other than feeble gestures and useless platitudes. What is needed urgently is the initiative of *Statesmanship*, - leadership on the international scale in capturing the imagination of people in solving these problems threatening humanity and the biosphere alike.

The reasons that no such statesmanship has emerged, despite the urgency of the situation, may be cited as under: firstly, because governments are too often narrowly concerned with their own internal vested interests; secondly, because there has not yet developed in the world an international political consciousness amongst ordinary people which is capable of being enforced, despite fifty years of the United Nations and its many ancillary organisations; thirdly, because environmental issues have not yet become central to the thinking or philosophy of mainstream parties; fourthly, because of the false ideology of growth as promoted by the orthodox economics establishment; and fifthly, because the nature of contemporary capitalism and its manifestations on society is so different from the theory of capitalism as it is commonly understood, that the former is not properly comprehended by either the general public or established political parties themselves.

Hence the resulting situation today is that we are surrounded by a plethora of so-called *peripheral* political issues which instead should take on the status of *central* political issues. These "peripheral" issues are, in fact, already central to the political thinking of the majority of thinking people in the developed world. This fact is especially reflected through the following: firstly through the strength and mass-following of a multitude of single issue pressure groups; and secondly, through the low-

1-6

esteem in which mainstream politicians and political parties are held generally. This is a clear indication that mainstream political parties need to update and transform not their image or presentation, but rather their philosophies and approach to the world.

6 Political parties of the right may be forgiven if in concentrating on more immediate national issues they adopt a lower international profile, but such an approach cannot be excused the parties of the left. Socialism must remain in essence a movement with international interests irrespective of where it operates. This is not only because Socialism should be concerned with humanity as a universal concept, but because of the practical factor that a world riven with injustice and suffering is bound sometime to be thrown up against those peoples who enjoy greater comfort and security. The self-interest of pursuing the international ideal is therefore to be found in safeguarding stability and peace. In this light internationalism may therefore be seen as amongst the most pragmatic requirements of any nation state.

It is a curious fact, often demonstrated by recent history, that the most impoverished countries are always able to raise sufficient capital to engage in wars of attrition, even though they may be incapable of feeding their own people. This illustrates the ubiquity of war, and the volatility of nations everywhere on the planet. There never was "A war to end wars," and no amount of horrors, howsoever publicised, has ever contributed to the diminution of the warlike instinct. The presence of war can no more be banished by moral precept than can quarrelling amongst children by the same means. No wars are accidental in origin even though they take on this appearance in retrospect. All wars are causal in origin, and those causes may be found in the four following circumstances: in the paucity of resources for existence; in inequity in the distribution of resources; in resulting resentment arising from either of the above; or in initiatives to counter acts of aggression. Even unprovoked wars against harmless neighbours, or wars of imperialism are accountable to these causes.

Thus German aggression in the last century was due to the psychological state of a young nation formerly surrounded by predator powers in the previous ten centuries, envious, and emerging too late to enjoy the overseas spoils of her Western neighbours. The gentler imperialism of Britain was stimulated by the injustice of primogeniture, and the need of younger siblings of great families and the landed gentry to venture into projects of enrichment in attempting to rival the status of elder brothers. The growth of Rome was due to the instability of land ownership, the over-concentration of an urban population, and eventually, the decline of agricultural productivity and dependence on colonial imports - particularly grain from Egypt. The Viking invasions, as with very many wars, was simply due to population pressures in the Scandinavian

2-1

peninsula.

All these causal factors not only illustrate the volatility of nations existing on a finite planet, but the underlying function of Socialism in the pursuit of justice in attempting to remove the root causes of war. The purpose of internationalism, therefore, is to promote an all encompassing world stability which reaches even into our own homes in warding off armed conflict. To summarise the failures of the economic systems of both East and West in the post-War period, we may conclude with the words of David Korten when he wrote that, "both Communism and capitalism have failed to live up to their ideal in practice. Communism vested property rights in a distant state and denied people any means of holding the state accountable for its exercise of those rights. Capitalism persistently transfers property rights to giant corporations and financial institutions that are largely unaccountable even to their owners."[8]

CHAPTER 2
The Crisis of Socialism In A Changing World

"The great irony is that capitalism's victory over Communism seems to be coinciding with capitalism itself succumbing to a *rentier* cancer."

F.Harrison, M.Hudson, G.J.Miller & K.Feder, *A Philosophy For A Fair Society*, Shepheard-Walwyn, 1994, p. 8.

1 - Does Socialism still exist ?   2 - Sanitised top-down Socialism   3 - Ineffectiveness of the backward-looking hard left   4 - Labour leadership fearful of Socialism's watershed   5 - Restrictions on free communication brought the downfall of East bloc Socialism   6 - But its failure to fulfill consumer needs capped its unpopularity   7 - Failure of Old Socialism in the industrialised West   8 - Victory of the pragmastic left in the face of globalisation

1   The previous chapter has shown that Socialism as an international movement has a function to perform which is integral to its central purpose, i.e. the welfare of humanity, irrespective of intervening boundaries created through the accident or artifice of society. Parties of the right, in better focusing their image in attracting the electorate, often claim a similar purpose, but if their aims are analysed with clarity, it will usually be found to have little substance. This is because they are committed to more exclusive national interests.

---

[8]   David C. Korten, op. Cit., p. 312.

2-2

In a close and dangerously interdependent world, as we find today, Socialism is therefore particularly apt in meeting the political needs of the future. There is a common realisation of this fact, reflected in a leftward movement amongst peoples throughout many areas of the globe. But Socialism cannot be taken for granted because of this. This, too, is understood ! The winning of elections by the left, or the ingenuity of spin-doctors, is not sufficient to maintain the growing bandwagon of the Socialist movement. It is not even sufficient to maintain the existence of Socialism itself !

If the truth be known, then at the present time, it has to be said that Socialism is in crisis. There is something paradoxical in the current situation, for whilst the left is firmly entrenched electorally in many leading industrialised countries, and seemingly, continues to go from strength to strength, it is questionable as to whether Socialism exists at all in any real sense. In any event, it may be found to be unsatisfactorily definable by contemporary statesmen- and women and leading politicians of the left. Of course any politician, when asked, will blithely produce his answer, but soundbites or slogans, however cleverly delivered, fall far short of convincing argument.

If it is not a contradiction in terms, the intellectual creativity of those supporting the ruling parliamentary left, in speeches, pamphlets, books and articles, is devoid of ideas, philosophy, or long term direction. It is instead comprised of nose to the grindstone policy statements, self-congratulatory analyses of achievement, and careful pragmatic responses to every event and difficulty. There is a dryness, superficiality, and neatness about this approach which seems to belie integrity itself, for the overwhelming desire to please, crushes out entirely the desire to explain or understand, or to point to a greater long-term purpose.

Such an approach, of course, is in keeping with the technique of spin-doctoring or good advertising copy, and its presence is explicable for two reasons: firstly, for electoral success in refraining from "frightening the horses," i.e. in ensuring the permanent erasure of the unpopular image of Old style Labour; and secondly, because there was no new philosophy to replace that which had been apparently discredited. Whilst many on the left were appreciative of this approach in the pre-1997 election period, on the understanding of sound strategy, it was nonetheless assumed or hoped that the Labour leadership had discreetly formulated a concealed programme held close to its chest until the moment ripe for its revelation to an interested public in the post-election period.

2   Those on the left, particularly activists in the Labour party, anticipated with optimism the day when this concealed card would be openly revealed,   to usher in an exciting period of enlightened discussion on the purpose and direction of New Labour

2-2

and New Socialism. Now a long period has elapsed since that happy outcome in May 1997, and still no philosophy or grand strategy for the future has been presented to the public. Consequently, many on the left feel "high and dry," disappointed and directionless, particularly in view of the increasing centralisation of the Labour party and the diminishing status of constituency parties in policy making, all of which was symbolised by the removal of the party's headquarters from the friendly Walworth road premises, to the totally inaccessible and security guarded floors high up in the Millbank tower block.

The party has even become shy of the term "Socialism," seemingly unaware that in doing so, it has deprived itself of the one adjective describing its very purpose. The term "democratic Socialism," however, has become acceptable providing it is used sparingly, but then the term "democratic" used in this context has a suggestion of Newspeak about it in view of the increasingly top-down authority of the party, in conjunction with the development of a Presidential style of government. At one time the party was flooded with cheap-printed literature emanating from many quarters on many levels. Much of this may have been of indifferent quality, but it did offer a forum for debate, it was democratic, and it did stimulate discussion.

Today, from its headquarters, the party pushes out expensively produced literature on glossy paper, which in layout and design, and the array of smiling faces beaming out from the well-presented illustrations, have more the appearance of advertising brochures than well-argued pamphlets. It goes without saying that these beautifully produced publications are full of good cheer, but any recipient with a modicum of intelligence must feel imposed upon and offended, as if victims of an unwarranted propaganda campaign.

Few want a return to the undisciplined and anarchic Labour party of a decade or more ago, but a sanitised top-down party is no answer to the future, and it is already fraught with dangers threatening sometime to topple the leadership. No one knows the true feelings or opinions of the majority, or significant sectors, of the membership of the New Labour party, but there is undoubtedly a seething undercurrent of resentment amongst rank and file activists at the suppression of free opinion. This is expressed through a variety of bodies, such as the Labour Reform Group; The Centre-Left Grassroots Alliance; the Campaign For Labour Party Democracy; Labour Renewal Network; and the Campaign For Socialism (Scotland). Militant and similar peripheral organisations have long since passed into history, whilst the Fabian society, the official think-tank of the party, is controlled by such an exclusive tightly-knit group as to be wholly inscrutable, and then it only seemingly produces publications licensed and

2-3

blessed by the moguls of Millbank.

3   There is, however, one particular movement of opposition within the Labour party which needs special mention, but it is of questionable value in raising new issues for debate. This is led by the old-established weekly newspaper, *Tribune*, which whilst on the one had proclaims itself as the "only" newspaper of the Labour party (albeit of "the independent left"), on the other hand, carries forth the standard of Old Labour with such force and vitriol, that hardly a single issue is without its lampooning caricatures by Martin Rowson of Tony Blair and his "Babes." The presence of such a newspaper may indeed be satisfying to the cunning wizards of Millbank on two counts: firstly, on the grounds that its existence demonstrates "healthy" opposition within the Labour party; and secondly, on the grounds that such criticism demonstrates to all "right thinking people" the utter futility of such particular effrontery to the powers that be. The secret message to the membership, in the eyes of Millbank, therefore, is that if such aggression can only entail the regurgitation of old ideas and concepts from an earlier era, then better no opposition at all - but anyway, recognise the right to its existence for it is "harmless!" Better that than the *actual* launching of fresh ideas !

The truth, of course, is that the mainstream opposition of *Tribune* is an unhealthy symptom of the Labour party's intellectual life, since it entails a looking backwards rather than forwards to a uniquely changing world. It yearns for the spirit of the past; worships the heroes of the past; and cherishes a cloth-capped proletarianism whenever the occasion arises, e.g., during industrial disputes or when writing about depressed areas. *Tribune* undoubtedly retains a firm loyalty amongst a large sector of Old Labour activists, and in fairness, it does accept contributions from different spectra of the party, but its old-fashioned spirit; its resentful banner headlines; its chip on the shoulder attitudes; its scurrilous cartoons which are too distasteful to be amusing; and its crudely cheap utility style layout, make it anathema to the typical man or woman of the 1990s.

Its style and content is an irrelevance in equal measure to both the sophisticated Labour party leadership in Millbank and the average elector in the age we live in. The *real* or core criticism of the *Tribune* newspaper, however, is not to be found in the above remarks, but rather in its deadening and reactionary conservatism, which opposes the floating or discussion of new ideas simply because they might offend the gods in the ancient Socialist pantheon. New ideas always tend to be uncomfortable to the warmth of hard-held prejudice, and therefore they are best avoided. With regard to the Marxist left (covertly supported by *Tribune* and other Labour party supporting groups), Fred Harrison and others noted that "academic Marxism has moved more towards becoming a theory of language, of literary and ideological deconstruction .

2-5

rather than analysing the quandaries of modern *rentier* capitalism."[9] It is the latter economic issue, of course, which is paramount for our age.

4   The contemporary Labour party does not augur well for the future, since a reforming political movement needs to be a creative entity in constantly meeting and effecting change in society. It cannot successfully exist like an army, managed by *apparatchiks*, concerned only with efficient bureaucratic mechanisms and party discipline. If it is so managed then decay will soon set in, the symptoms of which would be intellectual stagnation, rigidity of thinking, intolerance of the unknown, and eventually, inability to meet the actual changes in the evolving structure of society. It is an undisputable fact that the Labour party today opposes and fears internal debate. If this was not so then the present structural changes would not be in place. In any group, community, or nation where free speech is suppressed or frowned upon, there is anyway eventually dissent and fragmentation.

The Labour party's fear of discussion as to its purpose and direction is not something that has simply been imposed arbitrarily by its leadership. It has arisen through the crisis of Socialism itself. It is probable that the current leaders of the Labour party do not even know what should constitute the meaning of Socialism for the future. They are fearful of the watershed and the options ahead. They are concerned to avoid the shoals and shipwreck of a wrong direction, for they are sufficiently aware to perceive that the Socialism of the past is dead and buried, and that something new and quite unknown must lie ahead.

The present crisis of Socialism is of overwhelming historical significance, and in the epochs ahead may be seen as presenting a turning point comparable with the Reformation, the Industrial revolution, or the emergence of democracy itself. But from our own narrow perspective in living out the present, it is a turning point the significance of which we may never be fully aware. The Socialism of the future, in both temperament and detail of purpose will bear little resemblance to that of yesteryear.

5   The crisis of Socialism has arisen from two main causes and from two directions in the world: from the Communist East and from the social democratic West.

The collapse of the Soviet Union and the fall of the Berlin Wall followed in the wake of the inability to modernise in the face of the new information and computer technologies, which were dependent for their existence on free communication. The totalitarian system of Communism, which had been the pride of generations, and was

---

[9] F.Harrison, M.Hudson, G.I.Miller & K.Feder, *A Philosophy For A Fair Society*, Shepheard-Walwyn, 1994, p. 8.

2-5

viable during the era of vast proletarian identical task workforces engaged in heavy industry, could not meet the challenge of the constantly changing smaller unitary production methods of highly trained technicians and engineers. The authoritarian pattern of ruthless discipline, and thought control, of the old industrial sociology could not be adapted to the new conditions, and consequently, there was a breakdown of confidence and initiative in undertaking even the simplest tasks.

This, perhaps, is a situation difficult for Westerners to comprehend, but in highly authoritarian societies, as in Eastern Europe and elsewhere, there is a crippling inability to take individual initiative. This stems from the obsessive fear of undertaking unauthorised acts and the punishment which follows, and in circumstances where the smooth top-down lines of communication are no longer possible, there is paralysis, lying and indifference. In understanding the threat of the computer, it should be borne in mind that for the greater part of the Soviet period, there were no freely available telephone directories, no proper indexed city plans, and no unlicensed typewriters for domestic use. These conditions stemmed from the state's fear of the consequences of free communication.

Discontent with state Socialism was wide throughout the East bloc during every period of its history, and an iron curtain around the entire territory was an essential tool in preventing escape or population leakage. In the eyes of some internal critics, the system was not even perceived as Socialism of any variety. Fedor Zniakov, for example, in his *Samizdat* 'Memorandum' circulated in May 1966, described the Soviet economic system as "super-monopoly capitalism," with all significant ownership concentrated in a single centre.[10] It is doubtful if all the propaganda weaponry of the Soviet Union was sufficient to achieve real thought control, and it is now believed to be unlikely that Lenin's boast, taken over from the Jesuits, that the adoption and education of a 7-year old would guarantee life-long party loyalty, had much substance in reality. This is because the human mind is more moved by one gram of experience than a thousand grams of proselytism. What is known is that cynicism was widespread throughout the privileged exclusive Communist party elite, many of whom are now promoting the very reverse of Socialist ethical purpose. As the inheritors of a bankrupt and fragmented system, but with their hands on the levers of financial power and know-how, many have acceded to the leadership of criminal tax-evading commercial networks, rapidly contributing to millionaire self-enrichment but achieving little in building the productive infrastructure of their economies.

---

[10] Quoted from Paul Johnson, *A History of The Modern World*, Weidenfeld & Nicolson, 1991 ed., p. 677.

2-6

Thus the East bloc was brought to its knees through technological change, but had it encountered the greater fortune of existing in a more static world, it might have lasted for a thousand, two thousand, or even three thousand years, as with the ancient monarchies of Egypt or Sumeria. This is because the Soviet Union operated one of the most effective systems of control known to history. But the longevity of a regime is no criterion for its popular support by the majority, or for its system of justice - and of course democracy, as a system of government, played no part in Soviet decision-making.

6   Perhaps the main ground for dissatisfaction with the Soviet system was not to be found in its social oppression, appalling as this was, but in its inability to offer consumer choice. As the orthodox principles of Socialism forbad the free market as a capitalist "evil," consumer products and services were offered through the beneficiary medium of bureaucratic departments. This was judged the only fair way to promote production and distribution in serving the market place. The outcome was the inability to serve consumer demand from every conceivable aspect, even after the late Kruschchev period from when it was decided to transfer the emphasis of production from defence purposes to the domestic sector.

Not only were shop assistants (who saw themselves as part of a bureaucracy)often rude and arrogant to customers, but stores and shops were flooded with identical products at infrequent intervals between periods of dearth, when shelves were left empty apart from unwanted merchandise gathering dust in a deteriorating condition. Little attempt was made to create attractive displays. Meanwhile, food shopping was a nightmare, not merely because of queuing and unanticipated alternations of abundance and scarcity, but because of the complex procedure in making purchases, entailing separate queues for collecting product tickets, till payments, and counter service.

All this was a logical outcome of orthodox Socialist theory transferred into practice, by senior planners in government departments who were usually isolated from the everyday life of the ordinary housewife. It not only illustrates the stupidity emanating from authoritarian practices, but contrariwise, the wisdom and intelligence emanating from free choice and interaction in a democratic environment encouraging discussion, experimentation, and the opportunity for disagreement and wrong decision-making free of censure. In summary, as William Keegan has remarked, "the search for new profitable opportunities, which is linked with the continuing efforts at innovation in capitalist economies, was simply not part of the Communist culture. There was no

2-8

incentive either to improve the product or to maintain the plant."[11]

7   Disillusionment with and the eventual breakdown of orthodox governmental Socialism in the West may be traceable to a somewhat earlier period, viz., from the late 1950s onwards. The repudiation by the Social Democratic party in West Germany of Marxist economic theory in 1959, to be replaced by the new concept of the Social Market economy, was a significant landmark in European history. Meanwhile, the gradual realisation of the failure of Nationalisation policies in Britain over a longer period of time, confronted government and the Socialist movement with a crisis of confidence on policies which were central to Socialist purpose. Soviet style totalitarian state Socialism had anyway been repudiated in the West, but if Nationalisation policies implemented in good faith within a democratic framework were to fail, what then ?

In those countries with multi-party systems, usually relying on coalitions, as France, Italy, or Finland, such crises of confidence did not usually occur within their splintered parliamentary groups to the left of centre. This was because in societies where several Socialist parties worked and competed alongside one another - especially in conjunction with proportional representation - each tended to safeguard its own doctrinal integrity, only needing to bear the brunt of realistic policy decision-making in administrative-coalition type situations. Hence such parties were and remain protectively insulated from the rough and tumble of governmental politics, and so are allowed to evolve more slowly, usually according to the purely intellectual decision-making of their memberships.

By the close of the 1970s Socialism in the West may be said to have reached the nadir of its fortunes, for whilst in Britain it marked the dawn of the Thatcherite era, in those Continental countries which retained administrations nominally supporting the left, the question was raised as to whether Socialism still existed in any real sense.

In practice, the vaguely defined concept of the social market economy meant little more than the need to intervene occasionally in the capitalist process, but the extent or circumstances of such intervention went no more beyond the declaration of defending employees' rights and promoting co-determination (*Mitbestimmung*). As long as the economy was maintained on an even keel with steady growth, the idea of the social market economy satisfied all sectors committed to the industrial process, but as soon as choppy waters were reached, doubt and mistrust gave rise to division .

8   Consequently, by the start of the 1990s, the successful participation between the two sides of industry, which had flourished for so long throughout Continental Europe,

---

[11]   William Keegan, *The Spectre of Capitalism*, Vintage, 1993, p. 82.

2-8

and served as an inspiration to Britain and other parts of the world, began to display deep cracks in its unity. This followed in the wake of sharp rises in unemployment, particlarly following the economic difficulties in uniting the two halves of Germany. Leading industrialists throughout the Continent suddenly repudiated the consensus which had worked so well throughout the previous 50-year period, and attracted by the new ideology across the water, began to openly embrace the principles of Thatcherism.

This, of course, was not only encouraged by witnessing the experience of Thatcherism on the British economy, but more significantly, by the apparently inevitable growth of globalisation, accompanied by ruthless market forces which swept all before it like a tidal wave. It seemed to many as if a new era had been entered, and that the social market economy no longer met up with the new reality. The old had to give way to the new!

These changes, and the fears they engendered, naturally contributed to the electoral successes of the left by the mid-1990s, but it was a left which had lost its confidence. It knew it had won the allegiance of the electorate, not through the love of Socialism, but as the lesser of several malignly perceived alternatives. These new governments would need to tread warily on a field of unbroken egg shells. Whilst on the one hand Socialist governments were popular, and seemingly secure for the longer term; on the other, they too (as with the business community) seemed constrained - if not imprisoned - by the ubiquitous financial might of global market forces.

In addition, they no longer knew what Socialism meant, and were forced to adopt a short term pragmatic approach, at the same time ditching principles in place of spin-doctoring and clever advertising copy.

20

CHAPTER 3
Why Representative Democracy Is Reliant On Constructive Political Philosophy

"In a democratic age history tends to become a series of popular apologies. Grote began it in England with his defence of the Athenian people for the execution of Socrates. But the false idea that the people can do no wrong is as absurd as the notion that the king can do no wrong."

A.F. Pollard, *Factors In Modern History,* Constable, 1910, p. 87.

1 - How academic influences have undermined free thought   2 - Contemporary academic environment not conducive to constructive philosophy   3 - Differences between policy making, spin-doctoring and general principles   4 - Plutocractic power is eroding the principles of the left   5 - Four reasons calling for a constructive philosophical approach   6 - Representative democracy dependent on such an approach   7 - As only then can those elected be held accountable for their promises   8 - A constructive philosophy empowers the electorate

1   There are many in the Socialist camp who question the need for Socialism to be supported by a set of coherent principles. They feel no anxiety about a Socialism free of philosophical theory, and hence are unworried by the underlying questions already raised in this book.

The attitude or complacency of these people, it is argued, is very wrong indeed. With regard to the principles for maximising democracy or people power within a representative system, this chapter may be taken as the most important in the book, and despite the possible intricacy of several passages which follow, I would ask readers to give them particular attention in view of their importance to the central thesis. We live in a very pragmatic age - certainly in the Anglo-Saxon world - and there are many reasons for the present situation. The anti-intellectualism in the face of general constructive theory stems primarily from the current academic environment, but in the labour movement, it is also analogous with the traditional impatience of trades unionism with abstract discussion.

The scepticism of 20th century British philosophy, especially of the analytic school in confronting Idealism (which was well established in universities in the earlier decades of the century); and later, of the logical positivists from the 1930s onwards, went well beyond the bounds of the esoteric faculties devoted to their study. The scepticism of these schools was so powerful in its influence, as to break through the barriers of philosophy, in the sense that generations of students in the social and other sciences were brought into public life unable or unwilling to express or formulate ideas for fear of their contradiction or ridicule on the grounds that they might not be upheld

3-1

by the Verification principle, or some other such tenet laid down by Wittgenstein, Ayer, or others.

By these means several specialised schools of philosophy went well beyond their remit in overflowing into other spheres of intellectual activity. Consequently, in the spontaneous realm of the formulation and exchange of ideas, amongst an educated elite, the facility for thought itself was undermined. The heavily guarded barriers of doubt effectively destroyed the very tools for freedom. The outcome was manifested through the following: great issues were either not discussed, or passed over lightly at a superficial level; debate was trivialised by the pun or cheap point-scoring; and a short-term pragmatic approach was applied to problem-solving.

Perhaps the greatest irony of this tendency was that the foremost of these sceptical philosophers, who was personally brought into contact with most branches of the analytic movement, viz., Bertrand Russell, was also one of the most imaginative and provocative thinkers of his age. But this was only because his life was split into two identifiable careers: firstly, as an innovative mathematician and professional philosopher who set out to demolish the established ideas of his youth; and secondly, as a popular teacher of philosophy and author of numerous controversial books in which he often shot from the hip in expressing feelings of the moment, sometimes, even, indulging in the luxury of writing arrant nonsense.

The pertinent point is that the subject matter of most of these books covered serious social issues or the discussion of concepts crucial to society, but there is not the slightest suggestion that he was ever constrained by the Verification principle, or any other of the intellectual limitations he helped to promote during the course of a long life devoted to sceptical philosophy. Therefore, whilst on the one hand he fearlessly allowed himself unlimited intellectual freedom in the expansion of ideas, on the other, he has to be held accountable in some part for the generations of timid thinkers and even mental cripples emerging from our universities. The conclusion to be drawn is not that Russell, or any of his associates were hypocrites, but rather that any philosophy when pushed forward to its extreme in everyday life is absurdly misused. I do not believe that any of the philosophers of the analytic school ever intended that their teaching should be used or abused in the way it was, even though the universality of its message must have been flattering in their eyes.

Some highly-technical schools of philosophy, as specialisms, are best left to themselves - as indeed are certain areas of science - if they are not to exert a mischievous influence on society. This is not merely because they may be beyond the ken of laymen, but because they are only properly concerned with complex technical

3-2

questions internal to their own disciplines. Therefore, if they are popularised, they are too easily misunderstood and misinterpreted at a level for which they were never designed to be comprehended.

This is certainly the case with the philosophy of Russell and G.E. Moore, at the start of the present century, which initially was formulated specifically to refute the Idealism of Bradley, Bosanquet, and others. The same may be said of the analytic school, established in this country a few years later in 1912. The major branches of 20th century British philosophy have all been critical, primarily concerned with the definition of meaning and linguistic questions, and invariably opposed to constructive philosophy or Idealism which dominated thought throughout the 19th century.[12]

2   Hence it may be perceived that such branches of philosophy were never intended to be carried over to the social sciences. They were irrelevant for such a purpose. This is because the social sciences, and especially effective political thought, is dependent on a constructive philosophical approach. Before outlining the reasons for this, and reviewing the present tendencies of mainstream political life, which is so barren of general theory or ideas, there is one other intellectually constraining factor in the world of academia which must be touched upon.

It might be anticipated that a constructive political philosophy would best emerge from either the world of active political life, or that of academia. But the problem with politicians (at least in the late 20th century), is that although they are perhaps amongst the best talkers and rhetoricians of any occupational group, they are too close to the hurly-burly of day-to-day action to take a broader in-depth view of society's underlying needs. Although their appreciation of practical issues would be of value, their long-standing involvement with the viewpoint of a single party is too likely to narrow their philosophical perspective.

Academics, meanwhile, are hindered by another factor. The intensive specialisation of knowledge in the post-War period; and the exclusive and jealous safeguarding of each specialism; and the often vicious rivalry of closely associated specialisms - sometimes indirectly promoted by the pressures of external commercial, political, or other vested interests, has undermined both the integrity and universality

---

[12] It might be concluded that a shadow was cast over the final years of Bertrand Russell, seen in the light of the serious philosopher, or that he came to doubt the value of his most important work. This is, anyway, suggested by the following reminiscence: "The best years of my life were given to the Principles of Mathematics, in the hope of finding somewhere some certain knowledge. The whole of this effort, in spite of three big volumes, ended inwardly in doubt and bewilderment. As regards metaphysics, when, under the influence of Moore, I first threw off the belief in German idealism, I experienced the delight of believing that the sensible world is real. Bit by bit, chiefly under the influence of physics, this delight has faded." Bertrand Russell, *Autobiography*, Allen & Unwin, 1967, Vol. II, p. 160.

3-3

which supposedly is the overriding consideration of academic life.

This is especially the case in the field of the social sciences, where I have personally encountered over the years, frequent difficulties with a number of academics in consulting on over-lapping socio-economic questions, which could not or would not be discussed beyond a certain point, since they infringed on matters of which these specialists claimed they were either ignorant or uninterested. This sharp division between different academic disciplines is most accountable to the huge and unmanageable increase in the bulk of knowledge. Its outcome has been detrimental to the vital need for maintaining an overview and healthy inter-connections between different spheres of knowledge, but the creation of such an overview has in all probability been hindered by the speed of acceleration in the accumulation of knowledge in the separate disciplines.

It can clearly be seen that the formulation of a constructive political philosophy is work which is best taken on by a polymath, but polymaths are scarcely to be found amongst contemporary academics, and it is anyway unlikely that an academic would be either sufficiently competent or prepared to take on such a daunting task. On whose shoulders, then, should fall such a responsibility ? There is no way in which this question may be answered, beyond conjecturing the need for sufficient relevant knowledge (which in itself is impossible to define), and the will of the individual to pursue such a task.

3   By way of preparing the groundwork in demonstrating the necessity for formulating a constructive political philosophy, it would be useful to view the current circumstances of political life. A distinction has to be made between the separate activities of promoting political ideas and the frenetic work of churning out policy documents. Political parties may produce a surfeit of policy documents, and endless discussion papers - as indeed they do, and yet convey the impression to the public of being without direction or proper purpose. Such political parties, as we have today, seem uninspired, soulless, or cynical, and even when they are successful through the ballot box (which is usually in the wake of negative voting) they fail to carry through the impression of support by a loyal and convinced majority.

Policy statements are no substitute for general principles. They may be well drafted, practical, and even appealing to those they seek to benefit, but if they are not supported by the underlying principles of a general theory, they are lifeless and uninteresting. Consequently, policy documents, which are at the very forefront of legislation and practical political life, pass by the attention of the general public as too time-consuming for passing study. Meanwhile, in place of general principles the public

3-4

is regaled by the spin-doctoring of skilled oratory during the conference season, or to clever advertising copy during other periods of the year.

This apprehension or reluctance of political leaders to formulate or discuss general principles has penetrated even the think-tank of the Labour party, the Fabian society. We have already noted how the work of this association is held jealously in the hands of a small coterie, but it is the one body in the Labour party which might have been expected to float new ideas in underpinning the Socialism of the future. Its approach, instead, through the topics of its debates and publications has remained purely pragmatic, whilst eschewing entirely the consideration of general principles. When it seeks to achieve a high profile, it is usually through controversial issues, often peripheral to Socialism itself, with topics of sufficient interest to raise the eyebrows of *Daily Telegraph* readers, so ensuring some publicity in the broadsheets. It is no wonder, therefore, that New Labour has not yet identified exactly what this Newness is !

An interesting aspect of policy documents today, produced by conflicting parliamentary groups, is their decreasingly partisan nature. Many such documents may be cited which might have been produced by any parliamentary group. The terms left, right, or centre, carry little meaning any more. Many Liberal Democrats claim to be left of the present Labour party. There are also "wet" or national consensus Tories holding views to the left of policies actively promoted by the Labour government. It is also conjectured that the Labour government is prepared to push through legislation that the Conservatives would have never dared embark upon. It is difficult to imagine, for example, that the Student loan legislation, or changes to the Legal aid arrangements, or cuts in the Disability allowance, would have progressed so smoothly had the Tories remained in power. In a certain sense it may be seen that the Labour government is continuing the work of the previous administration only under more propitious circumstances.

4   An interesting criticism levelled at the present government is its increasingly "Presidential" style, and by this is meant a growing similarity with the American system of government. That is, power is becoming more concentrated in the hands of the Prime minister and his cabinet, whilst back-benchers in the party are kept on a tighter leash, and parliament is otherwise left impotent as fewer policy questions of real significance are exposed to either open discussion or a vote. But there is also another and more significant comparison with the American experience. Underlying political principles are fast slipping away from British parliamentary parties as they have long since disappeared from those in America.

3-4

Although in America Democrats may be perceived as the party of the left, and Republicans as the party of the right, these distinctions have little meaning. This is not only because the parties themselves are free of ideological tincture, but of greater significance, because both are controlled by and accountable to powerful financial and commercial vested interests. This is no less true of Democrats than Republicans. Not only was the Clinton administration obliged to curtail some of its promises and best intentions in the domestic sphere due to the pressures of big business, but more recently in the international sphere, it was forced to use threats and heavy-handed methods towards the EU in imposing prohibitive tariffs on the importation of European goods in promoting its banana trading interests in South America.

Meanwhile, British political parties are also increasingly dominated by big business. From the time the Labour party climbed into bed with Rupert Murdoch and subsequently formed close alliances with other questionable business interests, it not merely compromised its principles (which anyway had to be eliminated beforehand) but restricted its ability for movement in the sphere of practical politics. A breakdown of the occupations and financial interests of Labour party created peers over the past ten years, for example, might present an interesting exercise. Many would fall into the category of so-called "industrialists" i.e. commercial lawyers and accountants, being chairmen or shareholding directors of major conglomerates and other corporations. It would be pertinent to enquire into the integrity of these men (for I believe that no women are yet included in this specific category referred to) *vis-à-vis* their commitment to the purposes of the Labour party, or in what real sense they hold themselves to be Socialists.

A further factor regarding the American experience reveals that when its system of government is examined with closer scrutiny it may be found to be no longer a democracy in any proper sense. An electoral system, or the right to vote, is not and has never been regarded as in itself a sufficient criterion defining democratic government. After all, ancient Rome had warring class-based political parties and an electoral system, but it was in no way a democracy. It was instead an oligarchy of wealthy interests, for only the privileged were entitled to stand for election. Likewise in contemporary America only the privileged can stand de facto if not de jure for influential positions in national life.

But the determining factor defining America as in no real sense a democracy is not the personal expense of political activity in standing for Congress or the National Assembly, but rather that all political decision-making is over-ruled by the financial power of business interests whenever these are felt to threaten the will of the giant

3-5

corporations. In this way representative government is reduced to becoming the poodle of big business. In reality America is a plutocracy cleverly disguised as a democracy through the myths and history of her earlier traditions.

As noted above, Britain is meanwhile following fast in the same direction, not wholly through the attempts of big business to buy up the political system, but conversely, through hanging up the red lamp to buy the love of financial and trading corporations. This activity of the political left is a uniquely new form of prostitution. If Britain is not yet to be categorised as a plutocracy in the American sense according to this criterion alone, then another shaft to our pride in democratic freedom was delivered by an eminent elder statesman more than twenty years ago who denied Britain's status as a democracy, claiming that on constitutional grounds she was instead an "elective dictatorship."[13]

This is the picture of political life as we see it today, not merely in Britain but throughout the industrialised West. In the light of this, we may again ask the question as to the need for a constructive philosophical approach to politics and more easily see the urgency of attempting to present an answer.

5   The purpose of a constructive philosophy in the sphere of politics is fourfold: firstly, to give long-term direction to what is intended, particularly with regard to the final outcome to be achieved; secondly, to ensure the integrity of both the means and end in struggling towards this purpose; thirdly, in promoting unity amongst those committed to the cause; and fourthly, in facilitating both a concept and an organisational basis for its achievement which may be applied successfully through the means of representative democracy.

The first factor, viz., the need to comprehend fully the end purpose, or final cause of a series of actions (i.e. towards Socialism), is an appeal for a teleological approach to politics in this particular context. Only by such means can the *best ends* be sought after. All political activity should therefore be guided in the light of this final outcome, since "human conduct, insofar as it is considered rational is generally explained with reference to ends pursued or alleged to be pursued; and human thought tends to explain the behaviour of other things in nature on this analogy, either as of themselves pursuing ends, or as designed to fulfil a purpose devised by a mind external to nature."[14]

---

[13]   See, Lord Hailsham's, *The Dilemma of Democracy*, Collins, 1978.

[14]   Encyclopaedia Britannica, 1963 ed., Vol. 21, p. 892.

3-5

It was long ago argued by Aristotle that in fully explaining a thing, it is not only necessary to take account of the "material," the "formal," and the "efficient" causes, but also of the purpose for which the thing existed or was produced, viz. Its "final" cause. Although a teleological approach is uncommon in the post-enlightenment era, in the context of upholding a constructive theoretical approach to politics, it has practical relevance in helping to make for effective representative government. If there is no clear vision of what Socialism is to be in its final form, then it is liable to be understood or misunderstood as anything or nothing. Therefore a constructive philosophy embodying a practical description of the Socialist society needs to be formulated as a vision and long-term purpose for all those committed to the cause.

The second factor, viz. That a constructive political philosophy ensures integrity of both means and ends in struggling towards a given purpose, stems from the clarity of direction given by the final cause, i.e. the rationale and description of the desired Socialist society. This infers that there has to be a basis for building a dialectic, i.e. foundations for investigating the truth of opinions within the context of the purpose to be achieved. This means that all those committed to the cause are guided by a set of objective criteria as to the path which lies ahead and the aims to be achieved. This objective criteria ensures that those who stray from the path do so knowingly, and not only betray themselves to themselves but to others in the movement. This is simply an appeal for the formulation of clear and firm principles. It is made in the light of the fact that modern political parties are so devoid of principle, that unscrupulous individuals with unauthorised or foreign vested interests, gain entry and promotion within parties using them for purposes contrary to their true intention. The presence and influence of such objective criteria is therefore necessary in safeguarding the democratic will of the electorate.

The third factor, viz. The promotion of unity amongst those committed to the cause, springs from the spirit of fraternity engendered by the inspiration and clarity of a philosophical outlook which is constructive and complete in its striving for best purpose. In illustrating this situation, history has often demonstrated the occasion, in both political and religious life, when people from contrasting backgrounds are united as brothers and sisters in a common cause. A contrary situation is illustrated in those movements lacking constructive principles where there is division and conflict.

The internal relationships of the Labour party today, for example, are far from healthy. Because the Labour party lacks an underlying philosophy, it is both demoralised by a sense of uncertainty as well as riven by widely differing if not conflicting interest groups. The fact that the party presents an image of being at peace

3-6

with itself to the outside world is little consolation. Its disciplined aspect could well be an illusion in presaging the calm before an eventual storm. No situation in any organisation is ever static, and if tensions are mounting secretly in the hearts of the many, sometime in the future the dam is bound to burst. For these reasons, therefore, the formulation and establishment of a constructive philosophy for the Labour party is an imperative for the future.

6   The fourth factor, viz. The need for a constructive philosophy in facilitating effective representative government, is quite separate from those already considered above. But before looking at the problems of representative democracy, we must first glance at direct or *real* democracy. In so far as institutions have developed until the present time, direct democracy is only workable amongst small communities or miniscule states, e.g., in the ancient world as in Athens or Samos, or in the modern world as in the Cantons of Switzerland. The Greeks suggested that approximately 3,000 citizens was the optimum number to facilitate the efficient operation of a democratic state.

Direct democracy not only entails the meeting of all citizens in a central square or *Agora* for political discussion and decision-making on a collective basis, but a system of rotation for citizens in compulsorily fulfilling government posts and other duties. Although such *systems* of government may have been ideally democratic, the communities themselves were far from fully meeting the democratic ideal, since in both the ancient and modern world, women were excluded, and in addition, in the ancient world there was a large slave population without citizen rights, although for the most part humanely treated, and often enjoying the status of tradesmen, teachers, artists, clerks, etc.

In the contemporary world direct democracy is an impracticality. Sometime in the future, however, in an age when higher educational standards have been achieved for the majority in creating a culturally classless society, and when the internet and computerised systems are available in every household, means may be devised for cleverly effecting direct democracy through sophisticated forms of referenda. The prospects for such a system of government might only arise after the broadly-based vested interest parties as we know them today have long since passed into oblivion.

At the present time the notion of government by referenda, despite its theoretical justification as the only true mode of direct democracy for the future, is so foreign to contemporary politicians that it is pooh-poohed as both undesirable or impossible to initiate. If such scorn is taken as reflecting the fear of redundancy amongst politicians themselves, then that is explicable but not excusable. There is no way of anticipating

3-7

the twists and turns of future progress, for predictions about the future when read long after their occurrence, have usually produced a comically distorted view of historical development.

In the meantime, therefore, we are bound to maintain sound systems of representative democracy as a good second best, but effective representative democracy is conditional on several essential factors. In a representative system there needs to be present an interconnected on-going free channel of two-way communication, passing through the three components constituting a democracy: viz., the electorate, or those who empower authority; the elected representative, or the media through which such power is transferred; and the legislative and executive branches of government as exerted by the entire administrative system. Thus bureaucrats are rightly denominated Civil servants, but by the same token, elected representatives should similarly be seen in no lesser light than as Servants of the public will.

In ensuring the existence of democracy in any real sense, it is not sufficient that representatives merely stand for lazily-defined groups of people, but that they stand for clearly identifiable political parties. But not even that is sufficient in itself. A political party without clearly defined principles, or which represents different interests in different parts of the country (as in America) immediately severs itself as an interconnected on-going free channel of communication between the authorisers of power, the medium for its transference, and the different branches of government which enact that which has been authorised.

7   When electors vote for a representative, in the context of any meaningful democracy, they do not vote for a personality but for a set of principles on which impinges a practical end purpose and set of policy aims. The importance of the principles are not only that they underpin the action which is eventually to be achieved, but that they act as constant pointers or reminders to the three component parts of democracy. The necessity for this arises from the fact that whilst an action plan is perceived in a different light by the three component parts of democracy (viz., by electors from the viewpoint of need; by representatives from the viewpoint of enhancing party status and power; and by the government agencies from the viewpoint of practical implementation), underlying principles remain constant in quality and purpose, irrespective of the group by whom they are perceived.

The reality of the above situation is made evident when promises or policies for any reason, unanticipated or otherwise, cannot be fulfilled in whole or part. What happens in such circumstances ? If a party is bereft of underlying principles, then broken promises are conveniently pushed aside and forgotten, and the authority of the

3-8

electorate is reduced to nothing, for mediating representatives cannot be held accountable except through non-election at a later period. If, however, a party is bound by guiding principles, then mediating representatives are put under exceptional pressure, and a second best alternative contributing to the same purpose, will need to be sought out and substituted. By these means the electorate remains empowered.

In any event, there will always be occasions when it is difficult to implement the will of the electorate, not necessarily through the over-optimism or ambition, or guile of political parties in directing the electorate towards false hopes, but through administrative practicalities, the sudden upsurge of conflicting vested interests, or adverse unanticipated events. In such circumstances there may arise conflict, or grounds for misunderstanding, between the party political group and the permanent civil service. Again, in such a situation, if the ruling political party is devoid of principles, the matter is easily settled by pushing aside and forgetting awkward issues. In that event the electorate is dis-empowered, often without knowledge of the fact if negotiations between the government and the civil service are held in camera and withheld from public knowledge - as so often in Britain. If, however, the ruling party is influenced by a set of principles (and these too as a guiding purpose are of course as a point of duty implemented within the practical aims of the permanent administration) then there is an intelligent basis for constructive discussion and compromise between the two components of government. The outcome will then usually maintain the empowerment of the electorate.

8 It must be reiterated, that in ensuring the on-going empowerment of the electorate, it is not sufficient for a political party to be guided by a set of vague general principles, for these would allow too broad a basis of interpretation to be meaningful. It is important that such a set of principles be incorporated within a constructive political philosophy embodying an end purpose, for only through such a doctrinal framework would the principles stand out in sufficient defining clarity, as topics for inspiration and intelligent discussion.

In such an environment, every individual, irrespective of his or her place in the community, would be bound by a common understanding of the aims and purpose of the political movement in question, and each according to personality and temperament, would be the judge and interpreter of the political construct presented to the electorate. In summary, representative democracy can only be meaningful as truly democratic if there is a common understanding and an on-going two-way channel of free communication running through the body politic as to the aims, means, and purpose of political activity.

4-1

These beneficent circumstances may be all the better comprehended by contrasting them with the situation in those societies where political life has degenerated into pragmatism, and guiding principles have all but disappeared. America, where the financial and commercial interests of big business have taken over the two great political parties, is a prime example of the latter. In that country, representatives standing for election are forced to promote not a set of political principles but themselves as personalities. A good set of white teeth, a cheery smile, a glint in the eye, and a good figure, are more important than presenting political substance. Of course speeches have to be made, but the content of high oratory is usually confined to local issues, or attacking the failures of the opposition, or self-congratulatory forecasts, or a set of hyped promises with little intention of their fulfilment.

By no stretch of the imagination can the consequences of such an electoral system be properly described as the workings of a democracy. This is because none of the conditions for the democracy of representative government, cited above, are present to ensure its viability. The situation in America, however, gives us no grounds for complacency. This is because Britain is following fast in the same direction.

CHAPTER 4
The Dichotomy Between Intention And Actuality In The Realm of *Realpolitik*

> "It is the task of the leader to anticipate. It is not sufficient for him to claim that the crowd went the wrong way. It is his job to find the right way and to lead the crowd."
>
> Peter F. Drucker, *The Age of Discontinuity,* Heinemann, 1969, p. 190.

1 - Morality is imposed as the thought control of rulers   2 - How progress is achieved through conflict   3 - But there is a flaw in the Old Socialist concept of class struggle   4 - Dialectical-materialism has prevented the formulation of a constructive philosophy   5 - A new methodology for ensuring a constructive approach to politics   6 - Difficulties arising from the divide between intention and actuality   7 - Conflict between popular and proper political decision-making

1   Having considered the worldwide crisis of contemporary Socialism, and the theoretical basis necessary for the soundness of any healthy democratic political movement, there is one other introductory theme to be covered before considering the sociology of Socialism. This concerns the world of *Realpolitik.*

There is a huge gulf dividing the world of political theory or ideals from that of political actuality. It is a gulf which has always existed. Bacon's contention that "It

4-1

is as hard and severe a thing to be a true politician as to be truly moral,"[15] or King Lear's sardonic cry to the blinded Gloucester, "Get thee glass eyes; And like a scurvy politician, seem To see the things thou dost not,"[16] are statements which may as well have been uttered in ancient Athens, or in our own time, as in that of the Jacobean period. It speaks badly for politicians and the profession of politics. All leaders in government, even those with the highest reputation for moral integrity, are sometime forced into guile, pretence, or ingenious deceit, and often with reluctance, they have been forced to use violence or bloodshed in preventing the break-up of the state.

Despite that, all politics in all regimes purports to be for the common good, but the common good may be interpreted in an infinite variety of colours. In the theocratic nations of the Oriental monarchies, where kings ruled as gods-on-earth, the good of the state was concentrated on the welfare and after-life of those rulers. There is always a distinction, in both notion and actuality, between rulers and ruled (even in democratic states) and often these take on subtle forms. In 16th century Catholic Spain, for example, the population were seen as "Servants" of the King, whereas in Protestant England of the same period they were no more than "Subjects." It is rulers, of course, who are arbiters, as to what is the good of the community, and a moral overlay is always given to uphold that good.

But as morality is subjective and no more than the unconscious imposition of custom as to right or wrong acts or thinking in a community (and so should never be confused with ethics which entails a deeper and objective study of right and wrong) there also develops in society a contrary morality of discontent - the morality of the oppressed. This latter morality is usually a morality of thought rather than action, but even though it is the morality of the oppressed, it is no more objective or justifiable as a basis for ethics than the imposed morality of a ruling elite. This factor is of crucial significance and linked to the central thesis of this book. Morality, therefore, is no more than a weapon of thought control used by conflicting vested interest groups in society.

In view of this conclusion, how then are men and women to justify right and wrong in the sphere of political action ? In the pre-democratic age the only criterion was the might as right of constituted authority in upholding law, in preventing the ills which result from anarchy. Peace and smooth relationships between all sectors of

---

[15] *Advancement of Learning*, Bk. II.

[16] Act IV Sc. 6, 1, 174.

4-2

society was the ideal to be achieved. Thus Machiavelli, who was an experienced politician, living in an age of exceptional turmoil, bloodshed, and treachery, sought to advise princes that any means were justifiable in strengthening authority and crushing revolt as a lesser evil than weak government resulting in anarchy. In a sense he was the first "spin-doctor," for he appreciated the need for effective propaganda and "good image" in securing and maintaining the loyalty of subjects. As a proponent of practical politics, his philosophy is as relevant today as when it was formulated 500 years ago.

2   But in the post-democratic age something more is needed than simply the justification of power as an end in itself. In the absence of invoking moral force as a starting point for political first principles, since the former lead invariably into dark cul-de-sacs and are self-defeating, structural forms need to be devised based on objective sociological criteria, which not merely contribute to the concord of society but also to justice understood as democracy. As demonstrated below, it is impossible to conceive these objective structural forms through an appeal to right or wrong, or through the ordinary conflict of vested interests which are promoted (as we have said) through the overlay of moral values. This is because the latter, as we shall show, always leads to disequilibrium in society.

At this point it is necessary to outline the modern and most convincing interpretation of the forces of history, as a first step in comprehending the nature of practical politics. Until the middle of this century conservative liberal thinkers, and Oxford historians, etc., tended to deny that history had any perceivable purpose or direction. With the development of the social sciences over the past fifty years, the Marxist interpretation of history, or historical-materialism, is accepted in outline although not in detail, across the entire spectrum of political thinking. Marx is now recognised as a seminal sociological thinker without whom it is impossible to make any sense of our current predicament in its historical perspective, although as with many great minds, there are gaping faults in his analysis.

Marx as an economic thinker, however, as we shall demonstrate in a later chapter, needs to be seen in quite a different light, for although he offered a devastating critique of 19th century capitalism, he did not embody in his work (nor can it be inferred) an intellectual basis for the criticism of capitalist conditions which were to develop in a totally unanticipated direction. Consequently, the many conflicting interpreters of Marx, the economic thinker, up until the present day, have been engaged on the futile task of attempting to breathe new life into sacred texts which were blind to the realities of the modern world.

The conflicting forces of history and the process of progress towards more

4-3

complex forms is derived from the dialectics of Hegel, whereby Thesis leads to Antithesis, and Antithesis to Synthesis, which again becomes a Thesis in an on-going cycle. This process of conflict between opposites, and the tendency of opposing forces to polarise and self-destruct through the emergence of new forms and new truths, reflects the fact of all conflict and all history. Despite embodying a kernel of truth, all extremes prove detrimental in themselves, and it is the nature of struggle that compromise should be the outcome. History, therefore, is built on a huge superstructure of unending struggle, whereby all groups and concepts are composed in equal measure of truth and falsehood.

Class struggle is the instrument of progress according to the "science" of Marxism, for Marx had already proclaimed the "end of philosophy" and repudiated the term in the context of his own teaching. He correctly demonstrated that the class struggle intensified when a certain stage was reached in the capitalist process, and he argued that Communism, the ultimate stage in the Socialist struggle, could only finally be attained through capitalism experienced in its most dynamic and advanced form. The overthrow of the bourgeoisie and the victory of the proletariat would be accompanied by the end of class struggle and the disappearance of the state. As soon as Marx entered the realm of prediction he lapsed into utopianism - another term he used with contempt in describing "non-scientific" forms of Socialism. Marx's criticism of capitalism in entailing ever-greater concentrations of wealth into fewer hands remains valid to this day, but the nature of capitalism and the sociology of work, and especially the structural development of society, have changed in ways that could never have been anticipated by Marx, and consequently, many of these factors have invalidated much of his sociological and economic thinking.

3   Integral to the theory of class struggle is that all values arise through class consciousness. This is a realistic approach to understanding society, and is in alignment with the scepticism, we have argued, in which moral values should always be held. Marx explained that wrong values, particularly those detrimental to one's own class, were due to a false consciousness, and the inability to see through the false values imposed by a ruling elite. Again, this is sound analysis, but a reservation has to be drawn as to the exclusiveness of economic factors in influencing thought. Power-lust, love, hatred, madness, and other psychological states, not accountable to economic factors, are also significant driving forces, marking turning points in history. There is seemingly a determinism in the development of society, and free-will counts for little in the context of political or social progress.

There is, however, a flaw in Marxism, and also, in the entire Socialist movement

4-3

· with regard to its dialectic. Whilst on the one hand it is based on a deterministic and seemingly inevitably process, claiming to be scientific rather than philosophical, on the other, it is the subjective victim of its own self-fulfilling prophecy. That is, the call to fight and push forward the Socialist struggle, and the conscious implementation of that struggle, must be distinguished as something quite separate from the determinism conceived as a general principle. In other words, some critics have posed the question, if Socialism is inevitable then why is it anyway necessary to fight for it ? Another relevant question, often posed is: by what criteria do Socialists assess the Socialist validation of their struggle, or how do they align the outcome of that struggle with the general principle or prophecy of its determinism ? These questions have frequently been asked by Socialist thinkers and activists over the past eighty years in the wake of disillusionment at the outcome of Socialist revolutions.

The flaw in Socialism up until the present time is that it has in practice been amongst the most subjective of political ideologies, for it is hard to imagine more subjective political principles than those which are consciously based on class interests and the promotion of class hatred. The resentment to which this gives rise, and the chip on the shoulder attitudes permeating so much of Socialist literature, inevitably distorts the perception of a wider reality and narrows considerably the vision for intellectual thought.

Furthermore, it gives rise to intense moral feelings or values, which are false in all their essential manifestations. For example, the sickening sentimentality of both Marx and Engels in glorifying the proletariat as a class with intrinsic virtues is a distortion of objective fact. The condemnation of individuality as a bad trait as contrasted with collectivism or co-operation as solely desirable qualities, is again a perverse attitude in view of the many qualities needed in a community. Even the acquisitive instinct and striving for wealth are virtues to be promoted in society for the benefit of all, providing such qualities are socially constrained.

The vision of the world from the perspective of an oppressed underclass may energise the process of hatred for the oppressors, but it offers a very limited aspect towards a constructive approach for the future. Even if the values of the proletariat are to be seen as ends in themselves, the hatred of Socialism for the bourgeoisie is greater than its love for proletarianism, and the psychologically negative aspects of hatred is a poor starting point for understanding either humanity in its broader context, or the nature of truth. As H.W. Spiegel has contended, "Marx's strength resided in his destructive criticism, not in his constructive ideas. ... Why did he excel in destruction? Because, as Bertrand Russell once put it, his aim was more for the unhappiness of

4-4

the bourgeoisie than the happiness of the proletariat."[17]

4   Dialectical-materialism, or the so-called "scientific" method of Marxism, has been central to Socialist thinking, and remains influential in Socialist thought - usually implicitly, in a world retreating from the old dogmas. But it is questionable as to whether the term "scientific" has much validity in this context in view of the outdated mechanistic interpretation of materialism, and the many false conclusions and distorted views of history and recent events to which it led. If the end purposes of dialectical-materialism leads to false conclusions, then its claims as a scientific method are illusory rather than real. Early Marxists were conscious of the need to treat the method as scientific, and because of this, they avoided any attempt to describe in detail the structure of Socialist society as it might ultimately appear.

This was because any such descriptive attempt or construct would clearly be perceived as unscientific, and Marx was derisive of those who indulged in what he saw as "fantasising." Socialists were instead to concentrate on stoking up the revolutionary embers, in bringing the body politic to fever pitch, and its desirable outcome. But, again, the impracticality of such an approach - certainly from the perspective of hindsight - can be appreciated *vis-à-vis* its failure to plan and put in place those necessary structures for the long-term success and smooth management of a Socialist society.

Furthermore, it is doubtful as to whether any method which can properly be described as "scientific" should be applied in the consideration of political principles. This is because political principles and the social sciences, in which they need to be embodied, are so wide-ranging and include so many imponderables, that their consideration defies any method which could possibly lay claim to the scientific. The study of politics, therefore, entails many sciences, but collectively, or overall, the study of politics is not a science. In the 19th century, when research into the social sciences had hardly been embarked upon, and the study of the unknown aspects of humanity offered an exciting vista into the future, it was flattering - and certainly rash - of men of the calibre of Comte and Marx to imagine themselves as scientists, working on principles similar to those of the Listers, Bessemer, Bunsen, Faraday, T.H. Huxley, or Darwin. If their assumption to the status of scientists was not arrogant, it was certainly illusory. In any event, dialectical-materialism as a system of ideas with a veneer of the scientific, was no invention of Marx. It was taken bodily from the philosophical system

---

[17] H.W. Spiegel, *The Growth of Economic Thought*, Duke University Press, Durham & London, 1991, 3rd ed., p. 477.

4-5

of Hegel, and turned on its head with a materialistic interpretation. And Hegel was a philosopher - albeit of the Absolute - laying no claims to the status of a scientist.

The argument in this book is that the Marxist and broadly accepted Socialist dialectic (i.e. the method used for investigating the truth of opinions), viz., the pseudo-scientific methodology of dialectical-materialism, embodies an intellectually limiting system which blocks the possibility of formulating a constructive philosophy for a successful Socialist society. It is argued, furthermore, that materialism as a philosophical (or "scientific") system is ineffective and so invalid, as a mode for investigating truth or falsehood; but that is not the same thing as arguing that materialism (or concrete) criteria should not always be applied in laying down the foundations for political principles.

5   Therefore, the stance taken here is that philosophical idealism remains an essential tool for constructive thought, without which it is impossible to think through constructively all those varied factors necessary in formulating a sound basis for political theory. As George Havens has argued, "one of the most neglected lessons of history is that the most idealistic thinkers, if their feet are firmly planted on the ground, are in the long run the most practical."[18] It should be noted, however, that upholding the philosophical idealist position does not imply a defence of the abstruse methodologies of Bradley, Bosanquet, and others. As the eminent philosopher, Mary Warnock, has argued, the metaphysical thinking of the idealists often failed to validate the justifiable and admirable ends they had in view. For example, she blames the "extraordinary literalness" of Moore for his not understanding what the Idealist philosophers were attempting to do by their use of a metaphysical ground for ethics.[19] Consequently, idealism as a school of philosophy, retains a significance placing it far above those other schools which subjected it to such withering scorn solely on the grounds of its methodology.

The eminent historian of sociology, Ronald Fletcher, has argued powerfully that, "the teaching of the philosophical 'idealists' - from Hegel to T.H. Green - possessed an important kernel of truth. They ... thought of the actualities of nature and history as the gradual *actualisation* of an initial *idea*; the *realisation* of the *potentialities* of spirit; and they believed that individual human beings come to their own realisation of the qualities of spirit, realising their own fulfilment, in so far as they experienced the

---

[18]   George H. Havens, *The Age of Ideas*, P.Owen, 1957, p. 51.

[19]   See Mary Warnock's *Ethics Since 1900*, OUP, 1962, pp. 46-47.

4-6

objective embodiments of these qualities (greater than they) which had to take shape, as an outcome of the many-sided quests and conflicts of history, in the *institutions of society*: in the 'totality' of the state in their own time.[20]... Hegel may have failed - but is there any other philosophy of history basing itself on the primacy of spirit or mind as the fundamental ground of reality, which has succeeded any better than he did ? The answer, as far as I am aware, is - no !"[21]

Idealism simply recognises that reality is to be found in the supremacy of ideas; and as ideas are an essential component of thought, and thought is the process of intelligence, any system opposed to idealism, at once turns the lock against the capacity for constructive thought. Of course ideas or constructive thought may at any time be abused as nonsense, or in the pursuit of nonsense, but the purpose of thought is the use of a sound intellect, not merely through the employment of common sense, but of equal importance, in the light of relevant knowledge, reasoning, and a good moral temper. The nit-picking and loquacious opponents of philosophical idealism in the 20th century, have succeeded (as we have already suggested) in throwing out the baby with the bathwater in what amounts to an attack on free speech and the intelligent development of ideas.

Hence the critique of dialectical-materialism, as well as materialism in its broader context as a methodology for thought, hang ultimately on their intellectual limitations as a basis for constructive political theory. The suspicion may consequently be raised in the minds of some (because of the broader uses of idealist argument) that such a stance may allow religious or metaphysical-type reasoning to creep surreptitiously under the political door to objective rational truth. No such notion is remotely intended, for as stated above, and elaborated in more detail later in the book, the methodology for political discussion should remain both concrete and crystal clear.

6   The above arguments, made in this chapter, point in the direction that the first purpose of practical politics should be to lessen - and ideally, to close the gap between intention and actuality in the business of government. Certainly, the criterion of good as well as popular government is the successful alignment of intention with actuality. Unfortunately, this is seldom achieved because of the complexity of the world we live in, and when it is achieved, it tends more often to be in times of war rather than peace.

It is, however, of overriding importance that political movements and their

---

[20] Ronald Fletcher, *The Making of Sociology*, Nelson, 1972, Vol II, p. 220.

[21] Ibid., p. 168.

4-6

leaders should constantly bear in mind the problems posed by the divide between intention and actuality. Failure to maintain such an awareness leads inevitably to one or several of the following situations: firstly, to self-deceit as to means and ends; secondly, to disillusion and cynicism; thirdly, to self-corruption and the corruption of the political group; and fifthly, to the failure and collapse of political power as the vacuum is filled by a competing faction.

If a political party is to avoid corruption through conflict, surrender, or compromise, with competing forces, then its active membership must be sufficiently aware of *Realpolitik*, and the necessary attitudes and action needed in responding to competing pressures. Those who fail to bend because of the rigidity of their ideological convictions (or principles) will anyway be destroyed - or pushed into insignificance. This is because of a poor political sense which equates stubbornness with unreality. In the stress of political life it is vital to have the flexibility to bend in response to the oncoming storm, and even more necessary to have the resilience in returning to original principles, or a proper line of action, once the storm has passed. But political integrity through difficult times cannot be maintained unless a firm grasp is kept in view of what distinguishes the intentional from the actual.

This is best illustrated through reviewing the type of vicissitudes confronting political parties and their leading figures. There is often a conflict of choice, particularly in democratic communities, between promoting what is perceived as a proper course of action as opposed to a popular course of action. In what direction should the politician exert his energy ? As democracy necessarily entails the will of the people, it might logically be argued that the politician should follow the popular path, but representative government creates a more complex situation. Underlying political principles should always be upheld as the first purpose of government, but sometimes there is a choice between following second-best short-term or ideal long-term courses of action. The long-term interests of policy should be followed whenever these are pacticable, i.e. not blocked by opposing vested interests.

Furthermore, it needs to be recognised that popular government is not necessarily best government. Such questions usually arise from either of the two following factors: firstly, the selfishness of individual interests will always override the necessity of working for the common good, e.g., low taxation will always be preferred to higher taxation, and the exertion of free choice may often endanger safety or health, or pose a nuisance to others. Speed limits and restrictions on the consumption of undesirable substances, may be unpopular and restrict the freedom of many individuals, but nonetheless may better serve the *total* interests of the community. Secondly, the

4-7

technical complexity of managing a state often entails the imposition of legislation or administrative acts which are difficult for large sectors of the public to appreciate due to a lack of background knowledge. This applies in the sphere of changing interest and exchange rates, as well as to the multifarious factors contributing to the input of the many forms of taxation.

The really astute politician, well versed in Machiavellian principles, is also aware that following the popular course can lead to disaster and self-destruction at the polls. The electorate are everywhere - even in the best democracies - fickle, short-sighted, bloody-minded, and obtuse, to an infinite degree. Gratitude to politicians or political groups for benefits rendered is rare or non-existent. The average elector is not only contemptuous of the politician, regarding him as "in it for the make," but has a vicious streak, and would want to prove the politician wrong, even in the absence of any fault. The consequence of this (as often experienced in local government) is that a group has successfully improved, at low cost, the amenities of a town, only to be attacked on spurious grounds by the opposition, for over-spending.

Accusations are always taken on their face value by an uncritically-critical electorate, with the predictable result that the ruling authority is thrown out of power at the next election. What would have been the course of a more astute authority ? To eschew any popular measures in anticipation that they may rebound against those responsible for their initiation ? To avoid expenditure on anything beyond the bare essentials ? To repress any imaginative inclination for improvement for fear of unexpected consequences ? There is no general answer to these questions. The politician must be sufficiently thick-skinned "to suffer the slings and arrows of outrageous fortune." The only defensive mode of the politician, or the group, against the seemingly unfair blows of the electorate, is through the formulation of constructive principles for the party. Then, after the elapse of time, and a period a political integrity, a bond of trust is enabled to develop between the electorate and its following.

7   Even in the most democratic of representative systems, government is often forced to adopt a condescending attitude in assuming the dark ignorance of the majority. Such feelings of superiority amongst permanent civil servants and politicians is only made morally excusable through the good intentions of sound political principles and the determination to carry through their purpose. The gap between governed and those who rule can only be narrowed by ensuring ever-higher standards of education. It also has to be noted that democracy in any meaningful sense can only survive amongst a people which has not merely achieved a certain level of political consciousness, but also a sufficient level of general education.

4-7

In the second half of the 20th century, the question has often been asked: should a people unfit for self-government be granted the benefits of democracy, even though it may lead to a situation further undermining their economy and living standards ? Since it is a sensitive question only confronting guilt-ridden de-colonising powers, the answer has always had to be a resounding "Yes," with the assuaging adjunction that it is anyway impertinent to judge as to whether or not a people is ripe for self-government. Again, there is a gap between good manners or tact and meaningful objective opinion. What has occurred in reality in the post-imperial period is that the European powers, like Pontius Pilate, have callously washed their hands of an awkward and embarrassing situation. Nevertheless, the underlying principle of the *right* to democracy (although not to democracy itself as a living long-lasting system of government) is that it may be put to any use its people choose, including even, as often witnessed in the present century, its self-destruction.

Besides the difficulties of political movements in power confronted by the pressures of opposing groups, business interests, the need to consider minorities, etc., there sometimes occur great questions of moral choice in decision-making. What, for example, justifies war as a practical consideration ? Is public outrage, or what Oliver Wendell Holmes called "called the inflammation of the public conscience" sufficient to justify involvement in armed conflict ? If populism and the immediate satisfaction of the democratic will is to have its way, then the answer must be, Yes.

But regret or soured hopes may soon follow in the wake of strategic failure or the unanticipated horrors of war. The outbreak of the First Wold War, for example, was universally acclaimed by Allies and Axis powers alike, as a popular event; but the Second World War was universally met with gloom and foreboding (even in Germany), and yet the declaration of war by the Allies in the Second War has been generally regarded as a more justifiable event than the First. Many still argue that the First World War should never have been allowed to occur. All this points to the occurrence of popular misjudgement in questions of armed conflict. The only criterion a government may apply is its conviction for eventual success, but official predictions in matters of war have always been notoriously unreliable.

A final question which may be considered, and it is no less significant than any other with regard to the gap between intention and actuality, is the acceptability or non-acceptability of the image created by the ideology of a political movement. In other words, does the unacceptability of a party's image in itself invalidate the underlying truths of a political movement, or is it only a reflection of a false understanding by the public? Such a question is of particular relevance to the contemporary Labour party.

5-1

Old Socialists would argue that the public have a wrong perception of the party, are oppressed by a false consciousness, or otherwise fail to appreciate the "true" image of "real Socialism."

The greater probability, however, is that the party has failed to move with the times, and that the unacceptability of its image, not so much reflects the falsity of the image and the need to change appearances, as an underlying fault in the Labour party and Socialism itself. This is a topic to which we must now return in the next chapter.

CHAPTER 5
The Missing "Gene" of Socialism

"The ultimate test of a set of economic ideas - a system, if the word be allowed - is whether it illuminates the anxieties of the time. Does it explain problems that people find urgent ?"

J.K. Galbraith, *Economics And The Public Purpose*, André Deutsch, 1974, p. 198.

1 - Importance of retaining the original purpose of Socialism   2 - Antipathy between business and non-business people   3 - The cultural factor of business aptitude amongst different peoples   4 - The failure of countries with a low business aptitude   5 - Why ruling elites have everywhere disdained the business instinct   6 - Business-as-work closer to Socialism than to traditional elites

1   During the hectic formative period of New Labour, some time after Tony Blair had been elected to the leadership, it was necessary to calm the apprehensions of Old Labour stalwarts who felt their party was being transformed beyond recognition.

Tony Blair consoled his anxious supporters by maintaining that although great changes were being made, the "old values" of the party would nonetheless remain firmly in place, and hence there was no cause for concern. As to whether Tony Blair actually meant that the old values would remain in place is a question which can never be answered. No one attempted at the time to define precisely what those values were, and anyway, there would have been argument as to their interpretation.

The reality, however, in meeting needs arising from the transformation of society over the past fifty years, is that New Labour and New Socialism will need to take on a number of new and very different values, whilst ditching others. What is quite certain is that the old values will not, and cannot, be maintained in promoting the Socialism of the future.

If, on the contrary, Tony Blair had instead contended that the original end

5-1

purpose of Socialism would be maintained in promoting the Socialism of the future, he might have stood on firmer ground, but would then have aroused consternation amongst all sectors of the party. But then Tony Blair fulfils his role as an effective politician, and it is not the function of politicians to philosophise, or to inaugurate new ideas, or to take on the mantle of a social scientist. The role of a politician, as we have demonstrated in the previous chapter, is to operate within the framework of a political movement in promoting its practicable ends by any necessary means. There has been much discussion in the media as to whether the new party leader is promoting or ruining Socialism, but in view of the difficulties facing any politician in times of change, it is premature - and would be unfair - to judge one way or the other.

A point has been reached when we must now define what we mean by Socialism, and having grasped the concept and the end purpose in view, the remaining chapters of the book will be devoted to developing the practical implications of Socialism for the future.   Socialism is defined as "a political and economic theory of social organisation which advocates that the community as a whole should own and control the means of production, distribution, and exchange."[22] This is the original and complete definition of Socialism, and no attempt will be made to interpret it in any other light. An initial response might be to raise eyebrows and conclude that this is a return to the principles of Old Labour and Old Socialism. But to offer an alternative definition would be an attempt to pervert Socialism's true purpose. If the Labour party has not already repudiated the idea of the community owning and controlling the means of production through its re-writing of Clause IV, then the Fabian society certainly has, but in doing so, it has by necessity also repudiated Socialism.

The problem with the above definition (and it is held in this book as the only viable and desirable definition), is that it evokes a variety of undesirable images: e.g., the failures of Nationalisation as practised by post-War Labour administrations; Soviet collectives; the appropriation of private property and the rounding up of the Kulaks; and ideological dogma in regard to the management of business. If, however, a more precise and up-dated version is given to the terms included in the above quotation, a very different picture may emerge. What must be the underlying purpose of democratic Socialism ? Surely the economic empowerment of all people in the community, but this is not to be achieved through any of the ineffective or stale old measures of the past. In conjunction with people power, the egalitarian ideal should be pursued, but this does not entail clipping the wings of initiative or well-being of the middling majority, but

---

[22] *Oxford Encyclopaedic English Dictionary*, OUP, 1991, p. 1377.

5-2

rather in restraining the threat of monopoly power, which destroys competition and choice, and greedily accumulates ever more wealth and power into fewer hands.

2   Before looking ahead at the future of Socialism it is first necessary to enquire into the underlying reason for the failure of Socialism worldwide up until the present time. Why has it been so difficult to establish in practice such an ideally just system for the government of humankind ? No satisfactory answer has been given to this question. Many have contended that Socialism has never been tried, arguing instead that only perversions of its true purpose have been attempted, i.e., state Socialism, dictatorship by patronising bureaucracies, etc. Although these latter allegations may be true as superficial assertions, it still does not explain the underlying reason for the failure of Socialism.

Innumerable Socialist experiments have been tried over the past 200 years, including those which should have satisfied the sensibilities of those demanding Socialism in its most unadulterated form, as, for example, as tried in communes in Europe and America throughout the 19th century. Such ideal communities seem always to have failed as soon as a particular individual or authoritative group emerged, and then encountered popular resistance to new ideas or modes of government. Meanwhile, revolutions have often broken out followed by the sincerest intentions of creating democratic and egalitarian societies, and latterly, with the intention that they should be specifically Socialist, but after a short period, best intentions were either lost sight of, or pushed aside as impracticable, before reaction set in. The argument, therefore, that Socialism "has never been tried" does not stand up in the light of historical fact.

It is in managing the economy where Socialism has always met failure. A point is reached when either the business community finds itself oppressed or in a recessionary situation, or in East bloc style dictatorships, when the economy collapses, usually in the wake of crop failures and famine, as in China with the Great Leap Forward, or in Russia on frequent occasions during the Soviet period. Socialism's real economic problem is that it takes the process of wealth creation for granted - as something ever-present - to be relied upon as a natural constituent in any community. The truth is that wealth creation is nothing of the sort. In world terms, it is instead, a rare and delicate plant.

The industrialist, Sir Peter Parker, and at one time a Labour party parliamentary candidate, has been scathing in his criticism of the movement *vis-à-vis* its relationship with the world of industry, when he wrote, "the intellectuals of the party, in true Oxbridge style, had been bred with at best an indifference to how industry worked, or at worst a contempt, and the trade unions saw the manager as a mere bargainer on the

5-2

other side of the table, or as the steward of capitalism, a Malvolio figure of fun. Efficiency and competitiveness were problems remote from this pantheon of the movement's gods; distribution was their issue, not production. Both intellectual and unionist questioned the motivation of the manager. What were managerial values ? Only money."[23]

Socialism's attitude to wealth creation springs from two factors: firstly, through its concern with the fairer distribution or re-distribution of existing resources, or the creation of future wealth by fairer means; and secondly, as a movement involved in class struggle for the appropriation of wealth for the proletariat. In practice, of course, Socialist movements have transformed their thinking and strategy over the past fifty years, but because of the resistance of tradition, their underlying attitude to the problem of wealth creation remains in essence unchanged.

This attitude constitutes a major handicap in understanding an essential living element in the working of any successful community. The error of Socialism (or Socialists) is to comprehend wealth creation, or business, in terms of a simple mechanism which may be adjusted or altered through the intervention of bureaucratic controls. Those who create wealth, or manage business on the basis of profit, are seen as engaging in activity opposed to that of promoting the more equal distribution of wealth, since their motives are personal and hence selfish. They are therefore perceived with suspicion and as opposed to a beneficent re-distributive agent, such as a Socialist government. The Socialist attitude to wealth in the abstract, is generous if not prodigal, whilst the business attitude to wealth is by necessity the reverse of this, i.e. frugal and accumulative. At once a psychological divide and grounds for conflict can be seen between the Socialist and business approaches to the nature of wealth creation and the uses of wealth.

Socialists, and a large proportion of the non-business community, particularly middle class public sector employees and those in education or the NHS, and those who describe themselves as "working class," see business as at best a tainted occupation, self-serving, with an overlay of trickery and deceit; and at worst, as ruthless and unprincipled, and totally against the interests of the community if not kept under the tight leash of government control. But underlying these feelings is a fear of business as an inscrutable process which defies understanding. The non-business person asks him- or herself, What is that unknown or mysterious quality which marks out some to be always successful in business whilst others are always doomed to

---

[23] Sir Peter Parker, *For Starters*, J. Cape, 1989, pp. 120-121.

5-3

failure? It certainly is not knowledge or intelligence in any ordinary sense, and no amount of training will turn a non-business person into a business person, any more than will a writing school create a Shakespeare or a James Joyce.

3   The truth is that wealth creation, or the business instinct, is creative in the same sense that poetry or painting is creative, except that business is a far more widespread activity in the community. If the business instinct is not an inherited factor, it is certainly a cultural aptitude within a community. Some peoples have a high aptitude for business, whilst in others it is almost entirely absent. The distinguished historian Theodore Zeldin has interestingly observed that "the Muslims were the first to produce a book in praise of commerce, *The Beauties of Trade*, by Ja' far b. Ali ad-Diminshqi, in the 12th century, arguing that trade is 'the best of gainful employments and the most conducive to happiness."[24] Amongst the Jews or Chinese the aptitude for business may be seen to reach levels of genius. The aptitude for trading has always been strong amongst Semitic peoples, e.g. the Phoenicians or Carthaginians, and in our own time, amongst the Arabs, but only the Jews amongst modern Semites have developed business in all its forms to the greatest success in a modern industrial society. The highest aptitude for business can only be developed in city cultures (or civilisations), and the phenomenal industrial success of mainland China in our own time could not possibly have been achieved without the presence of those qualities inherent in 3,000 years of Chinese history.

Success in wealth-creating business is therefore not merely a question of know-how or technique, but of attitudes to the world and underlying moral values. Of overriding importance is a sense of realism, and a practical ability to seize on situations where profit may be derived from sale or purchase. The creative instinct of business is not to be found through "taking advantage" or "exploiting" a customer, for that would be failing to perceive the proper business purpose; but rather in appreciating opportunities for mutually beneficial exchange, which reflects a far greater pragmatic understanding and a better intelligence than trickery or sleight of hand. Contrary to the common perception of the non-business community, the ordinary business person does not see him- or herself as engaged in exploitation, or accumulating wealth as an end in itself, or in aggrandisement, or even as striving for growth, but more simply, in struggling for survival.

This is reflected in the constant wariness to ward off failure, or the ever-present threats of the competition, and the need to conserve resources. The ordinary business

---

[24] Theodore Zeldin, *An Intimate History of Humanity,* Sinclair-Stevenson, 1994, p. 156.

5-4

· person is only a big spender occasionally out of necessity, and otherwise minimises expenditure in striving for success. In attitude he tends to be dismissive of grand or abstruse ideas, and showiness or pomposity, since these things are a distraction from the down-to-earth facts of business. As a successful business person he may be amongst the most religious of peoples, e.g. the Jews, or amongst the least religious, e.g. the Chinese, but in either case, nothing will divert him from an attempt to understand the world as it is in all its goodness and nastiness.

Those peoples in Europe with the most natural or strongest business instinct are the Dutch and the Swiss, who are constantly alert as to new ways of increasing profit. Even business failures amongst their number maintain an obsessive search for new projects and modes of money-making. The Greeks and Armenians are similarly endowed, although working in societies with a lower standard of living. Those peoples in Europe with the least ability for business are the Slavs (except for the Czechs), and the peoples of those two countries on the opposite longitude, Ireland and Finland.

Can generalisations be made about peoples with a strong business instinct, and those who seem to lack it ? A review of world history clearly reveals that those cultures most closely resembling democracies, e.g. oligarchic city republics with a relatively large middle class and a degree of freedom for international trade, invariably - and as would be expected - enjoy a strong business instinct. Athens, and her allies, would be the prime example taken from the classical world. History would seem to indicate that business cultures only flourish in those states which either do not attempt to intervene too closely into the lives of their peoples, as in ancient China or the Ottoman empire; or which themselves are plutocracies, as with Venice or Genoa, or the numerous Hansa cities on the western and northern seaboard of Europe, and scattered throughout Germany.

4   The business instinct is weakest in those countries where the state tends to dominate the lives of their peoples, usually with military obligations, as in ancient Rome, or during the 1500 years during which most of Europe was oppressed by the feudal system. This is because such societies are dominated by bureaucratic values, and their peoples become dependent on an employed status (irrespective of whether their work is rewarded or not with a money payment), or else they live on free handouts from the state, as began to occur in Rome from the second century BC.

Feudalism was maintained for the longest period in Germany and Eastern Europe - the Hansa city states standing out as islands of progress, prosperity and enlightenment in a sea of gothic ignorance. When the industrial revolution did reach Germany in the last quarter of the 19th century - as also in Japan, another feudal country, in the same

5-4

period - it had to be pushed forward by agencies of the state. Consequently, Germany and Japan, as well as other countries, were to develop a form of capitalism very different from the laissez-faire mode in Britain or American.

The reason for the poor business instinct of the Irish and the Finns may be traced to similar historical circumstances: for whilst Ireland was ruthlessly exploited by England, Finland was somewhat less exploited by Sweden, but suffered the worse fate of a buffer territory, marched over and plundered for centuries by the warring armies of Sweden and Russia. Although the Irish and Finns are very different peoples, both have successfully promoted the well-being of their peoples through major organisational initiatives: the Finns through the world's largest co-operative distribution networks, from the beginning of the present century, and the Irish, more recently, through commitment to EU subsidies and business start-up schemes.

Until the Mongol invasions of the 13th century, the Russians enjoyed a relatively high degree of civilisation, comparable with that of any other European culture of the Mediterranean, but from the 13th until the 20th century they remained in abject serfdom - if it is accepted that the official abolition of serfdom in 1862 compounded rather than relieved the misery of her people. This, together with famine, poverty, and ignorance, compounded by frequent major wars throughout Eastern Europe, ensured that their peoples could never develop a proper business instinct. Many Westerners are astonished at the glaring contrast seen today between the Chinese and the Russians. Why should the Russians, they ask, who after all have supposedly been a European power since the reforms of Peter the Great at the end of the 17th century, fail to create a modern free market industrial state; whilst the Chinese, an Oriental despotism closed off from the rest of the world until the present century, within a 10-year period glide into adopting all the habits of thought and succeed in creating a capitalist system hardly less sophisticated than those of America, Holland or Japan ?

The answer is simply to be found in the contrasting history and habits of thought of the two peoples. The dull mentality of the serf-like Russians only allowed them to sink into a morass of criminality as soon as they were brought into opportunistic contact with the West after 1989. The intelligence and natural business acumen of the Chinese, on the other hand, held down and dormant for almost fifty years, quickly allowed them to build an industrial infrastructure, and their people to play the stock market with a confidence and circumspection equal to that of investors in America or Britain, soon after the reforms of Deng Xiaoping in 1978. The two peoples are endowed with quite separate qualities due to the fortunes and tragedies of their long history.

5-5

5   In summary, the wealth creating process necessarily reflected through the business instinct, and success in business following from this, is only found in countries allowing a sufficient degree of socio-economic freedom, and the benefits of civilisation following from this. It is worth remarking that the anti-business ethos currently found in the industrialised West, particularly amongst middle class public sector workers, is always ready to draw a sneering comparison between the philistinism of business activity and the cultured world of the arts. The truth to be found in any period in world history, however, is that the flourishing of the arts, irrespective of whether it be sculpture, painting, music, literature - or philosophy, *only* follows in the wake of commercial or industrial expansion. The two are so closely related as to be inseparable with regard to their existence. It should be noted, therefore, that business exists in society as a positive and civilising force.

That is not the same thing, of course, as saying that business is perceived by the establishment, or the cultural elite of a people, as a worthy or status-giving occupation. Quite the contrary ! In all great civilisations (apart from America and Semitic cultures) business or money-making has been held as a despised or very much a secondary-status occupation. Even in China, amongst a people who were the most astute and proficient in business, the educated Mandarin class looked down in disdain on the wealthy merchants or those who earned their living through trade. In Britain, the Administrative class civil service, and the entire Oxbridge establishment (permeated for centuries with the snobbish values of Plato and Aristotle on what constituted the proper role of a gentleman) are bastions of the anti-business ethos. In the original caste system of Aryan India, the *Shudra* or artisan class, were placed on the fourth of bottom level of society.

The contrasting attitudes in which wealth creation or business may be regarded: i.e either as a despised activity of low status; or as an essential accompaniment to a high level of civilisation, are psychologically interesting in reflecting social mores, and will be of significance in developing the thesis of this book. What accounts for the negative feeling and attitudes of ruling elites to wealth creators and the business community? Is not the elite in any community most indebted to its wealth creators, without which the products of prosperity would not be available ? Why, then, do ruling elites disdain those who produce for them their most valued commodities ? The only satisfactory answers to be found are in the psychological manifestations originating in the disdain of labour itself.

Those privileged mortals who do not work, or do not have the capacity to work, irrespective of whether this entails earning a living or undertaking household tasks,

5-5

secretly fear the hypothetical idea of the need to work because of their helplessness and dependence on others. Because of this dependence and the fragility of their lives, reliant on a huge subservient class, the relationship between those who give and take orders can only be secured by widening the gap in society. Since humankind is everywhere the same in physical and emotional needs, artificial or illusory means must be used in widening the psychological and class divide. The subservient must be made to respect their masters and mistresses, and this is best achieved by lowering the perceived social and market values of skill, effort, and initiative, of those obliged to work, without diminishing the actual occurrence of these qualities in the community.

This is best done by ensuring that work itself is given a low status in the community, and that the characteristics of those who exert effort, e.g. a rapid step, hurried speech, calloused hands, or a bent back, are subject to ridicule or disdain. A rapid step, or hurried behaviour of any kind, are characteristics which have been disdained in civilisations across the globe. In Rome it was always regarded as the mark of a "slave." In further marking the divide between workers and non-workers, courtly manners, special and expensive clothing, sumptuary regulations, and isolation in fine houses, were used to emphasise the difference. In pre-1912 China the fingernails of the privile d were allowed to grow six inches long so that work or simple tasks were anyway made impractical.

Another reason why the non-productive classes disdain the world of profit and business is an underlying fear of the risk factor. In the eyes of those reliant on a regular pay packet, or other income from an assured source, those whose lives are dependent on risk seem to place themselves in the hands of an inexplicable or mysterious force. If risk-taking is no more than merely a gamble, then surely it is stupid, but if risk-taking seems always to reap its reward, then surely it must be crooked. By what standards of fairness do those engaged in the seemingly underhand activity of risk-taking deserve such high rewards for their efforts? The explanation, of course, in answering the above, is firstly, that risk-takers are engaged in creative activity (as we have already explained the nature of business); and secondly, that risk-taking is anyway an essential component of wealth creation in benefiting the entire community. The creativity of business can no more be interfered with than that of the painter or sculptor - except, of course, when it adversely effects the economic, social, or environmental interests of others.

In historical perspective, it needs to be emphasised that both work and commerce were lumped together by ruling elites as equally despised activities. No clear distinction was perceived, by the highly privileged, between oppressors and oppressed

5-5

within the world of work. Such differences were not thought worthy of recognition, since both sides in such a divide were equally disdained as an underclass of artisans and money-grubbers. That is why some prominent Tories in the 19th century had no compunction about a patronising sympathy with the plight of the working class and taking a stance against the "vulgar" new bourgeoisie. They were so distanced from the world of commerce that they did not see this as eventually compromising or threatening their own interests. The support of the Tories for working class interests in the last century was made evident by Alexander Macdonald, the miner's leader, when he declared in the 1870s that, "the Conservative party have done more for the working class in five years than the Liberals have in fifty."[25]

In the modern age, because of the influence of democracy and the transformation of society, it is no longer viable for ruling elites to denigrate the activity of work within their own circle, but commerce or business generally, is still regarded with suspicion and intensely disliked by a huge sector of the community. Deep-seated attitudes of the past 2,000 years have not simply evaporated. They have merely adapted to meet changing conditions. Hence the princely Mandarin in ancient China would be as loathed to acknowledge that the treasured ornaments in his garden were accountable to something as vulgar as competition and the profit motive, in exactly the same way as a primary school teacher in contemporary England would be as loathed to acknowledge that her or his wages were only made possible through the process of wealth creating business. The sorry fact remains that the teacher, the hospital worker, or the University professor, is as reliant for his or her salary on the wealth creating activity of business than was the King, the Prince, the Bishop, or some other non-productive functionary, of former times.

Oxbridge as the elite centre of education and culture in Britain, and as the training ground for leadership in all the professions - and particularly government, is still, in a subtle way, perpetuating the values of a slave society as found in the classical world. But strangely, and it is a huge irony, it finds an ally in the ideas of Socialism, which not merely despises business, but has set its sights on destroying the entire capitalist system through which business is able to operate. The Oxbridge sympathy for Socialism stems partly from the intellectual attitude of the latter in setting the world aright, as opposed to the empiricism and hit-and-miss approach of the despised business community in its approach to politics.

But as Oxbridge is also a bastion of privilege, its relationship with Socialism is

---

[25] W. Churchill, *History of The English Speaking Peoples*, Dodd,Mead & Co., NY, 1966 ed., Vol. IV, p. 292.

5-6

ambiguous and covert. It is no coincidence that the idealists and master spies, originally known in the 1930s as, The Apostles, were a group of men from privileged backgrounds, attracted by the intellectual ingenuity of Marxism and the Soviet experiment. Their innocence of the practicalities of the world, *vis-à-vis* political realism, complemented the rarefied air of the exclusive cloisters. More usually, however, Oxbridge intellectuals of the left steer more towards a conventional career in the senior branches of the civil service.

6   Since commerce and business in most civilisations throughout history, have been despised activities, and their practitioners denied status or recognition as morally significant contributors to the community, this suggests that commerce and business have themselves been oppressed. In the sense that they have been prevented from dominating, or contributing on a more equal basis, to the underlying value systems of cultures, this is certainly true. Why is this ? The obvious and only answer is that commerce and business ultimately represent the values of Work (i.e. skill, effort, initiative, imagination, intelligence, etc.), whilst ruling elites have represented the contrary values of freedom from Work (i.e. convention, honour, leisure, and the God-given permanence of the status quo).

Clearly the values of work more closely approximate to Socialist ideals than those values of ruling elites, since Socialism by necessity promotes the interests of those who work, and is concerned with all aspects of fairness in work. In view of this, should not commerce and business therefore be integrated into the value system of Socialism ? The only stumbling block to pursuing such a course are the ills of the capitalist system through which commerce and business are obliged to operate. Consequently,   Socialism has been unable to disentangle the positive and negative elements in both capitalism and business, and because of this, the latter is regarded as something necessarily to be disdained along with the former.

This Socialist situation is further compounded by negative attitudes to work emanating from two other directions: firstly, from religious tradition explaining the obligation to work as a curse and the outcome of the fall ("in the sweat of thy face shalt thou eat bread," *Genesis*, iii, 19); and secondly, through envy of the rich and privileged, and the desire to appropriate their value of leisure as an ideal for themselves.

All these conflicting values have not only brought psychological confusion to the direction of Socialism, but have blocked its capacity to build a constructive philosophy for the future. Such a philosophy can only be formulated through fully incorporating the business process as central to Socialist doctrines, and to achieve that is the purpose of this book. Socialism's failure to appreciate the business instinct as essential to the

6-1

success or fulfilment of any community, signifies its missing "gene," and this in turn has crippled the purpose of Socialism, dooming it to repeated failure after every new experiment or revitalising attempt at change.

CHAPTER 6
How Values May Advance Or Hinder Societies

"Enlightenment philosophies of history tell us that countries modernise by replicating Western societies. These philosophies and the theories of modernity they supported had already been falsified by Japan at the start of the 20th century."

John Gray, *False Dawn: The Delusions of Global Capitalism*, Granta Books, 1998, p. 170.

1 - Conscious and unconscious values call for sociological analysis in defining the true nature of associations 2 - How values may unknowingly pervert the purpose of an organisation 3 - Political values should be sociological rather than theological 4 - Examples of the mischief of theological values when applied to politics 5 - Faults of Old Socialism derived from cultural tradition 6 - Pervasiveness of value systems and the need for change 7 - The self-destructive dualism in Western civilisation 8 - The road to social harmony

1   All societies have values, both conscious and unconscious, which act as underlying motives in their behaviour and direction. Different cultures and civilisations have widely varying moral codes and ideas as to what constitutes the Good, and these vary both according to the evolution of cultures and to different modes of direction by cultures on a comparable level of civilisation. Even within civilisations each society has a moral code or value system which differs in subtle ways from those of its neighbours, and these we describe as national characteristics.

Unconscious values are those which would seem to contradict the values of a society as perceived by itself. Thus the British may see themselves as honest and transparent in their dealings with others, but their neighbours, through past experience, may find them scheming and perfidious, and so hypocritical. Until 1945 most of Europe may have perceived the Germans as warlike and expansionist, but the Germans may have seen themselves as merely taking justifiable revenge on neighbours for wrongs committed over the previous centuries. There is much truth and falsehood in all such perceptions, but it is indubitably true that no people sees itself exactly as it is.

Associations within a society, social, religious, cultural, sporting, political, and other, also have their conscious and unconscious values, formed through the characteristics of their memberships and relationships with external bodies. The fact

6-1

that any society or association transmits unconscious values means that it can only be properly understood from a sociological perspective. In other words, the aims of a belief system of an organisation fails to explain its existence in any meaningful sense. An organisation can only be explained in terms of its place and relationship with other social groups of a complementary, contrasting, or competing nature.

This particularly applies to religious or political type organisations. Churches, for example, crystallise the value systems of class groups or localities as a social bonding agency, and have little to do with the prescribed theology of the particular church, and even less to do with the teachings of Jesus Christ, although these latter are convenient props on which to hang the cloak of identity. Whilst a village church is little more than a friendly or support society for local inhabitants, the Anglican church in its wider aspect, has been described as the open social club for the upper classes - usually for those with Tory sympathies. The Methodist and Baptist churches, meanwhile, constitute social gatherings of the go-getting lower-middle class.

All this is confirmed by the fact that post-Reformation church history is also the history of social change and the transformation of classes. The interconnection between religious belief and economic behaviour, as a subject for sociological study, was analysed long ago by such scholars as Max Weber in *The Protestant Ethic & The Spirit of Capitalism*, and some years later, by R.H. Tawney in, *Religion & The Rise of Capitalism*.

In response to declining church attendance and religious belief, the clergy have sought to popularise their message by transforming their role from a leadership to a patronising attitude. This has taken the form of concentrating on the myths of Christianity and simple analogy with everyday life, whilst ignoring its theology, or ethics, or intellectual arguments as to the nature of God. The content of teaching as taught in seminaries, for example, has little resemblance with what is heard from the pulpit. A sharp distinction is drawn between knowledge judged fit for the clergy (the secrets of "priestly power") and that which is to be dished out to lesser mortals comprising their congregations.

This supercilious attitude of the clergy to the intelligence of their flock, in a greatly changed society with higher educational standards than heretofore, has probably rebounded against their interests or success as transmitters of the Christian message, if not as social linkage agencies within their respective localities. The change in the role of the clergy from religious leaders in a proper sense, to that of social bonding workers, is not intended as criticism in itself, except insofar as it diverges from the intended or original and stated purpose of their particular religion. A new agnostic

6-2

clergy is now emerging in the Protestant church, especially in Germany, which is prepared to turn over many of the old beliefs in meeting the needs of an increasingly secular world.

2   The above sociological illustration of the current situation found in many Christian churches was made to demonstrate several factors found in most major organisations seeking to influence the thought or behaviour of great numbers of people, viz:-

1 . The stated aims or purpose of an organisation may in reality be different from that   proclaimed.

2. The outcome of an organisation's purpose may differ from its intention for any number of reasons.

3. The underlying belief system and strategy of an organisation may be confidential to the closed circle of its leadership.

4. The doctrines of an organisation may be adapted, or so coloured, to suit the needs of a wider membership.

5. The leaders of an organisation either compromise or risk compromising their integrity when acting as a medium between its underlying doctrines and those which are to be transmitted for popular consumption.

6. The aims or purpose of an organisation may be transformed or perverted by forces beyond its own control.

7. When this occurs, an organisation will often use self-deceit in denying the nature of the said changes taking place.

8. Unconscious values tend to preponderate, or take over, in those situations when an organisation experiences widespread change.

9. When an organisation encounters external forces of such strength that adaptation to the challenge is no longer sufficient, it will splinter and disintegrate following a period of internal strife.

10. In the last resort, it is not integrity or best intentions which maintain the life of an organisation, but its ability to maintain *reality* in a changing world.

Sociological observation may point to the fact that religious-type organisations are no less dishonest than those which are political, and insiders are well aware that the politics of Cathedral life in almost any part of England is no less vicious, and fraught with pride, jealousy, intrigue, and deceit, than that found in the most contentious political movement.

6-3

Large social organisations, therefore, are not necessarily what they seem or purport to be. Christian missionary expeditions, for example, in the light of their history over the past 500 years, might more correctly be understood as instruments for social control in easing and complementing imperial expansion. Meanwhile, Anglo-Saxon freemasonry, despite its charitable and beneficent ends is in reality little more than a tightly knit organisation of the privileged and powerful and their willing minions, to conserve *guan xi* (business connections) amongst their own number, in excluding outsiders and undermining the free market.

In view of the gloomy picture which may be drawn above of the real world as it is, how best may organisations maintain their integrity to themselves, and of more importance, to the wider community ? At the risk of being accused of repetition, the answer may only be found through formulating a constructive philosophy which takes into consideration internal contradictions and other factors facilitating an objective understanding. The opening chapters of this book have already laid out the groundwork for such a constructive philosophy. We must now turn again to the question of Socialism and the values of which it is comprised.

3   An interesting contrast may be made. Whilst on the one hand Socialism is highly subjective, since it chooses to see the world from the narrow and restricting perspective of a particular class; on the other hand, it claims to represent the highest ideals of humanity. The values of Socialism are undoubtedly, in theory, of the best kind. They assume the intrinsic goodness of humankind, and would be aptly suited to angelic beings existing on a higher plain. The problem with Socialist values are their impracticability. Human beings are intrinsically neither good nor bad, but morally neutral, although capable of great goodness as well as wickedness. The falsity of Socialist values is that they are theological rather than sociological. That is, they are concerned with aspects of goodness in the abstract, rather than with actual aspects of human nature in all their complexity. Consequently, when theological values are incorporated into a political system, contradictions arise which soon break out into conflict, and these in their turn lead inevitably to frightful evils.

For example, an attempt at establishing a moneyless economy (assuming that the love of money is the root of all evil), may be the first step towards creating Armageddon. Equality may reflect the theory of perfect fairness, but its enforcement through sumptuary regulations on dress is felt as tyrannical, since most prefer to express their personality through distinctive clothing. The suppression of individuality may be suited to the purposes of a Buddhist monk, and its pursuit is certainly on the path to achieving the collective ideal, but it is a disastrous value in striving to construct

6-4

a modern industrial society as we have already pointed out in the second chapter.

Theological values are bound to fail, since in themselves they are empty abstractions, and invariably, are opposed to human nature. Whilst, for example, equality, self-effacement, unending generosity towards all and sundry, humility, and a permanent feeling of altruism, are fine as ideals from a collective standpoint, as soon as they are presented to the individual, they are kicked against as an intolerable intrusion into personal freedom. The only individuals who approach such perfection are mostly drawn from the pages of fiction, such as Dostoevsky's Aloysha in, *The Brothers Karamatzov*, or Prince Myshkin, known as *The Idiot*, in the novel of that name, and they anyway usually met a bad end. A decade following the end of seventy years of Soviet Communism, and the conscious attempt to educate a society into perfect virtue, it is hard to imagine a country with a higher proportion of nasty people of mortal danger to one another.

4   What value system, therefore, may be used in constructing a workable or successful Socialist society? We have said that humankind is morally neutral, although capable of great goodness and wickedness. It should be noted at the same time, however, that beneath the surface, all societies are in a constant state of turmoil. This is due to the difficulties of relationships between different-thinking individuals in all situations in life. The unceasing Will of the individual is never satisfied, and as Schopenhauer has argued, creates the unhappy situation of a war of all against all. All individuals tend to harm or be a nuisance to one another, or to the state, or to the groups to which they belong, but this harmful or nuisance factor is often unintentional or even unknown by those responsible. In the economic sphere this harmful factor becomes very much greater, but even then, it does not necessarily incur moral culpability.

For example, a businessman may build an enterprise which grows from strength to strength, giving employment to great numbers of people. He sees himself as a beneficent agent and pillar of society. The enterprise reaches a stage of growth beyond the consequences of which the entrepreneur is ignorant. Work and the logical pursuit of a single purpose, viz., wealth creation, narrows the vision of the businessman. Eventually, a stage is reached when the enterprise exerts an ill-influence in many directions: wages fall below a level of fairness or just comparison with other earners; plants are moved overseas necessitating loss of jobs in the home country; monopoly undermines desirable competition; pollution begins to damage the environment; overwork damages the health and family life of middle managers; and eventually, inefficiency and industrial decline threatens the survival of the enterprise and the

6-5

employment of the workforce. There are naturally many other situations in the sphere of economic life when individuals or managing groups may unknowingly or unintentionally harm or present a nuisance to their fellow beings.

The above entail real and serious issues for the community, but they are not resolvable through sitting on a high moral horse, or through evoking grand ethical principles - preferably backed-up by the authority of theological claptrap. This is because such an approach always distorts reality, and whilst it is effective negatively, as a rhetorical tool in attacking perceived ills, it achieves little in resolving issues towards a constructive outcome. Religious-type values are only concerned with the opposing abstractions of good and evil, and are mischievous when applied to the world of politics, leading usually to hypocrisy. Political issues, as we have argued above, are not so much concerned with good and evil, as convenience and inconvenience, or benefit and dis-benefit, and hence sociological values should be understood in the light of these morally neutral qualities.

The religiously inspired values of Marxism, and the entire Socialist movement, are therefore a menace to reason and common sense, and this can be seen clearly through the demonisation of the bourgeoisie and the fantasising idealisation of the proletariat, which amount to no more than rhetorical stances in promoting the class war. It would be useful to look more closely at the development of Socialism and the place it occupies in Western civilisation. Only then may we grasp the subjectivity and shaky foundations of its moral base.

5   Karl Marx, although nominally brought up in the evangelical Lutheran church, following the conversion of his parents, came from a well-to-do family and was descended from a long line of eminent Rabbis. His father was a lawyer and an intellectual, with a serious interest in philosophy, and although Karl was only six years old at the time of the family's conversion, the founder of "scientific" Socialism was essentially a Jewish thinker in the structure of his thought, in the dialectical approach to problem-solving, and most significantly, in his millennial ideals. The Talmudic thinking of Marx is everywhere reflected in the passion and style of his writing. But of more relevance is the fact that the moral principles underlying Marxism, and all Socialist movements which were to develop later, are central to the traditions of Western civilisation, as developed through the growth and spread of Christianity into every aspect of religious and intellectual life.

The unending dualism in the struggle between good and evil, with its resultant heightening of conflict in religious, political, and other situations, is unique to peoples to the west of the Near East in the post-classical period. Everywhere monotheism

6-6

destroyed toleration, replacing it with dogma and fanaticism. Moral values were no longer relative qualities dependent on differing situations, as seen in the civilised philosophy of Greece and Rome, but absolutes brooking no discussion, the infringement of which brought damnation and death. All these attitudes were no less Christian than they were Jewish - except that the later Christian influence tended to exaggerate and worsen those tendencies which compounded the difficulties of humankind. Finally, the Messianism of Judaism was carried over to anticipation of the Second Coming.

Sociologically, within the framework of Western civilisation, Socialism as a moral force may be said to be replacing Christianity. Whilst the writings of Marx convey the force of a Biblical prophet, all subsequent Socialism has a certainty and moral conviction which seems to go unchallenged, despite the failures of practical Socialism worldwide. This is only because there remains a divide between practical Socialism, or Socialism in power, and the ideal or its theoretical purpose. In other words, the end purpose is seemingly so good, it is felt that not too much anxiety should be given to the gaping chasm between theory and practice. To leave Socialism in such a quandary, however, is most unsatisfactory.

The problem of Socialism cannot be taken further without considering the question of values. This is because the missing "gene" of Socialism cannot be inserted without a revaluation of values. Without that Socialism has no chance for success.

6   A value system is taken for granted as something, which in the nature of things, is everlasting, unquestioned, and irremovable. This is because we have known it since earliest childhood, and it permeates every corner of our civilisation. We feel it is something worse than sacrilege to question the basis on which it stands. The prejudice and subjectivity of our narrow lives blinds us to the possibility of wider horizons. And yet value systems do change, and as we noted, they differ considerably from one civilisation to another. At the present time, in the industrialised West, values (if not the value system) are changing more quickly than at any other period in history. But the value system within a civilisation or culture, changes at so slow a pace, that it is rarely noted by people during their own lives.

Value systems are vital to the survival of civilisations, since it is only through the breakdown of the former (irrespective of other causes, primary or peripheral), that civilisations decay and eventually collapse. For example, the values supporting slavery, state benefits, luxurious living, and Christianity, all contributed to the decline and fall of the classical world. Those values supporting an arrogant assumption of superiority to all other peoples, the fossilisation of custom and belief, and latterly, restrictions on

6-7

foreign trade, led to the decline of ancient China. It is apparent that civilisations have immutable characteristics, and it seems that one or several of these, which may be traceable to their early history, and which at one time served their interests well, eventually act as instruments for internal decay and subsequent ruin.

That is why the consideration of value systems is so important in trying to understand our own future. If Christianity was a major factor for the destruction of much that was best in the classical world (i.e. most of her literature, speculative thinking, and historiography), it would be tragic to anticipate that an unchanged Socialism, the natural heir to Christianity, might some day bring about the decline of the West. It could be argued that Socialism, or more accurately Communism, almost brought the downfall of Russian civilisation, if the latter, as seen by Arnold Toynbee, is categorised as quite separate from the civilisation of Europe (or the West).

The problem confronting us, as stated earlier, is the need to integrate the business ethos into the kernel of Socialist doctrine. The business process is seen as dangerous and unpredictable, its repercussions liable to lurch destructively in any direction, in destroying jobs, communities, ecological systems, or even triggering the outbreak of war. That is why it is feared and loathed by so many in the non-business community. But the business process also reflects the unpredictable, wild, and electric energy of human nature, which is as intentionally creative as it is inadvertently destructive. The answer to the problem of human nature is not to moralise and bemoan over the cursed and wretched state of humanity with wringing hands, in a Biblical-like fashion; or to take a Procrustean-like approach in stretching or lopping off the limbs so that we may fit the Socialist bed, but rather to design appropriate channels into which all the diverse energies of people might flow without causing harm or hindrance to others.

7   But to enable this requires a changed approach to thinking, which our present value system does not allow. The clinging curse of dualism, permeating every nook and cranny of our civilisation must be discredited forever. As a moral force it is traceable to the theologies of both Judaism and Zoroastrianism (the conflict between Ormazd and his evil twin Ahriman), and as an intellectual influence, it is traceable to the Greeks, i.e. in the separation between mind and matter, form and content, etc. The intellectual aspects of dualism are no longer a threat to the soundness of modern thinking, since philosophy and psycho-analysis have long since disposed of such futile debates between mind and matter; but as a moral force, dualism is no less a threat to reason and common sense than it ever was.

Because of our intellectual tradition dictating our thought patterns, here in the

6-7

. West, it is difficult to imagine a world free of the prejudices of dualism. When we learn that such physical activities, as Sumo wrestling or the martial arts, also have a spiritual dimension as understood through the beliefs and practice of Zen Buddhism, at first we are surprised and find the assertion incomprehensible. If, however, we learn that the cultivation of a loving sexual experience through improved technique and consideration for the pleasure of the partner, is also held to have a spiritual dimension, then this is entirely in keeping with modern Western ideas on a healthy sex life. The old Christian values distinguishing spiritual love from material lust, which aroused psychological conflict in preventing the development of loving relationships for almost 2,000 years in the Western hemisphere, have now been discredited forever and are recognised for the evil which they always were.

The evil of moral dualism, as we have said, is that it polarises issues, distorting them out of their true context. The consequence is that underlying problems are not analysed nor even perceived, but aspects of them merely targeted for attack and destruction. As T.E. Lawrence has noted - and it does so much to explain the political extremism in the contemporary world in the conflict between Arab and Jew: "Semites have no half-tones in their register of vision. They are a people of primary colours, especially black and white, who see the world always in line. They are a certain people, despising doubt, our modern crown of thorns."[26] The principle of Socialist strategy, underpinned by dialectical-materialism, is that the class war should be pushed forward, and that the desired end purpose will be achieved inevitably through struggle, without any need to bother one's head in advance about the necessity of formulating a constructive philosophy. It is hard to imagine a more futile or stupid approach to problem-solving, and yet that is the logical outcome of moral dualism.

Perhaps the greatest impediment in attempting to incorporate the business ethos into that of Socialism are the underdog and other-worldly values of Socialism. Again, these are theological values, transferred directly from our Judaic-Christian tradition, and in paraphrasing Nietzsche's criticism of Christian morality (Which apply to no lesser extent to Old Socialism), such values, "feed upon and foster weakness, life-weariness, and *resentiment*, poisoning the well-springs of human vitality in the process by 'devaluing' all 'naturalistic' values."[27] Such envious, aggrieved, bitter, irritable, and chip-on-the-shoulder attitudes fill the pages of almost any Socialist journal or

---

[26] T.E. Lawrence, Introduction to Charles M. Doughty's, *Travels In Arabia Deserta*, J. Cape, 1926 ed., p. xxi.

[27] *The Oxford Companion To Philosophy*, Ted Honderich, OUP, 1995, p. 621.

6-8

newspaper.

Those nurturing such feelings or thoughts are far more concerned with the destructive task of kicking over the last remaining struts of the establishment, than with the constructive task of creating a new order for the future. Such values as these people harbour would be quite unsuited to incorporating the business ethos into their own narrow belief system. Meanwhile, the other-worldly values of Socialism, its Messianism expressed through the utopian belief in the disappearance of the state following the annihilation of the bourgeoisie, would sit uncomfortably with the down-to-earth practical values of business.

8   What is needed in our own civilisation is harmony in reconciling conflict between individuals and groups, so allowing an objective understanding to develop in helping to resolve more peacefully chronic issues. It might be useful to glance afar at other civilisations in searching for a paradigm. Certain scholars in the West, such as the eminent Japanophile and industrial sociologist, Prof. Ronald Dore,[28] have identified Confucianism as a philosophy which might be adapted to Western needs, particularly in the sphere of industrial relations. Ronald Dore, who has written about the dire influences of dualism in stirring the pot of conflict in Western civilisation, has an intimate knowledge of Far East cultures.

There are many aspects of Chinese civilisation which are beginning to be felt in the West, in the global village of today's society, e.g. the theories of Yin and Yang; herbal remedies and acupuncture in the realm of medicine; Tai Chi and other fitness techniques; Feng Shui in regard to promoting harmony through design, but the most important aspect of all, that of Confucianism, has yet to be popularised and promoted in healing the wounded soul of the West. Confucianism is a school of philosophy which has developed over hundreds of years. Its relevance may be seen in its down to earth approach to the problems of humankind, and the need to promote harmony in human relationships. It emphasises the values of education (and hence, perhaps, the resulting success of innovation and industrialisation in the Far East), and it recognises the need to avoid, what our 18th century forebears would have described as *enthusiasm* in religion. Confucius expressed this with the profound exhortation that we should "respect the spirits, but keep them at a distance."

Good manners, benevolence, and moderation, are values desperately needed in the contemporary West. As a practical philosophy Confucianism could be adapted and

---

[28] See Prof. Ronald Dore's article, "The Confucian Remedy For Industrial Success," *Government & Opposition*, Vol. 20, No. 2, Spring 1985, pp. 213-214.

7-1

utilised, firstly, as a mode of communication between groups or individuals with conflicting interests; and secondly, in addressing substantive issues in themselves and designing means for their real resolution. Confucianism may indeed prove a useful tool as a first step in incorporating the business ethos within the main framework of Socialism.

In this chapter we have called for a revaluation of values, but have hardly touched on the question of what those values should be for the Socialism of the future. It is a question to which we shall often turn in later chapters of the book in carefully constructing a value system for the Socialism of tomorrow.

CHAPTER 7
New Values In The Wake of Social Change

"The grandest system of civilisation has its orbit, and may complete its course; but not so the human race, to which, just when it seems to have reached its goal, the old task is ever set anew with a wider range and a deeper meaning."

Theodor Mommsen, *History of Rome*, Bentley, 1894, Vol. I, p. 5.

1 - Social conditions of benefit to Old Labour (or Old Socialism) 2 - Reaction against the old values 3 - Consequences of the demand for greater brainpower 4 - Changing sociology of work 5 - Individualism an inevitable outcome of social change 6 - The middle-middle majority and the proletarian minority 7 - Why Socialism is unattractive to the new middle class

1   The above critique of Socialist values, as we find them today, amounts to a critique of the unrealism of Socialism in failing to meet the needs of actual changes in society. No amount of ingenious intellectual argument can succeed to persuade if its message is felt to be irrelevant or dated. Marxists and other old-style Labour party intellectuals are therefore flogging a dead horse when they harp on about the old issues and the old philosophy from a class-based standpoint.

Good or intelligent Socialists are aware that sound Socialism is always realistic. It meets changes in society by changing itself, so that the two interact and evolve together. Dialectical-materialism, as modified in meeting contemporary standards of the social sciences, remains the sociological basis for the realism of Socialism. Rigidly doctrinaire Socialists, both Marxists and others, have misapplied sociological factors by looking backwards and glorifying past traditions and mind-sets, often from a sentimental standpoint, and consequently, they have lost grasp of time and slid back to a former era. That is the reason for the failure of Old Socialism as a practical school

7-1

of thought at the present time.

Our present purpose is to look at those changes in society which have made contemporary Socialism such an unattractive proposition in the industrialised West. The problem of Socialism today, *vis-à-vis* forwarding the class struggle, stems from the transformation in the structure of society over the past fifty years. Up until the 1960s industrialised peoples saw themselves as pyramid formed societies. Class differences were visible in terms of dress, living standards, and material possessions, and speech and educational levels were far more a differential of class than they are today. Slum areas were sprawling, dark, dirty, and depressed, lacking many of the facilities now everywhere taken for granted.

The factor which most emphasised the pyramid formed society were the huge factories, mines, and dock- and shipyards, employing thousands, many engaged in identical type semi- or unskilled work. Poor housing, long hours, indifferent pay, arrogant managerial attitudes, and the feeling of being "at the bottom of the pile," naturally engendered resentment and grounds for Socialist activity. The view of a well-to-do and comfortable middle class, and above that, an upper crust of ostentatious spenders and night-clubbers living off *rente* and not needing to work, inevitably aroused feelings of injustice and envy. In the light of such conditions, the explanation of society in terms of the class struggle was attractive in holding out hopes for a better future.

Socialists, both Marxists and others, could organise for discontent with a free conscience, although even then bitterness twisted a true perspective of reality in making for intellectual dishonesty amongst the far left. Intensive debates during the 40s and 50s - and later, amongst trade unionists and other groups up and down the country, gave rise to internal conflict and bad feelings throughout the labour movement. At that period mainstream politics was more polarised than today, since the middle classes feared the threat of the workers, and both the Conservative and Labour parties, although naturally in a state of flux, had clearly defined principles, and the loyal support of substantial memberships long since lost. The Cold War may have added to the fear and tension between left and right, for the Soviet Union was held up as either an example of "progress" or of "totalitarian horror," according to ideological belief.

Most of all, support for Socialism was aided by the values of collectivism, which occurred naturally in the workplace and in working class communities. In the old back-to-back slum housing areas there was a spirit of togetherness and mutual help in many situations in life. In communities where private transport was still a luxury, people were thrown together socially whether they liked it or not. Neighbours interrelated

7-2

irrespective of mutual feelings, but trust and loyalty to the community emerged as overriding values. Credit was given by the corner shop, borrowing and lending small amounts of cash was an everyday occurrence, and outsiders were looked upon with suspicion until accepted by the community. In this environment the Labour party was not so much an external factor in peoples' lives, as a natural part of their thinking, a topic of serious discussion, and a place for socialising in the many workers' and trade union clubs.

2   That world is now long gone and forgotten, and to the younger generation, it might never have existed. The stories of suffering and heroic struggle which had passed down from one generation to another as oral tradition for so long, suddenly encountered the deaf ear of complacency. But even these facts failed to stir the doubts of Socialist stalwarts. "Let conditions worsen, and they'll come back," they consoled themselves. "This is merely the happy interlude before the storm!" The belief in dialectical-materialism, or at least, in the simpler intellectual conviction that the eventual outcome of Socialism was a foregone conclusion, never deserted Labour party activists. But in truth something very different and unanticipated was occurring in society, transforming its total structure. Changes occurred taking peoples' sympathy away from the central values of Socialism. And these changes were not simply accountable to a rise in living standards. If they had been, in themselves, they would have been of little threat in undermining belief in core Socialist values.

Two tendencies were developing in society: firstly, the growth of a new kind of individualism; and secondly, the structure of society was losing its pyramid form as it changed into an egg-like structure set up on its thicker end. These changes began within the working class itself from the 1950s onwards. Rising living standards did not merely entail a wish to replace want with plenty. The new consumerism was more complex than simply a desire for acquisition. It wanted to express a feeling of rebellion against the past, not merely against its drabness and monotony, but even against the identity of class itself. The Teddy boy culture was the first popular expression of working class youth rebelling against the status quo. The fact that Teddy boy dress was inspired by the Edwardian era of fifty years before, clearly indicated a yearning for a more colourful and affluent image. More interestingly, however, was the mental development of those who adopted the Teddy boy culture in later life. Twenty years on, they were no longer Teddy boys, but neither had they reverted to their old working class life-style. They had been transformed into something quite different. They had cast aside the exotic image of their youth, but with maturity, and in its place, they had settled into an entirely new ethos as to their place in society. Many may have mutated

7-3

into the new Essex man - brash individualistic small-time (and not so small time) entrepreneurs with strong Thatcherite leanings.

Many other factors contributed to the increasing individualism of the working class. Huge tower blocks became the homes of those displaced by bomb or slum clearance. Tower block flats had none of the accessibility or social intimacy of the rows of small housing leading directly onto the street. The groups who had stood and chatted by their doorways, or watched their children play ball games in the street, or stared or beckoned at passers-by, became a thing of the past. The new flats, often many stories above street level, isolated families and individuals. Added to this was the fact that domestic life was changed to a much greater extent by the arrival of television than it had been by the radio. Entertainment or leisure became more passive and home-based than in an earlier era. Parlour games, singing, and even conversation gave way to sitting many hours before the TV set. The minimising of social contact not only engendered greater self-absorption, but dulled the senses to external stimuli. What happened to other people, foolish or tragic, was other peoples business, interesting perhaps, but not of worrying concern. In the wake of ennui and feelings of alienation came a declining interest in political or social issues.

3   Meanwhile, during the boom years of the 1960s, industry became geographically more diffused. Increasingly, manufacturing became smaller scale, dependent on electricity or gas supplies from the standard grids, and so no longer reliant on contiguity with the massive coal deposits in the Midlands, the North East, or the North West. In response to this changing infrastructure, new towns were built, or overspill areas created around existing towns and villages throughout the country. Overspills entailed the emptying of the old, often slum areas, in the great city centres of London, Manchester, Liverpool, etc. Following this dispersal of the population to often rural areas, and to different and better kinds of housing, there was a further breakdown in working class solidarity, as communities became smaller and more heterogeneous.

As the second half of the century progressed, gradually, the entire sociology of work was transformed. With the advance of technology, the demand for brainpower increased in all occupational spheres, amongst white collar no less than blue collar workers. Manual, unskilled or semi-skilled tasks were taken over by more complex CAM (computer aided machinery) in the age of information technology; whilst the general clerk of a former era, with basic skills in writing and numeracy, disappeared forever, to be replaced by computer operatives, not only knowledgeable in using different software programmes, but qualified as executives in a specialised occupation.

In meeting this demand for skills, not only was it necessary to reach "A" level

7-4

standard, but to progress onto a university course in one of the innumerable red brick institutes for learning established in the post-War period. Eventually, the demand for respectable degree courses became so great, that by the 1990s, polytechnics throughout the country had to be up-graded to university status level. A university education was now a requirement for occupations as varied as those of a junior manager in a supermarket, to an operative or maintenance engineer in a CAM manufacturing plant. Thus, within a 60-year period, the completion age for a basic formal education had been raised from 14 to approximately 23. Hence 7 years of additional education was desirable in obtaining and fulfilling the requirements needed in embarking on the career of an average occupation.

A university education was no longer the privilege of the middle and upper classes. Changes in technology and the industrial infrastructure had created a situation whereby educational standards needed to be raised throughout the entire population simply to ensure economic survival in a competitive world. The raising of educational standards did not arise as a political or party political issue. No such decision was taken in fulfilling the natural rights of "working people" for a better chance in life. It came as a necessity, irrespective of the government in power, in meeting competition and the need to maintain a reasonable balance of payments. The new red brick universities were therefore classless, as those from every background were thrown together, and forced to socialise on equal terms.

The success of the emergence of a new classless culture may be gauged from the ease of social mixing, as well as from the evidence of student newspapers and other publications, if these are taken to reflect general or majority opinion. This classlessness and ease of social mixing was in great part promoted by the BBC, with the introduction of announcers and commentators speaking a classless accent of English, and later still, with the introduction of those speaking supposedly with regional accents, but which in reality were usually a pastiche of regional dialects. Gradually, Southern, Oxford, or Queen's English became anachronistic, usually only spoken by the older generations, and by the young, only in the privacy of their own families or exclusive upper class circles. The criterion for the new standard English, imposed by the BBC, was simpy based on the clarity of pronunciation for the easy comprehension of all.[29]

4   Changes in the workplace especially bore a direct relationship with those of the politics of the left. Trades union muscle, particularly with regard to strikes and other forms of disruption, had always drawn its strength from the collectivist ideals of the

---

[29] Where the BBC fails miserably as a public service, it should be noted, is in its misuse of grammar.

7-5

giant work places employing many thousands, in the mines, shipyards, car factories, etc. The appeal to resentment and revolt was always easier when great numbers could be addressed by powerful orators carrying a tannoy aloft, who were then called upon to make a show of hands in authorising a down-tools or a go-slow. With changes in technology, and especially with the dispersion of industry, it was not only more difficult to organise industrial action, but more seriously, to recruit in building up trades union membership from one plant to another. Consequently, trades union membership slumped by three million within a 10-year period by the mid-1980s.

The most difficult problem of all facing the Labour movement in the industrial sector was the changed relationships between workers and management. The stratified divisions between shop-floor, management, and clerical staff in the bad old arrogant times up to the 1970s (when even use of the wrong toilets was a punishable offence), was fertile ground for promoting confrontation between bosses and workers. But in the smaller plants of a later date, new and quite different relationships had developed. The highly skilled operatives in the new plants might be technicians or university graduates, and their chief executives might also be maintenance engineers, who on the odd occasion would dirty their hands by climbing underneath machinery. There was therefore no longer a significant - if any, divide between shop-floor and management, and as the chief executive was seldom likely to be an owner or even shareholder of the plant, in those situations when the plant was threatened with relocation, acquisition, or closure, he was likely to see a closer connection with his employees than with a distant and ever-feared corporate office.

In those situations when there was a closer comparability between education and skills, a shorter chain of command, and the need to communicate on a two-way level between shop-floor and management, socialising and trust on an almost equal level would develop as a natural outcome, during lunch breaks and after hours. Company loyalty would be both felt and expressed, by those on the lowest rungs of the ladder, and where all are held in respect for the level and speciality of their skills, there is an equalising of status and flattening of hierarchy. Consequently, any attempt at trades union penetration was likely to be met with mistrust and rejection.

5   Meanwhile, the living standards of the working class had been so transformed over the previous fifty years, that the majority no longer saw themselves as belonging to such a category. This had occurred through an equalising of living standards in terms of acquisition of certain specific benefits enjoyed by the majority. These may be listed as the ownership of a central heating system, wall-to-wall carpeting, the equipment of a modern kitchen, hi-fi, TV and video recorder, car, and house or flat

7-5

bought through a mortgage. These constituted comforts and levels of convenience denied all previous generations, irrespective of status, and no individual, however wealthy, is capable of enjoying physical comforts beyond a certain level of pleasure. None of the above material benefits any longer confer or reflect status in the community. Therefore, a family living in a renovated working class area of Preston, but with all modern conveniences, and providing that they are in full employment, could claim that they live as good a life as any King or Queen - or that they desire no better. Of course a palace may be more sumptuous; caviar and champagne may be more costly than lasagne or beer; and Ascot may be more elegant than the local dog track, but who can compute the degree of pleasure of any of these things against the other ? In the real world, price is no gauge of value. Raising material standards in a community may induce self-satisfaction and complacency, but few other characteristics of significance. Other influences must be sought in explaining further changes.

The growth of individualism has marked the most significant transformation of the working class, but again, this individualism has not arisen through selfish or egoistic motives, but through the influence of inevitable circumstances. A sharp increase in the diversity of occupations has marked the post-War period, and this has been especially applicable to the employment prospects of the working class. As the old manual, unskilled, and semi-skilled jobs of the masses disappeared, so too did loyalties to old workplaces and particular occupations which had been passed down for generations from father to son. New and varied occupations needed to be sought in strange environments. In every family each sibling sought a different occupation according to his or her ability or inclination, and so individualism needed to be developed in meeting this exciting challenge. Every person was obliged to do his or her "own thing," not out of the spirit of adventure, or a wanton love of free choice, but out of necessity. Collective values, therefore, came to be seen as hindering initiative and personal development, and many new attitudes were adopted in progressing towards a new, and hopefully, better future.

Further education and competition to enter new spheres of employment were in themselves individualistic pursuits, in breaking away from the collectivist mould of the old society. But it was in the sphere of leisure where individualism found its most widespread expression. Those who had emerged from the old working class, now living in dispersed areas, and dependent on private transport for commuting, supermarket shopping, and delivering and fetching children from school, were also no longer restricted to their locality with regard to free time pursuits. With the demise of working men's clubs (for women had usually been excluded) and the closure of many

7-6

thousands of public houses in every part of the country, a wide range of other more purposeful leisure activities took their place, such as: the fitness gym; the health club; evening classes covering every conceivable interest; squash, volleyball, etc., at the many new sports and swimming centres; gardening and DIY, in the wake of more spacious living conditions of the new house-proud owners on the new estates, etc. All these benefits contributed to changing attitudes.

In the wake of greater alertness or career progression; and the accumulation of ever-more material possessions; and the awareness that employment or job-security for the rising generation would not be a foregone conclusion; and that the examination success of school education was anyway becoming increasingly important, came ever-more responsibilities at work, in the home, and in regard to children. All these pressures inculcated an individualism which naturally mutated into a quiet sense of pride, since personal decision-making seemed increasingly to decide success or failure in life. There was no collective ideal or identifiable community, on which the individual could any longer rely. There was a nodding acquaintance with neighbours, but beyond that, there was little interest and less knowledge about other occupants in the tidy new estates. Whilst there was a declining interest and growing contempt for party politics, there developed instead an intelligent interest in directly relevant economic factors, such as interest rates as they effected mortgage payments; exchange rates as they effected foreign holidays; globalisation and industrial policy as they effected jobs; and environmental factors as they effected health and general welfare.

6   All these factors, arising from acquisition and individualism, resulting from the force of economic circumstances, transformed a former proletariat into a new middle class within a single generation. Research studies have now conclusively demonstrated that the vast majority of the population perceive themselves as middle class, providing the specific question is not put on an "either or" basis, when in recognising a debt to social origins, the more self-effacing course is taken in opting for a "working class" description. Nevertheless, the former proletariat is now essentially middle class in all its characteristics and attitudes.

What is left of the true proletariat may only be found in isolated population pockets , usually in the midlands or north, amongst mining communities and depressed inner city areas, and also in tinier population pockets in towns and villages throughout England. It has been estimated, for example, that a small Suffolk town of 33,000 has a proletariat of 750, i.e. 2% of the population, most of whom reside on a salubrious well-kept residential estate with restricted access. The problem, however, is that many of those residents are not only burdened by unemployment, alcohol or drugs problems,

7-6

or are ex-prisoners, but that they harass, rob and injure one another to such a degree that the estate exists in a constant state of turmoil. No amount of expense or effort by the local authority in renovating or repairing buildings, maintaining tidy grass verges, or establishing children's play areas, has succeeded in reducing an underlying resentment, or engendering a sense of gratitude in helping to re-elect a Labour borough authority.

This particular proletariat is apolitical in the sense that no legally recognisable inducements of electioneering can bring it to the polling station to cast a vote. If such a situation may be replicated in many parts of the country (and there is no reason as to why it should not), then it has to be concluded that those at the bottom of society are so disillusioned by the existing electoral option of the left, that they constitute what may be described as an anti-Labour party minority. In the eyes of such a proletariat, their disillusionment may carry some grounds for justification, but the will of 2% of the population cannot hope to resurrect the ghost of Old Labour or Old Socialism.

The new middle class, on the other hand, chooses to disdain its origins, having a fear and horror of the past. It wants only to forget the past - burying it through enjoyment of its recently acquired material acquisitions. It often displays the characteristics of a *nouveau riche*, feeling superior to the older generation, and treating parents or grandparents with a patronising attitude, and sometimes good-natured ridicule. The older generation respond, sometimes, with gruff comments, feeling isolated and pushed to the margins of a society it no longer understands. The confidence of the new middle class rests on the assumption that it constitutes the majority of the population. It is no longer an underclass.

In this new egg-shaped society, those at the bottom of the pile are a minority composed of the isolated remnants of the proletariat, and single mothers and the unemployed who may stem from any level in the community - for contemporary unemployment is no longer class-based as it predominantly was in the 1930s. Meanwhile, above the middle-middle majority sit a declining proportion of ever-richer individuals, but the new structure of society fails to arouse the sense of injustice or resentment as that found in a pyramid formed community. Whilst the gap between rich and poor continues to increase, and is now wider than it has ever been for more than a 100 years, the contemporary structure of society has meanwhile created a huge barrier of complacency and self-satisfaction between the poor and the very rich. Such is the irony of the self-regarding prosperity of a middle-middle majority. This is partly why the Labour government lost four consecutive elections, despite the appalling economic failures of Tory administrations, and unemployment rising to levels unknown

7-7

for almost sixty years.

7   The primary reason for the Labour party's failure to make headway during these disastrous years must therefore be traced to the peculiar structural transformation of society and the attitudes of this new emerging middle class. The Labour party continued to promote Socialist values when the electorate could no longer respond to them. The psychological response of the majority to the emotive appeal of the left had been changed forever. The appeal to resentment (often interpreted as self-pity), or anger against injustice towards the poor, or the need for collective values in marching shoulder-to-shoulder against privilege and wealth, rather than arousing sympathy, generated disgust. There were many reasons for this:-

1. Economic ills were perceived as not so much accountable to the Tory government as to other economic forces beyond the control of government;
2. Party-political allegiance patterns had anyway been totally transformed, for whilst many ex-working middle-middle class people became ostentatiously Thatcherite or Tory in repudiating their own class origins, a huge proportion of the old middle class, especially in the medical and educational professions, moved leftwards in support-ing either Labour or the Liberal Democrats;
3. The appeal of Labour was de facto, if not intentionally, addressed only to those at the base of society; and,
4. Most significantly, the individualism of the new middle class altered its entire ethos in those situations confronting its economic interests.

This last factor must be considered in more detail, since it contradicts Socialist sociological theory on winning the class war. Socialist theory is based on the increasing accumulation of wealth into ever fewer hands (and this is incontrovertible), in conjunction with the enlargement of an oppressed and resentful proletariat which eventually will break out into revolution. What we are now witnessing in reality is an oppressed middle-middle majority, which because of its possessions and relative sense of security in an insecure world, is not to be seduced by the warnings and predictions of Socialist analysis. This is not so much because of any error in the analysis itself, as the overall tone of the message and the emphasis on "working class interests." The latter assumption is taken as impertinent in sullying the perceived class status of this new sector in the community. The majority regard themselves as middle class, and will not tolerate the patronising description of themselves as "workers," "working class," "brothers," or "comrades."

7-7

Furthermore, even when these new middle class people encounter real economic difficulties, such as unemployment, the repossession of their homes, or bankruptcy, they cannot be relied upon to react in the same way as might their parents or grandparents in resorting to Socialist-inspired activity. This is because their attitudes, varied obligations, and life experiences have unfitted them for such a response. Their acquired individualism; their sense of fatalism within an economic risk environment whose benefits and dis-benefits they fully accept; an awareness that their difficulty may be partly of their own making; and a particular feeling of personal pride, which inhibits daring to expose misfortune, inclines them towards self-isolation, paralysis, and depression. In a political context, this may be seen as the down-side of individual values, but as the outcome of sociological reality, it is useless to bemoan their existence as politically disadvantageous to the left. Middle class values will always repudiate the call of proletarian collectivism.

The transformation of society, therefore, has made the application of Socialism as we have known it, an impracticable task. At this point, it might be thought as if Socialism could have no future as a powerful reforming movement; or as if history, as in the eyes of Francis Fukuyama, had come to its end. But history, as we shall show, has a long course to run yet before its too soon predicted conclusion. This book will demonstrate that Socialism has a huge and vital task to accomplish for the future of humankind, but it is a task as yet unanticipated by political gurus. In subsequent chapters we shall reveal issues of conflict quite different from those of the past, and the immense struggle facing the future.

CHAPTER 8
The Work Environment And The Wider World

"Those who manage the global flows of capital are driving down the wage-levels of their tax-paying employees. Wages as a share of national wealth are declining worldwide; no single nation is capable of resisting the pressure."

Hans-Peter Martin & Harald Schumann, *The Global Trap*, Zed Books, 1997, p. 7.

1 - The social problems of work, unemployment, and unpaid labour   2 - The psychological value of work 3 - Questionable value of the Protestant work ethic   4 - The healthier non-Protestant attitude to work 5 - The work environment in the East and the pre-Reformation period   6 - Disillusionment of middle and senior ranking executives with working conditions   7 - They need trades union representation   8 - Meritocratic values may hinder the disadvantaged   9 - Employment empowers the individual as an economic unit in the community

1   Before entering into a discussion of broader economic issues, it is first necessary to consider the nature of Work as it effects different aspects of viewing society. Work in the context of its relationship with the wider world needs to be discussed at this stage of the argument, as otherwise prejudiced or wrong notions of its purpose or value may be apprehended as soon as we embark on a discussion of its economic implications.

If the good of humanity is to be considered in its widest perspective, it is not sufficient to view the world of work merely as found within the capitalist system, or as if effects the interests of one or several sectors of the community. The values of work as perceived in contemporary Western industrialised societies are of relatively recent origin, and because of many new and unexpected social issues contingent on the world of work, e.g., that many are overworked whilst their peers are deprived of work; ills stemming from great population movements in the search for work; conflicts of loyalty between work and family induced by employer pressures; and the anticipated possibility that great numbers of people may never experience full time employment, necessitates that the nature of work should be considered in the broadest sociological light.

It may be in the interests of powerful corporate capitalism, in those countries where capital is concentrated and managed on a global basis, that an increasing proportion of the population is made dependent on the dole. If, for example, the currency of a country, or economic area, is maintained at so high a level in ensuring inward investment for speculative purposes, then manufacturing and most productive activity in the sphere of tangible goods is inevitably driven abroad because of excessive costs. In that event the dole is supported by capitalist interests, as it is already in Britain and other countries, and as it was in ancient Rome, in enabling the continued

8-2

accumulation of capital through speculation or overseas robbery. What social ills emerge in a country dependent on Income Support ? Even if Income Support was raised to a level allowing for a decent standard of living, would it then be socially desirable ?

Is there such a thing as the right to work ? This is a question studiously avoided by all politicians. In view of the pessimism over future employment prospects, it is too embarrassing to face. Old ideas on the values of work are still nurtured gently by the establishment, and in accordance with such principles, half measures are taken to ensure that the majority *seem* to have work, or are searching for work, and a host of unsatisfactory schemes are proposed, launched, operated, or relegated after a time, concerned with work-sharing, so-called skill training, or volunteering, which usually means unpaid work for charitable-type organisations. The Department of Social Security makes no distinction between paid and unpaid work in the context of its obligatory declaration in signing for the dole. In its eyes, all work is suspect on the grounds that it is only undertaken for gain ! In any event, huge numbers of people are engaged in unpaid work, but they are usually middle aged or elderly and have private means.

But that does not discourage the DSS from attempting to inveigle penniless young people into taking up unpaid work with innumerable charitable status organisations involved with woodland conservation, caring for the disabled or elderly, assisting slow readers or teaching the illiterate, working with disturbed youngsters, gardening for the bedridden, etc. Those with private means are fully entitled to engage in unpaid work if they so choose, but is it right that the indigent unemployed should be set to unpaid tasks - howsoever keen they should be for the work experience ? By so doing, are we not surreptitiously moving in the direction of creating a new kind of slave economy ? The value of work is not merely to be seen in the accomplishment of specific tasks, or in the pleasure of undertaking them, but in learning to manage one's personal economy.. Hence when young people are engaged in unpaid work, even if they gain from a genuine training scheme, they are deprived of a monetary reward and the opportunity and responsibility this entails in learning to manage personal finances.

2   In the past work has always been seen as central to economic life. It is, and must remain, the essential linkage between capital and production. Some foretell the end of work for the majority in the belief that information technology will take over most manual, clerical and computing tasks, but nonetheless, the underlying principle remains that the human factor of labour is still the essential link between capital and production. Human choice and changing needs will always necessitate the demand for work. It is

8-3

the human capacity for an ever-changing culture and development in transforming all available materials, which distinguishes humankind from other animals and has given rise to the nature of work. In no other species is there a consciousness of work as a purposeful activity. Work not merely confers dignity on humankind through its sense of purpose and achievement, but also through its giving a sense of identity to the individual in connecting him or her as a valued member with the rest of the community.

The essence of work as a valued sociological factor to the dignity of humankind is not dependent on the cash nexus. In primitive moneyless economies there is competition for the right to specific tasks which confer status irrespective of material rewards which may be attached to them. In modern societies the respect or honour in which an occupation is held bears little resemblance to its level on the earnings scale. The same may be said of the value or usefulness of an occupation to the community. A scientist, artist, or inventor may be ill-rewarded for the eventual outcome of their efforts; whilst a life-saving fireman, paramedic or surgeon, may in the eyes of some, successfully complete tasks for which no monetary reward would be sufficient. Wage rates of differing occupations are not linked to any great objective criteria, nor can they be. The market is a hit and miss affair, and trades union muscle is no justification in itself for what is achieved.

What is unquestionably of importance is that work should be made to serve the needs of the community, rather than the demands of capital or specific interest groups. This raises many questions, for there are aspects of work in modern society which are not merely psychotic but self-destructive. In this respect modern society has much to learn from our ancestors in the pre-Reformation period, or from peoples living in the East and Far East.

3   The Protestant work ethic has for several centuries been upheld as a great social value in contributing to growing prosperity, to the advance of industrialisation, and to the internal development of the free individual. It has certainly accounted for these benefits. The consciousness of its value has been reflected in literature since the close of the 17th century, following the optimism of the Glorious Revolution, with such varied writers as John Locke and Daniel Defoe - the latter especially through his novel, *Robinson Crusoe.* The Protestant work ethic was glorified in innumerable works, both religious and secular, from then onwards, culminating in peaks which may be cited through the work of the Calvinist theologian, Jonathan Edwards, in mid-18th century America; through the writings of Samuel Smiles, a hundred years later in Britain, through such books as, *Self-Help, Thrift,* and, *Duty*; and again in America, in our own century, in the post-War period with books, rallies, and individual development

8-3

courses, emanating from such diverse sources as business organisations, political groups, and varied evangelical church bodies.

The Protestant work ethos permeates all North West European societies, and the northern continent of America. It also permeates communities with large Catholic populations, with complex histories, such as Germany, Switzerland, and France. In Germany it is due to the *Kulturkampf* in the Imperial post-unification era; in Switzerland to the penetrating influence of Calvin and Zwingli, in reaching the Cantons to the south and east; and in France to the spirit of the Huguenots, which was never entirely crushed despite the revocation of the Edict of Nantes. In strongly Catholic societies, such as Austria, Spain, or Ireland, the Protestant work ethic is entirely absent, and consequently, attitudes to work differ considerably. This is not to suggest that people in Catholic countries work any less hard than those in Protestant countries, but only that their relationship with work is formed on a different psychological basis.

The work ethic is so deeply entrenched in the belief systems of many Western peoples, that as with other sacred icons, its seems almost churlish to call it into question, and even worse to indicate it may amount to a malady of the human psyche. But this it is. The author has to confess, that for the greater part of his life, because of cultural conditions within the world of industry, as well as common prejudice, he has accepted the values of the Protestant work ethic as belonging to the benign natural order of things. This belief he can no longer uphold. The Protestant work ethic, it must be revealed, because it falsely apportions best human values, is one of the great lies of our time. Its significance can perhaps best be understood through tracing its origin in Calvinist doctrine.

The principle of predestination announces the divine foreordaining of all that will happen in the world. But it goes further than that. It states that salvation or damnation are also preordained events - God-decided even before the birth of the individual. Consequently, the individual is helpless to change the course of an event that is too terrible to contemplate. Good deeds may achieve nothing, and faith is insufficient. The credibility of predestination is convincing, and easy to support with rational argument when carried over into the sphere of secular life. This is because all of us are sometime brought into contact with those who are perpetual failures in life, and others who always succeed. Whilst those who succeed are held up as heroes, and become worthy of emulation; those who fail, become subject to ridicule or pity, and are consigned to oblivion.

It is easy and quite natural, therefore, to transfer such secular views of humanity to the theology of the afterlife. From the era of St. Augustine until recent times

8-4

mainstream Christianity has estimated that approximately 85% of those born will eventually be consigned to eternal hellfire, and since Calvinism did not allow for the saving grace of purgatory, the prospects of death are more terrible than the worst terrestrial existence. The heavy weight of this gloomy theology on the shoulders of simple middle class artisans in the 16th and 17th centuries was so great as to cause a psychological crisis necessitating an escape from an intolerable situation. That escape was found - could only be found in work as an obsession, and the accumulation of capital as a great defensive barrier against the future.

4   The Protestant work ethic therefore developed as a virtue in itself. Any activity which could be interpreted as work within the exchange system, and particularly the accumulation of capital, was seen as a virtue, and the harder and more successfully the individual worked, the greater the virtue. The loss of employment, on the contrary, not only entailed a material loss, but more hurtful, a loss of self-respect and deep feelings of guilt. In America, for example, where the psychological implications of the work ethic are felt most strongly, the response to loss of employment, irrespective of whether it be through negligence or a recession, is typically self-blame, accompanied by depression and profound feelings of guilt.

The Protestant attitude to work is essentially aggressive, hectic, and compulsive. The typical image of the square-jawed, loud-mouthed, and boastful executive is purely the product of the Protestant work ethic as encouraged by hard-task masters in the northern hemisphere. Over the past fifteen years, the drive to work harder and longer hours has accelerated with the pressures of downsizing, and the threats of unemployment in an increasingly friable world. In the selection process for the totally committed, many employers in America and elsewhere, give preference to candidates who are divorced or separated, on the grounds that this is the best proof of both mobility and preparedness to ditch families in favour of the more important priority of work. It may be asked, is this desirable for the health of society, or for the good of the rising generation ? Is there a point when work-obsession becomes a social disease in the community ?

The contrasting attitude to work in Catholic cultures is interesting. It is undoubtedly more balanced and mature. As already stated, there is no evidence that those in Catholic countries work less hard or less effectively than those in Protestant cultures, even though they may be less hurried or demonstrative in their working style. The Spaniard or the Irishman feels no need to prove to friends, acquaintances, or the casual observer, that he is a good or conscientious worker. Work is simply a natural every day occupation, and may be taken for granted for what it is. To be demonstrative

8-5

about one's keenness for work, or effectiveness in completing a task, might invite ridicule or the suggestion of vanity. Likewise, the status of unemployment to an Italian or Irishman, conjures up no feelings of embarrassment or guilt. He will refer to his joblessness as something not out of the ordinary, or any cause for unnecessary concern. After all, a job is only a job! There are more important things in life. If you're short of a penny or two, cut your purse according to your cloth, and go on enjoying life to the full! What's the sense of keeping up with the Jones's ? That's a fool's game, and doesn't make for happiness! Those are the words of a philosopher musing over a pint of guinness, in a remote Irish pub.

Such casual attitudes to work, when heard for the first time, by an Englishman or American, strike as startling confessions. How can one really be so casual about unemployment ? Those from Protestant cultures, especially from middle or upper ranking occupations rarely admit to an unemployed status. Any lie or invention is preferable in covering up the truth. The most commonly told story of business executives, for example, is that they are engaged in "consultancy contract projects." This is a happy let-off for every eventuality, since they neither admit nor deny to being employed or self-employed, whilst "consultancy" is such an innocently generalised term as to have little meaning. But which is the healthier attitude to the world of work: the relaxed frankness of the straightforward Catholic or the deceit and secretiveness of the guilt-ridden Protestant ?

5   A glance at work attitudes in the Far East might also be enlightening. It is the Chinese, Korean, and Japanese industrial economies which are most dynamic and innovative today, despite their recessionary problems, and yet their working style is the reverse of demonstrative. Good manners and Confucian values call for modesty and self-effacement, and the rumbustiousness and showiness of the American approach, not only evokes ridicule, but horror at the folly to which humankind may sink. Leadership is quiet and discreet, and in Japan at shop-floor level, discussion and decisions on better working practices pass upwards for endorsement and official implementation within the enterprise. Meanwhile in China, *guan xi* or connections, are necessary in developing relationships between one company and another. This is to ensure trust, and secure, honourable, and long term business success within an extended network, for it is recognised that the failure of one might adversely effect the profits of all within a complex system of obligation and exchange.

Chinese business worldwide remains family based and personal, and this limits its growth and range of activities within a manageable scale. High risk factors tend to be avoided in favour of practicality and the certainty of the known. Throughout the

8-5

East, the hurry and bustle of Western work practices, is looked upon with askance and suspicion as a sign of immaturity. This is possibly because business in the West is still a relatively new and exciting experience. Europeans are still learning to break away from the mind-set and dependency of a militaristic or feudal society which bound them for 1,500 years. The Chinese, on the contrary, have a trading culture of more than 3,000 years, and so business and work attitudes are so deeply ingrained as a natural part of life that they arouse no self-consciousness.

In referring to work attitudes of those from Catholic cultures, we are of course turning to pre-Reformation or medieval patterns of employment. In the middle ages work attitudes (but not necessarily work effort) was far more relaxed than in the modern era: there were no clocks dictating the divisions of the day, and tasks were carried out as need allowed between dawn and dusk. In addition to Sunday, innumerable other Holy or Saints days were laid aside for merrymaking or feasting, rather than as "rest" days for quiet and meditation, for the gloomy Old Testament "Sabbath" (still in the memory of those living today) was the later invention of puritanical Protestants.

Even until the 17th century much office life was still conducted, what to modern eyes would appear in a lackadaisical fashion, employees coming or going according to the abundance or scarcity of tasks to be completed. Offices had an open plan appearance, closed meetings were the exception, and there was informal access to those in authority - much like office life in Arab countries today.

In the middle ages, which was not a consumer society in the modern sense, the concept of the Just Price decided retail costs, and detailed regulations and inspection tried to ensure correct weights and measures as well as correct pricing. As long as the currency remained stable, which it did for the greater part of the medieval period, this remained a workable system. Laws forbad usury (i.e. the lending of money at any rate of interest), although such laws were ineffective in the face of market forces, and consequently, interest rates reached extortionate levels in the real world.

Medieval economic theory and work practices, particularly with regard to the creative freedom of the artisan, were romanticised during the Victorian era as the idealised alternative to soul-destroying industrial capitalism. In the second half of the 19th century, the medieval economic system even inspired Socialism, especially as reflected through the later writings of the former art critic, John Ruskin, and the designer and poet, William Morris. But neither Ruskin nor Morris had an authoritative grasp of economic or social issues, and the conditions of the modern world are so changed that it is difficult to elicit paradigms from the middle ages for our own times,

8-6

other than the generalised observation on the need for state intervention in maintaining business activity.

6   The above review of work attitudes, across cultures and historical periods, helps to put our own situation into perspective. And there is already change on the horizon in the industrialised West. Today the Protestant work ethic is very much under threat. For a variety of reasons, Americanised work attitudes are beginning to break down.

The huge transnational corporations have now become so powerful that increasing numbers of people are realising that, on balance, they may give rise to more ills than benefits to communities everywhere. Their unaccountability is sufficient to condemn them on the grounds of their inhumanity and that power corrupts, and that absolute power corrupts absolutely. The instability of globalisation, and the transfer of jobs from one part of the world to another at the drop of a hat, makes for job instability at all levels in the industrial hierarchy.

The driving force of employers, on the rewards for effort and achievement, through the pursuit of the work ethic, has now become a sick joke, for the higher the status in the hierarchy, the greater the instability of employment. Chief executives of industrial plants, for example, now have an average tenure of between eighteen months to three years. Over the past fifteen years, with high rates of unemployment, and a plentiful supply of well qualified graduates willing to fill posts at salaries well below their established market level, employers have become increasingly mean, callous, and contemptuous towards their employees - especially those in middle and senior management unprotected by trades union arrangements. Executives are still expected to work many hours of unpaid overtime, or to take home every night a bundle of reports for reading and study. Many perks, once taken for granted, are now being gradually withdrawn, or heavily taxed, such as cars, expense accounts, and membership of relevant clubs and institutes. After-hours socialising between different levels of executives is now far less frequent than before, or discouraged, whilst the traditional Christmas dinner or dance, is now for many companies a thing of the distant past.

Meanwhile in America, the illusions of the ever-expanding pioneer economy offering prosperity to all, is fast coming to a close. The West has long been opened up, and there are no more unclaimed spaces for ownership claim and profitable exploitation! The sudden realisation that the world is, after all, a finite place, is coming as a terrible shock to the psyche of many Americans, whose only understanding of business is of unending growth. With the catastrophic decline of manufacturing; with the Far East buy-outs of business and real estate; and with the polarisation of society into rich and poor, a cold draught is running across the American continent. For the

8-6

first time Americans are needing to look inwards and more deeply in searching for new turning points for the future. Innovative thinkers, on economics and the social sciences, are floating ideas, launching pressure groups,   and designing web-sites, on the sustainable economy, environmental and monetary reform, etc., which are beginning to influence even the mainstream political parties. The reaction against colossal waste, pollution, crazy speculation, and downsizing was bound sometime to occur.

The new generation of executives everywhere are very different from their forebears. Firstly, they have not grown up in the optimism of the immediate post-War period; secondly, the majority are no longer from the old middle class, and so do not share entirely the comfortable values of their predecessors; and thirdly, financially, they are far less secure. In Britain this is partly because on graduation they are often heavily in debt due to the new Student loan system, and will need five, ten, or fifteen years to repay for their education; and in addition, each middle class generation in the post-War period is relatively poorer than that of its parents or grandparents, due to rising tax levels, and increasing economic egalitarianism amongst the middle layers of society constituting the majority of the population. As Peter Drucker has noted, "the hidden conflict between the knowledge worker's view of himself as a 'professional' and the social reality in which he is the upgraded and well-paid successor to the skilled worker of yesterday, underlies the disenchantment of so many highly educated young people with the jobs available to them."[30]

All these factors have tended to make the new middle class more sceptical of achieving affluence; more cynical of grand promises; more careful or realistic in assessing their role in an organisation; more reluctant to conform to required patterns of behaviour; more prepared to jump at short notice from one enterprise to another; and more ready to rebel for their benefit should the occasion arise. Again, it should be noted that these characteristics have not emerged purely through the upbringing or educational environment of the younger generation, with its emphasis on the need to safeguard personal rights, but through the total environment and conditions of contemporary society.

This factor is emphasised, since some employers choose falsely to blame the younger members of their workforce for "lacking sufficient loyalty or commitment," when true blame should lie on their own shoulders, or at least, on the shaky characteristics of the industrial system. Such employers, or the rentier capitalistic system, has created a rod for its own back. Loyalty and commitment can only be given

---

[30] Peter F. Drucker, *The Age of Discontinuity*, Heinemann, 1969, p. 259.

8-7

in exchange for benefits, and those benefits are lacking. What the new generation of executives require is job security, a genuine career path, and acknowledgement of their true worth.

7   All the above economic factors have prepared the middle and senior management sectors of industry, working at plant level (i.e. those separated from the corporate office), for trades union membership and activity. As Robert Taylor has argued, "the chronically insecure condition in which workers find themselves in today's labour market suggests trade unions ought to be much more in demand in the workplace to carry out their fundamental purposes as protectors of people at work than possibly at any time since before the First World War."[31] All that is needed is the catalyst to arouse the right political consciousness, so that psychologically, middle and senior managers, including even the chief executives of manufacturing plants, will be drawn into fighting for the right to better working conditions. The involvement of middle and senior management in the struggle of the labour movement would push even further the reforms of trades unionism in meeting the changing sociology of work. The trades unions would need to transform their image for purposeful action in attracting this new constituent to their membership. The style of middle and senior management industrial revolt would be very different from that of the proletarian activity of the past, but in its own way, it need be no less militant.

It would be a trades unionism operating within a different cultural ambience, and its need is demonstrated by two simple facts: firstly, the senior executive today is as helpless in deciding his own fate as the shop-floor worker; and secondly, that proportionally, he has no less to lose, in the event of redundancy, than any other employee on his payroll. Since the chief executive or senior manager has further to fall, and usually more to lose than the shop-floor worker, he is more likely than the latter to lose home, wife, and family, since he may be a shareholder, and will almost invariably be denied another chance to hold a comparable position. The shop-floor worker, on the contrary, will usually be more consolable because of the greater chance of other opportunities, and the lower perception of disgrace. The characteristics of this new trades unionism for the middle and upper echelons of industry will be elucidated in later chapters.

There are other miscellaneous but no less significant factors to be considered with regard to the nature of work in relation to the broader aspects of society. For example: how hard should people be obliged to work ? Should there be limits on

---

[31] Robert Taylor, *The Future of The Trade Unions*, André Deutsch, 1994, p. 6.

8-8

pressure placed on the individual ? This is an issue now facing employees at every level in the organisation. Competition, especially today with low wage overseas economies, not only in manufacturing, but perhaps more commonly, in the field of computer programming, graphic design, and the general management of software, has led to increasing or impossible pressures for employees in the West. Should there be legislation on health grounds to restrict pressurising practices, in addition to limiting hours? Where is the median line to be drawn in determining acceptable and unacceptable work practices ? These are questions demanding study and resolution.

8 Since the majority of working hours of most are engaged in work and commuting, it is desirable that all forms of labour should be made as agreeable as possible, through creating a pleasant environment, through inducements or rewards, and through a proper career structure in giving a sense of long-term purpose. But unskilled and disadvantaged employees should also be given inducements and the prospects of a long-term purpose, for a society which is only based on meritocratic values is grossly unfair, and cannot possibly fulfil the aims of true Socialism. The problem with Blairite Socialism today is that it is too ready to substitute meritocracy for old style privilege, unaware of the fact that the former can itself mutate into a new form of privilege and injustice. It is, for example, iniquitous, as we generally find in Britain today, that unskilled work should be rewarded according to a fixed hourly rate irrespective of other factors. This demeans the dignity of work whilst ignoring the needs of the individual. It is desirable that a lesson should be taken from Japan on justice in the workplace. Hourly rates for unskilled work should be increased according to age and length of company service, together with further increments for suggested efficiency improvements endorsed by management, so that even the most disadvantaged might benefit with a long-term purpose built into their careers.

It should be recognised by all sectors of the community (and especially employers) that work is not the most important aspect of existence, but life itself. The workaholic is not simply a problem to himself but to society, since he neglects wife, family, and friends, and the need for his own inner self-development. It is not the function of colleagues to prompt the workaholic to relax his efforts, for that would be an impertinence amongst equals in the environment of the workplace where co-operation and competition should be in harness in making for success. It is, however, the function of the good employer to remind the workaholic of his other obligations in life. Anyone deserving the status of an employer should have sufficient responsibility to transcend his role in becoming a disinterested observer of the world. The employer should be a person of maturity and balance, who occasionally may even be dismissive

8-9

. of the values of profit and work.

The above indicates that there are circumstances when the wild and hectic dynamism of business needs to be constrained by the state and trades union activity for the health of the community. Such constraining forces, have of course, always existed through legislation covering every aspect of business: viz., anti-trust legislation or competition policies; health and safety regulations; and the entire body of commercial and company law.

9   In conclusion, it has to be noted that an employed status is an essential requisite in the democratic community in empowering the individual as an economic unit. Hence a Socialist government should set out to achieve nothing less than full employment, and this may be set at 97 1/2%. Not only is full employment necessary as a collective force in empowering realistically democratic government (as will be explained in the following chapter), but in securing the rights and prosperity of the individual as a living part of the body politic. Some leading Socialists (e.g. Clive Jenkins and Barry Sherman)[32] have argued, either out of fatalism or utopianism, or both, that the unemployment of the leisure society will be an inevitable factor of life, and because of this should be welcomed.

There is hardly a socio-economic prediction which could be more horrific than this in alienating one half of society against the other. No amount of leisure activity, however varied or pleasurable, can possibly hope to give a sense of purpose to life; any more than could an exclusive diet of expensive chocolate truffles hope to satisfy the craving for a more varied nourishment. All leisure societies, whether rich and cultured, as in 18th century France and England, or debased and poor, as in ancient Rome, point to the immorality and aimlessness of their existence. In the words of Jeremy Rifkin, "the notion of being a 'productive' citizen is so imprinted on the nation's character that when one is suddenly denied access to a job, his or her self-esteem is likely to plummet. Employment is far more than a measure of self-worth. To be under-employed or unemployed is to feel unproductive and increasingly worthless."[33]

Purposeful work, within an exchange system, is as vital to the status, self-respect, and dignity of the individual, as is oxygen to life itself. This is because no government sleight of hand, no benefits, and no grand declarations, can succeed in establishing the un-discriminated equality of the unemployed, alongside their more

---

[32] In, *The Leisure Shock,* Eyre & Methuen, 1981.

[33] Jeremy Rifkin, *The End of Work*, G.P. Putnam's, NY, 1995, p. 195.

9-1

fortunate brothers and sisters contributing to the welfare of the community. Therefore, every individual should have the right to a job comparable with his or her ability, but unless it is recognised by the state as a human right alongside other established rights, such a cry would remain an empty voice in the wind.

CHAPTER 9
People Power In Transforming The Economy

"The financial system is *our* financial system; the conventional economy is *our* economy; and both have a responsibility to serve us - and we have a right to seek their reform."

Michael Rowbotham, *The Grip of Death*, Ian Carpenter, 1998, p. 254.

1 - Representative systems too easily mistaken for democracy at work   2 - The unhappy situation of the nationalised industries   3 - People power and what it means   4 - Non-class based social struggle of the future   5 - Meaninglessness of class distinctions in the Economic Sector Struggle   6 - Global forces threaten the interests of all   7 - Securing the interests of the Productive economy for all

1   In the fifth chapter we acknowledged that the true nature of Socialism entails the ownership and control of the means of production, distribution, and exchange, by the community as a whole. The failure of Socialism in the past, in both East and West, has stemmed from the fact that representative systems alone have been used in pushing forward Socialist measures.

In the third chapter we argued that representative democracy is the only practicable form of democracy in an industrialised state at the present stage of society's development. The future, as we noted, might facilitate advanced forms of government through referenda, but only after society had become more egalitarian; had achieved higher levels of education; and had become more politically cohesive.

It was also noted that representative democracy was very much a second best alternative to direct or Athenian styles of democracy. In the modern era, political parties are therefore very much representative organisations, and because of the consequent domination of parties with regard to all aspects of political life, bad habits of thought have come to see all politics in terms of representation. In view of the fact that all kinds of committees are comprised of delegates for every conceivable purpose, and that all voting activity is concerned with appointing individuals to undertake tasks on behalf of others, this is not surprising.

9-2

Real Socialism, however, cannot be introduced into society purely through a network of representative institutions, and the great mistake of Socialist activists everywhere, is their obsessive love for committees and sub-committees, and rules and procedures, under the false impression that this necessarily advances the underlying cause of democracy. It does nothing of the sort! Too often, as we all know, it feeds the power-lust and self-importance of ambitious and loquacious functionaries. Socialism has always implied the implementation of democracy in its best or ideal form, i.e. in empowering the least privileged members of the community alongside all others of which it is composed. The problem of Socialism is that it has consistently failed in this through confusing the means of representation as the purposeful end of democracy, which clearly it is not.

Most great representative systems of Socialist governments designed to advance the power and interests of the people have been fraudulent, and because of this they have met with failure and opposition. The Soviet system, comprising a complex network of committees, utilising all the voting systems of democracy, was in reality a party dictatorship over every aspect of life. The contempt which Communism had for business was self-fulfilling in destroying or preventing the growth of a sound economy serving the needs of the populace. Pride in economic achievement was measured purely in terms of productivity levels for specific classes of goods: e.g. the number of shoes, tractors, shirts, spades, or brooms, which had been produced annually or within the current 5-year plan. Productivity levels in themselves are meaningless in measuring the success of an economy, since they take no account of over-production, or the production of unwanted and useless goods.

As the Soviet economy was not market-led, or responsive in any sophisticated sense to market needs, the temptation by the peoples' representatives controlling industry to over-produce was too great to resist. Rewards and different categories of official Hero-worship were generously accorded the over-producers. Soviet domestic economic policy may have been undertaken in the name of the people, by the people, but by no stretch of the imagination was it for the people or of the people, since production policy was exclusively a matter for the party hierarchy. The consequent inertness and insensibility of Soviet life is evident in almost any street scene or illustration of the epoch.

2   In Britain, meanwhile, the nationalised industries of the post-War period were hardly less-loved than the great production ministries of the East bloc powers. They were in theory managed and part-owned by employees for the greater benefit of the community, but widespread discontent marked them out as workplaces where

9-3

industrial strife was especially acute. In reality the nationalised industries proved a bonanza for the employment prospects of middle class Oxbridge graduates seeking comfortable sinecures until retirement. The fact that bureaucratic procedures were allowed to take precedence over the need to make profit, lifted the pressure from those who directed their course. The exclusive gin-and-tonic brigade managed the nationalised industries, partly with the connivance of civil service confidentiality procedure, and partly through the arrogance of their assumed superiority. Ordinary working people had no more say in the organisation or managment of these industries than did Soviet workers in factories in deepest Siberia.

The situation was compounded by the muscle of strong left wing unions which had no inclination to play along with the pretence of "people-inspired industries." Bosses were still bosses and needed to be opposed on the grounds of advancing the class struggle. Any attempt at crossing the dividing line between labour and capital, or shop-floor and management, was still class betrayal. The result was that British Socialism was divided against itself for one decade after another in the post-War period, with unions confronting Labour administrations. The last of these unsavoury and uncompromising stalemates occurred in 1979, bringing with it the downfall of the Callaghan government and eighteen years of Tory rule, and four failed general elections for Labour. The public had become exasperated by Socialism's internal squabbles, and was unforgiving in turfing out the last administration, which might aptly have been referred to, as "Old Labour."

3   Real Socialism, i.e. Socialism as Socialism, or Socialism as democracy, necessitates the achievement of people power. People power, as defined in this book, does not entail representative authority, which amounts to little more than transferring power from one agency to another, but rather the direct exertion of power by each individual. Nothing less can be affirmed as meaningful as either truly Socialist or truly democratic. It may be asked as to why mainstream Socialist movements have stopped short of advancing people power as defined above.

Syndicalism in France and Guild Socialism in this country have approached the question of people power in the workplace, but something more than that is now intended, and in any case, neither of these movements may correctly be referred to as mainstream. The idea of people power has failed to influence mainstream Socialism for the following four reasons:-

Firstly, because parliamentary groups are constrained by opposing vested interests with regard to discretionary limits on their thinking;

Secondly, because insufficient thought has been given to the actual

9-3

mechanisms of economic power within the infrastructure of society;
Thirdly, because Socialists still perceive the community as divided
into two irreconcilable factions (although New Labour would wish
it were not so); and,
Fourthly, because people power is only practicable after a certain level
has been reached in the evolution of society.

The realisation of people power requires a transformation of political attitudes with regard to the exertion of power. Socialist or left wing attitudes lay emphasis on the need to fight injustice and oppression. Its motivating force is resentment against a dominating power which is ill-understood, and from this perspective emerges frustration, anger, and thoughts which are predominantly negative. The miners' struggle in the 1970s, or that of the Midlands car workers in the same decade, or any of the other great industrial conflicts of an earlier period may be cited as examples. The attitude was to demonstrate, strike, work-to-rule, picket, etc., in forcing an opposing group to give in to a specific demand. The attitude is exactly that of a screaming toddler to a parent. The left wing demonstrator, of an earlier era, would be as horrified at the suggestion of participating in the management process, as the toddler would be at supplanting the role of the parent.

The attitude of people power is quite different. It need be no less rebellious, and it is still against the oppression of a stronger or higher authority, but there all resemblance ends. It has a clearer vision of what is ultimately required. Its confidence lies in its knowledge and expertise. Its feelings are not so much those of resentment or ill-usage at the hands of others, but rather anger and contempt at the ignorance of those in authority. Its thoughts are predominantly positive, in the sense that it seeks to grasp power away from superiors, in transferring the management of power to itself. Its rationale for such seizure of power is not primarily based on arguments for greater "justice" or "fairness," but rather on arguments in promoting greater efficiency for the enterprise or institution, in benefitting the community in total. Such subjective arguments, in promoting self-interest or promotion, are therefore kept strictly subordinate to those of the public interest. This may be described as the pattern for middle class rebellion, which eschews any suggestion as to its limitations, in the quiet assurance and pride of its superiority to those in power.

The rebelliousness of people power is therefore far more responsible than that of older forms of industrial unrest. Whilst people power is inspired by a constant vision for the reconstruction of society, or a part thereof; proletarian rebellion never rises above the expression of mere discontent. The latter is inspired by frustration, it is

9-4

fought through threats, and it is resolved through the granting of a favour extended by another. People power, on the contrary, is inspired by enlightenment, it is fought through negotiation and scheming, and it is resolved through displacing another group with its own abilities and know-how. It has no need to be indebted to another for any of the successes which it gains. It is seemingly autonomous or independent, and only indebted to its own knowledge and ability. As it is never suppliant or servile, it tends to be impatient with moral justification based on human rights or wrongs. But people power cannot be exerted - nor even conceived - without having first attained collectively a high educational level.

4   The appropriate stage in the evolutionary development of society is now being reached when people power may be realised successfully. This is facilitated through the narrowing skills gap between employers and employed, and all that is really required is the political consciousness to initiate the struggle for the eventual seizure of power. The motivating power and responsibility for such a struggle is therefore not justified by mere human rights or the need for a fairer society, important as these are, but more significantly, by creating a more workable or efficient society, often concerned with countering such dangers as environmental threats.

Many such issues do not therefore easily lend themselves to a class-based interpretation, if at all, and so the social struggles of the future will take on characteristics quite different from those in the past. They are battles which may need to be fought with no lesser intensity than those of the earlier industrial revolution, but since the protagonists will be multi-class rather than uni-class, as in the conflicts of the past, the nature of anger and opposition will be markedly different.

Social conflict in the future, in advancing the cause of Socialism, will cease to be class-based, in the older sense of the term, for two reasons: firstly, because of the miniscule number of people representing the class interest to be fought against; and secondly, because of the lack of identifying features characterising the minions serving their interests. Those minions may fall into two main categories: those who are reluctant to serve the interests of their masters; and those who are simply unaware of the position which they occupy in the new and invisible divide parting the two economic interest sectors of society.

These minions may comprise collectively of individuals taken in equal measure from every sector of society, and in occupation may very from accountants, land speculators, lawyers, doormen, butlers, cooks, hoteliers, dentists, merchant bankers, venture capitalists, or stockbrokers. It has to be noted, however, that most of the above occupations may also be found supporting the other side of the political divide. The

9-5

only other recurring characteristic of these minions may be an insensitivity to social issues, a tendency towards self-interest, or a general light-headedness on knotty matters, all of which are natural human traits, and may be found amongst those of any political or other persuasion.

5   Class struggle as properly understood, and as reflected through the experience of history, is only definable through the clear definition of class interests and class characteristics. When we speak, for example, of the bourgeoisie or the proletariat, or the patricians or the plebeians, these not only conjure up distinct images, but reflect both economic conditions and economic interests which lend themselves to depth analysis. We are now entering into a unique epoch of history. The social conflict of the future will not lend itself to a class-based definition, for the reason that in the advanced industrialised countries of the northern hemisphere and the Far East, the class to be fought against will be so dispersed and so few in number as to have no other signifying characteristics than its own extreme wealth.

The ownership of extreme wealth alone cannot in itself elicit a predictable political response, or lend itself to a meaningful class classification. This is because of the variation in personality of those who possess wealth. Some may be flamboyant, but others may be retiring; careless in appearance; confused by their status and at one time penny-pinching (e.g. Bill Gates); have a strong social conscience and hold left wing views (e.g. Richard Branson); set out to save the world through promoting green issues (e.g. James Goldsmith); preach a doomsday scenario with regard to globalisation (e.g. George Soros); or live in such isolation, poverty, and filth, that they succumb to disease and death (e.g. Howard Hughes). Extreme wealth is as rare a condition in humankind as it is conducive to eccentricity. To define those of extreme wealth, on those grounds alone, as belonging to a distinctive economic class would be meaningless. The only really significant factor is the means by which wealth is attained. The new social divide in society does comprise a significant sector of those owning great wealth versus the rest of humanity. We have spoken about the minions of this class, in the defining sense that they serve this class, and the interests of this class, but they are not *of* this class.

Because of all the above factors, the social conflict of the future cannot correctly be referred to as a class struggle, but rather as an Economic Sector Struggle. This is because the struggle will be waged predominantly against a financial-commercial system, which because of its power and ubiquity, transcends the discretion and reach of individuals supposedly concerned with its control. Hence it is understood that processes, and the products of computer technology concerned with the management

9-6

and transfer of financial assets, have overridden rational planning or social need to such an extent, that an evil genie has been let out of the bottle.

Of course individuals are involved in these processes through a mixture of accident and design, and should - and do take blame for some of the disasters for which they are responsible. Nick Leeson may be cited as every small cog in a big wheel who nonetheless succeeded in bankrupting one of the oldest and most famous merchant banks in the City of London. His case was an example of the irresponsibility of the system in managing financial assets rather than the irresponsibility of an isolated and foolish individual.

But the big fish - the directors and chairmen of conglomerates and financial institutions - can under no circumstances be exculpated for the ills and disasters for which their organisations are responsible. They should not be protected by limited liability. Neither should they be protected by the excuse of unintentional consequences, nor the inability to predict an outcome, nor the incapacity to control events that had spun out of control. All blame for disasters, not of a natural order, must finally be cast on the cause of a human agency. Machines or computers do not rule the World ! That is the fiction of fantasy. Computers need programming and operatives to press their keys. The instability of the world trading situation today is accountable to three factors: firstly, the irrationality of stock market speculation; secondly, the speed of transactions which take no account of the need for caution or deliberation; and thirdly, the unaccountability of the system which removes any inhibitions, moral or otherwise, as to consequences.

6   The forthcoming Economic Sector struggle may be referred to as a Social (although not a class) conflict, solely on the grounds that the minions supporting the economic interest to be fought against nevertheless represent a human collective albeit without distinguishing or identifiable characteristics. It is a human collective which through the accident of occupational situation sets it at variance with the rest of the community.

What is the source of this economic conflict, and where are the lines to be drawn for this new divide in society ? In the answer to these questions will be found the core economic factors for the Socialism of the future. In a sense we shall be returning to traditional Socialist values, in promoting the cause of labour and productivity versus irresponsible speculation and the accumulation of capital into ever-fewer hands. Irresponsible speculation is defined as that which destablises financial markets; withdraws assets from healthy productive plants; invests in passive assets like land and property, with their inflationary values; and downsizes or closes plants in specific

9-6

locations.

The great economic divide in the world today, overriding all other interests, is that between Corporate or Conglomerate interests versus subsidiary enterprises, i.e. primary, manufacturing and service industries at their productive working level. The globalisation of the transnationals represents the system on the world stage, and although no country escapes the ruinous tentacles of international capital, they are effected in different ways according to the level of social and industrial development. Poorer and less developed countries are always exposed to greater damage, and the ruination of their economies and the suffering of their peoples is usually in direct proportion to the beneficence of lending (or more correctly of investment) of the great powers. As John Gray has remarked, "it is no exaggeration to say that the global freedom of capital, which is a distinguishing feature of our current circumstances, effectively demolishes the economic foundations of social democracy.[34] ... Globalisation weakens or undermines the bargaining power of organised labour. Public financing of the welfare state is constrained by dependency on global capital markets, which limit to a narrow range national governments' leverage over interest rates and exchange rates." [35]

In Britain the ills of corporate power or globalisation are predominantly manifested through de-industrialisation and unemployment. An explanation of how this is advanced will be reserved for later chapters. Here we are only concerned with stating the problem as it effects the new social divide in society. American and British business follows the corporate pattern, and over the past ten years, the more benign Continental form of capitalism has given way to the aggressive Anglo-Saxon mode of business with the spread of transnational activity. The pattern of corporate business entails the ownership of dozens or hundreds or subsidiary enterprises, controlled with regard to their financial policy from a central office. When a corporation owns a varied portfolio of companies, differing say, from a chain of hairdressers to engineering workshops, it is usually known as a conglomerate. A conglomerate may own several separate groups, in which case there would be three layers of authority: the plant (or factory) head office; the group head office; and the conglomerate head office.

The corporation or the conglomerate is listed on the stock exchange in its own name, in representing all its owned subsidiaries. The first purpose of the corporation

---

[34] John Gray, *Endgames*, Polity Press, 1997, p. 23.

[35] Ibid., p. 28.

9-6

is to ensure the maximisation of its share value as well as paying sufficiently generous dividends to shareholders. Any legal means, and some which are borderline (such as rigging share values), are used to ensure these ends. The long-term prosperity of separate subsidiaries is not a priority, as the energy of the corporation is necessarily concentrated on the collective valuation of the group. Apologists for the corporate system sometimes argue that separate enterprises are afforded the benefit of a protective umbrella, so that in hard times, the group may reallocate financial sources for where support is required. But in the real world this rarely happens. The subsidiaries of a corporation are always dispensable, and treated like cards in a poker pack. The corporation is constantly searching for new opportunities, and there is an on-going process of acquiring and selling enterprises in the group. The sole purpose of subsidiaries is that they should be made to contribute sufficient profits to shareholders.

The problem with the system is that many types of companies are sluggish or slow to produce profits of a sufficient level in satisfying the requirements of the corporation, but this does not in any way indicate that such companies are necessarily inefficient or badly managed. It indicates rather that the speed and level of profits accrued differs according to the nature of the business activity. For example, estate agency, mortgage lending, banking, venture capitalism, stockbroking, and insurance, are highly profitable within a short time period. Many service industries which are labour intensive, but require little capital investment, occupy an intermediate position within the scale of profitability.

Manufacturing and primary industries, on the other hand, such as mining, require substantial and constant investment in keeping ahead with technological change. Consequently, their profitability levels - or the time taken to achieve sufficient levels of profitability, is a headache to financial planners in corporate offices. The result is that in the Anglo-Saxon economies, manufacturing and technology receives a raw deal in the hands of investors. Will Hutton pointed out a common misconception when he wrote, "Britain's 'success' in attracting inward foreign direct investment is trumpeted from the rooftops, but every pound of investment that entered Britain between 1991 and 1995 was on average trumped by half as much again leaving the country in British direct investment overseas."[36] Preference is given to promoting those easier activities concerned with financial services or enterprises requiring a low rate of investment. Manufacturing is regarded as a high risk gamble - which it is when under-invested - and

---

[36] Will Hutton, *The State To Come*, Vintage, 1997, p. 5.

9-7

so like poor orphans, manufacturing enterprises are exposed to the constant instability of acquisition and sale, for the profits which may be squeezed out of them in the short term. Often this takes the form of asset-stripping or closure, for the sale of land and plant for a more profitable purpose.

All this explains why in the post-War period British productive industry, has in relative terms, performed so poorly by comparison with our competitors in Continental Europe or the Far East. If Germany or Japan had had to rebuild her industries in the post-War period with the handicap of financial dependence on such institutions as the London stock exchange, or the risk-averse British clearing banks, they would inevitably have dragged far behind even the productive levels achieved in this country.

7   In the industrial sphere today there is therefore a sharp divide between corporate interests and those of productivity. Corporate interests, which are purely speculative, are concerned with making money out of money, and the process not only enriches the few, but over a period of time accumulates wealth into ever fewer hands. Productive interests, on the contrary, are purely social, since they are concerned with producing essential or other goods demanded by the market; with promoting industrial efficiency and maximising market share, in benefitting an ever-larger customer base; and with promoting fuller employment opportunities.

The internal struggle between corporate and productive interests may be witnessed in almost any subsidiary enterprise, even though senior management may cover-up or disguise its intensity. The chairmen and senior management of industrial plants are therefore pulled in two directions: i.e. by the need to serve the longer term ends of their enterprises, through up-dating equipment and methods, improving efficiency, and seeking to maximise market share; versus the short-term ends envisaged by the corporation, in maximising profits for every twice yearly accounting period for the payment of dividends; repairing rather than replacing equipment; and economising on the wage bill through salary freezes, redundancy policies, etc.

In strengthening its authority, corporate policy often entails sacking the all-round industrial chief executive (usually an engineer), and replacing him with a young accountant, sent down from the head office with a free hand to root out and dismiss all managers not falling into line with the spirit of the new financial management. The final irony is that such new management succeeds in squeezing out its predicted profit levels, but only by bankrupting the enterprise within an 18-month period. This, tragically, fails to upset the corporation, since with a constant flow of new acquisitions, those companies put into liquidation (which after all, satisfactorily fulfilled their required function) are soon forgotten.

9-7

The purpose of New Socialism, therefore, must be to arouse a new consciousness with regard to this conflict of economic interests, which is not simply a difference of interests amongst industrialists, but pin-points the root cause of all social injustice dividing rich and poor in the world today. The viability of arousing this consciousness to a level for political action may be summarised through the following:-

1. The diminution in the differential of earnings amongst productive workers employed in industrial plants, ranging from chief executives down to shop-floor operatives;

2. The diminution in the different skills levels between top management and shop-floor workers in CAM plants;

3. The diminution in the differential of cultural background and general education between management and shop-floor.

4. Smaller plants and fewer employees tend to generate more trust and friendlier relationships amongst all levels of staff;

5. Globalisation is exacerbating all the worst aspects of corporate business through the de-industrialising policies of downsizing, transferring plants abroad, and promoting home-based unemployment; and,

6. Corporate policies and the isolation of its office from the technical minutiae of managing a productive business, is creating a widening divergence of understanding between the conflicting interests of investor-directed financial management and the maximising of market share on a commercially viable basis.

Arousing this Socialist consciousness may only be achieved successfully through the formulation of new political values in advancing the coming struggle. This matter will be discussed in later chapters.

Meanwhile, the concern of this chapter must remain the different aspects of people power. It is right that people power should find its source in economic activity and in the workplace, and concern itself with issues, the consequence of which, effect us all. The time has arrived for the democratisation of industrial plants. People power in industry should be a responsible and constructive force for greater efficiency and success, linked to employee shareholding arrangements in ensuring tighter commitment to the enterprise.

The purpose of employees must be to support their chief executives and senior managers in the on-going and often covert struggle against corporate power. Socialist governments should put in place industrial credit investment institutions (modelled on those in Germany, France, Japan, etc.), in preparation for encouraging subsidiary enterprises to seek their release from corporate control, so they might in future be

10-1

. managed for their own best interests and those of the community. An open conspiracy between government and grass roots industry, but necessarily reliant on the efforts of people power, would eventually succeed in whittling away the corporate empires, as the financial control of their former subsidiaries was transferred to the protective umbrella of industrial credit banks.

As skill and educational levels rise, people power may be introduced through direct democratic procedures, into all work places in promoting more efficient and profitable practices, better working conditions, and products and services of greater benefit to the community.

CHAPTER 10
Autonomy And The Limits of Democratic Power

"The model of growth currently in force in the world economy is creating, not alleviating, poverty and environmental destruction."

Joshua Karliner, *The Corporate Planet*, Sierra Club Books, San Francisco, 1997,
p. 51.

1 - Representative democracy as yet unable to cross national frontiers   2 - Failings of the EU as an instrument of democracy   3 - Internationalism used by global forces for an ulterior purpose   4 - Internal and not global trade is the guarantor of survival   5 - Conflict between the interests of people prosperity and globalisation   6 - Democratic power must be mobilised against global forces   7 - How this would be achieved

1   In the opening chapter, we already indicated that in the realm of practical politics, ideological movements concerned with the general business of government, even when internationally oriented, are constrained in their organisational activities by geographical factors. This is a significant question to which we must now return in greater detail. Only single issue movements can organise successfully internationally.

Democratic Socialism calls for people power, and the latter calls on the individual to exert direct (and not merely representative) democratic power in the sphere of work, party politics, and many other spheres of life. The exertion of rights and choice in the fields of free association, bringing up our children, buying and selling property, re-locating, and laws allowing or restraining relationships with others in different situations, etc., are all manifestations of people power or its outcome. The individual, as Aristotle remarked long ago, is a political animal, but he is a very different political animal in each nation state - even amongst contiguous countries with similar cultural histories.

10-1

Quite apart from differences of language, historical tradition, law, culture, or religion, the most significant difference politically dividing one people from another is the overriding difference of political temperament and view or interpretation of concepts. These variations give rise to constant misunderstanding, not only by the media in reporting back on events, policy statements, etc., but between politicians and leading statesmen themselves. Almost nothing is written on this problem (partly possibly out of courtesy of one country to another), although it is of overwhelming importance to international relations. Not only such broad concepts as Liberalism, Conservatism, and Socialism, conjure up quite different images in different countries, but also political terms commonly used in international relations take on different shades of reality.

These variations arise through different traditions, for abstract terms, universally used in political language, only take on a concrete reality within the mind through the remembrance of images from past historical experience. To take an historical and extreme example, there is a world of difference between the nominal Liberalism of the arch-nationalist, virulent anti-Semite, racist, and hater of Britain, Heinrich von Treitschke (one of the most highly respected academics and parliamentarians in Wilhelmine Germany) and his contemporary, the British Liberal W.E. Gladstone.

A further difficulty arises not only from differing interpretations of concepts, but from variations in national character and behaviour. Just as habits of thought give rise to varying modes of honesty and dishonesty in each individual, so every nation is honest or dishonest in its own particular way - or is seemingly so in the eyes of its neighbours. All these factors give rise to communication difficulties between states, and particularly amongst economic power blocs which supposedly engage in close co-operation.

The success of governmental democracy is not only dependent on a people achieving a sufficient level of education and political awareness, but also on a homogeneous consciousness, understanding, or acceptance of the political system as it impacts on the welfare of society. Hence a governmental democracy, or parliament, ruling several countries not bound by a common political tradition, is either an impossibility (if untried), or a failure when implemented. One might hazard such exceptions as the multi-national parliament of the Austro-Hungarian empire, but it was not a democracy in the true sense but subservient to the imperial bureaucratic system.

Even countries bound by a long tradition, and similar language and culture, tend to break apart as soon as they develop a sufficient level of democratic and national consciousness. Norway's independence of Sweden in 1905 might be cited as such an

10-2

example, or the regionalisation of states towards a separate national consciousness may be cited as others: e.g. Bavaria in Germany, or Wales and Scotland in Britain. Therefore, although democratic forces may lead countries to splinter into regions, no way has yet been devised of enabling effective representative institutions to cross national frontiers or transcend the nation state.

2   The problems today in uniting the countries of the EU are therefore particularly acute. The perception of this is partly overcome by the yawning gap dividing the European Commission from its parliament. Whilst the parliament is a remote and feeble assembly whose members are connected by a tenuous thread with their uncomprehending constituents; the Commission (with its secretive association with national governments) is an arrogant body crazed with issuing an unending flow of directives effecting every aspect of our lives. At the present time the EU does not begin to approach the requirements of a democracy in any proper sense, primarily because the public does not feel its interests are represented, or that the representatives can in any meaningful way be held accountable for the acts of the Commission. This is not intended as criticism of the EU *per se*, but only in the context of its failing to meet the required standards of representative democracy. It is acknowledged that the EU is instrumental in bringing many miscellaneous benefits to this and other countries, e.g., through legislation in the workplace, the minimum wage, and judgements in correcting injustice through the European Court.

Despite the proliferation of international bodies stemming from the United Nations, as well as from the EU, democracy and people power still very much remains the exclusive prerogative of nation states or regions within them. If, therefore, we believe that all political power should be democratic or people power, as opposed to bureaucratic power, or the power of elected bodies which do not realistically reflect the will of peoples, it is right we should be sceptical of transnational political organisations. This is because bodies which are not effectively democratic, or held constantly accountable by the critical eyes of an electorate, are particularly prone to corruption by powerful financial or other interests, such as those of a state much stronger than its neighbours. Already we find that the EU is rife with corruption, as it is buffeted by the vested interests of forces accountable to no external authority. The recent resignation of the twenty European Commissioners was but the tip of an iceberg.

A shadow is therefore being cast over the ideal of internationalism in the sphere of practical politics. Internationalism must always remain the ideal of Socialism, and justice and prosperity for peoples worldwide must be its ultimate purpose. No good Socialist may rest so long as there is poverty or suffering in any part of the world. But

10-3

this does not mean that internationalism should be used as some kind of icon in knocking those forces which seemingly are opposed to it. If history has demonstrated that up until the present time the nation state is the limit to which all-round governmental democracy may be extended, then some note should be taken of that fact, if we are not knowingly or unknowingly to pass political power into the hands of bureaucratic elites which de facto become dictatorships in their own right. Hopefully, in the future, means will be found for devising realistic democratic structures which transcend national boundaries, but as yet that time has not arrived. We shall again turn to this topic of the geographical limits of governmental democratic power in our discussion of the principle of Nationality which we distinguish from Nationalism in Chapter 39.

3   It is perhaps an irony that the torch of internationalism has been snatched out of the hands of the Socialist movement, and is now being carried forward by the forces of corporate capitalism. Weak-minded or unthinking Socialists - many in leadership positions in politics or the trade unions - are being "shamed" into recognising that they are lagging behind in their ideas of modernism. In uncertainty about the future, and with a confused mixture of thoughts, they are recognising the forces of globalisation, not necessarily as ideologically acceptable, but as an inevitable consequence of events. This suppleness of mind has only been made possible through the huge hammer blows against major Socialist economic policies over recent decades. With the present ideological vacuum, Socialist leaders no longer have the gumption to oppose major trends irrespective of their origin or direction.

Consequently, a gloss is put on the idea of globalisation. It is convenient to accept it with the minimum of fuss as a *fait accompli*. In the end, it is argued, all differences will be levelled out as economies and exchange rates will be reduced to a common denomination. Only time will heal all ills in the intervening period. The only alternative of Socialists to this approach, is a fatalism which argues that no practical steps may be taken to oppose globalisation since capitalism is all powerful and omnipotent. The purpose of this book is to oppose such fatalistic pessimism through bringing the greater part of the business community into the Socialist fold in opposing the very ills of the capitalist system. Without such a strategy it would indeed be impossible for the labour movement to confront this world-threatening phenomenon.

In view of the above, it is worth noting the words of Noam Chomsky when he wrote that, "the Bretton Woods institutions ... that are being made 'the centre of gravity for the principal economic decisions that affect developing countries' are marked by 'their undemocratic character, their lack of transparency, their dogmatic principles,

10-3

their lack of pluralism in the debate of ideas and their importance to influence the politics of the industrialised countries' - whose dominant sectors they serve, in reality.[37] ... GATT, NAFTA, and the like are called 'free trade' agreements. That is a misdescription. Firstly, the term 'trade' hardly applies to a system in which some 40% of US 'trade' is intrafirm, centrally managed by the same highly visible hands that control planning, production and investment.[38] ... As for 'world trade' well over a third is already 'intrafirm,' that is, centrally managed commercial interactions, not trade in any serious sense."[39]

In returning to the first of these alternatives, i.e. "that everything will turn out all right in the end," the blindness and absurdity of this optimism is easy to perceive. The theory and practice of globalisation entails the constant search for cheaper manufacturing processes in lower cost locations. The inevitability of the practice is not so much dictated by manufacturing enterprises themselves, as by investing institutions seeking greater profits for shareholders in a competitive environment. If the promoters of an enterprise fail to find a cheaper process or a lower cost location, then the competitors of that enterprise will find them first.

It therefore follows, as we find on a daily basis, that jobs are taken away from the older more affluent economies and passed to poorer territories with lower exchange rates. Jobs are taken away from those with a good living wage and decent standards of employment, and often given to those who are paid slave wages in factories with minimal health and safety regulations. The products of Western industrialised countries have become meaningless in terms of the originating brand as a source of manufacture, since so-called British or American products are as likely to have been produced in China, Indonesia, or Brazil, as in the home country. Home-based assembly operations add further to the confusion, as imported components are then put together, with a "made in England" label seeming to falsely justify the origin of the product.

Those promoting the interests of the great transnational corporations will attempt to prick the consciences of Socialists critical of global forces. They will argue that now is the time for those on the other side of the world to benefit from the advantages of industrialisation and consumerism which follows in its wake. Why should not competition be allowed to benefit the peoples of the Third world, in the same way it has

---

[37] Noam Chomsky, *World Orders, Old & New,* Pluto Press, 1994, p. 179.

[38] Ibid., p. 180.

[39] Ibid., p. 185.

10-4

benefitted those in the privileged West ? Does not globalisation promote an economic egalitarianism throughout the world, and is that not the core purpose of Socialism ? Furthermore, these leaders of corporate capitalism will suggest that opposition to globalisation is unrealistic; attempting to turn back the clock; reactionary; or simply against the inevitable laws of progress.

4   When the facts of globalisation are considered in their proper context, it will soon be found that all the above arguments are spurious. No modern Socialist would deny the benefits of industrialisation or a free market economy to any peoples of the Third world. But it is not necessary to sacrifice the interests of one half of the world in fufilling the needs of the other. It is not right that the 200-year struggle of the labour movement for desirable standards in the realms of work and domestic life should be foregone in placing peoples in another part of the world on a debased level in the industrial system. That is not progress, but on the contrary, industrial regression. The powers of corporate capitalism are in no position to lecture Socialists on the correct road to Third world prosperity. Their so-called loans or investments to the Third world through the agency of the IMF or the WTO, have proved a millstone around the necks of the peoples of Africa, and central and south America, as well as elsewhere, bankrupting their economies. Due to the greed for profit, investments were made in activities for which the level of their industrialisation was quite unfitted, and loans were hamstrung by conditions which prevented there ever serving the needs of ordinary people. As the eminent French historian, Fernand Braudel, has noted, "if the Third world is to make any progress it will somehow or other have to break down the existing international order."[40]

Globalisation is an agency for world chaos rather than progress. All viable economic activity is finally traceable to productivity in goods or services, but it is in the productivity of goods where the wealth of a community is ultimately found. This is because we are all dependent on food, clothing, and shelter, and all other needs whether material or other, are contributory in a subsidiary sense to these basic demands for survival. In the recent past, much nonsense was written about the post-industrial society, whereby the advanced countries moved over to concentrating on high value service requirements whilst the business of manufacturing was left to the more backward Third world economies. Now even this conveniently happy myth of transnational capitalism has been laid to rest when it is realised that software management and computer programming on behalf of Western based companies may

---

[40] Fernand Braudel, *Civilisation & Capitalism*, Collins, 1984, Vol. III, p. 542.

10-5

be undertaken in Bombay, or elsewhere, at a fraction of home-based costs.

The truth is that no country in any part of the world is able to hold onto a monopoly of skills or expertise in any industry, irrespective of whether it be in goods or services. The fact that Britain may dominate the world in certain sectors of insurance, or maintain amongst the largest financial services sector anywhere in the world in international finance, is no guarantee that this will continue forever into the future. The assumption that specific skills or expertise are intrinsic and exclusive qualities of particular nationalities is not only delusive but dangerous nonsense. I can well remember when it was "safely predicted" that the British motor cycle industry; the production of white goods; and that of vehicles, would never meet with serious competition from abroad.

Is there any lesser reason now why current predictions on the job-creating information industries should not also meet with crushing foreign competition ? There is a school of economists, who in moving along with the interests of transnational capitalism, preach that Britain should only concentrate on the production of high technology products already "proven" in export markets. This of course contradicts with the other reality of Britain presented as a low-cost low-skill assembly centre for advanced Continental technology. It will be argued in this book that British business should engage in any manufacturing or other activity quite irrespective of its technological sophistication or skills required. Anything that is job-creating is worthwhile and viable, and it may be the function of the state to protect home-based industries as they are already protected in many advanced industrial countries.

5　　Today in Britain we witness a situation when ever more jobs are lost to foreign competition irrespective of their level of expertise. Furthermore, these jobs are no longer merely lost in manufacturing, but also in highly skilled service or information industries - in fact any mental tasks which may be transmitted to any part of the world via a computer network. No work is secure from being territorially uprooted and transferred abroad apart from retailing and other personal services such as hairdressing, beauty treatment, etc. I was about to add dentistry and medical services to this list, but in central Europe, there has been a flow of patients to Hungary in benefitting from much cheaper dental treatment, whilst medicine also is contributing to a special kind of tourist industry in several parts of the world.

There is a hazy notion in Britain that the economy may somehow be carried on the back of the profitable financial services industry in inward and outgoing investments, but it is an absurdity to imagine that a population of 57 million may be sustained through a mix of rentier activity (the fortunate minority); Income Support

10-5

made possible through heavy taxation wherever taxation may be levied; and the oppressed wages of a poor and an over-taxed service sector. This is the direction in which the country is currently moving, but despite all the profits of the financial services sector, bankruptcy would be made inevitable through the mounting imbalance of payments for essential imports.

The ultimate criticism of globilisation is that the great transnational trading conglomerates, and the work of the financial institutions maintaining them, are unaccountable to any nation state or to any other democratic or controlling authority. There is no way in which states or political power may control or intervene in this new trading situation. There are two reasons for this: firstly, because such trading activity is autonomous; and secondly, because (as we have earlier noted) its directional power and energy is even beyond its own control. This is because of the purely market forces of investing activity. Not even the most knowledgeable or wisest seer in business can predict market conditions for tomorrow, let alone next week, next month, or a year hence. This criticism, of course, is moral, since it is based on the assumption of the democratic right of people to intervene in the business process.

The leaders of our great corporations and institutions may laugh at this criticism, pushing it aside at a brush stroke, on the grounds that democracy does not lend itself to the movement of market forces. They will retort that such criticism is purely theoretical, based on a hypothetical situation , and hence unanswerable. Finally, they will explain that the world is as it is, and that the forces of globilasation can no more be altered than the turning of the tide, and that trust must be put in its eventual beneficence. The most intelligent apologists for globalisation will adopt the Marxist dialectical approach on the grounds that it constitutes an inevitable or logical process in the development of capitalist systems, and that therefore it is senseless to worry about its eventual outcome which as a problem will only face those of a later generation.

None of the above defensive stances of the leaders of corporate capitalism can stand against our underlying criticism of globalisation. The fact remains that globalisation presents a colossal threat to the well-being or prosperity of peoples worldwide, and irrespective of whether or not business may be subjected to democratic intervention, any decisions which may be taken collectively by a people in good faith and after due deliberation, become authority through their own will. Socio-economic crises may give rise to any conceivable changes, and there is no reason why the democratic will of peoples should need to wait as supplicants in the ante-chamber of the great transnationals. The latter have had their way for too long. Socialism, over

10-6

the past decades, has been impotent and barren of ideas due to its internal crises. Old Socialism is dead! Long live the New Socialism which must take up and carry forward the torch of social justice and people prosperity.

6   Democracy is a process of self-determination, and repudiates the fatalism of those prepared to be moved along by a tide for good or ill in no particular direction. The purpose of a constructive approach to politics is to confront problems effectively as they emerge, and not to retreat in the face of seemingly insuperable issues on the grounds that "fate" or the "natural course of events" should be allowed to override human will. Because of the geographical limits of democracy as an agency of political power, the ills of globalisation can only be confronted on a two stage basis: firstly, through each country exerting its autonomy to its own best advantage; and secondly, through co-operation between an ever-widening circle of discontented states.

The idea that the peoples of the advanced industrial countries should be expected to prosper in a world economy seeking to reduce all costs for products and services to a global minimum is an insult to their intelligence. Contrariwise it may be argued that all peoples have a natural obligation to maximise their self-sufficiency through extending the productive sector. It is important to distinguish clearly between the Real economy and the Phony economy. The first is concerned with the productivity of goods and services, whilst the second is concerned with speculative activity and the profits thereof. A country relying on its phony economy is a hostage to fortune. When and if the bubble finally bursts, it will realise too late it has not the wherewithal to produce for itself the most basic goods for survival. That is why every country should maintain a high level of productivity for its self-sustainability. Ensuring high levels of productivity in every corner of the world is the best insurance for peace and stability.

The old philosophy of laissez-faire taught that increasing interdependence between states through international trade contributed towards strengthening peace, on the assumption that no country could survive without the products of its trading partners, and that consequently it was in the interests of all countries to maintain peace and stability. In a world, as we see today, where international trading has reached crazy proportions: in distorting or destroying the structure of economies; in dumping merchandise into countries where such produce is already available in abundance; in sweeping away the self-sufficiency of the poor in exchange for profitable exporting cash crops; in promoting a trading system which predominantly benefits traders and investors in pushing exotic or luxury goods onto reluctant consumers; not to mention the pollution and wastage of energy in needlessly moving such quantities of matter from one part of the globe to another, the opposite argument now definitely applies.

10-7

The consequences of over-trading in the second half of the 20th century have undoubtedly led to the outbreak of innumerable wars and civil strife in many parts of the Third world, and to the equally tragic results of desertification; the loss of the water-table; the growth of unemployed shanty town proletariats; and famine. These ills are usually referred to as the capitalist exploitation by the rich countries of the poor peoples of the south, but more specifically, it really refers to the acceleration in international trade.

The road to democratic Socialism, as an international movement, can only be pursued by each country seeking to promote its own material interests according to its circumstances and level of industrialisation. Such interests should at all times only be pursued with the idea of benefiting the bulk of the population as a first priority, and not those of traders or such abstractions as "industrialisation." Productivity for domestic consumption must be the priority of any government seeking to raise the living standards of its people. This may be through developing the primary industries, i.e. agriculture, forestry, fishing, mining, etc.; the secondary industries, i.e. manufacturing; and the tertiary or service industries.

Productivity policies must be aimed at achieving full employment, and this may entail holding back on advanced industrialisation in favour of promoting intermediate technology or traditional modes of production. In promoting full employment policies, every country needs to reserve the right to impose selective tariffs and control exchange rates.. The tragedy of the loan system to Third world countries in the post-War period, is that it has involved investments in major capital intensive projects, such as the building of dams for hydro-electric power, or advanced technology industrialisation, and these schemes have too easily lent themselves to the corruption of bribes and commission arrangements paid to greedy dictators and their henchmen.

7   Every people has the right to the latest developments in science and technology and to developing these, as it sees fit, for its own industrial purposes, in maximising productivity for its people, for the earnings accrued through international trade. There is no way in which the spread of technological knowledge may be blocked, and the imperialistic concept implied in dividing the world between countries which supply raw materials, and those which manufacture, is long gone. If all countries sought to maximise their production of tangible goods, or sought to maximise production for their own needs, and in so doing strove for full employment and higher living standards, there would be a considerable diminution of unnecessary international trade. Furthermore, the economic situation of such a world, where countries sought self-sufficiency would contribute to greater peace and stability, as there would be lesser

10-7

jealously and rivalry amongst nations, and the pattern of essential international trade would contribute to a nice balance of interdependence and autonomy.

But we must conclude this chapter by returning to the question of confronting the threats of globalisation. Only through the efforts of democracy can the power and accumulated wealth of the great transnationals finally be broken and returned to the ownership and control of the people. The struggle may be arduous and protracted but may be achieved through careful strategy and co-operation between nations. The following steps would need to be taken:-

1. Within each country statistical research and publication of all those globalising factors which contribute to or deduct from national wealth creation as it touches on the interests of the majority.

2. The formation of a growing federation of states pledged to fight globalisation and return the ownership and management of business to the people.

3. The establishment in each country of industrial investment credit banks (modelled on those successful financial institutions in post-War Continental Europe and the Far East) in preparation for funding national enterprises.

4. The establishment of alternative tightly regulated stock exchanges, based on the Swiss model, promoting national enterprises. Dealings on such stock exchanges would be restricted to the authorised newly established or reformed banks, and only securities officially introduced could be dealt in; the banks working on commission and technically as responsible principals even when representing third parties; and business would be transacted daily between members by direct negotiation without jobbers or their equivalents being employed.

5. The establishment of Independent Enterprise Boards, responsible to the DTI (or equivalent bodies in other countries), to encourage and oversee the smooth transfer to industrial plants and other businesses from the financial control of corporations to that of the newly founded industrial investment credit banks.

6. The introduction of strategic tariffs on imports in conjunction with protecting National Enterprises, i.e. those which are already independent of group control, or have been liberated from the constraints of corporate management.

7. The preparation by central banks of an alternative emergency currency for use in the unlikely event of currency slippage through global transactions; such preparations to be set in place under the umbrella organisation of a bank owned and controlled by the said federation of states pledged to counter the ills of globalisation.

10-7

8. Legislation enabling the seizure by states of corporations, or their assets, in emergency situations, for immediate re-sale or transfer to private ownership.

The above measures would be taken in the light of protecting current City of London investments, through negotiated changes with leading financial institutions, in minimising the shock effect.   Such protection would not be motivated by New Socialism's love for the City, but rather through the first priority in protecting the investments of the ordinary citizen. Through a careful system of checks and balances, a dual economy would therefore be put in place enabling the gradual transfer of assets from an international (or speculative) to a national (or productive) base.

*

PART II

Socialising Productive Capitalism

"Industrial changes imply social changes and necessitate political changes.
Progressive societies outgrow institutions as children outgrow clothes."

Henry George, *Social Problems*, Kegan Paul, Trench & Co., 1889, p. 7.

New Labour has not yet begun to address the underlying problem of its relationship with capitalism as it exists today. It has declared itself as pro-business, but what does this really mean, if anything, from a Socialist standpoint ?

The following five chapters set out to describe the parameters for pro-business Socialist principles. This has only been made possible by analysing the nature of contemporary capitalism, and differentiating between its benign and malign characteristics. That is the first step. The second is for Socialism to take over capitalism from within, and use the system for its own purpose. In other words, Socialism should cease to confront capitalism *per se*, and neither should it hope to achieve its ends as an external agency through relying on checks and controls on the workings of capitalism.

Why is it desirable for Socialism to take over capitalism for its own ? It is not only desirable but essential in establishing a benign self-regulatory process for the benefit of the entire community. It is now recognised right across the globe, and across the full spectrum of political systems - from Beijing to London - that market forces must be allowed a degree of freedom in satisfying the consumer needs of peoples everywhere. A Socialist self-regulatory inbuilt process within the capitalist system, would be far more effective in controlling the abuses of capitalism, than any amount of external controls, and the disruption and misunderstandings to which they often give rise.

Only now with the present evolutionary development of capitalism, in conjunction with the higher educational standards facilitating the emergence of the Responsible society, is it possible to socialise Productive Capitalism. The term Responsible society refers to a workforce, from the basic to the higher grades, which is prepared to invest in and participate in the management of the employing enterprise, with the same commitment as directors or senior management.

The practicality of how this is to be achieved is the subject matter of the following 23 chapters. Of course such a responsibility carries its own burdens, but if people are to own and control the means of production, distribution and exchange in any meaningful sense, then this has to be the Socialism of the future.

***

For 18 years the Tories had it all their own way. This was certainly not because of their "successful" management of the economy, for their 18-year rule was an unmitigated disaster, devastating to industry, whilst pushing unemployment levels up to those of the 1930s.

It therefore has to be conceded that the Old Labour party failed as an effective opposition between 1979 and 1997. If there was a slide into poverty and the interests of the majority were forfeited, then Old Labour must take a fair share of the blame for failing to convey a convincing image or to project sufficiently attractive policies.

There were many reasons for the difficulties of the Labour party over the past couple of decades: the changing structure of society with its fresh aspirations; the transformation in the pattern of employment and the new sociology of the workplace; and perhaps most significantly, the failure of the party to keep its theoretical framework ahead of the tremendous changes to the financial-industrial system. It was these changes which not simply "threw" the Labour party but Socialism itself. The financial-industrial system took on a form and exerted an influence that was never anticipated in an earlier era. This meant, firstly, that Old Labour aimed its shafts at the wrong targets for attack (i.e. at an outdated model of capitalism); and secondly, it failed to attack the new model of capitalism which was actually responsible for unemployment and all the misery it caused.

The major problem of Old Labour was its entrapment in a contradictory situation: on the one hand its beliefs were set in a time-warp of an earlier age; and on the other, it was trapped in the bureaucratic framework of accepting the financial-industrial establishment as something to be "worked with" rather than opposed, irrespective of its harming majority interests. This led to confusion and intellectual paralysis, whereby those on the left continued to promote outdated values and policies, for lack of a better alternative; whilst the moderate majority resorted to a principle-free pragmatic expediency, since they could see no other common sense course for progress. The net result was predictable: in the eyes of the electorate, an unconvincing Labour party.

If the following chapters succeed in reaching their mark, then a breath of fresh air will sweep through the Socialist movement, for the problems of yesterday remain those of today. The following five chapters present a way out from the entanglement of the Labour party in the complexities of our contemporary situation. Whilst repudiating all the old-fashioned ideas which have lost their conviction with today's majority, the analysis and proposals which follow remain entirely Socialist in the ends they seek to achieve. For example, the need for a classless egalitarian society; for people power; for the effective representation of functional groups; and even for the ownership *and* control of the means of production and distribution by employees of their employing enterprises, are advanced as priorities for the future. The spirit and context in which these things are to be achieved may differ from the traditional environment of Socialist struggle, but that does not matter if the ends are to be the same.

The ideas and proposals in the following chapters have been formulated from a down-to-earth practical viewpoint. Radical economic interests are no longer those which merely attract the working class. The time has conveniently arrived for the middle classes to be radicalised and brought into support the labour movement. To achieve this, the class struggle as it has existed in the past, needs to be repudiated. The enemy is no longer to be identified as a "bourgeoisie" but as a Rentier capitalistic elite, exploiting the wealth creation of the majority.

Furthermore, this Rentier elite is not to be identified with the totality of business interests, or those of the majority of business people, but only with corporate business (of a certain kind) and the financial sector, which together undermine the productive wealth creation of individual enterprises. Hence the Labour party must seek actively for the support of the business sector - appealing even to senior management of conglomerate subsidiaries. How will the Labour party secure the loyal support of chief executives of manufacturing and other enterprises ? Through the following measures: by seeking to counter de-industrialising monopoly and the unemployment that follows in its wake (for senior managers are at the sharp-end of job losses no less than shop-floor workers); assisting subsidiaries towards independence from their corporations for a more stable and long-term profitable future; by initiating the establishment of responsible deficit-funding institutions for the smaller business; and by working for the transformation of the clearing banks, so they might take on functions comparable with those of Japan or Germany in serving the needs of industry and the majority of our people.

There must also be an end to conflict between management and shop-floor. Instead, both should unite their common interests in confronting the exploiting power of corporate capital, i.e. the exploitation (or attrition) of productive enterprises; of labour at every level; and not least, of national interests. Meanwhile, the trades unions would continue their existing functions, whilst extending membership to management, with whom they would co-operate in friendly partnership.

The ownership and control of industry by employees, through co-determination and varying forms of shareholding, would be achieved partly as a logical consequence of the above, but also due to the following factors: the smaller scale of enterprises of the future, with their highly skilled technicians and engineers, and costly capital-intensive machinery, will lead to greater interdependence in the management process of these firms, resulting in the development of partnerships or other forms of personal financial commitment. The newly emerging sociology of the robotic industrial workplace will inevitably engender greater trust and closer links amongst its more egalitarian-situated personnel, leading to a greater willingness to invest or take on a directorial role.

All the above ends, as advocated in the following chapters are Socialist in the best traditional sense, even though they are to be achieved within a differing framework from traditional Socialist struggle. But that framework is contemporary, and it is unlikely that Socialist aims are to be achieved in any other way in the conceivable future - if at all. It is no longer good enough for Labour party supporters - and I have particularly in mind those on the far left - to sit back and wait for the millennium. That kind of dreamy musing is only playing into the hands of those we seek to vanquish, since it deflects from the need for intelligent action.

Perhaps even more important: the guiding socio-economic principles in the following pages will help to bring democracy back to the labour movement. Since the War, all parliamentary groups have increasingly forfeited principles in lieu of expediency and soulless pragmatism, and it is this which has been responsible for so much widespread cynicism.

CHAPTER 11
Labour's Lost Majority

"Sound economic literature makes ... no appeal to the passions or
desires of the people as a whole. The poor do not read it, and the
rich, as a class, make no effort to understand it."

Ernest J.P. Benn, *The Confessions of A Capitalist*, Hutchinson, 1925,
p. 17.

1 - The Labour party's dilemma   2 - Socialising productive capitalism   3 - Our methodology   4 - Failure of
Socialism's dialectic   5 - The new majority   6 - Classlessness of today's economic oppression   7 - Failure of Labour's
electoral appeal   8 - Lost to Labour gained by Tory   9 - But Tories fail to promote the interests of this majority   10 -
The new oppressed not attracted by Labour

1   The Labour party finds itself seemingly in an impossible dilemma: it must either
revert to older Socialist principles, haunted by Marxist economic theory; or
compromise with capitalism through the pragmatism entailed in accepting the mixed
economy. Whilst the first alternative is strong on principle, but weak in grasping the
particular situation of our time; the second amounts to expediency without direction.
Neither alternative brings satisfaction, for neither succeeds in solving substantive
issues, nor inspires the electorate or party membership.

It might be suggested that such a dilemma faces any party of the left elsewhere
in the industrialised West, but as we shall show, Britain is placed in a strangely unusual
situation. This is because her financial-industrial system must be clearly differentiated
from those of her partners in mainland Europe or the five dynamic Tigers of Far and
South East Asia.

The dilemma is compounded by the Labour party's position within the particular
structure of the British political system. As with any movement of the left, it arose in
response to social oppression, but the dual-party nature of our parliamentary system
with its unique cross-benches, has generated such a polarisation and intensity, that both
adversaries developed highly subjective ideologies whereby appearances preponderate
over reality. Consequently, party interests have swamped the need for a deeper
consideration of underlying or substantive issues. In such an environment, failed
political principles maintain a credibility long beyond their shelf life.

Furthermore, the polarisation within Old Labour accentuated the existence of
these alternatives: for whilst those on the parliamentary left saw the "betrayal of
principles" as surrendering to the Conservatism of the opposition; the mainstream

11-3

majority, in the name of modernity and "common sense" saw no other option than to forge ahead in rejecting the failed ideas and experiments of the past. There is little compromise between these opposing views, and almost no way out towards constructing an alternative Socialist philosophy.

2   But if a distant view is taken, away from the bustle of political life, a third alternative may nevertheless be perceived - untried in practice, the concept unexplored - involving the socialisation of productive capitalism. This does not entail, as the notion might at first suggest, a compromise with capitalism. It is instead a call for Socialism to take over certain attributes inherent in the capitalist and business process, utilising these for the greater good of the community. To those able only to comprehend Socialism in terms of class conflict, or as an opposing half within the democratic system, this will at once present the picture of an impossible contradiction. Is this to turn Socialism on its head ? How can Socialism be made the promoter of capitalism?

     This book not only sets out to demonstrate the possibility, but furthermore (in view of the present development of society and our industrial infrastructure) that it indicates the next logical step in the development of practical Socialism. The discussion will not be based on hypothetical theory but on empirical data.

3   This brings us to the methodology to be followed. There are two directions from which political issues are approached. An issue may either be treated substantively, i.e. from a disinterested viewpoint, as having a separate and independent existence; or else expediently, i.e. assessed according to the mood of the electorate or the party in power. In our democracy, unfortunately, it is usually the peripheral non-party issues alone which are treated substantively; whilst the great economic and other questions of the day are so covered over or distorted by the guise of party doctrine, that their underlying reality is concealed. The substantive treatment of major issues is predominantly the preserve of learned societies and other specialised bodies promoting supposedly disinterested purposes. It is only party politics, with its vested interests and prejudices, which exposes issues to the colour of its particular distorting mirror.

     The emphasis that modern political organisations place on the expediency of electioneering techniques in assessing popular opinion has an especial irony. On the one hand, the methods for investigation gathering, which should be accurate and scientific in contributing to more effective democracy, are geared to the knee-jerk reaction of immediate response and the shorter term; whilst on the other, the consequent outcome of incompatible pieces of legislation piled one on top of the other, fails to make for satisfactory government. This results from the pragmatic approach to policy making.

11-4

In an earlier era, by contrast, principle played a stronger role in the life of political movements. Whilst principles imply a degree of authoritarianism, they also entail an agreed body of doctrine and a direction for the future. Hence political parties had a greater predictability, and their memberships a greater loyalty. In the words of Prof. Nisbet, "Politics in our own era has become as nearly devoid of genuinely ideological divisions as is possible to conceive. ... Today the political scene is occupied by strategies and tactics, no longer by principles emerging from the three great ideologies (i.e. Liberalism, Radicalism and Conservatism) which for so long were the stuff of politics in the West."[41] Therefore, the policy-making and direction of the Labour party today is predominantly principle-free with regard to specific socio-economic theory, and consequently, its membership is lukewarm in loyalty - if not actually apathetic. The Tory and Liberal Democratic parties, it should be noted, are similarly placed.

These introductory remarks contrasting the substantive and expedient approaches to politics are important in view of the study which is to follow. A high degree of objectivity must be attained if definitive arguments are presented. As we have seen in Chapter 7, the class-based appeal of Socialism in the past has contributed to an introversion in the understanding of our socio-economic predicament, not merely because of the exclusive concentration on class interests, but more significantly, because of the failure to appreciate the psychological mechanism of the business process as an essential component for Social Wealth Creation. Hitherto Socialism has excluded, through a blind spot in its intellectual credo, a huge dimension of the human experience necessary for the success of social organisation. The purpose of this book is to correct that deficiency for the greater success of the Socialist cause.

The socialising of productive capitalism, as here advocated is concerned with substantive issues, but from these emerge measures aimed at widening the appeal of the Labour party. It is not the primary purpose of this book, therefore, to enquire as to what policy-making best contributes to maximising the popularity of the party. Such an approach would lead to superficial or facile conclusions. We are here concerned only with the formulation of several scientific-like basic principles, from which all practical Labour party policy may be developed as a natural or logical consequence.

4 By way of leading into the topic of socialising productive capitalism, it is necessary to enquire into the causes of the malaise of the Labour party as we find it today. The contraction of the Labour party and the collapse in the support for Socialism

---

[41] Robert Nisbet, *Twilight of Authority*, Heinemann, 1976, p. 47.

11-5

is not merely a reflection of conditions in our own country. It is a worldwide phenomenon.

It stems from the occurrence of unanticipated economic situations which Socialism has not only been unable to resolve, but is even unable to perceive within the context of its philosophical approach. There are two reason for this: firstly, Socialist predictions have failed to materialise as once expected, for it has transpired that historical-materialism , far from serving as a reliable crystal ball, merely fulfils the anodyne function of offering meaningless but sanguine explanations for any turn of events. Secondly, and more significantly, progress has developed at such a speed and complexity in transforming the nature of capitalism, that political thinkers have been unable to keep apace in comprehending its true significance. It appears as if the transformation of our industrial infrastructure has simply embarrassed the Socialist movement.

Consequently, whilst Socialist analysis has been locked into the doctrines of the past, its logical solutions to substantive issues have become increasingly less relevant to the practical world. As Rattray Taylor has observed, "ideas have an extraordinary persistence. We continue to repeat shibboleths for years, then suddenly wake up to the realisation that what we are saying has long ceased to make sense. ... Ideas block progress more effectively than steel doors."[42] As the credibility of old beliefs have been stretched to their limit, yet nonetheless retained as intrinsic to the cause, Socialists have been falling away from the movement, or losing the tough conviction which made for earlier success. Meanwhile, the ditching of doctrine by the pragmatic modernists is no answer to the need for up-dating Socialism. It amounts to an expediency which is a flight from thought.

5   For an understanding of the dire predicament of today's Labour party, we must turn away from an introverted contemplation of Socialist thought, and instead consider the structural and social changes in the community at large. The greatest bar to the wider appeal and success of Socialism today arises from the call to the class struggle. Whilst on the one hand it may be difficult to imagine a non-class based Socialism, on the other hand, the call to class struggle is so antipathetic to the feelings of the majority, that it is self-defeating. From another perspective it has to be said that any movement of the left must appeal to all those desiring change out of discontent for any reason. In the words of Charles Carter, "it is ... possible that a country might be becoming richer, but the level of satisfaction of the majority of its citizens might be falling - both because

---

[42] Gordon Rattray Taylor, *Rethink: A Paraprimitive Solution,* Secker & Warburg, 1972, p. 227.

11-7

they see a few people becoming very wealthy, and because (though not actually poorer) they feel cheated of reasonable expectations."[43] This, however, is unlikely to be the contemporary situation. Vast numbers of people are now experiencing the erosion of their assets through no fault of their own.

Hence the Labour party has a purpose to fulfil, more ethical or justified, than the alleviation of envy. The most widespread problems effecting Britain today are those of unemployment and the associated evils of private and corporate bankruptcy, housing repossessions, and the slow impoverishment of many millions. These evils accelerated over an 18-year period during which a long-continuing Tory government oversaw the de-industrialisation of our country leading inevitably to the worst unemployment crisis since the 1930s.

It is true that this period was interspersed by a crazy lending phase, during which money chasing money was mistakenly interpreted as "business expansion," but during all these years, the ruin of the economy accelerated, and the government responsible nonetheless won four consecutive elections. This does not speak well for the appeal of the Labour party. It underlines the fact that a disillusioned electorate chose to vote into power the lesser of two undesirable alternatives.

6   The reason for Labour's failure in the recent past was due partly to the wrong emphasis given to these major ills. This in turn is part due to the latter being of a kind that are masked from public view. Unemployment, slow impoverishment, and even bankruptcy and repossession, as they touch the unaffected majority, have become invisible evils in contemporary Britain. The net curtains remain in place irrespective of the circumstances within. There are no demonstrations and no hunger marches - not a whisper of protest from that great majority who feel the heavy hand of economic oppression.

When the breaking point is reached then suicide is commonly resorted to. There is no other escape, except the breakdown of family life and the loss of mental stability. These are not merely the unseen but also the unspoken socio-economic evils of our time. And since they effect the entire spectrum of society (below the very highest levels) in almost equal proportion - the new self-styled middle class no less than the traditional poor - they take on a classless dimension.

7   It is not suggested that the Labour party underplays these issues out of choice, but rather that it overplays those of the impoverished disparate minorities, since the latter better illustrate the class-based interests of the party. Although the Labour party

---

[43] Charles Carter, *Wealth*, New Thinker's Library, C.A.Watts, 1968, p. 17.

11-8

today may refrain from proclaiming overtly the class war, its ideology remains entrenched firmly in the old divisions of class. Because of the egg-shaped structure of today's society (and other factors cited below) the class-based attitudes of Socialism are self-defeating to its cause and good intentions.

Whilst not doubting the worthiness of all those minority interests promoted by the Labour party, the level of their projection in advancing Labour is counter-productive. This is because the party is perceived by the electorate as both narrowing its constituency and its sphere of social interests. When, therefore, Labour confronts the wider electorate, its appeal is met by a cold or embarrassed response - if not contemptuous disregard.

This is not because the electorate is inherently unfeeling or inhuman, but because in a political context, it chooses not to empathise with a call it feels is untypical of the problems of society at large. As the average citizen may neither be homeless, nor a single parent, nor disabled, nor racially discriminated against, he resents the call to identify with such minorities, repudiating the assumption that his needs may be boxed into the same category of wants. The average citizen has other aspirations, and although he may be charitably disposed, he feels his democratic choice and obligations to the community must be based on a degree of self-interest, without its necessarily going so far as to endorse the "invisible hand" of Adam Smith.

More significantly, the Labour party's minority-interests approach conveys a subliminal message having little to do with the targeted minorities themselves. More powerfully, it appeals to resentment, negative feelings, and the need for dependence on collectivist authority.

The average citizen is also well aware that the electoral exploitation of minorities must have an ulterior motive, since once a government is in power, it cannot take these as the measure for its legislation in the name of the majority. As resentment, negative feelings, collectivist ideals, and class war, arouse fear and ridicule amongst today's individualistic majority, such appeals are met with a blind eye. In a very different situation, e.g. in response to the call of specific charity, other feelings would be evoked. In such a context generosity more often wins the day - indeed, the British have been proven as amongst the most generous of peoples. Hence a clear distinction has to be made between the appeals of charity and those of a political ideology.

8   But the most significant loss to Labour has undoubtedly arisen through the emergence of that new phenomenon, Essex-man. So-called Essex-man (and this is a gender-free description) now found throughout the length and breadth of Britain, is not only included amongst the tens of thousands of new entrepreneurs in our society, but

11-9

also amongst ordinary working people whom the former employ. Essex-man regards him- or herself as either "classless" or "middle class," and perhaps because his recent antecedents formed the backbone of the Socialist movement, he finds himself antipathetic to every aspect of Labour's ideology.

Since he has pulled himself up by his bootstraps, striving against difficult odds, he has no intention of returning to that hated past of want and drab emptiness. As he is embarrassed by the thought of his early environment, preferring not to slight old associates and friends, the best way out is forgetfulness. Hence a break is made with yesteryear as other values are pursued. In the sphere of politics, a new spiritual home was easily found in Thatcherism and the Tory party. It fulfils his rugged individualistic needs, his hedonism, his rebelliousness against authority, and his contempt for the interfering "nanny" state. When Mrs. Thatcher declared that "Society" is a fiction - that only "individuals" exist, this struck a vibrant chord with Essex-man. If this was really true, then there is no such thing as the "working class." This salves the conscience - severing lingering doubts as to any obligations to a past life and the solidarity it might have meant.

9   These, then, are the new Tories - often dogged in their faith and contemptuous of Socialist "do-gooders." These are the people who have contributed to the successful re-election of four consecutive Conservative administrations which have decimated our wealth creating base as no other government in modern British history. Does the Tory party, therefore, serve the best interests of Essex-man ? The answer is a definitive, No! And here lies the internal contradiction.

The Toryism of Essex-man, as indeed with most of its supporters, stems from subjective feelings having little in common with the objective socio-economic reality. Although party political life is everywhere seen as an activity of propagandistic deceit, of empty promises and delusion, in contemporary Britain, with the slide of the economy, it has increasingly become a question of Appearances predominating over Reality. Horrible inflictions have been endured by Essex-man (as indeed by other population sectors) with regard to slow impoverishment, unemployment, and especially repossession.[44]

His debts have not only been oppressive but horrendous, and rising daily. He has seen no way out of his predicament except for a false trust in the optimism of political leaders. He has been urged on daily by the demanding drum-beat of "renewed confidence," and the patient vigil for "green shoots." There can be no return to the

---

[44] This was written in January 1994.

11-10

proletarian-like attitudes or loyalties of a distant past as we have noted in Chapter 7. It is simply a psychological impossibility. The boats were long ago burnt. History cannot be put into reverse gear - even though hypothetically it might offer a way out. The media has done its task and Socialism is portrayed as a parody of what it really is. To Essex-man the Labour party is a disparate collection of untamed interests of the under-privileged at the bottom of society. From a feeling of disdain, he cannot and will not associate with a calling so far removed from his own experience of life.

10   In the face of impending disaster, note must be taken of the psychology of those occupying the middle-middle ground comprising the majority of the population. A heavy millstone is the price for conformist individualism. The demands of privacy, self-help and decorum, means that aggressive solidarity is not an option. The middle class individual stands alone, taking full responsibility for his success or failure. When the going gets tough, a stiff upper lip is maintained, and a silent introversion is preferred to calling on the help of others. This self-imposed isolation is motivated by fear, confusion, the need to think through a situation, and most of all, by a feeling of shame at realising the impotence to overcome an awful predicament.

The stubborn individualistic pride of the cornered middle class seeks escape in the darker recesses of life. Either this leads to mental paralysis and the idle Micawberism of "waiting for something to turn up," or else a slide into petty (or greater) fraud and sophisticated crime of one kind or another. Somehow the system must be bucked, and a sharp wit used to cut through the bonds of legality. But at any cost, a low profile must be kept. Nothing is more shameful than publicity ! It is interesting to observe that the thousands of bankrupts, and those who are repossessed, merely sink into a mire of oblivion as if they had never existed. It is as if they had vanished physically from the earth.

It is even more interesting to observe that those many thousands of entrepreneurs who have surrendered their enterprises and livelihoods into the hands of receivers, have simply been swallowed up into a black hole of nothingness. There has been no protest against abuses, no call for a public debate, no organisation for reversing decline, and no attempt to float radical ideas for a new prosperity. None of these challenges of economic decline have acted as a stimulus to overcome adversity, but on the contrary have only further undermined any hope for the future. The socio-economic weakening of the middle-middle majority has only led to its confusion, mental paralysis, and a greater sense of shame.

The reason for this hopeless situation is that its real or substantive interests are as yet unrepresented - but it fails even to acknowledge that fact. It somehow assumes,

12-1

in its naive fatalistic way, that either one party or another must be understood to promote its cause. Thought goes no further. It must be the role of New Socialism to fulfil the needs of this unrepresented middle-middle majority.

CHAPTER 12
The Dilemma of Class Struggle

> "Doctrine ... has lagged behind reality. ... in spite of prolonged searching, no one has discovered a new set of guiding principles to take the place of old ones. The governments of the industrial world are adrift, unable to steer with the instruments they used in the past, but uncertain what instruments to use instead."

> David Marquand, *The Unprincipled Society*, J. Cape, 1988, p. 2.

1 - Class-based politics is unappealing   2 - Although Britain is a class-based society   3 - Defining social egalitarianism 4 - Marxism's inescapable influence 5 - Determinism a substitute for constructive theory 6 - Class war is now failing Socialism 7 - But in the past it fortified working class protest 8 - Naive psychology of the idealised proletariat 9 - Socialism's repudiation of the business process 10 - Earlier Socialists and their business sense 11 - Invalidity of profit theories 12 - Deficiencies of materialism 13 - Traditional Socialism has outlived its usefulness

1   We have looked at the changing structures of British society and found that the outcome is not conducive to promoting the traditional concept of class struggle as an instrument for change. Furthermore, we have looked at the psychological changes in society and found that a class-based politics is counter-productive, as the major socio-economic ills of our time cut across the entire spectrum of the community - excepting only for the wealthiest top minority.

There is every indication that if the Labour party (or Socialism) continues as a class-based movement, as it has always been in the past, it will doom itself to silent annihilation. If, furthermore, it chooses to project itself as the party of class war (or is merely perceived as such) then the certainty of its annihilation becomes all the greater.

What is the way out of this conundrum, if Socialism is to have any meaning or success for the future? We must turn to the philosophy of Socialism in examining its basic tenets as to their relevance and application for tomorrow. There cannot be a total break with tradition. If Socialism is re-defined without reference to its past then it can no longer properly claim to be called what it was before. Words cannot arbitrarily be made to change their meaning. If, however, respect is given to the connecting link of an evolutionary thread, and this is demonstrated with sufficient evidence, then

12-3

Socialism may retain its integrity to itself whilst appearing in a different guise.

If it can no longer exploit convincingly the divisions of class struggle, or project its cause as that of an oppressed majority, then in view of its intellectual credo, Socialism faces a huge practical problem in its appeal to the electorate. If Socialism is to be made appealing to the majority then it must have intellectual integrity. If its doctrines fail to convince its adherents as to their truth, or if it is apparent it is devoid of doctrine, there is little chance of Socialism being sold to the electorate at large.

2   There is something more to be said about the changed structure of society and the psychological changes following in its wake. Although the egg-shaped society has turned the class war as an instrument for the achievement of Socialism into an impossibility, and although the concept for the revolution of an underclass is a quite impractical aspiration, this is not to infer that we live today in a classless society.

Britain is still the most class-ridden society in the industrialised world, and although the criteria of class distinctions are in a constant state of flux, our country remains divided into finely layered levels of snobbery and petty privilege. Class distinctions are an evil since they everywhere give rise to resentment and unease, laying emphasis on false values with adverse economic consequences. Although British class divisions remain a good subject for the humour of the satirist, they can no longer be utilised in the field of political struggle - or only with the greatest circumspection.

The Labour party activist who dares to seize on class distinctions in thrusting forward his message, risks offending sensibilities which may rebound to damage the cause. As we have already indicated, and will further demonstrate below, the future supporters of the Labour party must be won in great numbers from the middle and upper layers of society. Whilst class divisions can no longer be utilised in the struggle for greater egalitarianism and social justice, they nonetheless originate from economic conditions unique to our country, and these we must consider below, since they are central to the topic of this book.

3   Whilst the pyramidal form of society is an affront to humanity and the ideals of democracy, the same cannot be said of its egg-shaped structure. As a general theory the latter would seem to have erased all sharp social gradations, whilst also offering a nice balance of upward and downward mobility, and the opportunity for all to achieve their reasonable aspirations. This is not to infer that a perfect structural ideal has been reached with the achievement of the egg-shaped society, for unacceptable differences still exist between rich and poor. A perfectly structured community might take on the form of a globe, in the understanding that the practical organisation of society cannot be based on an ant-like egalitarianism.

12-5

.   The human or animal condition will always form into a graded structure of authority. The springs of ambition and individualism contradict the demands of a levelling egalitarianism. Hence the need for egalitarianism must be met by the equation of freedom. The concept of an ant-like egalitarianism need no longer be taken as a serious proposition for the formation of society. The intellectual justification for such a concept was finally demolished by George Orwell more than 40 years ago; whilst the practical justification was surely obliterated with the collapse of the Soviet Union and its Communist satellites at the end of the 1980s.

4   In view of the above introductory remarks on the changed structure of our society and the unacceptability of traditional Socialist attitudes, the following principles must be considered from the traditional Socialist viewpoint *vis-à-vis* the thesis of this book:- 1. The class war; 2. The ownership of the means of production and distribution; and, 3. The dictatorship of the proletariat, or the ultimate source of power in the Socialist society. These entail, of course, the discussion of Marxist concepts, which are not irrelevant as some might allege. Although the methods of Marxism were excluded from the Labour party almost from the day of its inception, exactly 100 years ago, dialectical and historical materialism together with the other socio-economic principles of Marx and Engels, have exerted such a pervasive influence throughout the entire Socialist movement - in addition to influencing sociological thought in academic circles - that they cannot be ignored in this book on the future of the Labour party.

Even those most moderate Labour party activists claiming to loathe the tone and principles of Marxism, cannot for more than ten minutes elaborate on the aims and philosophy of Socialism without referring   (albeit unknowingly) to some tenet developed by either Marx or Engels. Marxism is as intrinsic to traditional Socialist thought as madder is to the colour red, for the one cannot be washed out without the other. Even though leading Socialists may recognise the invalidity or part collapse of many Marxist principles, the underlying influence of Marxist thought nonetheless retains its power. Although Marx claimed to establish Socialism on scientific principles (a claim long discredited by modern criticism) he did succeed in formulating doctrines that were scientific-like. No other Socialist thinker can claim to have established such a compelling system, and if for not other reason than this, his thought retains its pervasive attraction to the present time.

5   Every political philosophy divides into two parts: critical and constructive. The first is concerned with the analysis of causes giving rise to problems, whilst the second is concerned with their solution. The strength of Marxism lay in its criticism of 19th century capitalism, but it fails entirely as an instrument for criticism of Rentier

12-6

capitalism in the late 20th and 21st centuries. Furthermore, it failed in its constructive philosophy from the time of its inception.

Socialism is the greatest political protest movement of all time, but it has failed in finally resolving the great social issues in society in formulating a constructive philosophy. Such political thinkers as Plato or Sir Thomas More actually formulated constructive philosophies by describing in detail the kinds of societies they wished to see created. Karl Marx, on the other hand, was not to fall for such naivety. His approach was more ingenious. He devised a system for predicting the future, claiming this to be based on "scientific" principles. Having established the determinism of dialectical and historical-materialism (derived from an up-ending of Hegelian philosophy) it was unnecessary to attempt any practical description of the society to emerge eventually.

The great virtue of Marxism to the Socialist movement was that it presented a coherent body of doctrine claiming to embody the ultimate truth and the way ahead. It achieved this (as it only could) through the formulation of a cosmology, entailing the evolution of humanity through the struggle of classes, pointing finally to the end of history through the victory of the proletariat and the disappearance of the state. As an exercise in the attempt to define the source of social justice, and the way ahead, it amounted to an intellectual masterwork of genius. Its all-encompassing subject matter raised it to the imperative level of a religious creed. It is no wonder, therefore, that many millions in the previous century seized on Marxism as a religious cause, whilst its influence meanwhile extended far beyond those who would admit to Marxist sympathies.

6   Although Marx and Engels set out to formulate a "scientific" or objective body of knowledge, it soon transpired that this was based on questionable foundations. Whilst dialectical-materialism was cleverly designed to answer any intellectual objection, or explain any socio-economic political situation, it was the call to the class war that was to prove the Achilles heel of the Socialist movement. The historical determinism predicting the inevitable overthrow of the bourgeoisie and the final victory of the proletariat, together with all its intellectual trappings, was not sufficient to keep the Marxist corpus of knowledge, or the actions of its adherents, on the rails of objectivity. From the start there were cracks in the "perfect" system, and the frequent quarrels and "revisionist" groups, were merely a prelude to the day when the Marxist train would come crashing off the rails and lie in ruin.

The failure of Marxism and traditional Socialism as a constructive philosophy may be brought under five headings:- 1. Its subjectivity in conceiving society and its

12-7

needs from the exclusive perspective of the oppressed; 2. Its naive psychology with regard to human motivation and the foundation of happiness; 3. Its exclusion from the sphere of human activity consideration of the psychological mechanism of the business process, essential to the organisation of any exchange society; 4. The falsity of its economic principles; and, 5. Its epistemology. Each of these aspects may be considered in turn.

7   1) *Its Subjectivity*   The greatest contribution of Marxism as a practical philosophy stemmed from its effectiveness in arousing the consciousness of an oppressed working class to its miserable condition. This entailed designing a protest movement on the most efficient principles. It necessitated the idealisation of the proletariat as heroes in strengthening its sense of destiny and purpose. As society was seen as a pyramid, the eventual victory of the working class was to be achieved through its numbers and solidarity.

Although it presented an ideal medium for protest for better wages and conditions, Marxism was never received by the British proletariat in an undiluted form. In the 19th (and indeed in the 20th) century it was always mixed with the varied traditions of the older Combinations and the influence of the Free churches. Nevertheless, in an age of ruthless competition with its depressed wages, its unstable financial arrangements, and its alternately employed and unemployed impoverished proletariat, there seemed both moral justification for pursuing the class war and for upholding the prediction of capitalism's final collapse.

But the real victories of the proletariat through their own efforts, were industrial rather than political, and these were achieved in an unpredictable piecemeal fashion. Industrial action, usually through the strike weapon, brought improvements in conditions and wages. The working class were still too far away from the levers of real political power. This exacerbated their introversion, finding expression in greater enmity towards the bourgeoisie in stepping up the class war. The great irony of the 19th century is that it was a paternal High Tory party in parliamentary opposition to the ruthless Whig interests of trade, which was responsible for achieving many of the great social reforms throughout much of that period. This was an irritant to those who preferred to fight for their own cause rather than be indebted to the patronage of the class enemy.

Consequently, the millennial ideals of the class struggle became the substitute for actual legislative power. Early in the 20th century it was the Liberal administration of 1906-1911, which first introduced the great social reforms of state insurance against sickness and unemployment, the institution of trade boards for the fixation of wages in

12-8

sweated trades, and old-age pensions, etc. The young Labour party had meanwhile been set up in 1900 as a federation of trades unions, trade councils and local Labour electoral bodies, to serve in central and local government. The Marxist Social Democrats joined but immediately left the federation, and it was the trades unions which became and remained the dominating influence of the movement. Hence in an already class divided society, it was the vested interests of very specific sectors of the community which were promoted. It was seemingly to take the negative form of the Labour movement versus those of "industry." As the parliamentary battle lines polarised increasingly with the advance of the 20th century, the Labour party became ever more subjective in character.

8   2) *Its naive psychology* The lifework of Marx and Engels was almost solely concerned with the critique of the capitalist system as they found it. It would seem as if Marx's distance from the practical world of business, and his lifetime of desk research, engendered a fear of actually describing the kind of society he hoped ultimately to achieve. Marx was the antithesis of the practical man of the world, for having established his intellectual credentials through distorting the established conclusions of German philosophy, his life was devoted to producing an opus of many volumes of variations on a theme.

The repetitions of the critique of capitalism is woven out like the golden rope of the Norns to several million words, often relying on outdated or questionable data. That is not to suggest that the writings of the young Marx are identical with those of the mature man. There is a greater acceptance for the social writings of the younger man (on such themes as the corruption of the personality by possessions) amongst contemporary Marxists, than there is for the economic conclusions as elaborated in the three volumes of *Das Kapital*.

Marx saw the answer to problems solely through altering the power bases of the community, and this revealed his naive psychology. He sought the accession to power of an idealised proletariat. Indeed, both Engels and Marx, saw the working class as somehow possessing inherent virtues, placing them morally above the rest of the community. In this way they let slip the warning of David Hume, that the logic of an "as is" situation should not be transposed unknowingly into an "ought." That is, those who are oppressed by evil, and deserving better, are not made virtuous simply because the opposite is responsible for their misfortune. The intellectual argument used to justify the possibility of the virtuous society was that the socialisation of the means of production and distribution, together with the disappearance of competition and strife, would ensure the annihilation of evil.

12-9

In these contexts, the fathers of Socialism had little realistic appreciation of the human psyche, and the dependence of freedom, work, and happiness, on a fine degree of struggle. Their view of the ideal to be reached was theological and passive rather than psychological and active. Marx was a prophet in the biblical sense: he saw the proletariat as the righteous inheritors of the earth, much as the people of Israel saw themselves as the Chosen people of God. In the words of Paul Johnson, "Marx, with his highly detailed and imaginative presentation of the eschatology of capitalism, can be described as the last of the Judaeo-Christian prophets, or the first of the secular ones."[45]

The final outcome of the dialectical process was to be achieved through the imaginary situation of fairy-tale proportions: viz., the "withering away" of the state, law, money and the concept of economic value, since they would have lost their functions, following the accession to power of the proletariat. This was to mark the end of oppression in all its forms. Marx came no nearer than this in describing the practicalities of a fully-fledged Socialist society. This was utopianism carried to an extreme degree promoted by the man who frequently scoffed at the very concept.

9   3) *Its exclusion of the business process*   The greatest deficiency of Marxism, and all subsequent forms of mainstream Socialism, is the failure to incorporate within its philosophy the need for the business process as an instrument for Social Wealth Creation. Social Wealth Creation is defined as the economic activity fulfilling the needs and desires of the population through maximising distribution via the natural mechanism of the market.

The psychology of the business process is one of the most important elements in any consumer-choice society, without which the needs and desires of the majority could not be satisfied. The reason for Socialism's failure to integrate this process within its philosophy, is that it perceived business as exploitative and undesirable. The workers were perceived as being at the sharp end of bourgeois exploitation, for it was the latter who owned the means of production and distribution.

As Socialism was only concerned with the question of the re-distribution of existing wealth from the vantage point of the enviously deprived, it had little further interest in business as something to be pursued for a better purpose. The business culture was morally beyond the pale as far as Socialism was concerned. Hence it was either to be ignored or forgotten. There was no rationale to explain business activity within the Socialist (or any other) society, except as some kind of underhand, black

---

[45] Paul Johnson, *Enemies of Society*, Weidenfeld & Nicolson, 1977, p. 88

12-10

market, and highly undesirable swindling of the public interest.

Consequently, Socialism's answer to the question of fairer distribution was sought by means that were *external* to the business process. This entailed the implementation of artificial methods in the attempt to satisfy material needs. This either meant forcing the market into a straight-jacket, or abandoning the market altogether. Inevitably this led to consumer dissatisfaction as there lacked effective means for measuring consumer demand, and so the market was alternately cursed with shortages and excesses, indifferent products and services. This anti-business ethos was eventually to prove the undoing of Socialism worldwide as a practical long-term system for stable satisfactory government. Its external approach to the business process either entailed broadly theoretical or nebulous aims, such as the transfer ownership from the bourgeoisie into the hands of the proletariat (in practice into public bodies), or else, heavy-handed interventionism with little appreciation of the subtleties of the market.

10   The psychological mechanism of the business process and the necessary symbiotic relationship between producer and consumer were never properly understood in the 19th century. It was only from the start of the 20th century that serious study was given to the business process, clearly demonstrating that it constituted a vital element in free and modern societies. Such sociological research began in Germany and France, with the work of Max Weber and Emile Durkheim, and then in America (under the leadership of such outstanding thinkers as Thorstein Veblen), before reaching elsewhere in the industrialised world. Today a huge literature exists on the mechanism of the business process and its relationship to wealth creation. If it is surprising that none of this knowledge has been incorporated and made central to the doctrines of mainstream political parties in the industrialised world, this is only because the latter are still caught in the time warp of 19th century ideological thought, i.e. the age-old conflict between the Socialist left and the capitalist right.

If we look back to the pre-Marxian age of the early 19th century, we can indeed trace Socialist thinkers who were genuinely interested in the practicalities of the business process. Most notable amongst these were St. Simon and Robert Owen. Whilst the French Socialist and practical businessman, St. Simon, desired an industrial state directed by men of science in which universal association should suppress war, and society would be organised for productive labour by those most capable; Robert Owen actually established a near-perfect economic community for its time around the mills at New Lanark, incorporating educational and leisure facilities, together with a co-operative for the easy purchase of necessary consumables. Whilst St. Simon was a prolific writer on all manner of schemes in the world of work and industry; Owen

12-11

embarked on numerous practical experiments for the establishment of ideal communities in both Britain and America.

They flourished a generation before Marx embarked on his life's work for the Socialist cause, but both died disillusioned and unhappy men. The tragedy of both lay in the limitations of their intellectual vision, for whilst their practical efforts and courage deserve applause, St. Simon was a muddled thinker, whilst Owen had limited understanding of the social sciences, possessing a narrow speculative outlook. If, however, either or both of these men, with their understanding and appreciation of the business process, had been endowed with the broader education of a John Austin or a J.S. Mill, there is no knowing how this may have influenced the future direction of Socialist thought.

The emergence of Marxism was never a predetermined fact of history. It was only an imaginative intellectual product of human ingenuity, and no more a product of science than a clever sophist's work of logic. Socialism as we know it today is nothing more than an accident of history, dependent on the timely sequences of a thousand interlocking incidents, none of which need ever have occurred. No ideas are more than human invention, but their wide acceptance often gives them a greater credibility than deserved. This reminds us of Paul Roubiczek's contention that, "it does not matter ... how ideas arise, whether they are causes or effects; once they have come into being, they become realities which influence man's actions. ... To discuss ideas is to discuss realities."[46]

11   4) *The falsity of its economics*   It is supremely ironic that the most questionable economic principles of Marx were derived from the abstruse ideas of a speculator and Rentier capitalist, who was a prominent member of the London Stock Exchange and a parliamentary adviser to Sir Robert Peel, viz., David Ricardo. The Marxist theory of profit (as with that of the classical economists) is drawn from the theory that the value of a commodity depends on the amount of labour time necessary for its production. Profit conceived as the "exploitation of labour." is elaborated in depth in the third volume of *Das Kapital*. The blackness in which Marx painted the concept of profit, in both this work and elsewhere, has so struck the imagination that it still pervades the consciousness of all those on the left of centre up until the present time.

Profit is still imprinted on the minds of Socialists (howsoever mild in temperament) as the pervading evil of the business process. It is perceived as the great corrupter, stimulating greed, dishonesty and exploitation, wherever business may be

---

[46] Paul Roubiczek, *The Misinterpretation of Man*, Routledge & Kegan Paul, 1949, p. 5.

12-12

found to flourish. It is seen as the quality depriving business of the sympathy it might otherwise enjoy. These attitudes have done more to undermine the credibility of Socialism than any other aspect of its philosophy. Their inanity may be comprehended when it is appreciated that no business transaction, based on a neutral medium of exchange, can possibly be undertaken on a level playing field. Every transaction is either a profit or a loss, and no business can be maintained without the watchful eye of an accountant, balancing up one column of figures against another.

It should also be noted that the theory of profit as elaborated in the third volume of *Das Kapital* deviates from the logical consequences of the labour theory of value on which Marx based his earlier propositions, and this in turn, is yet another argument added to the body of proofs which has led modern theory to refute the explanation of value from labour time. If, however, the labour theory of value, and its derivative, the surplus value theory, are eliminated from the Marxist system, then this undermines completely the propositions demonstrating the inevitable collapse of capitalism as an objective economic necessity.

We shall see below that quite new economic principles need to be formulated and successfully propagated in meeting the unique conditions of Rentier capitalism at the close of the 20th century. In refuting the economic principles of Marx, we are not thereby promoting those of any possible adversary - and least of all those of the economist Ricardo.[47]

12   5) *Its epistemology* The epistemology of Marxism, i.e. its crude materialism and the reduction of events to economic causation, can no longer stand the rigours of contemporary criticism. Although no serious political movement, laying its cause on objective social values, can place its core philosophy on anything other than a set of clear economic principles, human motivation cannot wholly be explained in economic terms. The Marxist interpretation of events, through historical-materialism, has often led it into false and absurd interpretations of recent historical events. Many Marxist academics have simplified and distorted objective reality, in both East and West, by indulging themselves in long-winded and ingenious intellectual exercises giving a particular slant to history.

The reason for Marxism's faulty epistemology, arising from its materialism, is firstly because modern physics has overturned the old Newtonion science on which 19th

---

[47] The anti-industrial ethos of British business is summarised in the Rentier capitalistic argument of Ricardo that, "the more capital risks and undertakes, the less its relative income, the greater the income of the landowning class, which does nothing for the growth of civilisation." (M. Beer, *History if British Socialism*, Allen & Unwin, 1948 ed., Vol. I, p. 153.)

12-13

century mechanistic materialism was based;[48] and secondly, because of the complexity of psychological motives (e.g. powerlust, religious ardour, artistic or creative drives) cannot always be linked to the exploitation of materialistic or economic phenomenon. Modern psychology has demonstrated the greater complexity of human motives, often defying Marxist rationality.

For example, materialism cannot explain why a few offshore islands without mineral resources, whose people emerged from medieval feudalism just 120 years ago, should now comprise the mightiest industrial nation on earth. But it goes a long way to explaining the power of the spirit and the will to self-improvement. Likewise, it cannot explain why the two strongest nations in the immediate post-War period, with all the economic benefits of victory to dictate the political future, are now at the bottom of the league table in almost every sphere of economic activity. These things have little to do with the forces of materialism.

Furthermore, as Marios Camhis has observed, "materialism ... does not provide any safeguard against abuses, false or reactionary theories, and justifications for the domination of man by man."[49] The epistemology of New Socialism will therefore need to be based on a deeper understanding of the human psyche. The above concludes our five areas of criticism of Marxism and traditional Socialism as a constructive philosophy for the future. They are no more than a summary of arguments elaborated in depth in a thousand volumes on the topic.[50]

13   All this suggests that Marxist philosophy has outlived its usefulness, but our indebtedness should not be forgotten for its wider influence. The permanent value of Marx as a thinker, is not to be seen in the formulation of dialectical-materialism *per se*, but in introducing the dialectical approach in the understanding of history and society - a methodology not merely traceable to Hegel, but to Heraclitus and the Greeks. This is because, in the words of a member of the Old Guard, "dialectics sharpens our vision

---

[48] It should be noted that Lenin argued towards the end of his book, *Materialism & Empirico-Criticism*, that there was no basis for the view that materialism is rendered untenable by new discoveries in physics - especially with regard to the electrical theory of matter. His assertion that the new physics can lead to the discovery of new characteristics of matter and not to its disappearance, nevertheless leaves Marx's theory of materialism severely dented.

[49] Marios Camhis, *Planning Theory & Philosophy*, Tavistock Publications, 1979, p. 149.

[50] Amongst the best critical appreciations of Marxism and traditional Socialism may be found in Ludwig von Mises, *Socialism, An Economic & Sociological Analysis*, J. Cape 1951 ed., and H.B. Acton's, *The Illusion of The Epoch, Marxism-Leninism As A Philosophical Creed*, Cohen & West, 1955.

12-13

when focused on the study of facts and the laws of reality. ... It purges the mind of dogma, prejudice, preconceived nations and false 'eternal truths,' which entrammel thought and retard scientific development" or at least, it should do.[51]

Marx was a seminal thinker in the sphere of politics, on a comparable level with Darwin, Freud or Einstein, in their different disciplines. A huge gulf separates political thinking and the perception of the world in the pre- and post-Marxian eras, extending far beyond the realm of Socialist doctrines.

The greatness of Marx must be seen in his all-encompassing breadth in bringing universal experience within the realm of political understanding. His interpretation of human motives and the doctrine of false consciousness, were bold and courageous attempts to raise political thought to a higher level of objectivity. His approach was sociological in an age when sociology was still in its infancy. His deficiency, in retrospect, arises from the fact that he lived in an age before the development of modern psychology, and when Herbert Marcuse supplied a Freudian dimension to the corpus of Marxist philosophy 100 years later, it was already too late, for it failed to breathe life into an ideology which had been overtaken by the forward march of unanticipated change.

Although today we may detect the pitfalls of Marxist philosophy, and certainly reject its claim to scientific status, at the time of its formulation, it undoubtedly presented an honest attempt at creating an objective and definitive political philosophy for the future. Because of this, those who adhered to the movement could do so with conviction and integrity to their inner selves. They could commit their lives to the moral and intellectual truth of a cause with the intensity of religious belief. Today that is no longer possible. Today's Marxists and traditional Socialists are either myopic (i.e. insufficiently informed as to the objective nature of existence), or dishonest from a variety of motives - usually because they occupy a post or status to which they are indebted because of known beliefs.

The majority of contemporary Socialists, and may we add tentatively, activists within the Labour party,? are silent agnostics, with a pragmatic day-to-day approach to political issues. Is it any wonder then that lately the Labour party experienced a malaise and apathy it never knew before ?

An interregnum is now being experience by the labour movement. If the Labour party is to recover its conviction then a new philosophy must be formulated. Such a philosophy must be linked to the objective needs of our time, meeting the critical

---

[51] O. Kuusinen (ed), *Fundamentals of Marxism-Leninism*, Lawrence & Wishart, 1961, p. 106.

13-1

intelligence of social scientists and the goodwill of the majority.

CHAPTER 13
Social And Unsocial Wealth Creation

"Capital now moves across borders in such quantities and at such speed that the ability of national governments to formulate economic policy is seriously circumscribed."

Jeffry A. Frieden, *Banking On The World*, Hutchinson Radius, 1987, p. 162.

1 - The essence of Socialism   2 - Failure of public ownership   3 - So capitalism must be socialised   4 - Looking at successful and failing economies   5 - The two capitalistic systems   6 - Productive capitalism makes for Social Wealth Creation   7 - Whilst Rentier capitalism enriches the few   8 - When "growth" means de-industrialisation   9 - Pro- and anti-national economic systems

1   After the above critique of Marxism, traditional Socialists may well ask, What is left of Socialism to be fought for in the future ? Then again, we have suggested that if Marxism is repudiated, as many mainstream parties in the industrialised West have done over the past thirty years, then Socialism is liable to become anything or nothing. Others may argue that this discussion of Marxism in this book is irrelevant, since it is already "dead and buried," but as we have demonstrated, it is such a pervasive influence throughout the spectrum of the Socialist movement, that to ignore its doctrines would be to confine this thesis to the superficial level.

Having reviewed the bases of traditional Socialism, we shall begin this chapter by looking at the practicalities of Socialist government. This topic, and the question of people power, which is integral to practical Socialism, will lead us into our central thesis, viz., the need for socialising productive capitalism. The main body of the chapter will then describe the two systems of capitalism as we find them in the world today. But by way of introduction, we shall broaden and clarify our terms for the definition of the New Socialism for the new millennium.

As we argued earlier, the definition of Socialism cannot be made to rest on the vague generalities of the No-man's land of the mixed economy. And neither can it be left in the facile broader generalities of a benevolent egalitarianism. Socialism must be defined in terms which are contemporary and precise. The core economic (or scientific-like) principles of the New Socialism, enduing it with its own distinctive dialectic, will be elaborated in Chapters 14 and 15. Here we shall offer the five

13-2

definitive conditions necessary for the achievement of real Socialism:-

    1. Promotion of the interests of the majority, but only when these include consideration of minorities and the underclass, so that they may realistically benefit from equality of opportunity.

    2. A society ensuring the full development of abilities and aspirations, in seeking the best interests of both the individual and the community.

    3. Ultimate authority which is interventionist and impartial, i.e. independent of economic or other vested interests.

    4. Democratic government maximising the dissemination of economic and political power through the representation of functional groups.

    5. An ethos whereby freedom is perceived and experienced through egalitarian ideals, and the achievement of a classless but heterogeneous society.[52]

2   By way of leading into the discussion of how the socialisation of productive capitalism may be made central to Socialism, it may be useful to touch on the limitations of Socialism in the past to sustain successful long-lasting systems for the means of production and distribution. Socialism was always successful in the past as a convincing ideology, but invariably, sooner or later, it stumbled at the gates of practicality in the sphere of government in advancing its declared purpose.

There are seemingly few options as to how the people may own and control the means of production and distribution. Nationalisation, for example, was no less a failure in theory than in practice, for it entailed dictatorship by a smug, middle class, Oxbridge educated ivory-tower elite, over the better interests of the rest of the community. As Louis Heren so nicely expressed it, "top civil servants misconceived their role in society. They came into the service with what Balliol men used to refer as the unconscious realisation of effortless superiority, although they were almost entirely lacking in experience. ... They sought to govern the country according to their own narrow interests, education and background, none of which fitted them to govern a modern technological, industrial, pluralist and urbanised society."[53] Not only did nationalised industries fail in terms of gross inefficiency and cost accounting, but also in terms of good employee relationships. There was no attempt to involve workers in the management and development of their employing concerns. The industries were

---

[52] These five conditions will be elaborated in depth in Chapters 34-44.

[53] Louis Heren, *Alas For England*, Hamish Hamilton, 1981, p. 40.

13-3

. loathed by customers and workers in equal measure.

In criticising past Labour governments, or those of Socialist parties elsewhere in the world, we are not thereby suggesting that opposing parties existing at the time necessarily produced - or would have produced - better administrations. We are merely saying that Socialist governments failed to live up to their own expectations or those of their electorates. There is a difference in the perception of success between reforming and Conservative administrations: for whilst the first entail high expectations for the new and unknown; the latter can rest on maintaining the status quo since the electorate are more tolerant of their deficiencies. Hence in view of the natural conservatism of populations everywhere, governments of the left have a more difficult role in sustaining credibility and support.

As for the "dictatorship of the proletariat" in terms of managing the economies of Eastern Europe and elsewhere, the same criticism may be made as that of nationalisation. The only difference is that in the former Communist bloc countries, public or state ownership existed on a larger scale, and consequently, shortages, inefficiencies and corruption, were more widespread within the exchange or business system than in the West. In practical terms it entailed dictatorship by a privileged, Communist party bureaucratic elite.

3   As we have indicated, up until the present time, the approach of Socialism towards production and distribution has tended towards the artificial. This has been dictated by the theory of production for use as opposed to production for profit, which hitherto has always been upheld as the essential distinction between the Socialist and capitalist systems. Consequently, consumers have been seen as passive recipients of a market forced into a Procrustean mould.

The three dimensions of the psychological equation necessary for Social Wealth Creation are thereby ignored: 1. The psychology of the business process or entrepreneurship; 2. The nurturing of consumer desires; and, 3. The two-way symbiotic relationship between producers and end-users. There is of course a justified growing distaste for consumerism and waste-making trivia, and this is something that can never be entirely overcome in a free market economy, but the intolerable alternative would entail an end to free choice. If the free market has undesirable characteristics, this can only best be corrected by cultivating higher standards of desire.

How, then, can the Labour party resolve the problem of the free market without sacrificing Socialist integrity ? It must develop an approach towards production and distribution in harmony with natural forces. That is, Socialism must be made to work from within the business process, but only so that capitalism is not deflected from

13-4

serving the social needs of the community. This should not be achieved through compromise with the capitalist system - no meeting of minds with the mishmash of the mixed economy - but on the contrary, through socialising productive capitalism. A seed must be planted within the capitalist economy, so that by a spontaneous process, the different constituents contributing towards productivity are united in co-operating for a common purpose.

Let us look at the present structure of society and the present state of industrial relations. We have demonstrated clearly that there is no will for the class war, nor for any politics based even on the differentiation of class. In the sphere of industrial relations there is little desire for action likely to further endanger the remnants of British-based productivity, or exacerbate unemployment. Trade union attitudes today are light years away from what they were twenty years ago. Trade union leaders and shop stewards are everywhere concerned with the regeneration of industry, and if necessary, are prepared to think through the problems of their own bosses in finding answers to the mounting crisis. Note especially the work of the AEEU on both the national and local levels over the past ten years. A revolution is necessary - but of quite another sort from that envisaged in the past.

As Barrie Sherman has argued so well, "Unions are going to have to think the unthinkable and then act on their deliberations rather than offer excuses for why changes cannot be made or find a compromise which will give them the worst of all possible worlds. Unions must show that whilst their prime responsibilities must be to their members they must have some responsibilities to society as a whole too."[54]

4   Early in this book we inferred that our methodology would be confined to empirical criteria. Let us look at our toughest industrial competitors, and enquire if there are pointers for our future. Is there anything to be learnt from those who have succeeded whilst we have failed ? At least comparisons might give pause for thought. Our toughest competitors are defined as the Western countries of the European mainland, and the five Tigers of Far and South East Asia.

Why is it that these countries have consistently produced such successful productive economies over the past 40-year period ? Why is it that they have a far higher percentage of independent and small scale firms? Why is it that their governments are more supportive of home-based industry ? Why is it that their peoples now enjoy living standards higher than our own ? Why is it that their quality

---

[54] Barrie Sherman, *The State of The Unions*, John Wiley & Sons, 1986, p. xiii.

13-5

of further education for the majority is considerably higher than our own ? Why is it that their societies are significantly more egalitarian ?   Why is it that they have a smaller average range between highest and lowest earnings ?   Why is it that their societies are so free from inherited privilege and rank ?   Why is it that countries formerly authoritarian are now more democratic than Britain, in terms of societal structure, modes of government, and access to information ? Why is it that some of these countries enjoy pension arrangements infinitely better than ours, and sickness insurance benefits that are marginally better ?   Why is it that Britain has been hauled before the European Court, and had more judgements laid against her in human rights cases, than any of her other partners ?   Why is it that Britain was the lone EU member to resist signing the Social Charter ?   There were at one time only two parliamentary parties throughout the entire EU opposed to the Social Chapter: John Major's Conservative party and Le Pen's National Front.

These questions have often been asked before, and a medley of meaningless answers have been produced at different times, ranging from the "bloody mindedness of the British worker" to the "decadence of the nation."

5   There is one answer to explain all the above situations to which all our troubles may be attributed. Our competitors benefit from a different financial-industrial system. Whilst they enjoy the outcome of Productive Economies, the peoples of Britain   and America ail under a Rentier system of production and distribution.[55]

Two quite separate systems of capitalism exist in the world today: the Productive Capitalism of our toughest industrial competitors; and the Rentier Capitalism of the Anglo-Saxon economies. Although existing side by side in a free trading environment, in the longer term, the Rentier Economies cannot hope to compete in the struggle for greater market share. The peoples of north America are doomed to an absolute decline in living standards, solely because of their system of production and distribution, no less than are the people of Britain.

The two systems of capitalism have emerged as an accident of history in the sense that they were not consciously brought into existence to be what they are today. Therefore, if one system has proved socially, for the majority, to be better than the other, this was not out of design. Because of this, we should be cautious in attaching moral qualities to one in preference to the other, or in lauding particular cultures and peoples in a context that may be misleading. The evolution of progress is unpredictable and surprising. History is an accidental process, and great discoveries for bettering

---

[55] See Appendix A.

13-6

human improvement are often stumbled over like acts of serendipity, to be seized upon and refined and developed, for the benefit of the majority.

6   Let us define these two contrasting systems of capitalism as we find them in the world today. Both have their macro- and micro-economic dimensions. Productive capitalism insists that the primary purpose of an enterprise must be its own long-term success, and this is achieved through maximising market share in a free trading environment. This purpose is dictated by its mode of funding, for Productive capitalism is predominantly deficit-financed. This means that a partnership is entered into between an industrial credit bank and the particular enterprise, and because of the huge amounts of loan capital invested in many transactions, the risk factor has to be minimised almost to the elimination point.

Therefore the bank must not only acquire an in-depth knowledge of the borrowing business, but control the scope of its activities on a month-by-month basis. Since the enterprise is kept on a tight rein, it is prevented from unauthorised diversification, wheeling and dealing, or other extraneous activities. In exchange for this it is granted as much capital as required in fulfilling its strictly defined function as a modern, highly efficient and competitive enterprise in the world market.

Financial management is rational, and ultimately controlled by bank executives. As Ronald Dore, Britain's most eminent authority on industrial Japan, has so clearly demonstrated, "Japanese firms are *not* primarily defined as the shareholders' property. The directors are usually senior employees who have spent their lives in the firm, not outsiders appointed to care for the shareholders' interests. The resisted takeover is unknown in Japan, so is the conglomerate that trades in companies as if they were bits of real estate and not the livelihoods of a living community of people."[56] That is the micro-economic dimension.

In a country where deficit funding is an almost universal mode for financing industry, from the small factory employing a mere five hands to the major corporations, the state is obliged to play a highly interventionist role. If it failed to do this, then enterprises might face disaster, or the national debt run out of control. The prime function of government in all these countries is therefore to ensure the success of home-based industry. This is achieved through integrated industrial planning associations; · overseas commercial posts for guaranteeing export success; ad hoc subsidies in

---

[56] Prof. Ronald Dore, "The Confucian Remedy For Industrial Success," *Government & Opposition*, Vol. 20, No. 2, Spring 1985, pp. 213-214. See also, his illuminating book, *British Factory - Japanese Factory: The Origins of National Diversity In Industrial Relations*, Univ. Of California Press, 1973.

13-7

overcoming difficult competitive situations; the manipulation of standards institutions for the prevention of undesired imports, as well as a variety of other invisible import barriers; the financing of research and development; the establishment of first rate educational institutes from nursery school to university levels; and the right kind of low-cost long-term funding institutions for industry.

The outcome of Productive capitalism is easily predictable. As home markets must be secure before embarking on export projects, the maximisation of market share means that products and services reach down to enrich the lives of all sectors of the population. As business is diversified, with a large small-scale and independent sector, there is a greater spread of national wealth. To ensure a sound consumer economy, wages must be raised to absorb home-based production, and this in turn contributes to better living standards.

The modernisation of industry, in reducing unit costs and meeting competition, means that high standards of education have to be maintained in finding sufficient personnel to man the complex information and robotic technologies. Meanwhile, modernisation, far from creating unemployment and the spirit of Ludditism, leads to greater employment prospects. The five Tigers of Japan, Korea, Taiwan, Hong Kong and Singapore, have for long experienced the lowest unemployment rates in the world. Because Productive capitalism drives towards the egalitarianism of wealth, it contributes to what we describe as Social Wealth Creation.

7   Let us turn to Rentier Capitalism. Its philosophy is based on laissez-faire (or letting things be), and the primary purpose of the enterprise is the enrichment of its shareholders - openly propagated in America but promoted more covertly in Britain. A great emphasis is laid on the fact that the enterprise belongs solely to shareholders and directors, and there is a jealous possessiveness giving rise to a divide between management and shop-floor. The funding of the enterprise is unstable, if not fickle. It stems from the re-investment of internal resources, short-term bank loans, or the workings of the equity market and stock exchange. Financial management is directed by accountants who are usually confined to utilising the internal resources of the company. Consequently, in the face of pressures for modernisation, repairs are preferred to replacement.

The world of business is divided into three interest sectors: Financial, Production and Labour, and according to organisation and the division of profits, they may either work together as a unity, or be formed into any combination of alliances. In Britain, the Financial and Production sectors are united under the misleading heading of "Industrial" - misleading since it wrongly implies that finance is necessarily the friend

13-7

of industry. That is the political situation as we find it today, but history could have been different. As Bertrand Russell interestingly observed in the 1930s, "if wage-earners had not had votes, British politics since the war would have consisted of a bitter struggle between financiers and industrialists. As things were, however, financiers and industrialists combined against wage-earners, and industrialists supported the financiers, and the country was brought to the verge of ruin."[57] Our purpose is to redress this imbalance.

As manufacturing industry is fast changing and capital intensive, impossible demands have been placed on British industry over the past forty years. Serious funding on viable terms has simply been unavailable from any financial source. Consequently, manufacturers have long been forced into pursuing the short-term. As the payment of shareholders is the first priority, cuts are made in all directions. In the face of mass-market competition, British producers yielded to the self-deception of concentrating on the "superior" restricted market sector. As the British consumer decided that the "superior" product was over-priced and not as claimed, one industry after another went to the wall. Manufacturers then began to diversify in desperate efforts to maintain their solvency, but as the resulting products were poorly researched and unattractive, these too met with failure.

It was soon discovered that if money could not be made out of products, then money could be made out of money. Hence in the 1960s, enter the Speculators. The activities of Slater-Walker, and their progenitors until the present day, entailed the buying and selling of enterprises like cards in a poker pack. Few ailing independent manufacturers resisted the temptation to a sell-out, and the quiet life of a rentier existence it bought. Ever more corporate industrialists accumulated tens, scores, even hundreds of separate enterprises, working them for their shorter term profits, playing them against each other, asset-stripping some to finance others, and acquiring yet more for the purpose of putting them into liquidation, for the capital that could be raised through the sale of land and buildings.

As D.W. Noble has said, in summarising the ideas of the great American socio-economic thinker, Thorstein Veblen, "The factories ... were technically owned by the finance capitalists, and these men lived in an unreal, irrational, artificial world. Their values were still the predatory ones of the feudal past expressed as a desire for profits and not production. Their economic world was the world of paper money and abstract credit which had no functional relationship to the concrete fate of productive wealth.

---

[57] Bertrand Russell, *In Praise of Idleness*, Allen & Unwin, 1935, p. 77.

13-8

And they made their profits by sabotaging the productive economy to create fluctuations in this artificial money market which worked to their personal gain."[58] The capitalisation of enterprises in the Rentier economy is irrational, as firstly, businesses are not managed according to their best productive purpose; and secondly, well-run enterprises may be liquidated simply to accrue corporate profits in meeting end of year balance sheets for the reward of shareholders. That is the micro-economic dimension.

Rentier capitalism places its trust in the "invisible hand." This is a kind of divine influence supposedly ensuring that free market forces everywhere and invariably benefit all sectors of the community. It should be noted, in fairness, that the author of that concept formulated his ideas before the full development of the industrial revolution. The approach of government is therefore non-interventionist. Business is regarded as a private matter with which government should have little to do. The consequences of this attitude in the face of home-based de-industrialisation have been catastrophic to the British economy.

Rentier capitalism entails the accumulation of wealth into ever fewer hands and the slow impoverishment of the majority. For many years the City of London has acted as a magnet, sucking financial wealth into the narrow confines of the square mile, but its reinvestment for the community has been abysmal relative to its wealth creation, even though most of us have a stake in its activities through pension and life plans, etc. Its ubiquitous power has made it untouchable by government. The ultimate strength of the City in controlling the national economy is exerted through the direct influence of the Treasury. This is the government department to which all others yield, and no British premier of either party, has ever shown the will to prevail over its final word.

8 But the worst aspect of the City has arisen from its international interests. The great international financial and trading conglomerates exert a power in Britain that would hardly be tolerated by our Productive capitalistic competitors. Whilst the Productive economies are hemmed in by a range of rules and regulations in protecting national interests, in Britain international trading interests are afforded almost every conceivable freedom - something proudly acknowledged by the former Tory government. These great corporations are unanswerable to national authority or any other democratic voice. They are only concerned with their own expansion and self-interests as an end in themselves.

We must glance at these corporations noting the extent of their damage to the

---

[58] David W. Noble (contributor), *Thorstein Veblen*, ed. Carlton C. Qualey, Columbia UP, NY, 1968, p. 91.

13-8

British economy. It makes little difference as to the source of their ownership or "flag of convenience." As they operate on the world stage, owe no national loyalties, and are only concerned with pure money profits for the reward of shareholders, British-based companies are often uprooted to be planted elsewhere anywhere on the globe.

Although this means unemployment in Britain, and the loss of skills and industries, it has rarely been the cause of protest; in contrast to comparable episodes in mainland Europe immediately leading to government intervention. The greatest criticism of these corporations in Britain up until the present time, has arisen from their establishment of low-labour cost assembly only operations, so turning Britain into the "Indonesia of Europe" - the latter intended in the pejorative sense of "slave wage" conditions. It should be noted, however, that whilst the Indonesian labour force is upwardly mobile in terms of skills, wages and living standards, the British are downwardly mobile in all three in world relative terms.

Most ironic and dissembling have been the proud boasts of our own industrialists in proclaiming the advance and expansion of "British industry." These have usually been made to counter the gloom of political critics or other prognosticators of the economy, but the real meaning of these empty boasts is seldom understood. What they too often entail is the establishment of manufacturing plants by British conglomerates in foreign parts, employing foreign labour and skills, or worse still, that British-based factories have been moved abroad. All this explains the fact, long known to most of us, as to why the success of the City is only remotely connected with that of the *real* economy. Rentier capitalism is solely concerned with promoting the interests of the *phony* economy.

If we look at the internal infrastructure of our Rentier capitalistic system, it will be hard to find a voice prepared to speak up for the Productive economy, and out of the many hundreds of industrial associations, not one supports the cause of home-based industry. The reasons for this are interesting - even if astounding to the novice of our financial-industrial system. The majority of firms, both large and small, now belong to groups, and these groups in turn sometimes belong collectively to larger conglomerates. Influence proceeds downwards from the corporate offices to the dozens, scores or hundreds of subsidiaries, as to the profit targets to be met and expenditure limits.

The chief executives of subsidiary manufacturing plants - be they Chairmen, MDs, or merely factory managers (the title is irrelevant) - are stretched to their limits in facing impossible demands. But they dare not protest, and dare not speak the truth, for fear of losing their employed contracts. The world of business is pervaded with conformism and abject cowardice. The system must never be questioned ! Hence

13-9

these chief executives anyway eventually lose their posts. They sink with their ships, with a stiff upper lip, still saluting their leader responsible for their ruin.

With regard to the corporate leaders - our top British industrialists - the story is different, and since they are successful strivers in a failing system, they are blind to its faults. Their bland reply to the reproach of failing British industry, is invariably that, "We live in a tough world and lame ducks must be left to their fate. As industry exists in a global village, money will flow where the profits run fastest. Investors' profits alone must remain the criterion for decision-making." These are the reasons why British-based industry stands unsupported and alone in a friendless world. If top industrialists are in the vanguard of de-industrialising Britain, then where is the hope for our future ?

9   Let us now compare the two capitalistic systems. The Productive economy spreads wealth and raises living standards since it is based on maximising market share. The Rentier economy concentrates wealth in fewer hands since it is based on pure money creation and maximising shareholders' profits. It supports the mistaken notion that money is wealth, or what A.N. Whitehead cited as the "fallacy of misplaced concreteness."[59] Its worst aspect is that productivity, especially manufacturing, is investment-starved. We now live in a world where in the longer term the peoples of the Rentier economies will be doomed to a slow impoverishment through the inevitable victory of the Productive capitalist system.

A major reason for this is that Productive capitalism lays emphasis on the need to safeguard economic autonomy. Indeed, if the state is to use taxpayers' money in interventionism in ensuring the success of home-based industry, there would be little sense if it allowed a situation to arise whereby foreign business gained the upper hand. Rentier capitalism, on the other hand, is neutral with regard to questions of free trade. Consequently, foreign business may be allowed to dominate increasingly the British industrial scene, without it ever arousing concern from either government or the City. The outcome of this myopic ideology is predictable.

The terms of trade between the contrasting systems are not so much unfair, since each is based on its own self-chosen ideological grounds, but certainly unequal. The British manufacturing enterprise, even when blessed with all advantages, is doomed to eventual extinction as soon as it meets its match in the Productive economy. And this

---

[59] A.N. Whitehead, *Process & Reality, An Essay In Cosmology.* He says the fallacy of misplaced concreteness results from, "neglecting the degree of abstraction involved when an actual entity is considered merely so far as it exemplifies certain categories of thought." Free Press ed., NY, 1978, p. 7. See also pp. 20, 93 & 94.

14-1
is not because personnel, methods, or equipment may be wanting, but purely because the method of capitalisation allows no other alternative.

When the once mightiest free trade laissez-faire nation on earth is forced into blatant protectionism, in saving jobs and industries, this is not merely a contradiction of its own ideology, but a pitiful irony in its effort for survival.

CHAPTER 14
Protest For Prosperity

"The view of business as a game with special ethical standards is especially worrisome to people without much business experience."

Albert Z. Carr, *Business As A Game*, J.M. Dent, 1971, p. xv.

1 - The necessity of profit   2 - Undesirable Rentier profitability   3 - Desirable Productive profitability   4 - Assessing the validity of profit   5 - The goal of Socialist profit   6 - Ownership is nothing without control   7 - Employees must fight for ownership   8 - But primarily to save our industrial base   9 - Industrial solidarity for prosperity   10 - Promoting ability

1   The reason for the origins of the separate capitalistic systems is only explicable through the different circumstances through which their industries were first developed. Whilst Rentier capitalism developed as a spontaneous process out of societies with a strong moneyed middle class; Productive capitalism was forced through by the state in societies that either had not completely thrown off their feudal past, or lacked a class possessing sufficient liquid capital. The future outcome (or strange twists) that either system might take, could never have been anticipated from the beginning.

It might seem that Rentier capitalism contradicts all the social ideals and aspirations cherished by the democracies from which they originated. If we trace the evolution of Rentier capitalism from its beginnings until the present day, noted the gradual erosion of productive activity, we may describe it as the cancer of productivity. A crisis stage is reached in the history of capitalist production, when money begins to create money for its own sake, and thenceforward, this spreads like a parasitic growth, influencing every business decision, eventually infecting every aspect of the economy.

None of the above points the way to a New Socialism, other than to the general observation that Productive capitalism contributes to more egalitarian and democratic societies than the working of the Rentier economy.

Now we must look more closely at these contrasting systems in reaching the core argument of our thesis. What is the central mechanism responsible for all the

14-2

differences they bring ? It is to be found in the different criteria for profit. As we have argued earlier, Profit is essential for all business activity. There can be no such thing in the organisation of a modern society as barter or simple exchange without the intervening medium of money. As the value of goods and services fluctuate constantly according to changes in demand and other circumstances, Profit is bound to occur in the exchange process. Furthermore, borrowing and lending is at all times a necessity, and long-term loans cannot be realistically effected without the imposition of interest. Again, this entails Profit. There is nothing perverse with profits derived from interest providing that ultimately, within the framework of the community, they contribute to a good social purpose.

2   Profit becomes harmful only when the economy is diseased. It is then that usury grows apace; racketeering flourishes; shortages or excesses hit the market; work is scarce; and the operation of the free market in socially desirable goods and services begins to break down. In these circumstances, when capital cannot be utilised for its proper purpose, it accumulates into fewer hands and is used for purposes whereby it multiplies itself to excess.

This is through excessive interest or prices, or investment in passive assets like land and property for a higher return at a future date, or in other inflationary activities, or in modes of exchange unaccompanied by socially desirable productivity, or in criminal activities. In such Rentier economies, the highest profits are often derived from protection or extortion rackets, prostitution, drugs, tobacco and alcohol. Invariably in such societies, there is a polarisation between rich and poor, accompanied by oppression, want and misery. This is a description of an extreme form of Rentier Profitability as may be found in a Third world economy.

In the advanced industrialised world, in Britain and America, Rentier Profitability takes on a less dramatic form. The greater real social evils may flourish nonetheless amongst a growing underclass, but Rentier Profitability is marked throughout the larger body of society, by the decline of industry and business, in terms of quality and efficiency. Although prices are raised and quality reduced relative to the competition, in maintaining profits, failure and bankruptcy nonetheless continues to take its toll.

Eventually, in the face of this, academic schools of thought emerge arguing that manufacturing is inessential to "advanced" economies. This is taken as a welcome relief by hard-pressed governments, and so a greater emphasis is laid on the need for extending the financial and service industries. Rentier profitability is maximised in sophisticated forms through the inflated growth of insurance, life policies, equity plans,

14-4

and the aggressive sale of stocks and shares, and the proliferation of banks and building societies in dominating high streets throughout the land.

3   Productive profitability, as indicated by the term, links profit directly with the productive purpose of a business or enterprise, irrespective of whether goods or services are involved. It thrives within a given set of circumstances, ideally within the matrix of the Productive capitalist system. As it is dependent on a number of variables within the business enterprise, none of which can necessarily be measured against each other, it does not lend itself to the concise definition of a mathematical law. It is evident on the micro-economic level through examining the different mechanisms of the individual firm; and on the macro-economic level, through the policies of the state in conjunction with its financial institutions and industrial planning associations.

Productive profitability is most clearly demonstrated by analysing comparable enterprises from each of the economic systems, for then the differences are shown in most glaring contrast. Whilst in the one, circumstances contribute to the end of marketable production; in the other, they contribute to proprietors' reward. A Productive concern is a disinterested body existing as an en in itself. A Rentier concern is a subjective vested interest body existing for the ends of the different sectors of which it is composed.

The value of a Productive concern is that it contributes to the greater benefit of the community. Its value to itself arises from its greater rationality. The unselfish loyalty it inspires in those committed to its success leads to more equal reward in proportion to the in-put given. This means that justice, in terms of conditions and earnings, for all those committed to its activity, is the inevitable outcome of the enterprise which has reached a perfect equilibrium in terms of its Productive profitability. The pursuit of longer term interests are better for all, than the pursuit of shorter term interests which benefit one sector at the cost of another, but seldom the higher interests of the enterprise.

4   Let us now consider some of the practical implications entailed in assessing the Productive or Rentier profitability of an enterprise. The embezzling clerk is clearly engaged in Rentier activity, no less than the director who doubles his salary, or the spendthrift who daily dines his clients on champagne and caviar. These are blatant Rentier acts, contrary to the public good. Their eventual outcome leads to higher prices. Arthur Daley of the TV comedy series, *Minder*, for example, represents a typical small-time Rentier capitalist. As a type he would be less seldom met with in northern Continental Europe with its rational business structures, although he would not be unknown in Austria, the East bloc and southern Europe. Such persons are a

14-5

· nuisance for they create profits from questionable projects whilst producing little. They are too often parasites surviving off the Productive economy.

Profitability is best assessed by analysing the circumstances of the individual firm, for it is there where Rentier characteristics are manifested by type. The accounts and costs of a company should be subjected to scrutiny. As noted above, few British companies can progress along the line of ideal productivity, since they are caught within the framework of the Rentier capitalistic system, by short accounting periods, unfavourable taxation, unrealistic funding sources, poor government support, etc. Nevertheless, it remains a useful exercise in planning for an ideal future to assess the Rentier or Productive characteristics of British business.

All sources of wastage should be looked into, in addition to cost and profit margins, directors salaries and perks, shareholders' dividends, expense accounts, the utilisation of idle assets, the allocation of skills, time and motion factors, modernising equipment, etc. Then the company has to be examined with regard to its external relationships: What is its place in the market; ? What is its market share;? Are its products the best in the world market;? If not, why not,? etc. Constant research and discussion must be undertaken until definitive answers are found to all these questions.

5   In identifying the function of Productive profitability, we have found the key for transforming capitalism and the free market into a more effective mechanism for serving the interests of the wider community. It now only requires the use of that key in creating the New Socialism. The foundations would then be laid for a perfect union between freedom and social justice, resulting in the greater happiness of the community in total - not merely that of its greatest number. It has to be reiterated that the Rentier and Productive capitalist systems emerged involuntarily rather than through intention, and hence neither system, as found in practice, is truly pure.

As all societies and all systems are in a state of flux, the Rentier and Productive economies have characteristics borrowed from the other. The world recession has witnessed strange events. Economic pressures bring economic diseases in their wake. Whilst the Scandinavian countries and mainland Europe have lowered their defences against the scourge of the international corporations over the past few years; Japan has in a small way been corrupted by the greed of her new financial services sector. A country that built her infrastructure in the post-War period entirely through deficit funding, now sees her industries threatened by the vagaries of the stock exchange, whilst meanwhile, several millions of her private citizens have recently been swindled out of their investments and life savings. Rentier motivated greed brought about these losses.

14-6

With the benefit of consciousness and understanding, Productive capitalism awaits refinement into a perfect mechanism for the community. Socialism must complete this task, taking over capitalism for its own, lauding Productive profitability as its goal. This may sound a strange purpose to the traditional Socialist. Does this mean some odd pact with the enemy ? Is this the start of a new era when the lamb lies down with the lion - some mishmash compromise of opposites ? No ! It marks the start of a revolution in thinking. And the sign of greater battles that lie ahead between the de-industrialising Rentiers versus the Productive majority and those on the scrapheap of unemployment. The New Socialism may take the philosophy of St. Simon as a Socialist source for its inspiration.

6   The strands of our argument must be pulled together. We have shown how the old class-based politics is counter-productive and unacceptable to today's majority. We have shown how the rationale of traditional Socialism fails to explain the unanticipated problems thrown up by modern forms of Rentier capitalism; and we have outlined the practical failures of Socialist solutions, and the malaise to which this has given rise on a worldwide scale.

If Socialism is to retain its meaning or underlying purpose, it cannot rest its case on the neutral ground of the mixed economy. Such a mishmash compromise with the opposition may be accepted as an interim arrangement within the framework for democratic struggle, but it goes nowhere in advancing the cause of Socialism. We have argued at the start of these chapters that Socialism must retain its original meaning, "that the community as a whole should own and control the means of production, distribution and exchange." We have insisted that society must be free and democratic in the meaning that these words are understood in the West.

If all these conditions are met, a heavy responsibility is laid on the shoulders of the individual, but that is the price of freedom and fulfilling human aspirations. There will be little opportunity to laze in the dream of a cornucopia as advocated by several contemporary prominent utopian Socialists. The ownership of the means of production and distribution by the community, does not mean surrendering it into the hands of the state or nationalised bodies. That has been tried and failed. It leads only to dictatorship. Ownership without control has no more reality than any other fiction of unworkable representation.

We have identified Productive profitability as the key to a form of capitalism working for the benefit of the majority through a natural process, i.e. competition and free market forces. We have demonstrated how the psychological mechanism of the business process is essential in maintaining a society fulfilling consumer needs and

14-8

desires. But we have acknowledged that such a form of capitalism is unworkable without state intervention, particularly with regard to credit investment banks; integrated industrial planning associations; and the safeguarding of homed-based industry.

7   The structure of today's society, and its sociology and attitudes differ from what they were forty years ago. Circumstances in the world of work now demand a range of skills undreamed of in an earlier era. The demand on brainpower, skills, and creativity in the arts and sciences, has not only led to a greater division of labour, but to a breakdown of the old collective and proletarian values. New patterns of education and new interests have led inevitably to greater individualism. Following this are demands for greater openness in the spheres of government and the management of business. Knowledge is power and the majority know this. People are no longer prepared to accept the word of their doctor, or teacher, or lawyer as gospel. They want to find out for themselves - control their own fate. All this is a natural development towards democratising society.

It is also an inevitable first step towards the acquisition of the means of production and distribution by the population at large. Such steps are already far advanced amongst our toughest industrial competitors. In France and the Basque region of Spain (the Mondragon projects) there are many well-established productively profitable co-operatives in both manufacturing and service industries. The success of these is due to the business acumen and commitment of their shop-floor proprietors. This is practical Socialism led from the front by the drive towards wealth creation. But here we are not concerned primarily with co-operatives or other peripheral forms of business activity. We are here concerned with the transformation of the ordinary business, irrespective of whether it be a small independent manufacturer or a major plant employing thousands of workers.

Again there are precedents for embarking on their takeover by ordinary working people. We are not referring here merely to such enterprises as the John Lewis Partnership or the Scott Bader Company, but to the Co-determination (*Mitbestimmung*) and employee share-ownership schemes as found in many thousands of companies in mainland Europe, or the *Kaizen* of Japan, with its striving for perfection, for the benefit of all. If Britain is to achieve such successes a huge struggle must be faced. The vested interests of the Rentier capitalistic institutions of the City will fight tooth and nail against extending rights to working people. The threats to the City are too frightening to endure. The Rentiers have much to lose !

8   And here we reach the rationale as to why it is imperative for ordinary

14-9

employees to take over the means of production and distribution. It is not because of any inherent right, or because it is timely to do so, but because if the opportunity is missed, then productive industry and Social Wealth Creation will collapse in Britain. We have shown how through an extraordinary juxtaposition of circumstances, and the international dimension of contemporary business, that our own top industrialists are in the forefront of de-industrialisation. Who, then, can save our country and the livelihoods of our people ? Certainly not the politicians - not by their own efforts. Hence the majority must unite in the struggle for Productive capitalism. This puts the Socialist cause on quite another level.

It raises Socialism from the subjective level of class and the pursuit of vested interests, to that of the objective needs of the total community. In the words of R.H. Tawney, "industry should be subordinated to the community in such a way as to render the best service technically possible, that those who render that service faithfully should be honourably paid, and that those who render no service should not be paid at all."[60] There is little difficulty in ensuring such a struggle appeals to the wider electorate, but it is quite another proposition in assuming it appeals to traditional Labour supporters. New attitudes would need to be formed and new feelings cultivated. Older styles of resentment and stock stereotypes need to give way to an enlightened sense of confidence and belief in verities with a longer lasting value. There is no more room for the Fred Kites of this world. The acquisition of once hidden knowledge, formerly the preserve of an oppressing class, will endow New Socialists with feelings of equality with those they are forced to confront. One time wild beasts will seem as mere paper tigers.

A greater objectivity and the search for absolutes will sweep away the need for petty argument or the need to justify the cause. The intellectual and moral weapons in the ensuing struggle will assure victory almost before the battle has begun. All will give way before the advance of the Socialist cause. It will amount to a conflict between those who promote Social Wealth Creation and the needs of the community, as against those who would destroy it. The enemy would be left huffing and puffing in confusion, scratching around desperately for good reasons - lost for words to support their narrow and discredited vested interests.

9   In facing such a struggle it is vital that the trades unions and the Labour party pool their common resources. The trades unions, too, must undergo great changes, and already they are on the path to progress. Their attitude to major economic issues is

---

[60] R.H. Tawney, *The Acquisitive Society*, G. Bell, 1921, p. 7.

14-9

more objective than fifteen years ago. The unions would have much to benefit in transforming the nature of industrial conflict, not only in terms of enlarging their memberships, but also in winning popularity amongst the wider community. Let us look at the opportunities to be gained by our major unions in promoting the ends of Productive capitalism.

As the concern of the trades union leader will be full employment and prosperity, his first purpose must be the promotion of Productive profitability. Whilst still overseeing wages and conditions and the protection of established rights, these would be put into the shade by the ongoing activity of monitoring Productive profitability. Whilst negotiating for co-determination (or fully utilising these rights once won), and fighting for employee share ownership, the trades union leader would organise Profitability Inspection Committees. Trades union membership would be extended to include middle and senior management and on-site plant directors. As the ideals of the re-formulated union would be in accord with the highest objective ends of the company, directors would hardly be in a position to refrain from membership. Shop stewards would cultivate the friendship of the Chief Executive, and if the company belonged to a group, then the former would search out areas of conflict within the corporate office. The ultimate aim of the union would be to work for the independence of the enterprise from its controlling corporation. The most secure, efficient and competitive firms are those that stand alone, for only they can be best committed to their productive purpose.

If the directors or senior management of a company refused to join the union, giving it their support, then reasons should be identified. If the reason was that executives are in league by choice with the rentier capitalistic machinations of a corporate office, then a potential foe has been identified within the plant. If, on the contrary, executives have been threatened or frightened by the corporate office, then the union must adopt a sympathetic approach. It is then an occasion for the development of a clandestine relationship, so the better interests of the company may be developed.

If the corporate office, or in the event of an independent firm, its plant directors, adopt a reactionary obstreperous approach to the good intentions and excellent work of the union, then a serious confrontation may result. Employees may then be justified in nurturing suspicion. Secrecy always has an ulterior motive, and as rentier capitalistic tendencies should be fought, irrespective of whether they are actual or suspected, the union should organise its counter-measures. These should be low-profile - discreet and intelligent. Union activists should cultivate the confidence of managerial staff, in and out of working hours, in the canteen, pubs, and other leisure centres. Political attitudes

14-10

should be placed on file, and the propaganda of Productive capitalism promoted actively. Measures should be sought to expel from the company personnel or management uncompromisingly opposed to the doctrine of Productivity.

10   A major purpose of the trades unions in the future (and the re-structuring of industry and the new sociology of the workplace increasingly fits them for this task) must be the promotion of ability, or what the French Revolutionaries once described as *La carrière ouverte aux talents*, throughout all sectors of the enterprise. This is in view of the perverse ways in which many managers find themselves in positions of authority in tens of thousands of British companies. No companies in mainland Europe or the Far East operate selection procedures as subjective and absurd as those found in our own country. The appalling standards of British managers is still accountable to inherited privilege, nepotism, old boy networks, and the exclusive membership of questionable associations. It is still common in British manufacturing firms for subordinate management to hold total monopoly in all matters relating to business acumen, engineering experience, financial knowledge, and foreign language abilities. For the sake of national prosperity and greater employment creation, trades unionists must hunt down the incompetent (even when including top executives) and fight for their expulsion.

There will be occasions when unions are forced into high profile activity. This occurs when a company is threatened by a takeover, bankruptcy, or its voluntary or involuntary liquidation. Such circumstances usually arise through Rentier influences, and hence the union may find itself in conflict with the company. An appeal has to be made for public support. This is a time for industrial action, but not for the use of the strike weapon. There are two reasons for repudiating the idea of the strike: firstly, it alienates public sympathy; and secondly, it is anyway ineffective, tending to express the cringing resentment of the broken cause.

In situations when the life of the enterprise is threatened, employees should occupy the plant, cover its buildings with placards drawing attention to the crisis, and lock out corporate directors and those threatening the interests of the company. Such Advanced Industrial Action (AIA), which is dealt with in detail in Chapters 24 to 33, should preferably be carried out in co-operation with senior executives, and if possible, with the connivance of plant directors in keeping such action within the limits of the law. The media and other assisting agencies, should be invited into the plant, and day and night seminars held on the need for Productive profitability. The main task of the union, during the unspecified period of its occupation, must be to search for new buyers or other ways of saving the company.

14-10

As such an occupation must transcend the petty aims of vested interests, its primary purpose should be to arouse public sympathy and demonstrations of support. The ultimate moral argument and political justification for AIA must always be that the soundness of the Productive economy is a factor far transcending the narrow interests of nominal proprietors or their representatives. Health, welfare, education, pensions, defence, and other tax-dependent needs, cannot finally be made reliant on the caprice and incompetence of money-making de-industrialising rentiers misleadingly known as "top industrialists." Therefore, trades unionists engaging in Advanced Industrial Action must do so in the name of the community and the state.

The above indicates the ideological and practical role that trades unionists must adopt in transferring the ownership of industry from a purely rentier-motivated shareholder elite, to that of employee-ownership promoting the long-term productive success of the enterprise. It is justified in the words of Henry George when he wrote, "as to what is the just distribution of wealth there can be no dispute. It is that which gives wealth to him who makes it, and secures wealth to him who saves it."[61]

Such a transference of ownership does not necessarily entail the abolition of an external shareholding body (and certainly not with regard to the larger enterprise) but it does necessitate legal changes with regard to re-defining the powers of ownership. In the company of the future, employee share owners must have preferential control over external investors howsoever great their capital share. There is nothing wrong in a specific enterprise attracting as much external risk capital as it may, providing only that this is not used to threaten the productive integrity of the company.

If trades unionists are to promote this ultimate and greatest end of Socialism in seizing the means of production and distribution for the community, then they must develop parallel skills alongside all departments of management. This should pose little difficulty as, firstly, the complexity of tasks in the advanced enterprise anyway increases the demand on skills throughout all levels of work; and secondly, we are advocating the extension of trades union membership to all sectors of the workforce. It need hardly be added that anyone failing to adhere to the formulated doctrines of Productive capitalism should be ineligible for union membership.

In the better run company a common purpose should unite management and union for the prosperity of all. The company as an end in itself must be the measure of all activity as the criteria for the success of all. In this understanding an indivisible bond will be forged between British enterprise and its workforce.

---

[61] Henry George, *Social Problems*, Kegan Paul, Trench & Co., 1889, pp. 140-141.

15-1

CHAPTER 15

Increasing Labour's Support

"The role of the state in the economy differs everywhere, not only in its impact but in its form. Attitudes to fiscal morality differ. Thus it is almost impossible to speak in the late 20th century as if capitalism has common characteristics the world over."

Hugh Thomas, *An Unfinished History of The World*, Hamish Hamilton, 1979. p. 430.

1 - Tories are locked into promoting Rentier capitalism 2 - Socialists must confront the City 3 - Guiding investors towards British interests 4 - Identifying the enemy 5 - The insidious values of passive capital 6 - Productivity and social satisfaction 7 - The need for intervention 8 - The public utilities 9 - Britain and Europe 10 - Rentier capitalism and the Third world 11 - The task ahead

1   Having covered the industrial aspects of the New Socialism, and shown how new patterns of ownership may emerge as a natural evolutionary process, we must now consider the wider sphere of the community with regard to party political life.

If class struggle is to be eschewed, and the Socialism of the future is to be classless in its appeal, then where is there an enemy to be fought ? One will not have far to look. If the Tory party is examined in the light of everything it has done in the post-War period, and if the myths, promises and delusions of its ideology are separated from the actuality of its deeds, a clear picture emerges of its reality. The Tory party is concerned solely with the promotion of Rentier capitalism. It has no other interests. For eighteen years it has overseen the accelerating de-industrialisation of our country, and if it was still in power, it would continue to do so, since its promoters are the instruments of City financiers accruing profits either from home-based passive assets or unscrupulous (often ruinous) overseas investments.

All their promises of support for home-based industry have been without substance. It may be that there exist Tory politicians with a vague sentiment to promote home-based interests but they are locked firmly into the establishment of our financial-industrial infrastructure as it presently exists. Conservatism means resisting change. When they do embark on change it is never more than a "tactical withdrawal." The Tory party can no more promote the interests of home-based British industry than it can give elephants wings to fly. The short-termism of Rentier capitalism will always insist on the greater profits from the sale of assets of de-instrialisation, than having to endure the "losses" of investment for the longer term.

15-3

2   There is no contradicting the City's rationale, for the logic of its system demands obedience. Investors alone have meaning and in that lies the obligations and honour of the City. The City has its own logic and its own sanity, which in another place becomes illogical and insanity.   Hence there is little leeway for discussion or compromise, so creating a situation of inescapable conflict between Socialism and City interests.

This does not mean that the cause of Productive capitalism is without its friends in City circles. There are prominent bankers and others in the Square Mile who are deeply disturbed by the harmful social consequences of our financial-industrial system. But their opinions are seldom heard, for the City operates a closed and secretive system, holding a tight rein of discipline on its members. Threats soon follow in the wake of those daring to question established custom, for of all the institutions in our country, there are none so haunted by paranoia. The industrial task of Socialists, through the existing unionisation of bank and financial services employees, must be to generate a Young Turk revolution for promoting the Productive economy.

All these are reasons making it a categorical imperative that Socialism should project itself, and actually become, the movement promoting the better interests of business and industry. To succeed in this - in burying prejudice and winning over the electorate - the Labour party must proclaim the virtues of profit from the rooftops.

3   Where, then, is the enemy to be found in the body of society ? It might be suggested that our large investor class, with its fat portfolios, should be targeted as the enemy, since it is in their name that the City justifies the Rentier capitalistic system. But identifying such a sector as the enemy would be wrong. It is unnecessary and undesirable to upset the investing class. They are the pawns in a larger game. When the City cries "Murder!" at the threat of change, it is its own profits, not those of investors, which are closest at heart. The normal investor is an innocent as regards the machinations of financial power. He or she is well-meaning and patriotic at heart, and when he holds stocks and shares in companies alleged to be "British," he truly believes he promotes the export of British made goods, or helps secure the employment of British workers.

If the average investor in Tunbridge Wells or Bath was really to discover how his or her investments were misused, he would throw up his arms in horror. Therefore, to overcome this deceit, Socialists must fight for the re-definition of stocks and shares and general investment portfolios, irrespective of whether they are offered for sale to individuals or intermediaries, such as pension funds or other incorporated bodies. The discrimination must be with regard to home-based business activities on the one hand,

15-4

and foreign-based activities on the other.

Government publicity and tax inducements should weight investment activity in favour of home-based projects. Detailed planning would be necessary in making this a possibility, and as the City would attempt to frustrate every move, every loophole should be covered in ensuring the workability for this new re-definition of investments. The necessity for this reform cannot be questioned. It would protect the interests of investors, no less than those of the country. The well-meaning investing class must be brought into the Socialist fold, for they cannot be expected to see themselves in any other light than that of supporting British interests. It is incumbent on the Labour party to disabuse investors of their deceit by the City.

4   The public enemy may now be identified. It comprises those promoting the Rentier economy, and since they are found throughout all sectors of the community, they do not fall within the traditional Socialist definition of a class. Nevertheless, they are marked by a set of values which puts them at odds with Social Wealth Creation and the economic purpose of the wider community. The ideal of passive capital, and aimless leisure, which follows as a consequence, is particular to Britain if the comparison is confined to our toughest industrial competitors. The psychological damage arising from these attitudes has given rise to many studies over the past three decades.[62]

From the Socialist perspective, it is the anti-democratic ethos of pseudo-aristocratic values which calls for condemnation. They sustain dilettantism, and despise professionalism and those gritty qualities of concentration and effort essential for industrial success. Such attitudes lead inevitably to de-motivation and under-achievement in all spheres of production and distribution, and in academic circles have generated a distinction between *pure* and *applied* studies - something unknown anywhere else in the world.

Consequently, technicians, engineers and inventors (central to the requirements of Productive capitalism) occupy an inferior status in society. Teachers in Britain, meanwhile, especially since the education crisis of the 1980s, are at rock bottom morale, having fallen in status in exchange for a heavier workload in administration. Compare this with the pride and honour accorded teachers throughout Germany and Scandinavia. The manufacturer is so disdained in Britain that as soon as he accumulates sufficient capital, he sells out and becomes a Rentier, ensuring that his

---

[62] See especially Martin J. Wiener's, *English Culture & The Decline of The Industrial Spirit*, Cambridge UP, 1980.

15-5

children go into banking or financial services. Is it any wonder that our productive base has declined ?

5   It is important to outline briefly the origin of this anti-industrial ethos, so the Rentier foe may be more effectively fought. It is traceable to our long unbroken tradition of feudal land ownership (found nowhere else north of the Alps) together with the retained privileges of the hereditary aristocracy. Land ownership patterns in Britain are shocking in their inequity. The land survey carried out in Scotland towards the end of the 70s, revealed that a small group of landlords owned 12 million out of Scotland's total of 19 million acres. A similar survey to have been carried out in England and Wales was revoked by Mrs. Thatcher soon after her accession to power in 1979.

The British are the most landless people in Europe due partly to loopholes in taxation on the great estates. Great land ownership in both urban and rural areas, has not merely created an all-powerful Rentier class, but also depressed Productive profitability through excessive rent. Recent research has demonstrated that through this factor manufacturing has been weakened in its international competitiveness since Victorian times.[63]

The complexity of the class system, with its ensconced rules and customs, is maintained (albeit in a constant state of change) by Britain's long unbroken tradition of established authority and inherited wealth in land and urban property. Whilst over the past century the hereditary nobility have forgone or lost their political power in the Upper House, through a process of astute intermarriage with commerce, they have instead slipped comfortably into financial services, where they now exert a greater power than they ever held in the 19th century or the post-Reformation period. This is a hidden but nonetheless a real power, more significant than the political influence of the Commons, who are made to follow the path laid down by the financial establishment. The power of the ancient families, in conjunction with their minions, the lesser financial elite, is exerted through the Treasury and the Bank of England, as well as through a network of financial and other institutions (e.g. Oxbridge and the Administrative Civil Service) permeating down to effect the interests of us all.

It is the innate culture of this establishment which has long acted as an impermeable barrier to Britain's economic success. The emphasis on Rentier capitalistic activity, and the intellectual attack on manufacturing through the post-

---

[63] See especially Fred Harrison's, *The Power In The Land*, Shepheard-Walwyn, 1983, which makes interesting comparisons between the socio-economic effects of different forms of land taxation in various countries.

15-6

industrial theories of the 60s and 70s, have wrought havoc in their influence on major decision-makers in Whitehall. Only now are civil servants and parliamentary groups beginning to take a U-turn in this respect. It is the hedonism of pseudo-aristocratic values and their irresponsibility which have filtered down to corrupt every sector of society. The significance of this can only be properly understood through a close comparison with the societies of our competitors with their quite different values.

If the ordinary working person in Britain feels discouraged, it is because he sees the undeserving and leisured enjoy a better life. Although he retains a prurient interest in the foibles and life-styles of the petty-Royals and rich, the examples they portray are so beyond his reach, that they cannot and should not be upheld as a promise for his future. The British people deserve a better model on which to base their values than those of passive capital. We do not yet live in a society where the great Corsican assured every private the right to carry a Marshall's baton in his knapsack.

6   If the Labour party and the New Socialism is to create a more egalitarian and socially just society, it must not only create new values, setting out to destroy those which are discredited, but establish conditions whereby great aspirations are made realisable. The Labour party - as the name implies - is the political movement basing its ideals on reward through *Work*. That does not mean that work alone should be the basis for reward in society, for the accrual of interest from invested savings is both justifiable and necessary in building industry, but it does mean that the rewards of work should be in greater proportion to other means of income.

That is the situation we find in all the great Productive economies. If the Swedes, the Germans, the Swiss, or the Japanese, had been unable to fill their pockets in the post-War societies, they would never have been so diligent or successful in raising their quality of life. For these reasons Labour must project itself as the party of industry. If the New Socialism is to inspire, lead and control the society of the future, it must place as much emphasis on the obligations of the individual as on his rights.

The Rentier class comprise those hindering the practical aims of Productive capitalism. They may be listed as bankers, financiers and their employees opposed to desirable changes to our financial-industrial system; lending institutions or firms charging excessive interest; directors of conglomerates working for the shorter term, dependent on profits through asset-stripping, etc.; speculators profiteering through passive investments or inflation; those engaged in undesirable import activity, i.e. of finished goods or primary products that could be home-produced; swindlers in any branch of business; illegal protection agencies, and all criminal activity entailing a financial loss to either individuals or the community.

15-7

The great logic and virtue of Productive capitalism in promoting the happiness and good of the community, is that the more it is advanced, the more it diminishes criminal and undesirable business activity. This may be measured by comparisons of criminality (including non-property offences) between the Productive and Rentier economies. This is illustrated most glaringly by taking the Productive economy of Japan with one of the lowest crime rates, and comparing it with the Rentier economy of America with one of the highest.

Meanwhile, crime in Britain has increased in proportion to the acceleration of Rentier capitalism in the post-War period. The moral is to be found in the fact that the Productive economy is most natural and satisfactory to the human condition. As Voltaire observed long ago in his biting political satire, *Candide*, nothing so contributes to human happiness as productive labour since it gives meaning to life; and as Dostoevsky observed in his story, *A Gentle Creature*, nothing so depraves as employment in Rentier activity, since it too often thrives on the misery of others. These are aspects of economics, psychology and ethics, that must be explored by the Socialism of the future in its revaluation of values.

7   As noted earlier, Productive capitalism cannot be achieved without state intervention, and since in Britain this is dependent on transforming an opposing economic system, the degree of intervention needed is considerable. Employee share-ownership, for example, cannot be made effective and secure until such time as the state exerts a *dirigiste* authority over the private's sector. It would be unreasonable to expect shop-floor workers to invest in their employing enterprises - perhaps using their homes as collateral - until such time as the state had established integrated planning associations and other supporting agencies, in eliminating the possibility of business failure.

In view of the catastrophic decline of British productivity, emergency measures are necessary in regenerating manufacturing. In the words of Prof. Pollard, the most eminent economic historian of 20th century Britain, "it is at least arguable that the duty of government is to look beyond the micro-economic decisions of individual firms and to foresee macro-economic developments. If industry is hamstrung by institutional constraints only the government can be expected to alter the institutional framework."[64] Trade agreements need to be suspended during a period of temporary and selective import controls as specific industries are targeted for reconstruction.

Such import levies would be based on 100% ad valorum upwards, in addition to

---

[64] Sidney Pollard, *Britain's Prime & Britain's Decline*, E.Arnold, 1989, p. 258.

15-9

import deposit schemes on unnecessary imports. The allegation that protectionism would evoke retaliation is an argument no longer valid. It's an old bogey pulled out by the City whenever it fears that incoming investments might be put at risk. The overriding factor is that our balance of payments are so appalling, and our exports so diminished, that retaliation would be difficult to impose. In any case, the policy of selective import controls would be so designed as to eliminate damage to our export efforts. Unless such measures are taken, attempts at full employment policies are futile. Not until we have sufficiently re-built our manufacturing base can we afford to treble pensions (so giving the elderly a decent standard of living in the Autumn of their lives) and increase other welfare benefits.

8   In promoting an internationally competitive productive sector something must be said about the role of public utilities, as gas, electricity, coal, oil, water and telecommunications. The previous government promoted actively a policy of privatisation. There is nothing wrong with the principle of privatisation if it contributes to the public good, and its attraction is to be seen in the break-up of monopolies, the creation of competition, and the greater dissemination of wealth. But the privatisation of the public utilities entail hidden costs which are contrary to the public interest.

The Tory party's policies of privatisation are motivated by the desire to enrich the financial establishment, and secondarily, to marginally award the growing number of petty shareholders. Immense damage has been rendered to the British economy, firstly, through the privatisation of the utilities; and secondly, through the use of their resource as an excessive taxation revenue. If British industry and the private sector is to flourish, then the prices of the utilities should be reduced to levels comparable with our competitors - or less. As government has lost its revenue from declining manufacturing, it has now parasitically latched itself onto the essential utilities on which we are all dependent.

9   No Socialism can be true to itself unless ultimately it has an international dimension in embracing the interests of all humanity, irrespective of race, nationality, creed, or level of technical or cultural development. All peoples must be accorded equality and equal rights in their relationships with each other. In an ideal future there must be no exploitation and no domination, but to achieve this, practical steps must be taken now. This is because the tentacles of supra-national financial and trading organisations, together with the ineffective or undeveloped state of federal authorities, make it evident that if a country is to pursue the best interests of its majority, these can only be achieved through national autonomy. Recent history has demonstrated this fact, and as yet, no other political approach is practicable.

15-10

In an ideal future, international government may achieve the best chosen ends of the separate peoples represented, but such a situation is far from being realised. The heavy-handed bureaucracy, absurd contradictions, and unanticipated costs of EU membership is now a major anxiety to all its members. Hence there exists the paradoxical situation whereby we should support it in principle whilst opposing it in practice. This is not hypocrisy but pragmatism by compulsion. Out of the inextricable confusion of Brussels, and the breakdown of unsatisfactory arrangements, will instead emerge one-to-one agreements between different states. This alone can hope to settle such unexpected violent outbreaks against the landing of British lamb or fish in France, or similar dumping in Britain. French farmers or Scottish fishermen have every right to protest when their livelihoods are at stake, and if their own governments are impotent or the European authorities blind to the problems of their own making, then law-breaking will be all the more frequent.

As supra-national democracy, or European people power in settling Europe's problems, is far from a practical reality, then every European country must revert to its own resources in settling its endemic problems. With regard to our country, it is the British people alone who can hope to throw off the yoke of Rentier capitalism. No help can be expected from Europe. They have productive economic systems and cannot be expected to understand our very different circumstances.

With regard to the former East bloc countries, many of their present troubles stem from the appalling advice of Western bankers and politicians, and others with vested interests and an eye for future profits. Russia is rife with racketeers and swindlers impoverishing the majority. These Rentier capitalists owe their prosperity to the money-creation schemes dreamt-up by economists and financiers in London and Washington. If, on the contrary, the principles of Productive profitability, the break-up of monopolies, and the creation of new manufacturing enterprises through deficit-financing, had been undertaken from the start, Russia's present troubles would have been avoided. What she needs is a consortium of credit investment bankers to liaise with the directors of manufacturing plants in establishing a sound economy. But capital must be raised predominantly within Russia in avoiding the de-stabilisation of her currency or the exploitation of her people.

10 In the world struggle against Rentier capitalism and the oppression of peoples, a great task lies ahead for the Socialist movement, and if the Labour party is to take up the torch for Productive capitalism, it will exert a leading role in furthering the cause. This is because a moral responsibility lies heavily on our shoulders. As much of the misery in the Third world today, such as debt, the enslavement of women and children,

15-10

enforced prostitution, the poisoning of the environment, etc., is the direct consequence of the City of London, it is a moral imperative that Socialists should fight for bettering the condition of the oppressed wherever they may be found.

The encouragement of inward investments and the activity of lending are factors which have anyway ensured the over-valuation of the pound and damage to our exports. Inward investments from the Third world are often of very dubious origin and put to an even more questionable use. The corrupt dictator of every banana republic, every drug baron, mafia boss, Asian pirate, mountain bandit, and other big-time financial swindler, makes a bee-line for the City of London in depositing his ill-gotten gains. The profits made by these Rentiers are used to compound existing evils throughout the world, hold back progress, and enrich a privileged elite. Although the investments may somewhere be put to a good productive use, the profits are bereft of social purpose.

There are three major reasons for the irresponsibility of the City in its lending activity to the Third world. Firstly, usurious interest rates have demonstrated the impracticality of agreed arrangements. These have led to the compounding of Third world debt, in addition to huge losses to lenders, particularly by the big four banks. The British people are now paying for these mistakes through additional bank charges and the gross imbalance of our national debt. Secondly, project investment in the Third world is too often of the wrong kind, i.e. it is designed to enrich investors through high-cost capital intensive schemes, whilst failing to maximise local labour productivity.

More suitable would have been investment in low-cost intermediate technology, but this is unattractive to the City due to its lower financial return.. The virtues of intermediate technology may be brought under four headings:- 1. It is a greater disseminator of wealth amongst developing peoples; 2. It creates wider employment prospects; 3. It utilises existing local skills; and, 4. It is a lesser threat to the environment. This last point is linked to the factor that capital intensive industry in Third world areas has often led to ecological disaster due to:- 1. The lack of factory safety regulations or their disregard; 2. Paucity of relevant skills; and, 3. General attitudes, corner-cutting and corruption, making difficult the management of such enterprises along Western lines. The third reason for the City's irresponsible lending activity to the Third world stems from the fact that huge sums are simply whittled away into the pockets of commission agents, and other Rentiers with every conceivable claim.

The above is a lesson contrasting the Rentier and Productive economies within the Third world environment. The purpose of Socialists, in assisting the oppressed and

15-11

poor, must be to embark on work creation schemes for the majority. Bankers should be sent out from London (i.e. converts to Productive capitalism) to help establish credit investment banks for low-cost labour intensive intermediate technology projects. Such banks should be purely national institutions, forbidden involvement with foreign or international corporations. In this way, a sound local economy would begin to thrive. With time and the development of the social-industrial infrastructure, the intermediate technologies would evolve into more modern enterprises. Meanwhile, locally based currency would maintain and increase its value as it would be linked exclusively to Productive as opposed to Rentier activity.

The crusading task of Socialists throughout the wider world must therefore be the promotion of economic nationalism within the framework of international friendship. As pointed out by the eminent historian G.G. Coulton, "nationalism is a necessary and healthy step towards internationalism."[65]

11 Old-time traditional Socialists may object to the doctrines and policies set out in these five chapters. They will argue that there is "no mileage" in any of this for the Labour party today. They will look at the constituency of the Labour party membership, saying that manufacturing in Britain is anyway "finished." It is of little interest to Labour party members. The membership of the Labour party today is predominantly public sector, and admittedly, with large middle class support. These people do not want to be reminded of industry. "Getting your hands dirty" is not something for the future. All that belongs to the past and is best forgotten. Let the foreigners carry on with manufacturing whilst we stick to services. And as for ideals - let's look to leisure ! Unemployment's to stay, and that's an end to it.

These attitudes are based on the realism of the pessimist and the cynic. On their face value they are not easily contradicted. But in Chapter 11 we defined Appearance and Reality in the sphere of politics. Appearance is what most attracts, whilst Reality is the pain to be most avoided. All the corruption and deceit of politics stems from the pragmatism of those who have waived their principles and lost their faith. That is the situation of the Labour party during the interregnum of the present time.

There is, however, another realism - the realism of the optimist. This arises from the consideration of substantive issues irrespective of their appeal. It lays emphasis on the longer term approach to problem solving, as opposed to the shorter term approach of election winning. In these chapters we have shown how the Labour party may and should extend its appeal to a broader proportion of the electorate. The proposals have

---

[65] G.G. Coulton, *Medieval Panorama*, Cambridge UP, 1938, p. 57.

15-11

not been formulated from arbitrary intellectual theory, but from the dialectic and empiricism of socio-economic change.

There may be other told-time Socialists, however, who see in these chapters an answer to their prayers. As we argued at the start of our discussion on traditional Socialism, new proposals cannot be made without reference to the past. If Socialism is to maintain its meaning there must be the connecting link of an evolutionary thread. This we have maintained. The politically (although not socially) classless society described in these chapters, could be interpreted as the "proletariat" which has lost its economic and political power on the verge of taking over the means of production and distribution. Such a situation would anyway be preceded by the demise of class struggle - calling only for the final pushover of the Rentiers controlling our financial institutions. Then, again, we have described in practical terms how working people will achieve the ownership and control of the means of production and distribution. Such actuality may differ from earlier anticipations, but there is indeed a logical economic necessity in the thesis we have pursued. Are we presenting, therefore, nothing more nor less than the original dream of "scientific" Socialists ? If old-time Socialists can read into this the realisation of their hopes, then there are none within the labour movement who need quarrel with our proposals.

There is much that remains for discussion, and many difficulties lie ahead. In looking towards the future, the Labour party must choose between the easy path of expediency, or the rougher path of truth with all its knocks and animosity. In choosing the second road, surprise may be the outcome. Straight talking and the ring of truth, may appeal so strongly that the Labour party is hard put in confronting the flood of unexpected support. In the deepening crisis facing contemporary Britain integrity must finally win the day.

**

Part III

Establishing Socialist Business Values

"The assumption that the long-term common interest is best served by the efforts of each individual, organisation or society to maximise its own position in the short-term is no longer tenable."

Joseph A. Camilleri, *Civilisation In Crisis*, Cambridge UP, 1976, p. 228.

The following eight chapters are quite technical. They are concerned with the internal workings of productive enterprise - irrespective of the size of company. They may convey the impression of being addressed specifically to management accountants. But that is not their primary purpose.

The following chapters are especially addressed to anyone working on the factory shop-floor - or any other business in the world of commerce, or the primary extraction industries. They are designed to give a complete understanding, in concise and comprehensible terms, of practices which are desirable or undesirable in the world of industry.

By desirable or undesirable are meant those practices which contribute either to the long-term efficiency and prosperity of the business, and those committed to its success; or else to wastage, internal exploitation, bad management, corruption, and the misuse of resources, leading ultimately to uncompetitiveness and the decline of the enterprise.

What follows is therefore essential reading matter for trades union activists in studying the theoretical model for transforming our industrial infrastructure. The changed sociology of work in the wake of information technology, as described in earlier chapters of this book, calls also for great changes in the strategy of trades union activity for better working conditions and a true Socialist society.

If co-determination or participation, or partnership (the current buzz word) in industrial democracy is to be meaningful and not merely nominal, then employees must not only be prepared to learn everything about the economic circumstances and management of the enterprises which employ them, but also, have a clear purpose as to what is desirable or undesirable financial management, and moreover, be prepared to take corrective industrial action as need arises.

Whilst New Labour declares itself as pro-business, after more than two years in power, it is still widely blamed for "ignorance" in business matters. There is something far more ominous and worrying, however, which has occurred during these past two years. Two identical factors have repeated themselves after the election of Tony Blair, which also occurred following the election of Mrs. Thatcher in 1979: viz., firstly, the exchange rate of the pound has risen sky-high; and secondly, UK-based manufacturing, and exports of tangibles, have plummetted sharply. The question must be asked therefore, has the Labour party fallen completely for the invidious machinations of the City institutions so harmful to the majority in this country ? The following chapters will help to clarify this and many other questions.

16-1

CHAPTER 16
Introduction: Accountancy, Its Ultimate Function

"Freed of the most basic restraint of science - testing theory with facts - modern Western economics has completely lost its way. The theories of academic economists are utterly divorced from the grubby reality of daily commercial life. ... Unable to explain the awesome complexities of real economic life as experienced by workers and business people, where history matters and change is constant but largely unpredictable, Western economists have barricaded themselves inside their obtuse mathematical models."

Michael L. Rothschild, *Bionomics*, Futura, 1992, 9. 53.

1 - The potential of economic theory   2 - Failure of the economics establishment   3 - Industrial regeneration dependent on the accountancy profession   4 - The ultimate end of profit   5 - Why British business is locked into a "no-win" situation   6 - How the framework of business dictates the ends of profit

1   The accountancy profession has a great potential for reversing British industrial decline if it is prepared to explore the avenues of accountancy theory. The profession lies at the heart of business activity, but whilst it acknowledges its responsibility in many directions, the discipline that this imposes, too often restricts the vision for the better longer term interests of the enterprises for which it is responsible.

Accountancy practice is so constrained by the limits of company law and changing taxation legislation, as well as by the demands of a computing accuracy to the final degree, that rules and regulations often become ends in themselves in preference to the better purposes of the organisations they serve. This is the tendency that has given rise to the accusation of the "unimaginativeness" of the profession, as well as to the frustration and dislike it has aroused in those different departments of industry calling for change or greater re-investment.

The purpose of this chapter is to demonstrate why accountants should take the initiative in showing the way ahead, since they are endowed with the best overview of business activity, and they alone are privy to all the costing factors making for viability. Accountancy practice, of course, is preceded by theory. In the words of Frank Woods, "accounting theory provides a general frame of reference by which accounting practices can be judged, and it also guides the way to the development of practices and

16-3

procedures."[66] The ultimate purpose of such theory must be to improve the stability, long-term efficiency and growth of the enterprise in a highly competitive world.

2   If the above suggestions sound daunting to many in the profession, it may be useful to glance at the failure of those who have more traditionally set their minds to regenerating industry. The economics establishment is now in tatters. It has no new or practical proposals for the resurgence of British industry, and the failure of the political establishment has resulted from its dependence on hanging on the words of chosen economic gurus.

The problem with the economics profession is that it is too concerned with broad abstract theories or slick mathematical formulas which whilst possibly convincing on the macro-level, do not always make much sense when applied to the individual firm. Fiscal and monetary policies over the past decades, for example, have only had a marginal influence in effecting the health of business. Furthermore, economists usually operate from an academic perspective and are therefore far removed from the practicalities of the business purpose.

There is a great truth in the contention that the most successful post-War economies have been those blessed by the dearth of economists. If we turn to the Far East or north west mainland European economies, it will be found that their energies have been concentrated on the success of the individual enterprise. Having determined what makes for successful business, they have then designed dynamic planning associations, funding institutions, educational bodies, etc., all under the umbrella of the state, for maximising the success of the individual firm.

This is in sharp contrast to the British experience which has entailed the imposition of general economic theory of one kind or another, forming a framework into which the enterprise must be fitted, irrespective of its needs, in a Procrustean-like fashion. These are the reason why the accountancy profession must take up the gauntlet left in the gutter by the economics establishment. Post-War history has clearly shown that it is accountancy decision-making which is responsible for the success or failure of economies, and not the grand theories of so-called economic "science."

3   The clue to all our economic problems can only be found through analysing the nature of profit, and pursuing that concept of profit which best promotes the long-term interests of wealth creation. As accountancy is solely concerned with the nature of profit, the assessment of wealth creation should be a matter for accountancy alone.

The computation of profits are various and conflictual. They depend on the

---

[66] Frank Woods, *Business Accounting*, Pitman, 5th ed., 1989, p. 463.

16-5

purposes for which they are computed. The figure of profits in published accounts, for example, would be of little interest to the Revenue authorities who require a re-computation for their own specific purpose. Likewise, potential lenders to an enterprise require historical accounts presenting profits in yet another guise; whilst prospective purchasers of shares require even more complex accounts in presenting a basis for profit.

We are concerned with none of these bases for profit which have a narrower or subjective purpose, i.e. either to sell the company to potential investors, or to prepare a statement for tax avoidance. Although these activities may be central to much accountancy practice, they are not the ultimate purpose of the accountancy function. There is a concept of profit transcending these narrower purposes - more objective and essential to the very existence of the enterprise. And it is this higher concept of profit which should be central to all accountancy theory.

4 What is profit by this definition ? In what framework may it best flourish ? What is its purpose ? Whom should it benefit, or to what purpose should it be put ? In the words of Emile Woolf, "'profits' litters the financial pages of our newspapers, professional press and libraries of business texts, yet very few readers would feel competent to explain the precise meaning of the concept, which is after all the ultimate criterion for the majority of business decisions; nor would many wish to be faced with a demand to justify their calculations of it, whatever the context."[67] Nevertheless, in the cause of industrial regeneration, profit demands a definition in terms of purpose to be achieved.

Profit, objectively considered, demands that the company be managed as an end in itself, rather than as a tool of the constituent parts by which it is controlled. This is expressed in the use of profit towards the ends of long-term stability and growth of market share, and sufficient re-investment to ensure these.

5 None of these ideal conditions, however, are achievable through conscious intention alone. Every senior company executive claims to seek the "best long-term interests" of his enterprise, when in fact he does no such thing in practice. This indicates clearly that business is locked within the framework of set conditions dictating the ends of company success, but those ends cannot be taken for granted as being objective in themselves. For example, there may be a conflict over the interpretation of profit between the aim of expanding market share or adding profit onto a smaller turnover. That smaller turnover is usually assumed to have a higher quality or a

---

[67] Emile Woolf, *Auditing Today*, Prentice Hall, 4th ed., 1990, p. 579.

16-6

"specialised" demand in justifying its higher price, but again, history has demonstrated that such assumptions tend to be purely subjective.

The "long-term view" may also be seen as driving the firm towards "bankruptcy" when the interest on loans must be met within the shorter term. In that situation there is simply no practical alternative to the shorter term view in all decision-making, and on a day-to-day basis, it becomes a nonsense to attempt comparisons with the more successful strategies of Japanese competitors. But this is an occasion for those experienced in the down-to-earth occupation of accountancy practice, to step back and gain a wider perspective of world trading practices and their repercussions on our own business predicament. Accountancy theory must be explored and developed, for there is no other discipline with sufficient relevant facts and methodology at its fingertips to analyse seriously the question of British industrial decline.

6   Therefore, it may be seen that in terms of international trade, success or failure in business is predominantly dependent on the customary framework within which enterprise is obliged to operate. Hence the efforts, intelligence, or general competitiveness of those who manage or operate systems, is only of secondary importance. This is not intended as pessimism, and neither is it intended as a defence of the potential success of British management. It is only intended as a call for change to the systems within which we are obliged to work.

Profit for success (objectively considered) is interpreted in contrasting ways in different parts of the world, and these differing interpretations have brought startling and opposing results to the economies in which they operate. Business people in Britain and America may be no less energetic and aggressive in the pursuit of their own understanding of profit, than those in Japan or Singapore, but the outcome in terms of success or industrial productivity will nonetheless be very different.

But the analysis of these things is not a field of study for mere economists. They entail a scrutiny of business practices and an understanding of psychological motives going far beyond the remit of the academic in his ivory tower environment. It is a subject of study for the accountancy profession alone.

The ultimate purpose of profit must be to ensure a good social purpose: i.e. to enrich business, so that it in turn may enrich the community through the dissemination of wealth and ensuring full employment. That is the achievement of the dynamic Far East economies. But what is the actual mechanism enabling and ensuring their particular interpretation of profit for the longer term in maximising market share ?

It is to be found in the system of deficit financing whereby the constraints of lenders confine the activities of an enterprise to the specific task of its productive

16-6

purpose. The close partnership between lender (usually a credit investment bank) and borrower is only made possible by prior attempts to eliminate the risk factor. The lender virtually takes on the function of a management accountant, and since he is external to the company (which is dependent on his discretion) he exerts a power which cannot be crossed.

Meanwhile the risk factor can only be reduced to the minimum by ensuring that the company is managed on rational principles. This means that its marketing aim must be world effective competitiveness, since no other purpose could justify its long-term loan situation and the heavy responsibility which this incurs. This funding method applies to businesses both large and small throughout north west mainland Europe as well as the Far East.

In view of the undoubted historical success of this Productive capitalism, it may be seen that the Rentier capitalism of the Anglo-Saxon open financial markets cannot possibly hope to compete in the longer term. This alone is the explanation for the weakness of manufacturing in both Britain and America, as well as that of tertiary sectors of business.

All this poses questions demanding intelligent debate if economic decline is to be reversed. The problem touches on vested interests and the entrenched tradition of a long unbroken business culture - but these issues cannot be avoided. The integrity implied in the objective aims of better business must alone be upheld for the development of the future. But the task of research must be left to those practising accountants who are prepared to apply theory to the extensive knowledge already within their grasp.

CHAPTER 17
Britain's Toughest Competition: An Opposing Economic System

"Capitalism, we can now see, has two faces, two personalities. The Neo-American model is based on industrial success and short-term financial gain, the Rhine model, of German pedigree but with strong Japanese connections, emphasises collective success, consensus and long-term concerns. In the last decade or so, it is this Rhine model - unheralded, unsung and lacking even nominal identity papers - that has shown itself to be the more efficient of the two, as well as more equitable."

Michel Albert, *Capitalism Against Capitalism*, Whurr Publications, 1993 pp. 18-19.

1 - Non-sectorial business management economics a good starting point   2 - Economic theory too often confused with political   3 - Two non-compatible capitalist systems exist today   4 - Failure of the old economic theories   5 - The old divide no longer a useful criterion for investigation   6 - The need to compare successful and unsuccessful economies   7 - The identification of these   8 - Intellectual complacency over Anglo-Saxon industrial decline   9 - Need to re-define the capitalist system   10 - Economic causes must be sought to explain Anglo-Saxon decline   11 - Deficit versus equity funding distinguishes the systems   12 - Deficit funding an emotive issue in Britain   13 - Its effect on the business process is its significance   14 - It arose out of national necessity   15 - I.e. state intervention and aspirations   16 - Effectiveness of funding method most important factor   17 - Deficit funding dependent on minimising risk   18 - This achieved by banks entering into the business process   19 - And companies submitting to the constraints of a partnership   20 - This entails concentrating on a specific business purpose   21 - But also access to unlimited funding   22 - It influences business philosophy   23 - Comparison with the British company   24 - Accountancy constraints placed on the latter

1   A successful economy needs successful business but the extraordinary complexity of modern industrial infrastructures in a highly competitive world means that the ordinary firm can no longer be expected to flourish long-term unless linked to the commitment of a national purpose.

This book is concerned with the economics of business management, but it will be shown that this is essentially more wide-ranging than the narrow limits usually reserved for the topic. It is a question that not only extends to public policy and government but also touches on social issues.

The proposals formulated here for the regeneration of industry are of a non-sectorial kind, i.e. they cannot be said to appeal to any particular vested interest group in preference to another within the world of industry. This is because the underlying principles are concerned solely with the technicalities of the business purpose conceived as an end in itself.

17-3

This contrasts sharply, of course, with the mainstream business philosophy of laissez-faire, which explicitly promotes the interests of shareholders; as it likewise contrasts with the philosophy of an old-style Socialist-motivated interventionism, which aims to promote the better interests of employees and consumers. It is felt that such a non-sectorial business approach is particularly apt for our time in view of the increasing convergence of interests within the most advanced better run enterprises, quite apart from the contended validity of the economic principles in fulfilling their function.

2   Of course it has to be acknowledged that no economic theory can be separated entirely from questions of socio-political choice, but it also has to be remembered that the truths of the former are too often distorted by the vagaries of the latter. This contention certainly applies to the situation pertaining in our own time. Mainstream economic theory usually divides between those who support socio-political ideas to the right of centre, and so lean towards laissez-faire; or those who are left of centre, and so prefer some degree of intervention,[68] but both attitudes when linked to their ideological source, are today irrelevant in solving our most intractable problems. The final demonstration of this fact is seen in the deficiency of new economic ideas in public life, and in the dismal failure of government policy.

3   Furthermore, mainstream economic questions are too often concerned with peripheral which instead are mistaken for substantive issues, and the reason for this is that age-old ideological political thinking has failed to keep abreast with socio-technological changes which have made a nonsense of cherished political notions. For example, popular thought is still concerned predominantly with the relative merits of Capitalism *per se*, as opposed to some other system of production and distribution, usually of a Socialistic tendency. The argument of this book is that the greatest economic problem now facing Britain, and the rest of the Anglo-Saxon world, lies immediately at our feet.

In the world today are two quite separate capitalistic systems, and in the light of stable trading relationships, the one is incompatible with the other. All discussion of the relative merits of capitalism, or other systems, is therefore a deviation from the issues which *really* count. Hence this book is only concerned with the relative merits of the opposing capitalist systems, and the measures which may be taken for British economic recovery which stem from this analysis.

---

[68] It should not be forgotten, however, that the Conservative party also has a significant strand of interventionism dating back to Disraeli. Note especially the MPs who surrounded Harold Macmillan in the 1930s, and those who supported R.A.B. Butler in the post-War period.

17-6

4   In putting our present position into perspective, it would be useful to review briefly our most recent past. As we move (or have) moved towards recession, the continuing paralysis of economic thought as to the way ahead seems all the more astonishing. In the 80s, with the emergence of Thatcherism, in this country and elsewhere, there was a hard-line reversion to laissez-faire. But, as events were to prove, and as elaborated below, this was merely classical capitalism reverting to a decadent form. Meanwhile, Socialist economic theory lost the last remnants of credibility in significant parts of the world, whilst in the liberal West, it failed to adapt sufficiently in meeting the changed circumstances of the industrial infrastructure.

The transformation of that infrastructure to its present actuality was, of course, something that could never have been anticipated in the past, by those who either supported a form of Socialist interventionism, or by those who supported unfettered market forces; for the problems of the future can never be anticipated. Consequently, we are now faced by issues that do not lend themselves to the established economic mechanisms of the political system. Today, as government twists and turns in its tracks, we see a dog chasing its tail.

5   If, however, we analyse the true nature of our current economic problems in the light of reality, it will soon be seen that the age-old debate of interventionism versus unfettered market forces is a futile pointer to the way ahead. Out-dated politico-economic measures are now being applied to situations which they cannot successfully alter. The difficulty is exacerbated by the fact that economics is not a pure science, since the value systems of socio-political thinking often intrude to distort economic truths or the economic ends required. This, anyway has been the experience of history.

Furthermore, pure (or allegedly disinterested) economic thinking also has to be called into question, since it so often flies in the face of actuality or fails to achieve a promised outcome. All the abstract theories of money management promoted as cure-alls by the great gurus of the post-War period, and taken up by successive governments, have only culminated in miserable failure. Hence no attempt will be made in this book or regurgitate or invent such new simplistic but abstract theories as solutions for the future. Such paths lead to barren pastures.

6   This criticism may seem to place a block on all starting points towards investigating our most intractable problems, but its intention is to clear away the intellectual clutter failing to address the unique and unrecognised issues of our time. The starting point for such an enquiry should simply be to glance at the most successful economies in the post-War industrialised world, comparing them with those advanced industrial economies which have fared least well. Clearly the East bloc economies may

17-9

be ignored entirely in such an exercise. Hence we are only considering so-called capitalist economies.

The comparison has to be based on the typical characteristics of these economies over a 40-year period with regard to their change and growth. It must not be based on a photo-flash impression taken at any particular point in time, and even less must it be based on contemporary circumstances, quite apart from the distortions caused by the current world recession. This entails a strictly empirical approach to problem solving in preference to a more abstract intellectual investigation.

7 By this approach the following clear divide emerges:- Successful economies: the five Far and South East Asian nations of Japan, Korea, Taiwan, Hong Kong and Singapore, and the countries of north west Europe. This is by no means a definitive list, for Malaysia, Thailand and parts of Indonesia and coastal China may shortly be appended to the Far East section of this list; whilst northern Italy, Spain and Greece may be added to the successful economies of Europe.

The Unsuccessful economies are the United Kingdom and the other Anglo-Saxon cultures of the USA, Australia, and most of central and south America. Again, the list is not definitive for it might include most other economies with pretensions to advanced industrialisation. For the purposes of our comparison, however, it would be most apt to confine out attention to the Far East and north west European countries on the one hand, and Britain and America on the other, since these are economies on a comparable level of industrialisation where contrasts are most evident.

8 Over a 50-year period we have witnessed a one-way see-saw motion with the manufacturing bases of the two mightiest industrialised powers sink into relative followed by absolute decline; whilst their competitors either rebuilt their industrial bases from the ashes of war, or industrialised on the foundations of older-type economies, eventually far-outstripping their Anglo-Saxon rivals.

An early reaction to this phenomenon in the West was not so much disbelief as a convenient escapist complacency, with the emergence of the Post-industrial theories of Daniel Bell, A. Touraine, and others in the 60s and 70s; and more recently, the ideas of Alvin Toffler, all tending to undervalue the economic significance of the manufacturing sectors they chose to describe as the "older" economies. All these writers have wrought an extraordinary mischief in the minds of leading opinion-formers in the Anglo-Saxon world, and only now is there a realisation that desperate measures are needed to regenerate advanced manufacturing industry.

9 None of the above writers, and few other economists in the stricter sense, seem to have touched on the core problem undermining the failing economies of the West.

17-13

This, it seems, has been due to the blinkered attitude of either conceiving all major economic problems in terms of internal technical impedimenta preventing smooth-running capitalism, or else due to external opposition to the system itself. The possibility of the bifurcation of capitalism into two separate systems, and the need for the evaluation of each, seem never to have occurred. A clearer understanding of what confronts us today will soon reveal the necessity for refining our definition of the capitalist system.

10   The first step towards understanding our core economic problem must be to distinguish the general characteristics marking off the Anglo-Saxon economies from those of our toughest industrial competitors. No one would question the contention that both economic systems are intensely capitalistic, yet one of these systems fails miserably to meet the competitive challenge of the other. It is futile - and anyway invalid - to seek cultural reasons to explain the success and failure of the different systems, even though cultural causes may be of secondary importance. Irrefutable economic factors must be identified.

11   The most obvious difference between the economic industrialisation of our competitors and ourselves, is that the industrialisation of the former has been achieved predominantly through deficit funding, as opposed to the equity funding of the open financial markets. As we all know, the industries of both West Germany and Japan, were almost totally rebuilt in the post-War period through the deficit funding of joint-stock investment banks, but what is perhaps lesser known, is that all the other economies in this successful sector, benefited through similar forms of capitalisation. Although banks and financial institutions may differ in type and structure amongst our various competitors, it will be found that deficit funding has a long and estabilished tradition as a typical mode of ensuring industrial success. Now the question of deficit funding in both Britain and America is a highly emotive issue.

12   If the question is broached with most City financiers, or indeed, with corporate directors in the primary or secondary sectors of industry, a violent response is often evoked. Deficit funding is seen as somehow "rigging" the market, or laying too great a "stress" on the shoulders of funding institutions. It should be noted that no such suggestion is made in this book that City institutions in their present form should undertake such a function - nor could they - for they lack both the expertise and structure for a long-term approach. But however remote the prospect may be, the proposition is always pushed aside impatiently as a matter that is not up for discussion at any time.

13   It is not our purpose to enquire into the City's sensitivity to the suggestion of

17-15

deficit funding,[69] and in any case, we are not concerned with the relative merits or practicality of deficit funding *per se*, but rather with certain of its incidental benefits to the business process within the capitalist system, of which we believe the City magnates may have little awareness. It would first be useful, however, to explain the occurrence of deficit funding as an evolutionary factor within the economic system, for its emergence as a practical necessity and not as some kind of ideological monstrosity, may give it a trace of justification in the eyes of our City friends.

14   Deficit funding emerged as a necessity for the newly emerging industrial states, in response to the invincible competitiveness of the first industrial economies, during the second half of the 19th century. Whilst special reasons allowed Britain and America to industrialise successfully through encouraging a laissez-faire environment, e.g. most notably through the existence of a moneyed middle class able to utilise its savings[70] in funding the earlier technological stage of the industrial revolution, this was not the case with our competitors.

Firstly, our competitors had neither a sufficiently strong moneyed middle class, and secondly, they lacked suitable financial institutions. The only exception to this generalisation was Belgium and the Netherlands, and certain urban pockets of population in Germany and France. Thirdly, by the third quarter of the last century technology in the major industries had reached a level of complexity and cost that could not easily be met by the family savings that were sufficient to fund the simpler technologies of fifty years earlier in Britain.

15   Consequently, our future competitors in both Europe and Japan, who were determined to industrialise on a serious scale, were obliged to turn to the state for assistance. In every case the state was willing to respond in appreciating the national

---

[69] Nonetheless, this sensitivity may indeed be due to the long-standing failure of the financial markets and institutions to promote home-based industry because of the massive outflow of capital into overseas investments. With regard to this, see the following sources: A.K. Cairncross, *Home & Foreign Investment, 1870-1913*, Cambridge UP, 1935; G.D.H. Cole (ed.), *Studies In Capital & Investment*, New Fabian Research Bureau, 1935, W.P. Kennedy, "Capital Markets In Britain To 1914" in *Management Strategy & Business Development*, L. Hannah (ed.), Macmillan, 1976; J. Savile, "Some Retarding Factors In The British Economy Before 1914," *Yorkshire Bulletin of Economic & Social Research*, 13(1), 51-60, 1961; and, J.C. Carrington & G.T. Edwards, *Financing Industrial Development*, Macmillan, 1979.

[70] The following authorities may be consulted in demonstrating that family wealth and retained earnings were the principal sources of investment finance in the 19th century, in both Britain and America: P.L. Cottrell, *Industrial Finance 1830-1914*, Methuen, 1980; P. Mathias, *The First Industrial Revolution*, Methuen, 1983; F. Crouzet, *Capital Formation In The Industrial Revolution*, Methuen, 1972; R.E. Cameron, *Banking In The Early Stages of Industrialisation*, OUP, NY, 1967; and, L.S. Pressnell, *Country Banking In The Industrial Revolution*, OUP, 1956.

17-17

benefits of industrialisation. Help entailed the establishment of joint-stock industrial credit banks, promoting technical institutes and integrated industrial planning authorities, and perhaps most of all, national commitment to the success of the productive sector both at home and abroad.

Hence deficit funding emerged not as a theoretical idea but out of dire necessity. If Adam Smith remained the distant theoretical father of the Anglo-Saxon laissez-faire economies, then it was Friedrich List who was and still remains the inspiration behind the economic systems of our competitors - and the influence of his economic nationalism today within the Continental EU countries is in no way diminished by the supposedly cosy mutual benefits of the twelve.

16 It is our contention that the overriding priority of political institutions should be the successful funding of the productive[71] sector, howsoever this is achieved in best maintaining the interests of the *real* economy, and if this is to be through the instrument of deficit funding, then so be it. This is not an ideological stance but purely a matter of practicality as demonstrated through the experience of industrial economies assumed to be on a comparable level with our own. But as noted above, the significant fact of deficit funding is not to be found in the method itself, but in the secondary benefits as these effect the business process in all its major operations. And these consequences, be it noted, are not only reflected at the micro-economic level within the individual enterprise, but also at the macro-economic level in the dynamic promotion of the national economy.

17 It would be useful to glance at the specific characteristics of deficit funding as found amongst our competitors, and at a phenomenon little known in Anglo-Saxon societies. As deficit funding is available to enterprises irrespective of size or type, and as collectively, a huge proportion of national finances are invested in this way, risks against losses must be minimised from the start.

A highly rational and organised approach has to be taken with regard to the use of capital. Hence the "hunch" or intuitive approach to business is not only seen as irresponsible but ridiculous. There emerges a professionalism and a slow ponderous exactitude in decision-making, and a long-term planning that is almost military in its style and thinking. There is no gamesmanship in this process - it is far too serious for that - and this is what so contrasts it with the lighter atmosphere in the Anglo-Saxon

---

[71] Throughout this book the term "productive sector" or "productive firms," etc., refers only to the primary (i.e. extraction and cultivation) and secondary (i.e. manufacturing) industries. In other contexts, the term "productivity" includes the tertiary (i.e. service) industries also.

17-20

organisation. And these characteristics refer to business not only in Germany or Japan, but also in France, Scandinavia, the Netherlands and elsewhere.

18   Lending institutions in these countries, therefore, cannot afford to take "risks" as we generously understand the term. Hence measures are taken to diminish the risk factor almost to the elimination point, in all loans to the business sector. This means that banks are obliged to enter so closely into the business process as to act as the financial management departments of borrowing companies. In Germany, for example, bank executives sit on the boards of companies as Bank Directors, undertaking the equivalent function of Chief Accountants as found in British enterprises.

The commercial departments of these Continental and Far East banks, even on the most local level, have a sophistication and understanding of business unimagined in the UK. Since many of the industrial credit banks were established with limited funding from various sources, for the purpose of deficit funding, they were forced to broaden the framework of their activities from that of remaining mere depositors and lenders.

In addition, many started from the competitive position of having to offer lower interest charges and longer payment terms than those available from more traditional sources of borrowing. The Raiffeisen Bank in Germany, for example, was established to compete with usurious money lenders in the older medieval tradition.[72]

19   When a group of businessmen, in our competitor countries, initially approach a bank, it is not merely a question of presenting and seeking an endorsement for a business plan. The entire project must be comprehended by the bank in depth, together with all competitive factors, and then a partnership is entered into between the enterprise and the bank. And it is here where the most significant differences arise between the management of the British company and our competitors.

Whilst the British company would be left to operate freely according to the wishes of its board, subject only to specific financial constraints agreed with the bank; our competitors would be obliged to operate within the constraints of a very special partnership. This entails an interventionism and style of management that might not easily be acceded to by the traditional board of the British company.

20   Firstly, the partnership entails the management of the company for a very specific purpose, viz., the production of a defined category of products and the fulfilment of a specific market sector. The agreed market plan and the analysis of the competition,

---

[72]. See J.H. Clapham's *The Economic Development of France & Germany 1815-1914*, 2nd ed., 1923, pp. 221-224

17-23

designed to eliminate the risk factor to the minimum, ensures a greater concentration of purpose within all departments of the company. Consequently, diversification tendencies are excluded as an irrelevant distraction, whilst the wheeling and dealing mentality is made unthinkable. This intense, if blinkered, concentration on product purpose, which inevitably leads to the maximising of market share, ensures that the longer term is always held in view. All these characteristics are influenced by the method of capitalisation.

21   Secondly, if this partnership means the domination of the company by an external authority, this is more than compensated by unlimited funding if justified by need. Such funding, of course, is only granted on objective rational principles after closely assessing project viability and the loan and return on capital. If, during the process of this funding, the company finds its way into the pocket of the bank, so be it ! This is agreeable to all parties if the company: 1. Increases or maintains its market share; 2. Remains profitable; 3. Sustains the level of its remuneration for employees; 4. Succeeds in avoiding retrenchment; and, 5. Is judged able to repay its debts in the conceivable future.

22   Thirdly, and most significantly, this partnership between the bank and the productive enterprise not only exerts an influence that is manifested throughout every department of the company, but actually influences its business philosophy. As we have said, the Bank Director or his equivalent, amongst out toughest industrial competitors, takes the place of the company accountant as found in the Anglo-Saxon enterprise. The advantage of the Bank Director, however, is that in theory, he holds unlimited borrowing power for the company. Hence when the company looks to the longer term and the threat of the competition, it is able to pre-empt effectively attacks on its market share through timely investments in equipment, methods or personnel. Providing a rational case is convincingly presented, our competitors have typically seldom been denied the capitalisation required.

23   This assurance with all its back-up, has not only given foreign companies a tremendous confidence, but a dynamism and energy that seemingly gives them an invincible quality. Through this attitude every process in the company is professionalised in maximising efficiency. Compare this with the financial management of the Anglo-Saxon concern. Since the basis of that financial management entails a different method (and not merely one of style) it is only to be expected that the results should betray a glowering contrast. As the company accountant lacks the borrowing power of the bank executive on the company board, he is forced to utilise internal capital for all re-investment and other needs. And when borrowing is resorted to, it is

17-24

on such onerous terms - usually only for the short-term - that it is rarely taken up.[73]

24   Consequently, re-investment for machinery or expansion is constantly postponed. As the in-depth reports of sales engineers, marketers, etc., are constantly pushed aside by the financial departments of companies, accountants have called upon themselves an unenviable odium amongst colleagues throughout the Anglo-Saxon world. Such a reputation, it must be added, may indeed be unfair, as accountants are constrained within narrow and difficult limits; but such difficulties are seldom appreciated by colleagues who only witness the success of competitors.

If company accountants are unjustifiably subjected to the contempt and loathing of colleagues, and the constant butt of cynicism, this is primarily because the Anglo-Saxon business community has not yet awoken to the all-important distinction between the Productive and Rentier modes of capitalism as these effect the success or failure of industry.[74]

---

[73] See Appendix B.

[74] The British share of world exports of manufactures fell from 31% in 1913 to 8% in 1983, and according to the *National Institute Review,* 108, 70-84, GNP per capita in the UK was already half that of Germany, France, and Scandinavia by 1984. Britain's performance relative to her industrial competitors has been in continuous sharp decline, in both outputs and efficiency, since the 1880s. The following are a selection of leading sources demonstrating these trends: Charles Feinstein (ed.), *The Managed Economy,* OUP, 1983; Andrea Bolitho, "Growth," in, *The European Economy: Growth & Crisis,* Oxford, 1982; Angus Maddison, "Phases of Capitalist Development," *Banca Nazionale del Laboro Quarterly Review,* 1977; and Sidney Pollard, *The Development of The British Economy 1914-1967,* 2nd ed., Edward Arnold, 1969.

18-3

CHAPTER 18
When Money-Creation Hinders Productive Profitability

"The internationalisation of manufacturing and finance erodes a people's capacity to control its own affairs. ... this frenzy of mergers and acquisitions across Europe struck many critics as socially unbalanced, benefitting the chairmen, stockholders, lawyers, and others in those businesses, but offering little to people as a whole."

Paul Kennedy, *Preparing For The Twenty-First Century*, Harper Collins, 1993,

Pp. 53 & 263.

1 - Dirigiste policies benefit our competitors   2 - Characteristics of government commitment to industry   3 - It is solely motivated by the purpose of industrial success   4 - Effectiveness of government intervention   5 - Nothing allowed to adversely effect best national interests   6 - Misunderstanding to which this gives rise in Britain   7 - But our competitors capable of benign co-operation amongst themselves   8 - The rationale of Anglo-Saxon Rentier capitalism   9 - The rationale of Productive capitalism   10 - Origin of Rentier capitalism   11 - Separation between capitalists and producers   12 - Capitalist system independent of the state   13 - Emergence of laissez-faire ideology a natural progression 14 - Widespread cultural consequences of this   15 - The myth of open participation in the system   16 - The need for "Confidence"   17 - It is necessitated by the greater risk factor   18 - Instability of productive business exacerbated by conglomerate-type enterprise   19 - Self-defeating anti-intellectualism of the British business community

1   If we have outlined the micro-economic factors disabling British competitiveness as found in the typical productive enterprise, then only half the story has been told. The macro-economic conditions for our competitors are not only complementary to the activities of the ordinary firm, but actually promote the environment within which the latter could not hope to flourish.

If we take any of our competitors, irrespective of size or status within a trading bloc - it may be Norway down to Italy, or Sweden across to Singapore - it will be found that the government and administrative authorities of all such countries actively promote the home-based industries within their territorial jurisdiction through a variety of measures.[75] They achieve this not through nationalisation or pseudo-Socialistic measures, but through *dirigiste* policies. This means creative interventionism into the private sector, and as this contradicts laissez-faire philosophy, which has always been held as dogma within our own business community, it is perhaps a reason why the term

---

[75] The following are good sources demonstrating how the finance and economic ministries of France, Germany and Japan have directly promoted their home-based industries: Peter Katzenstein, *Between Power & Plenty*, Madison, Univ. of Wisconsin Press, 1978, and, Chalmers Johnson, *MITI*, Berkeley, Univ. of California Press, 1982.

18-4

dirigisme has as yet not found its way into our vocabulary.[76]

2   The success of the foreign competitive enterprise, therefore, is not merely indebted to the commitment of its credit investment bank, but often to a government that not only initiated the establishment of such a bank, but to a government that ensures stable and desirable exchange rates assessed through a multiplicity of interlocking planning associations.

Hence government not only oversees the success of home-based industry through creative intervention, but actually directs the productive economy through a variety of centralised and integrated bodies, all committed to the cause of ensuring a positive balance of payments. Such an explanation for our competitors' success is ideologically horrific to many British businessmen, for the only consciousness of many of government intervention was and still remains the experience of old-style Socialist control. Many can conceive of no other alternative than bungling inefficiency as soon as the state is involved.

3   The reality of our competitors' situation, however, is quite different. The motive for such intervention is not to stem the business process, or to restrict "capitalism" *per se*, and neither is it to ensure consciously a more even distribution of wealth; but simply to promote manufacturing success against all competitors, in maximising national wealth creation.

All the social benefits resulting from this form of productive capitalism, i.e. a faster circulation of money throughout the bulk of the population, a more even distribution of wealth, and higher standards of education and welfare, are thus peripheral benefits accruing naturally from the competitive business process. Seen from this perspective, therefore, productive capitalism occupies a moral ground through its intentions (or rather lack of them) that is no higher than that of rentier capitalism. At no time did productive capitalism consciously set out to create a greater distribution of wealth or a more socially just society.

4   In any case, this mode of interventionism is indirect and subtle, and quite benign in its approach to the business enterprise - indeed, if it was not, it would hardly be tolerated by those it was designed to assist. The legal relationship of the state to the central banks, educational institutions, inspection bodies, trade federations, and other agencies influencing commercial success amongst our competitors varies greatly, and is anyway irrelevant in the light of the universal overriding factor that the state de facto

---

[76] The word *dirigisme* will be found in some of our larger and better dictionaries, but nowhere is it given a full definition describing its proper meaning.

18-7

exerts a positive role in promoting the interests of home-based industry.

I have come across incidents, for example, when British equipment manufacturers have lost out to more expensive German competitors, through ad hoc subsidies granted by agencies of the German government stepping in at the eleventh hour to ensure a sale. Such orders have been won and lost through massive discounts of up to 25%. Such subsidising measures certainly overstep the ideals of laissez-faire, and I am sure they contravene the spirit if not the law of trading regulations, but as we should all know from our reading of the press, the demands of competition amongst our rivals take on a priority above all other considerations. This is a fact of productive capitalism worldwide, and if hypocrisy is to be overcome, then the law should be changed to suit this underlying reality. What is undoubtedly ineffective is to cry "Wolf" whenever our competitors contravene the spirit of the law, for they will only turn their back on any such accusation and shake their shoulders as if to say, "What does it matter ?"

5   Meanwhile, the regulations of National Standards institutions have been strategically used by a number of countries for protecting home products and keeping out imports. This has been achieved irrespective of EU membership status, for the activities of the dynamic business communities are always several steps ahead of the implementation of EU regulations which exist in a constant state of flux. The commitment to industrial success of all our competitors is so determined, that no laws, tariff agreements, or other impediments are allowed to stand in the way of their undaunted efforts.

6   All these factors would seem to indicate that our competitors "rig" the market, and in hard times, that is just the accusation that British businessmen are too ready to throw out. Top British businessmen - I mean the leaders of our conglomerates - are always fulsome in their praise for "Britain's friendly environment" as a centre for international trade, quite oblivious to the fact that there may be a darker side to *that* coin. They like to portray the British system as successful and benign in contributing to a greater world harmony; contrasting this with the "unfair," "cut-throat" systems of our toughest industrial competitors, threatening "anarchy" in world trading relations. As will be elucidated below, these are merely cultural prejudices stemming from contrasting systems of capitalism - not to mention differing attitudes towards the law.

7   The truer picture is that our competitors, despite their intense economic nationalism, are no less effective in sinking their differences in co-operating for a common purpose, than are the ideologically friendly laissez-faire countries. In fact they may possess this co-operative ability to a greater degree than ourselves. Witness the

18-10

· success of the Continental EU countries over the past 40-year period. Both large and small states have developed co-operatively in almost perfect harmony.

It is important, however, to distinguish clearly between economic and political nationalism, for the latter has become unacceptable in mainstream political circles in all the most advanced industrial countries. For example, whilst Germany exerts an intense economic nationalism, the expression of political nationalism from any part of the establishment has been taboo over the past 50-year period. Whilst Germany's businessmen behave like lions, their politicians seem as meek as lambs.

8 If we glance at Britain's contrasting economic system, there should be no surprise at our dismal industrial performance since the post-War period.

This is explained by the fact that our competitors promote a mode of capitalism, the rationale of which, is in direct contradistinction to our own, and it is from these factors alone that all resulting differences between the two systems can be explained. The rationale for Anglo-Saxon, or Rentier capitalism, is the maximisation of shareholders' profits. In the reception areas of many American companies, for example, prominently displayed and embellished in a fine copperplate script may be found a listing of the ideals of the enterprise, and the first of these is always the aim to maximise the return on shareholders' profits.

9 The rationale for the Productive capitalism of our competitors is de facto and invariably the success of the enterprise through maximising market share. These two systems, although by no means immutable, as qualified below, create such an incompatibility, that they can hardly be expected to coexist forever into the foreseeable future, since they rule out the possibility of trading on equal conditions, and this amounts to unfair trading relationships. Before elaborating on this latter contention, it would first be useful to return to the origins of these two conflicting modes of capitalism, since they can only be sympathetically understood within their historical contexts.

10 As the British mode of capitalism pre-dates the industrial revolution by at least 100 years, and as the system has evolved smoothly without any break in its continuity, it has to be said that it was never designed as a funding medium for industry.

Irrespective of whether we trace the unique system of British capitalism from the late 1530s and 40s, following the sack of the monasteries; or from the end of the 17th century, following the establishment of the Bank of England, capitalism predominantly entailed (and remains today) the activity of speculators, i.e. of wealthy men who were looking to invest their money in the projects of others, or else in the passive assets of land and property in the hope of a higher return through rent or sale at a later date. In

18-13

the 1530s and 40s there was a scramble for land speculation by courtiers and City merchants, but this was soon followed by investments in overseas trading projects and the establishment of Trading Companies managed under mercantilist principles.

11   In Britain there has always tended to be a divide between those who owned capital and those who used it for a productive purpose; the only exception to this tendency on a significant scale was during the earlier period of the industrial revolution. Hence it is unsurprising that capitalist philosophy in the Anglo-Saxon world should have always emphasised that its *raison d'être* was the return on capital, irrespective of other economic factors of a more objective nature. When producers were dependent as suppliants on an external source for their financing, be they manufacturers or Adventurer sea captains of an earlier era, it would not have been expected of them to ponder over the dependency of their relationship.

12   Furthermore, it has to be emphasised that those who initiated the capitalist process were always individuals, or groups of individuals, who acted independently of the state, even if in the earlier period their larger projects required licensing by the state. Hence these capitalists operated from an entirely subjective perspective; their only criteria for decision-making being self-benefit.

It is therefore not surprising that criminality on a vast scale early entered into their sphere of operations, most notably in the form of piracy in the 16th century, something which severely embarrassed the English government which the latter confronted with extraordinary difficulty. Meanwhile, the injustices arising from land speculation, with its dispossession and the creation of armies of beggars, need only be noted as social abuses that in no way retarded an accelerating economic process. The criticism of churchmen and intellectuals, like Sir Thomas More, were only to fall on deaf ears.

13   The emergence of laissez-faire as a systematic philosophy with the publication of Adam Smith's *Wealth of Nations* in 1776, and its early acceptance as an ideology by the Anglo-Saxon business communities, was not only a logical but an inevitable development from this mode of capitalism. The most significant aspect of the book is that it gave a moral justification to an *as is* situation. It certainly attacked what it saw as the abuses arising from the barriers to international trade, but it then went on to justify free trade as in all respects mutually beneficent. Trust in the "invisible hand" was upheld as the kernel of economic truth.

These contentions of a great moral philosopher were highly convenient to a nation at the dawn of becoming the Workshop of the world, and it is no surprise that the economic principles of Adam Smith were scorned in Continental Europe in the

18-16

generations to follow. When Britain dominated the manufactures and export markets of the world by the middle of the 19th century, the "economic truths" of Adam Smith, together with the "Manchesterismus" of the Free Traders and Richard Cobden, must have seemed very cynical to her European neighbours.

14   But stemming also from the philosophy of laissez-faire was something far more than mere economic principles: it was an attitude to life and a complete *Weltanschauung*, and unless we understand these latter factors, we shall never comprehend the real reasons for our contemporary blindness to our true economic condition. Laissez-faire, or letting things be, not only entails an intense individualism, an impatience with co-operative values, and the necessity for optimism, but belief in an economic system whereby any individual is able to participate freely in the capitalist process.

15   An opportunity is open to the humblest individual, but this belief is only made ideologically viable through the failure of Anglo-Saxon capitalism to openly recognise the difference between those who hold and lend capital on the one hand, and those who use it for a productive purpose on the other. The unity of purpose between capital and enterprise is conceived by laissez-faire philosophy as an inseparable component, the one unable to exist without the other. This conceptual distortion in the light of contemporary reality, of course, only exists in the popular mind, but it is nevertheless ideologically essential in maintaining confidence and justification for the Rentier capitalistic system. If, for example, a clear distinction was made between the owners of capital and the users of capital, as actually exists in the Anglo-Saxon world, then the moral basis for the Rentier capitalistic system would begin to fall apart.[77]

16   There is one aspect of this ideology, however, that extends beyond the realm of the popular mind, for it is intrinsic to the effective working of the system: and that is Confidence. Confidence in this context has now taken on an alarmingly mystical quality, for whilst it is based on no rational criteria, it is the one quality that government and top businessmen attempt to evoke as an essential factor for revival against all other odds pointing irrefutably to further decline.

---

[77] Small scale proprietorial business naturally entails a unity between the ownership and use of capital, but our argument is that the macro-economics of the particular capitalistic system, ultimately decides the success or failure of the total business community, as well as that of the rest of society. The greater drive towards acquisition and the erosion of the proprietorial sector within the rentier capitalistic system, constantly changes the pattern of ownership as it destroys the autonomous Productive careers of great numbers of people. The best that these producers (or ex-directors) can hope for after the event of acquisition is to slip quietly into the status of becoming comfortable rentiers. The psychological re-adaptation needed for an employed status is more likely to reduce them to ghosts of their former selves.

18-18

Confidence, therefore, is nothing more than an artificial self-delusive instrument for creating optimism in the face of a system now lacking rationality in its attempt to meet world competition. Furthermore, the notion that it is credible for Britain to "talk herself from a recession into a slump," suggested as a major danger by leading government officials and industrialists, is merely the gross absurdity of those refusing to turn their attention to the *real* problems of the economy. It is pertinent to note that this obsession with "Confidence" will not be found when searching through the business press of our competitors, as the latter are too busily involved in promoting the productive process.

17   Originally Confidence reflected nothing more than an earnest hope for the "ships' safe return to the home port" without shipwreck or hindrance; and subsequently, it came to mean a trust in the healthy state of the stock market against the multitude of unpredictable and often irrational factors adversely effecting shares. But the need for Confidence pervaded the entire business sector, as the risk factors for both lenders and borrowers were generally far greater than those experienced within the productive capitalistic systems of our competitors.

This is because of the greater divide between lenders and borrowers in the rentier capitalistic system, and because loans tended to be granted on the basis of "hunches" and trust in the character of those who were to direct productive concerns. The personalities of those who were going to utilise capital has always been given a closer scrutiny than the schemes they were responsible for initiating, simply because funding institutions have never had the time, inclination nor expertise to enter fully into the nitty-gritty of productivity. There has also developed a cultural divide between financiers and manufacturers from whom the latter borrowed, and this has given rise to much sociological study over recent years.[78]

18   The dominance of the risk factor, and the need for this magic quality called Confidence, has especially been furthered over recent years by the mode of capitalisation within conglomerates. The need of corporate   organisations to demonstrate profits and pay out generous dividends has placed impossible strains on the many subsidiary enterprises within their groups.

In the effort to quicken and maximise returns, a game of musical chairs has been . played out in the world of business, whereby productive concerns judged sluggish or not sufficiently profitable, have simply been sold-off, asset-stripped or closed down.

---

[78] The most notable study is by the American, Martin J. Wiener, in his *English Culture & The Decline of The Industrial Spirit*, Cambridge UP, 1981.

18-19

Hence the chief executives of plants answerable to a higher authority, have not only felt themselves placed in a situation of extreme instability, but subjected to financial constraints that were totally unreasonable bearing in mind the demands of their particular industries. The takeover of weak independent firms has too often entailed a move from the frying pan into the fire, because the corporate management of acquisitive concerns have had little understanding of the financial viability of long-term manufacturing.

19   The uncertainty and fear throughout the British business community arising from the decreasing feasibility of the rentier capitalistic system to promote productivity against the more effective systems of our competitors, has had a paralysing effect, leading to a closing of minds rather than to an environment more conducive to open discussion. As businessmen and women cling desperately to the ideology of laissez-faire, they can only resort to the Micawberism of hoping that "something will turn up," because their intense individualism and trust in the "invisible hand" militates against the idea of co-operation, or organised structural measures that might assist in regenerating the economy.

The anti-intellectualism of the laissez-faire philosophy, and the "hope against hope" and belief in "Confidence" has now amounted to nothing less than superstition, for superstition is only a combination of myopia and stupidity. As belief is stoked up by the business press that something is "just around the next corner," there is all the more impatience with analysis or solutions attempting to penetrate the root cause of our problems. Compare this with the rational capitalistic systems of our competitors that operate with the tidy mind and precision of a clockwork mechanism !

There are those who work in the dark and those who work in the light. How can we expect to compete on a playing field where the conditions so differ for the separate teams ?

CHAPTER 19
Irreconcilable Economies Within The Industrial World

"Big business in Japan after World War II organised itself to build political responsibility into its decision-making process, while successfully pursuing its own business interests. The Japanese big companies ... learned to start out not with the question 'What is good for business ?' but 'What is good for Japan ?'"

Peter Drucker, *The New Realities*, Heinemann Professional Publishing, 1989, p. 87.

1 - National versus International economic systems   2 - How these effect society   3 - Criticism of the City fails to identify the problem   4 - Crisis facing the Anglo-Saxon economies   5 - Incompatibility of Productive and Rentier capitalism   6 - Although mutable they remain distinct   7 - Historical comparison between the systems   8 - Rentier capitalism entails capital accumulation into fewer hands   9 - Financial reserves do not necessarily contribute to business efficiency   10 - Why deficit funding stimulates greater productivity   11 - The rearguard action of the lone laissez-faire enterprise   12 - Individualism versus Co-operation as cultural factors   13 - Complex technology puts a premium on co-operation   14 - Cultural factors must yield to economic necessity

1   The greatest impediment of all confronting Britain is the fact that whilst all our major competitors promote systems of economic nationalism, Britain promotes a system of economic internationalism. This requires precise definition.

It does not refer to the political system *per se*, but to the financial system pulling all the real levers of power behind the socio-political establishment. Much is spoken nowadays about the phony economy and the real economy. These equate respectively with the interests of the Rentier and Productive economies. Whilst appreciating the fact that international conglomerates are situated worldwide, it should be noted that their autonomous status differs from one country to another. Whilst in Britain they are granted an almost absolute freedom, amongst our competitors they are constrained or directed in such a way as to bring greater benefits to the productivity of the host country.

2   The financial institutions of our competitors lay overriding emphasis on investment in home-based industry. This is because of the closer link between government and those institutions, and also because the latter were often initiated by government for the specific purpose of promoting home-based industry. Resulting from this is full employment, higher living standards and a healthy balance of payments.

In Britain, because of our long imperial tradition, our financial institutions are internationally oriented in a very special way. The loss of empire has not made an iota

19-4

of difference to reversing this trend - in fact with the emergence of newly independent countries, there has been an accelerated surge in overseas investment - not to mention irresponsible lending on a massive scale by the clearing banks. For hundreds of years (well before the industrial revolution) the City has always been a law unto itself, and no government at its peril has dared to oppose it.[79]

3   Nevertheless, over recent decades, with our deepening relative and now absolute economic decline, and with the frightening sell-off of British industry to foreign concerns, and the transformation of one-time profitable plants into unskilled low labour-cost assembly only operations, increasing numbers of people throughout our country are asking, is this right ? The finger is pointed at the City, mumblings of complaint are heard, but because of the confusion in thinking, no specific accusations are made.

The increasing level of corruption charges made against the City, bad as these may be, are only an irrelevance, since they do not begin to identify the real underlying issues adversely effecting the economy. So, too, accusations of mismanagement against the City are no less beside the point than the conspiracy theories of vested interest groups. The City merely continues to progress along its traditional path, confident in its purpose, and oblivious to the widening gap between the phony and real economies. The justification for its existence is in its service to investors, and in that, its integrity is untarnished and its efficiency unassailable. Seemingly, there is no reason to question its complacent self-assurance.

4   The fact that two planets are destined to collide is something of which the City seems entirely unaware. It is an external factor, having little to do with the purely international ambience of the City's activities. The approaching planet is the threat of Productive capitalism. It is something which will not only hit Britain but also north America and the other Anglo-Saxon economies.

The decline of US manufacturing, in relative terms, has possibly reached a greater downturn than that in Britain. Americans today are haunted by the Japanese effect; deeply concerned that all their technological consumables emanate from across the Pacific. From being the world's greatest creditor nation fifty years ago, America is today burdened by a massive debt, in addition to growing unemployment, poverty, crime, and other social ills on a horrific scale. It may be asked, How has it been

---

[79] Note the pityingly helpless cry of that weak monarch, Henry III, to his Parliament in 1248: "I know that if the treasure of imperial Rome was to be sold, that London would take and buy it all. These London clowns, who call themselves barons, are rich to loathing. The City is an inexhaustible well." Quoted in J.E. Thorold Rogers', *Six Centuries of Work & Wages*, Swan Sonnenschein & Co., 1909 ed., p. 108.

19-7

possible for the world's top nation to sink so soon into such depths ?

5   Economic causes alone must be sought to explain these very economic factors, for an attempt at any other explanation would merely be an excursus into sociological fantasy. The only objective explanation that I can reach after more than forty years of hard practical experience in the world of business, in addition to many years of careful academic research, is that with the emergence of the Productive capitalistic system of our competitors, Rentier capitalism was doomed to eventual extinction. The two modes of capitalism are incompatible in a world open to free trade, for the one will destroy the other; as similarly Cro-Magnon and Neanderthal man could not survive together in mutual partnership on the same planet.

6   For a better understanding of what this means, we must take a closer look at the two contrasting modes of capitalism. As we noted earlier, neither system is immutable, and in examining particular countries in either camp, it will be found that neither system is pure in a theoretical sense. Furthermore, the systems are everywhere in a constant state of change. The rentier and productive capitalistic systems of Britain and America or Germany and Japan, are different from what they were forty years ago, and even more different from what they were 100 years ago. Nevertheless, the two systems, despite their degrees of similarity, as may be found in different areas, are sufficiently contrasting and incompatible in their modes of operation to be distinguished as two quite separate types of capitalism.

7   Although Rentier capitalism may claim the original status of "true" or "Classical" capitalism, and although its most ardent proponents may argue it is the only "proper" capitalism, this only applies in the context of the high point of the laissez-faire industrial revolution. Productive capitalism may trace its earlier origins to the Mercantilist policies of the Continental powers of the 17th century. Although contemporary Productive capitalism is vastly different in its economic influences on society from that of the 17th century, it may still be described as mercantilism with a veneer of free trade. Nevertheless, it has a long and successful legacy.

Rentier capitalism (in its most developed form) on the other hand, in the economic history of the modern world has a tradition of relatively short duration. It flourished in full flower, in the Anglo-Saxon societies, from the end of the 18th to the middle of the 20th century. Its success during this period in disseminating industrialisation on a worldwide scale cannot be questioned, even if the concentration of that industrialisation at its centre was severely weakened during the latter part of that period. A comparison between the two systems is best made in the light of contemporary conditions, for only now can they be contrasted in their most polarised

19-11

forms, as these effect the many aspects of society.

8   To describe Rentier capitalism as "money capitalism" would be a tautology, but what is really meant by such a term is the emphasis on capital accumulation. Rentier capitalism entails the control of capital into fewer hands, i.e. *vis-à-vis* the management of the Productive modes of economy. This accumulation of wealth into fewer hands is demonstrated in many ways: e.g., by the greater presence of joint stock companies; the greater tendency towards monopoly amongst a number of conglomerates representing a diversity of activities; a larger size in the average firm (when like is compared with like); higher salaries paid to directors; and a greater scale between the average of highest and lowest earnings in the industrial field, as well as in other occupational spheres.

9   It is only to be expected that deficit funded businesses would be less cushioned against exigencies than firms self-funded by proprietors or shareholders or profits held in reserve. And this has exactly been the case. It is not so many years ago when our own business press was flattering British companies on the grounds of enjoying a healthier situation than their German rivals, as the former traditionally held a fatter margin of capital in reserve. The complacency of this boast failed to take into account a comparison of the activities of British and German companies. The only sound criteria for measuring the potential success of a manufacturing firm is its intention and achievement in capturing greater market share, for even assessing growth on a year-to-year basis within the perspective of the world stage is a vain and meaningless exercise. This is because relative and not absolute growth has any meaning. If a company experiences an annual growth rate of 10% whilst those of its foreign competitors are 30%, that is no cause for self-congratulation. History has amply demonstrated that the company with plenty of fat tends not to respond effectively in the face of surging competition.

10   Why has this been so ? The reasons are not far to seek. As we have already noted, the deficit funded company is constantly under the pressure of an external source: viz., its bank, and the long-term programme of a contractual nature designed to guarantee commercial success. There is no possibility of diverting from the straight and narrow. There must be no diversification, and no opportunity for the butterfly mentality to take flight. In addition, the will of government, and an assortment of planning authorities, are all committed to the success of even the smallest enterprise. Compare this situation with that of the average British firm. It has its financial reserves, but it stands alone in an alien and dangerous world.

11   In a laissez-faire environment everyone stands apart. "Lame ducks" must go

19-14

under: that's the message of government.   The great moral value is a gritty individualism, and so when the going gets tough, there must be a stiff upper lip and a discreet silence. In difficult times the motto must be Caution, and so reserves are maintained. Of course, shareholders must be paid their dividends - that's the top priority - as otherwise investments might be withdrawn and placed elsewhere. Meanwhile, accountants must desperately scratch around for ways of demonstrating the greater valuation of the company. As for further re-investment in modernising the company, the answer has to be a decisive, No ![80]

12   The alternative, of course, is a butterfly approach to business. That means a crazy diversification implemented by a team of "half-amateurs," but as a high value is placed on individualism, the approach is not perceived as dilettantism. A flowery imagination is appreciated as an individual value, but in some countries it would be condemned as "eccentricity."   Across the North Sea, for example, the word "Exzentrisch" has a purely pejorative meaning - its existence arousing only a feeling of disgust and contempt. In societies where the greater moral value is Co-operation - it may be Japan or Sweden or Singapore or Switzerland (no less than Germany) - individualism is judged an ugly anti-social characteristic, best subordinated in the struggle for national wealth creation. This is a cultural factor distinguishing Rentier from Productive capitalism - possibly the most important sociological reality of all.

13   It may be, of course, that the increased complexity of technology and the industrial infrastructure, over the past 100 years, has turned the tables on us. That is, whilst individualism was undoubtedly of benefit to industrial society in the age of Crompton and Arkwright, it is far less so in the age of the blue chip. Whilst British inventors have a hard time in almost any circumstances, those of our competitors must usually co-operate in teams as the employees of specialised bodies. The successful entrepreneurial inventor is now a rare animal, as the costs of research and development (not to mention technological complexity) are so considerable, that co-operation and multiple-brain power is now essential for all stages of innovation.

14   Although the cultural differences between the Anglo-Saxon peoples and those of the Productive capitalist economies must be appreciated as a factor of existence, those differences must finally yield to an underlying analysis of economic causation. Cultural characteristics should not be confused with economic factors. Economic systems deciding the fate of peoples, should be judged primarily as the ultimate cause

---

[80] On the reluctance of British industry to invest, see OECD, *The Growth of Output 1960-1980*, Paris, 1970.

20-1
responsible for the material well-being of peoples. Few would doubt such a contention.

If individualism, for example, acts as a cultural factor in retarding an economic system - even if only through default, in failing to meet the competition of an alternative system - then individualism, in that particular context, should be condemned as undermining the well-being of society. Meanwhile, if the spirit of Co-operation acts as an incidental factor in oiling the wheels of the Productive mode of capitalism, then co-operation, in that context, should be upheld as a moral virtue. This, after all, is only a utilitarian argument. Nothing is gained by sentimentalising over the age-old memory of how a rugged individualism once glorified our historical past. The significant point today is that the Anglo-Saxon economies are falling to a stronger and more efficient system of production.

It is no time to justify the system that is failing us. If changes must be made to our attitudes and character in adapting to a new system of productive capitalism - and I do not think they need necessarily be so difficult or painful - then such changes must go ahead. After all, it is a question of survival.

CHAPTER 20
Rentier Versus Productive Profits: A New Criteria For Financial Management

"One reason ... for the general suspicion of business is that companies
do harm as well as good, and plenty of it besides."

Bill Emmott, *Japan's Global Reach*, Century, 1992, p. 25.

1 - Accumulated capital tends towards idle use   2 - Distinction between Invested and Active capital   3 - Financial movement promotes productivity   4 - Productive capitalism promotes the use of Active capital   5 - How Productive business utilises capital   6 - This contrasted with the Rentier business   7 - How the Rentier concern maximises money profits   8 - Need for refining the definition of profit   9 - Cause of Anglo-Saxon economic decline has never been clearly identified   10 - Distinction between Rentier and Productive profits   11 - On the validity of this argument   12 - Identifying the Rentier characteristics of an enterprise   13 - Multiplicity of factors prevents a concise economic law   14 - Value of Productive Profitability as a diagnostic tool   15 - As it goes to the heart of the objective business process   16 - It is the sole criteria for assessing sound decision-making

1   The contrast between the Rentier and Productive modes of capitalism is most clearly seen through an analysis of the use of financial resources, and this issue is central to the thesis of the present chapters.

As is clearly evident, Rentier capitalism entails the accumulation of greater financial resources into fewer hands, and wherever capital is accumulated it tends towards disuse. Accumulated capital may accrue interest or be used as collateral for

20-3

a specific purpose, but it nonetheless exists, for a longer or shorter term, in a passive or idle form.

Most economists would agree that in certain feudal societies in the pre-industrial age, e.g., in 17th century Spain, that accumulated capital was idle and hence hindered development; but they might be less willing to draw a parallel conclusion with regard to advanced industrial countries like Britain or America in the 20th century. This is because most accumulated capital in these latter countries is invested, and hence undergoing a *use* as capital lent for business development or public projects, or to accrue interest for future use in the form of pensions, the maturity of life plans, etc.

2 Nevertheless, a clear distinction must still be made between Invested and Active capital: the latter entailing either the movement of money from one individual to another, for the purchase and sale of products and services usually in the domestic sector, or else its *immediate* direction into specific productive purposes in the business sector. The distinction between invested and active capital, therefore, in the context of this discussion, is that the latter moves at a faster rate of speed.

It should be remembered that money is an abstract medium of exchange, only beginning to take on value through *use*, but it achieves a greater value in terms of national wealth creation through *direct use* or as active capital. It is disregarded by the majority, and certainly in a rentier capitalistic society, that money is in itself *not* wealth but only a medium towards creating wealth. Capital, as an economic term in the meaning of equipment, skills, and personnel invested for production, as distinguished from the mere accumulation of money, is correctly defined as wealth, but our purpose is to further dissect the meaning of capital used in reference to financial sources only.

3 If the above conclusions are true - and they have been reached through inductive methods and not mere abstract reasoning - then wealth creation is best promoted by ensuring (if not maximising) the speedy movement of financial resources. This means, of course, exerting a pressure on the majority of the population to buy and sell products and services, but *only* within the framework of stimulating UK-based productivity. And there's the rub !

This is where all governments have failed to correct the British economy, for fiscal policies only tinker with the money supply, and at best, create an "over-heating" of the economy which means the sucking-in of imports. That is why only structural measures can be hoped to regenerate productivity, but such measures would need to go beyond the powers within the usual remit of government. These structural measures entail identifying UK-based productive activities, and separating them for investment purposes, from all other business activities, so that the first could be promoted

20-5

.effectively. There can be no prosperity for Britain as long as the dog of the international markets is allowed to wag the national tail. Hence the present situation must be reversed.A further reason for the sluggish movement of money within the body of rentier capitalistic societies, arises from the constant effort of government to suppress wages and control inflation, but both these problems stem primarily from excessive imports. Imports have now become a ruinous burden on the public purse, and no political group is able or willing to offer a satisfactory solution.

Instead, parliamentary government (irrespective of party) is quite prepared to reduce the spending power of the ordinary citizen to protect the interests of foreign competitors as an alternative to import controls. In a Productive capitalist economy, by contrast, such problems do not arise since the promotion of home-based manufacturing prevents these ills. Consequently, economic policy allows the ordinary citizen a greater margin for expenditure above his immediate needs.

4   But this is only part of the explanation in illustrating how the use of financial resources differ within the contrasting economic systems. As we have already noted, Britain's vast accumulated wealth stems from her imperial tradition, and the particular characteristics of her rentier economy have influenced every aspect of financial management down to the smallest firm. We have already made general comparisons between the styles of Anglo-Saxon businesses and those of the competitors, but we must now observe more closely the differences in financial control and the contrasted outcome.

The deficit funded enterprises of our competitors are not simply more wealth creative and successful than their counterparts in the Anglo-Saxon world on account of heavier investment in modernisation, but because capital is forced to move at a faster rate of productive growth.

The fact that our competitors invest for the longer term, enjoying longer accountancy and taxation periods, might seem to contradict this contention, but that would be a misunderstanding of the true situation. All investment in machinery, methods and personnel, not expected to see a return on capital until after a prolonged period, entails the use of Active capital. Furthermore, all such investment is only undertaken in conjunction with a dynamic long-term strategy.

5   Deficit funded businesses use their capital as and when it is received, and so this becomes active capital. When profits eventually begin to accrue, these are used for re-paying loans or for further re-investment, after the settlement of immediate costs. Of course there are other shareholders in the business besides the bank, but their proportional significance in terms of status or control is on average minimal by

20-7

comparison with the Anglo-Saxon concern.

All these factors place great pressures on the enterprise - but of quite a different kind from those placed on the rentier managed business - but because the former is managed on strictly rational principles, it is usually destined for a successful future. As deficit funded businesses are granted low-cost long-term loans, the interest repaid on the latter should be deemed productive financial transactions, for the reason that they form part of an integrated financial package designed *primarily* to benefit the enterprise and its productive purpose.

6   Now compare this with the very different situation of the Anglo-Saxon enterprise managed according to rentier capitalistic principles.   It begins with a financial philosophy which is in reverse to that of the productive capitalistic concern, viz., that the first purpose of the company is to maximise shareholders' profits. This is not merely an abstract idea which begins and ends with a vague statement of purpose, but is actually implemented in every financial decision of the company. As will be seen below, it does everything to contradict the productive purpose of the company, i.e. the maximising of market share for a specifically defined product or service. In the Anglo-Saxon world the emphasis of the company's activities is driven towards pure money profits, howsoever these may be achieved.

There is nothing surprising in this, since the only interest of the shareholders and controllers of the company is maximising the return on investment. There is usually, of course, a complete separation between the owners of the company and those who manage it, and along with this, goes a separation of understanding and sympathy for the productive process. As regards the entrepreneurial concern, as soon as this is taken over and incorporated within a group, which is increasingly the case today in the Anglo-Saxon economies, then a divorce between the interests of the financial owners of the company and its true productive purpose almost invariably follows.

7   The following are common methods of maximising money profits whilst limiting the productive purpose of the company:-

1. Limiting the intended market sector for the sale of the product;
2. Assuming a superior image for the product which does not meet the reality of the existing competition;
3. Imposing an unjustified price-raising strategy;
4. Reducing the quality of the product in maintaining an established price level;
5. Postponing necessary re-investment in plant and methods;
6. Allowing relative wage levels to slide so that better workers are lost to other enterprises;

20-9

7. Factoring in products from the Far East or elsewhere, so that UK plants may be slimmed down;

8. Transforming a factory into an assembly only operation, so that the wage bill may be reduced in employing only semi- or unskilled staff;

9. Selling off capital assets to demonstrate the end-of-year profits for the company;

10. Diversification into short-term or unstable projects;

11. Rigging the share valuation of the company by whatever means; and,

12. Hiring and firing on the basis of buying in fresh skills cheaply and clearing out redundant skills, so that wage bills may be minimised and training costs evaded.

8   Now the purpose of every company *should* be to maximise profits, but in analysing and comparing the purposes and outcome of enterprises managed according to either rentier or productive principles, as we find them in the world today, it has become abundantly clear that the term Profit requires a finer definition than it has hitherto been given.

Business people in Britain and America behave as if the rentier mode of production existed in a self-enclosed world of its own. Perhaps they cannot be blamed for this as they have no other experience of alternative types of business. When British manufacturers factor in products from abroad, or cut back on investment, or resort to any of the other strategies listed above, they rationalise those actions as hard-headed realism. They are motivated solely by the need to maximise profits. If rentier capitalism existed in a self-enclosed world, then such strategies could be justified as sound; but in a world faced by the aggressive methods of productive capitalism, such strategies are doomed to failure in the longer term.

9   The core economic principles responsible for the decimation of productivity in the Anglo-Saxon countries have never before been properly exposed to the light of day. This is probably because their business communities have existed hitherto in the blinding light of laissez-faire ideology.

If one considers the cultural, social or political reasons usually given for Anglo-American decline, their absurdity becomes quickly apparent, for they are superficial and vague causes that cannot be linked to specific economic factors. They fail to offer a dialectic, i.e. a core principle approaching a scientific method for investigating the problem. This is not to suggest that cultural and other given causes are entirely without significance, but that they are subsidiary or symptomatic of the underlying economic causes - or at least they have to be understood as such in formulating a solution.

20-12

10   Profit, therefore, divides into two types, according to the surrounding circumstances in which it is created: there are Rentier profits, entailing the maximisation of profits for a beneficial purpose external to the enterprise; and there are Productive profits, promoting the longer term productive internal interests of the company. Whilst Rentier profitability has a shorter term view of the future and best flourishes in a usurious environment; Productive profitability is constrained by the moral purpose of labour linked to the fusion of capital for a specific productive purpose. The above principles and causes emerge entirely from the observation of concrete facts in the world as we find it.

11   It is important to underline this point as certain economic theorists might choose to question the validity of the above definitions. They might ask, for example, Where is the mathematical formulae to demonstrate the general principle ? When do Rentier profits merge into Productive profits ? Where is the borderline ? The answer to these objections is that we are here dealing with a multiplicity of facts that do not easily lend themselves to the concise definition of a mathematical law.

The totality of the company's efforts must always be held in view in deciding as to whether it is managed according to rentier or productive principles. False conclusions will be reached if the company is divided into component parts for analysis, or if an analysis does not take into consideration the surrounding circumstances in which the company is obliged to operate. For example, the best long-term interests of a company are not promoted when accountancy factors are given an overriding priority, as is usually the case in the Anglo-Saxon economies, for too often, other vital factors (such as strategic re-investment needs) are pushed aside conveniently.

12   Rentier and Productive profits may be seen in their sharpest outline when two comparable companies, one failing and one successful, are taken from each of the economic systems, and comparisons made: take, for example, a French, Italian or a German car manufacturer and compare it with a British car manufacturer; or take a Japanese computer manufacturer and compare it with a British computer manufacturer. A proper comparison entails not merely the internal management of the respective companies, but also their external relations with regard to taxation, government help or hindrance, other assisting bodies, other regulations, etc. After an exhaustive investigation, for anything less would fail to produce an accurate and balanced diagnosis, patterns and tendencies will emerge. From such a clinical examination, Rentier or Productive characteristics in the financial management of the company will appear, pointing to the need for ridding undesirable rentier characteristics within the

20-14

company in assisting its competitive struggle.

It should be noted, however, that the rentier characteristics of one company might not be deemed as rentier faults in another, for reasons of temporary strategy, or the different circumstances of an industry, or because of other balancing situations within a firm that complement or necessitate a characteristic that might otherwise be condemned as a rentier shortcoming. For example, manufacturing for the purpose of obsolescence is unquestionably a rentier practice, but there are justifiable circumstances (few as they may be) when the quality of a product may be reduced.

This occurs when the perception of a product loses it value in the eye of the public relative to the perceived value of other consumables. But such quality reduction is then only justifiable if it gives no rise for complaint or nuisance to purchasers. Some years ago in West Germany, for example, the products of a leading British vacuumware company lost their appeal to the market as the quality was "too high." German buyers demanded a materially inferior and cheaper product in meeting competition, and this the British company could not supply. The relevant factor deciding rentier or productive practices is always the maximisation of market share for the longer term. Such variable situations do not therefore lend themselves to slick economic theories.

These, then, are the reasons which would make the demand for a mathematical law defining Rentier or Productive profitability an absurdity. The multiplicity of facts and circumstances contributing to the success of a company *vis-à-vis* the problems raised by its competitors are so complex, that only *relevant* general tendencies should be sought in making a sound diagnosis in preparation for a cure. The existence of Rentier and Productive capitalism as two quite separate systems of production are facts that are no less evident than the existence of the sun, and mathematical formulae proving the existence of the latter adds nothing to the conviction of what we already know - and could only contribute unnecessarily to confusion. The post-War success of Japan and West Germany, and many other economies, is due to business practices quite different from those in the Anglo-Saxon world, and these practices we have identified and compared from an objective standpoint.

14   But the importance of Productive profitability extends far beyond its mere discovery as a fact in itself. As a concept it acts as an invaluable diagnostic tool in testing the health or sickness of any business concern, or privatised public body, or other association managed on a profit or loss account. Although the criteria when applied to assessing the financial management of a voluntary association would not exert the invaluable social benefits as when applied to great commercial enterprises, it would nonetheless be beneficial in avoiding waste and ensuring that expenditure is

20-16

put to a better use.

15   The value of the Productive criteria stems from the degree of its objectivity, for it goes to the heart of the business process whilst at the same time eliminating entirely all those subjective components of which any enterprise is composed. As a criterion assessing the sound management of a company, it is not concerned with the different interest groups or departments of an enterprise, such as workers, shareholders, middle or senior management, etc., but rather with those central factors bringing all interests into a unified whole.

The individual, for example, who chooses to support the rentier as opposed to the productive interests of the company, once those separate routes have been identified, is quite simply betraying the enterprise - irrespective of whether he or she happens to be the Chairperson or the tea boy. Hence the criteria is a great leveller of people, for it idealises the company as an end in itself so that those who would claim the right to "own" or "control" or "use" the enterprise for a selfish purpose must yield to a higher authority.

This, however, is not to suggest that it is always practicable to avoid the rentier capitalistic route, for the external constraints of a company within a rentier economy may offer no other alternative. But the criteria is nonetheless there for pointing out a better route for an ideal future. It is always of value as a marker for the truth, so that pressures for change may be envisaged in the right direction.

16   Although the concept of productive profitability may not easily lend itself to a concise mathematical law, for reasons already explained, the underlying principles have been sufficiently elaborated in these chapters to form the basis for greater in-depth discussion as the criteria may be applied to different sectors of industry. This is a vital task if serious measures are to be taken in reversing British industrial decline. It is an intellectual task that should be primarily opened to management consultants and advisers, and the accountancy profession.

Productive profitability is the sole criteria that should be used in discussing best business policy, for it will be found that all problems within the major organisation or the smaller firm, may be reduced to the question of rentier or productive motivated decision-making, irrespective of whether it is a question of re-investment, retrenchment, the design and manufacture of new products, re-location, increasing or decreasing salary scales, etc. The utility of the criteria is simply to be found in its concentration on the most relevant components of the productive business process.

21-2

CHAPTER 21
Building Structures For Prosperity

"The universal addition to growth and expansion is becoming stronger than all other ideologies. ... The idea that growth can be obstructive, unhealthy, or pathological is not entertained. What we urgently need ... is differentiation and qualification of the concept of growth."

Fritjof Capra, *The Turning Point*, Wildwood House, 1982, pp. 224 & 225.

1 - Criteria for successful economic policy once ignored the majority   2 - Rentier economies lean towards the older criteria   3 - Britain wracked by two "economies"   4 - Definition of the economic divide   5 - Why Productive economies are more democratic   6 - As contrasted with our own   7 - Strains between the two capitalist systems   8 - The 10 proposals for industrial regeneration   9 - Forestalling the objection of the rentier establishment   10 - On implementing the proposals   11 - The world recession presents an unpredictable future   12 - No suggestion to replicate specific conditions   13 - A dialectic for progress.

1   No general economic topic can be considered that ignores entirely social issues, and this is more true today than in the past. In a more historical period it was possible (or at least customary) to appreciate the economic decision-making of governments purely on the basis of the accumulation of national power *vis-à-vis* competitors, even though in the process immense hardship may have been inflicted on the majority who were trampled on.

For example, although we can still appreciate the wisdom of Colbert and Turgot as great economic thinkers and administrators, for both (especially the former) actively promoted Productive wealth in their struggle against rentier capitalistic tendencies, the environment in which they flourished in the 17th and 18th centuries took little account of the masses. Despite the underlying justice or equity of their intentions, their policies were unable to filter through to the bulk of the population. Today there is no longer a voiceless proletariat or peasantry whose condition may simply be ignored.

2   In the democratic industrialised world, therefore, governments of every hue are obliged to measure economic performance against the welfare of the majority - or at least, pretend to do so. Nevertheless, in the rentier capitalistic societies, because of the greater accumulation of wealth into fewer hands and because of the international trading culture, there is a leaning towards an older attitude in assessing the value of economic performance. In both America and Britain there is undoubtedly a social retardation in the approach to the economically disadvantaged , by comparison with conditions pertaining in the Productive economies of Continental North West Europe.

21-4

3   These factors exert an influence in the social and political spheres that transcends the level of mere party politics. Britain's financial imperial tradition, which as we have noted, remains unbroken despite the loss of empire, has given rise to two separate "economies" coexisting together - or at least, to two separate economic interests.

The relevant fact is that it is the imperial or international interest of incoming and outgoing investments, and the need to maintain a high value for the pound, that has always been given overwhelming preference by the Treasury,[81] and no British premier in the post-War period has ever been able to reverse that trend - not even for a temporary period. There is clearly a conflict of interest between the home and international "economies," and occasionally statesmen have burst out in exasperation against the latter. Back in the 60s, for example, Harold Wilson, exclaimed that, "the Treasury was always trying to hold down production."

4   It is only natural that the closed world of the City should turn its back on the nation as it looks out to the world in developing its "greater" interests. The City institutions are autonomous bodies and proud of that fact, since they see themselves representing financial markets in their freest form. They are only responsible to themselves, or rather to the Treasury, which de facto, they control.

Since all investing institutions, public bodies, trades unions, pension funds, etc., are linked to the City, the latter has immense power and might dispute the contention that actually two parallel economies coexist. Our argument, however, is that two economies have emerged through a situation of default: i.e. that the cash-starvation of home-based industry and its gradual demise and inability to compete, in conjunction with unemployment and increasing poverty, have reached a scale the effects of which our political institutions are unable to overcome, even though theoretically, the country may possess the financial resources to ease the situation.

Those resources, however, cannot be touched by government since their legal ownership lies elsewhere. There exists in this country today, two underlying separate and irreconcilable wills transcending the sphere of mere party conflict: viz., the Political versus the Financial; or Parliament versus the City. It is this situation which defines the

---

[81]   This is supported most vividly by the following: F. Longstreth, "The City, Industry & The State," in *State & Economy In Contemporary Capitalism*, C. Crouch (ed.), Croom Helm, 1979; and, Sir J. Stamp's "The Report of The Macmillan Committee," *Economic Journal*, 41, 424-35, 1931. The return to gold at an overvalued parity, in favour of the City, during the interwar period, for example, was one of the most damaging episodes to home-based productivity in the 20th century. It devastated our exports. This has been best illustrated by the following: D.E. Moggridge, *British MonetaryPolicy1924-31*, Cambridge UP, 1972, and L.S. Pressnell, "1925: The Burden of Sterling," *Economic History Review*, 2nd sere., 31, 67-88, 1978.

21-7

existence of two economies existing side by side, and these are constantly referred to by the media under the terms of "phony" and "real." In this way the majority of our population are sacrificed on the altar of international trading interests.

5   But the social effects of the rentier capitalistic system extend much further than those influences indicated above. Under the productive mode of capitalism, with its decentralisation and greater dissemination of wealth through the deficit funding of huge numbers of small independent businesses - as well as larger concerns - there is a more open and classless society, since a higher proportion of the population are drawn directly into the wealth-creating process. A greater exchange of information has to be made available just to ensure efficiency.

In a rentier capitalistic society, on the contrary, secrecy is not only more widespread, but much of it is institutionalised, not only in bodies of law like the Official Secrets Act, but in company regulations segregating information which in other countries would be freely open to inspection.

6   Much of this is motivated by the wish to suppress envy, but instead, it generates suspicion and resentment. Accumulated wealth on a vast scale cannot be maintained without safeguarding privilege. Britain's refusal to subscribe to the Social Charter, and the fact that she has been dragged before the International Court for Human Rights on more occasions than her neighbours, is no mere coincidence. Although such internationalised questions may be politicised in Britain as left/right issues, they are no longer seen in that light in Continental Europe, where they are accepted as basic rights across the spectrum as a matter of course.

All these differences between ourselves and our neighbours arise solely from the cause of our very different economic system. Although these differences may be seen predominantly as social or moral questions, they nonetheless possess an economic dimension, and so on all grounds should demand our attention. It should not be forgotten that the efficiency and dynamism of our industrial competitors owes much to the presence of social justice.

7   What practical steps are required in solving the issues raised in this book ? Firstly, full recognition has to be given to the fact that we cannot rebuild a sound economy without constructing a productive capitalist system. And neither can we participate as full and equal members of the EU without a Productive economy, for all our present problems with our European neighbours stem from the misunderstandings and difficulties of a different mode of production.

Furthermore, the trade war now looming between America and Europe results solely from the strains between two conflicting capitalistic modes of production. Why

21-8

should America wish to raise tariff barriers against her European friends unless she recognised her own productive failure ? She is desperate to ensure her own survival even if it means contradicting the lynchpin of laissez-faire ideology. As far as Britain is concerned, I do not think that the changes or reforms required need place too great a burden on the existing establishment.

8   First, there is the need to set up a system or an institution whereby investments in exclusively UK-based activities may be specifically identified. Within this category, primary and secondary industries should be distinguished from service sector activities, as potentially contributing more effectively to national wealth creation and a better balance of payments. State publicity, in addition to tax inducements, should then be offered in encouraging investments in the *real* economy. Such a strategy would need to be followed with particular care in avoiding the exacerbation of two parallel economies, for that would trigger the occurrence of Gresham's law whereby there would be a tendency for money of lower intrinsic value to circulate more freely than money of higher intrinsic but equal nominal value - or as it is more commonly expressed, for bad money to drive out good.

Second, UK-based productive plants, irrespective of ownership status, should be obliged to register on a special listing of the Dept. Of Trade & Industry. They should then be subject to inspection as to their productive profitability.[82] In the event of their membership of a group, exploratory moves should then be made for securing their independence as autonomous productive concerns.

Third, in addition to the establishment of credit investment banks of various kinds, serious measures should be taken to extend the commercial functions of the clearing banks, in preparation for the responsible deficit funding of productive

---

[82] Such inspections should be carried out particularly with regard to reluctance to innovate or expand. The historical aspects of this have been revealed in Neil K. Buxton's, "The Role of The 'New' Industries in Britain during the 1930s: A Reinterpretation," *Business History Review*, 49, 205-22, 1975; C.K. Harley's "Skilled Labour & The Choice of Technique in Edwardian Industry," *Explorations In Economic History*, 11, 391-414, 1974; and, W. Arthur Lewis's, "The Deceleration of British Growth 1873-1913," unpublished paper, Princeton, NJ. With regard to counteracting outmoded forms of work organisation at both managerial and shop-floor levels, see especially, A. Kilpatrick & T. Lawson, "On the Nature of Industrial Decline in the UK," *Cambridge Journal of Economics*, 4(1), 85-100, 1980; Leslie Hannah, "Managerial Innovation & The Rise of the Large-Scale Company in Interwar Britain," *Economic History Review*, 2nd ser., 27, 252-70, 1974; Barry Supple, *Essays In British Business History*, OUP, 1977; and, the Central Policy Review Staff's *The Future of The British Car Industry*, HMSO, 1975.

21-8

enterprises.[83]

Fourth, legislation should be initiated for different forms of employee share ownership and investment, designed to suit enterprises of various types and sizes. The creation of equity from housing stock should then be facilitated to promote these purposes. Employee investment and share ownership, however, could only be made to succeed on a realistic basis, in conjunction with co-determination or workers' democracy in partnership with management.

Fifth, employees should be entitled to on-going educational courses in furthering their careers, but in protecting companies from losses in such investment, the former should be bound by long-term contracts of employment entailing the payment of compensation fees in the event of job change. Such long-term contracts towards a status of permanent employment are common in Continental Europe.

Sixth, the government should initiate integrated dynamic industrial planning associations, into which all manufacturing federations should be merged, in preparation for transforming Britain into a unified competitive world power.

Seventh, the DTI should be turned into a financially self sustainable commercial organisation linked to our consular posts abroad, that should operate predominantly as effective trade promotion centres, as is already the case with our competitors. Such an ultimate act of privatisation would amount to the creation of Great Britain plc.

Eighth, government should give a top priority to ensuring stable and appropriate exchange rates designed to promote UK-based exports; and the international pressures of the City in counteracting such a tendency, should simply be pre-empted by building a sufficient level of wealth creation through domestic manufacturing.

Ninth, a high priority should be given to all levels of education, from nursery school upwards, to ensure that the majority of our population enjoy a standard of knowledge and skills matching that or exceeding any of our competitors. Current entry rates of our own population into universities and the remaining polytechnics, for example, need almost to be doubled if we are to match the educational standards of the Japanese or Koreans. The Singaporeans, meanwhile, are five times better educated

---

[83] Overhauling the banks so they might serve more effectively the interests of the *real* economy is a huge and responsible task. It is suggested that the in-depth studies of Carrington and Edwards should be used as a starting base for this purpose. They have produced the following 4 books concerned with this issue, all published by Macmillan, the first two co-authored by J.C. Carrington and George T. Edwards, and the last two by Edwards alone: *Financing Industrial Investment*, 1979; *Reversing Economic Decline*, 1981; *How Economic Growth & Inflation Happen*, 1984; and, *The Role Of the Banks In Economic Development: The Economics of Industrial Resurgence*, 1988.

21-11

than we are in terms of per capita entry into institutes of higher education.

Tenth, as a secure means of creating a pro-industrial ethos, the salaries of scientists, engineers, technicians, and others in the productive sector, must be raised relative to other occupational spheres, in alignment with conditions pertaining amongst our toughest competitors. From a study of advertised vacancies, for example, it will be found that export managers working for manufacturers in Germany earn between four and five times their counterparts in Britain. In addition, state publicity should be used in popularising employment in the primary and secondary industries.

9   The above proposals have been drawn up so as to minimise the possibility of treading on the toes of the rentier establishment, or at least, to forestall serious objection to the urgency or good intention of the proposals made. There is no hiding the ambitious range of the measures outlined but any lesser attempt would be futile. If only half the final intentions were achieved, it would prove a resounding success for our productive economy.

10   Two final remarks must be made on the above proposals: firstly, they are not listed in any order of priority; and secondly, they are complementary to each other in holding together as a unified plan. In other words, for example, it would not only be meaningless but quite wrong to encourage employee investment and share ownership unless government and financial institutions were at the same time realistically committed to the success of UK-based enterprises. How else could employees be expected to use their homes as collateral in investing in industrial enterprises? All the above proposals should be materialised on a controlled time-scale, and if one or several were blocked for whatever reason, the entire project should be deferred until a more propitious future.

11   The analysis and distinction we have made in this book between rentier and productive capitalism stems from the observation of actual conditions over a limited period, and as we have said, neither system is immutable. Both are undergoing a constant state of change, and the future is impossible to predict. In the Far East, over recent years, leading economies have been transferring large sectors of their manufacturing bases to lower labour cost regions, e.g. Japan to Korea (as well as to the rest of the world); Hong Kong to Guangdong province; Taiwan to Fujian province; and Singapore to Shandong as well as to Malaysia and Indonesia.

If these leading economies at the same time experienced a contraction of their home-based productivity, it might be suggested that these were signs of mutation into rentier capitalistic systems, but as yet, this has not been the case. Waves of new productivity are surging forward to replace that which is lost. Only in Singapore is a

21-13

. new financial capitalism seeming to swamp the economy, but this is not due to a loss of manufacturing productivity, but rather to the fact that banks worldwide have chosen to make it their South East Asian financial centre for growth in the years ahead.

In a world recession, as we are now experiencing, economic pressures can nevertheless exert strange and malign influences on the systems of individual states. In Continental Europe, over recent years, in contrast to the Far East situation, rentier capitalistic influences have begun to make some headway. It was against these tendencies that the eminent French economist, Michel Albert, issued his warning in a powerfully prophetic book, *Capitalism Against Capitalism*. Meanwhile, in Scandinavia, the traditional resistance to world-dominating conglomerates has begun to give way. It is impossible to predict how far these tendencies will advance, but it is certain that the long-term well-being and economic stability of the relevant countries will be adversely effected if rentier capitalism is allowed to fester unhindered. When local manufacturers lose market share and profits contract, then business people will scratch around for any means to turn a penny, even if the outcome of their efforts in the longer term is disadvantageous to the national interest.

12   As we remarked at the start of these chapters, in distinguishing most sharply the two capitalistic systems, we have looked at the economies of the leading industrialised nations and sought for what was most typical of their operation over a 50-year period following the Second World War. On the purely empirical evidence of what we have found, we have constructed both the theoretical and practical foundations for regenerating the Anglo-Saxon and world economies. We have sought to idea-lise an economic system the success of which has been proven by experience, but the proposals now put forward are not intended to replicate any particular system of the past. This is not only because change is a constant process, but because cultural circumstances will demand conditions specifically designed for our own needs.

13   On the political level - for if change is to be achieved, then economic facts must sometime be transmuted into political issues - we have formulated a dialectic for progress, viz., that Productive profitability should be upheld as the truth in measuring the soundness of all economic activity. This conclusion, of course, is independent of all traditional party ideology, but is perhaps all the more helpful in the prospect of uniting most sectors of our population in reversing economic decline.

As a course of investigation into desirable economic management, the criteria of productive profitability may be applied to investing institutions and to government policy, no less than to particular commercial enterprises situated throughout our country. In this, I believe, must be seen our hope for any future prosperity.

CHAPTER 22
How the Industrial Associations Are Failing British Industry

"The history of Britain's ramshackle array of trade associations is an industrial tragedy, a powerful cause of the downfall of our manufacturing. Competing nations had streamlined their processes of industrial representation, but in Britain manufacturing did not have a coherent voice as the crunch of competition came on us."

Sir Peter Parker, *For Starters,* J. Cape, 1989, p. 131.

1 - Home-based manufacturing unrepresented by any vested interest group   2 - This is partly because corporate policies do not necessitate maximising market share   3 - Corporate policies dictated by Rentier capitalism   4 - Assessing the contrasting capitalistic systems   5 - Industrial associations imprisoned within an "As is" situation   6 - Or else they are in conflict with one another   7 - Compared with the success of our competitors   8 - The problem with the CBI   9 - UK is asset-stripped by international conglomerates   10 - The impotence of small firms   11 - Failure of political institutions to support home-based industry   12 - What needs to be done

1   A public debate on Britain's real economic problem has never been more urgent than it is today. And yet despite the extent of present recessionary tendencies there remains a slim likelihood that the real or underlying issues will be more than cursorily skimmed over by the media.

There is only a sociological explanation for this unfortunate situation. It is a rarely disputed fact that political power (or the collective desires of the community) are pushed along by organised vested interest groups rather than by objective forces contributing to the better needs of the community. And it is sometimes a misfortune that the better objective needs of a community are not represented by any of its significant vested interest groups. This is certainly the case with British manufacturing.

If the objective interests of home-based manufacturing are taken to mean the growth and prosperity of the sector as a source for national wealth creation and full employment, it will be found that not a single significant body (out of the many hundreds in existence) represents those interests. There are two reasons for this. The first is that those vested interest bodies concerned with industry only represent one or several of its varied constituent parts, and often these are in conflict with one another. The second, and major reason, is that in contemporary Britain, the ownership and management of business is too often in separate hands and their interests fail to coincide.

2   If we take the second reason first, it will be found that the majority of

22-4

manufacturing firms are not independent entities working for their own clearly defined purpose but belong to a conglomerate with quite different aims in view. The overriding aim of the specifically Anglo-Saxon conglomerate organisation is to serve the interests of shareholders, and this is interpreted as maximising money profits within the shortest reasonable period of time.

This, in turn, calls for the short-term to have priority over the long-term. Consequently, the different parts of a conglomerate are treated as pawns in a chess game for maximising the profits of the group in total. Whilst some are strategically used for supporting loss leaders, others are simply stripped and wound-up in raising end-of-year capital to demonstrate the success of the group to shareholders.

Hence the rational management of individual firms is sacrificed for the dubious purpose of maximising the shorter term profits of the group. Consequently, the maximising of market share (the proper aim of all manufacturing enterprises) is limited by a blurred vision of the company's productive purpose; the restrictive policy intervention of the corporate body; and the scanty availability of capital for re-investment and expansion.

3   The philosophy governing these policies may be termed Rentier capitalism. It is manifested in every aspect of a company's management: e.g. in the limited vision of accountancy practices in conserving existing capital equipment as opposed to anticipating the benefits of investing in modernisation; decision-making reached through hunches and intuition as opposed to long-term rational planning; failure to invest sufficiently in training and develop employee commitment to the organisation; and an overall style of business that should be designated amateurish rather than professional.

Of course not all these characteristics can be blamed on the need for maximising the shorter-term profits of shareholders. Government policies - or the lack of them - must also take the blame for creating an unstable environment for manufacturing, e.g. through fluctuating exchange rates, or through crushingly oppressive interest charges. Nevertheless, all such policies form part of the general system of rentier capitalism specific to British business.

4   All these factors - and the need for distinguishing one form of capitalism from another - are displayed in sharper clarity when we contrast them with the business systems of our toughest international competitors, i.e. most the countries of Western Europe, and those of the dynamic Far and South East Asian economies, viz., Japan, Korea, Hong Kong, Taiwan and Singapore. All these countries not only have financial systems that invest heavily in long-term productivity and manufacturing, as opposed to

22-5

the safe or easy investments in land and property, but government policies which are interventionist, protective, and aggressive in finding foreign markets for their manufactured merchandise. This system may be denoted Productive capitalism.

There are clearly historical reasons explaining both contrasting systems of business enterprise, but whilst such reasons may be interesting to the social historian, neither should be justified in isolation or on their own merits. All such reasons to justify national business systems eventually become bogged down in the abstruse and subjective arguments of defunct political ideology, such as the overriding justification of "custom" or inexplicable definitions of "freedom." What really matters is the workability of such systems within an international context. If, for example, it is demonstrated that British manufacturing is going out of the window because of a rentier dominated economy, this should set off alarm bells in calling for a drastic re-assessment of the conditions in which our industrial infrastructure is forced to exist.

5   Returning to the first reason cited for the non-existence of any group promoting the objective needs of manufacturing, viz., that those bodies that do exist only promote one or several aspects of industry, it has also to be noted that we live in an "As is" world. This means that those organisations that do exist to promote some aspect of industry only seek to answer the immediate practicalities of a very practical topic; i.e. attending to the day-to-day possibilities of business within its existing framework. In the mental world of business there is little room - and less tolerance even - for the idea of theory. The first suggestion of speculative thought is immediately brushed aside as smacking of the "impractical."

What counts in business is the exertion of power - money-power in conjunction with business acumen and the right kind of practical imagination. All the rules of the game are pre-set by the financial framework of the society in which it is played. If that financial framework is not conducive to the success of a particular style or type of business, then it will simply not be embarked upon or will fail to flourish as a healthy growth. Hence all those significant industrial organisations that do exist, operate within an "as is" situation according to the pre-set rules of the game.

In this way they are able to "relate" comfortably with other bodies, and successfully fulfil their function within the understanding of the system. Seen from a more objective perspective or from the critical eye of an outsider, however, not only do they work within a very confined space but they fall far short of their proper purpose.

Take the most basic industrial organisation: the manufacturing and trade association, of which there are hundreds in the UK. Each trade association can only

22-7

be judged ultimately according to the success of the sector it represents. Therefore, the demise of manufacturing in so many fields must reflect the failure of numerous manufacturing and trade associations. No excuses can be accepted as valid, although attempted blame may be cast in many directions, e.g. on "unfair competition," "bad government policies," "dumping," etc. Hence it can be demonstrated plainly that these associations are not contributing to the best needs of their purpose, or indeed, to that of the community.

6   Turning to industrial organisations of quite a different nature, it will be found that some are set-up in conflict with others. There are a number of employers' federations, for example, that sell their benefits through services in fighting recalcitrant employees or trade unions, or assisting the representation of firms in industrial tribunal cases. Of course some trade unions are of little help to the world of industry when their philosophy is set out to oppose capitalism in any guise or form. What will be found nowhere, but is most needed, is a significant industrial association totally committed to integrating the best needs of labour and capital.

Unfortunately, we live in a society where the very idea of such an association would be laughed at by those from any sector of industry. This returns us to the topic that we touched upon at the start of the chapter: that the collective desires of the community are pushed along by organised (and conflicting) vested interest groups rather than by objective forces contributing to the best needs of the community. Not only does it reflect the underlying beliefs of British empirical philosophy, but more significantly, the emergence and nature of our particular democratic institutions.

7   But the idea of integrating conflicting vested interests towards the creation of a higher purpose is not something that has gone unresolved by our toughest industrial competitors. The Japanese, for example, have created work structures contributing to an almost perfect harmony in industrial relationships. This has developed from the adaptation of feudal attitudes to modern conditions as well as from Confucianism. In Germany, and elsewhere in northern Europe, a high degree of success in industrial relationships has been achieved through co-determination (*Mitbestimmung*) and by identifying the common purpose of capital and labour. This has been made possible through the widespread influence of Hegelianism.

In Britain, in answer to this, it will be argued by conservatives on both the left and right, that we are faced by cultural factors and entrenched tradition which cannot be overcome. This is a form of fatalism which merely rejects the idea of attempting change. It is also an irrelevant argument, for it implies we should adopt foreign patterns of thought *in toto* in changing our own condition. In this chapter no such

22-8

suggestion is being made. What is necessary is to float new ideas within the context of our own culture and then construct new institutions (or re-construct old ones) within which such ideas can develop and become a practical reality. It is therefore necessary for the leaders of our industrial associations to stand back and review their role within the wider context of society's needs so that they might make their own associations more demonstrably effective.

8   If one takes the larger organisations purportedly promoting the more generalised interests of industry, such as the CBI, it will be found that they are run by a number of internal vested interest groups to which the subsidiary more specialised departments within these organisations are dominated. For example, twenty years ago, W.G. Poeton broke away from the CBI taking some 300 firms with him and set up the Union of Independent Companies, claiming that the CBI no longer represented the smaller enterprise.

Just eleven years ago, Dr. Kevin Hawkins, took Lucas Industries, one of the largest CBI members, paying a subscription of £40,000 annually, out of that body, claiming that it no longer represented the interests of manufacturing be it companies large or small. Although the CBI has since taken some measures to rectify these deficiencies, and their attempts, it should be noted have been dismal, the organisation has remained dominated by service sector, and especially, orthodox banking interests. It might also be noted that although the CBI claims the independence of non-party affiliation, it is not helped by what is clearly perceived as mutual back-scratching between itself and the Conservative party.

If the CBI fails to represent effectively the interests of industry, then who can ? Since the world of industry is but a microcosm of society seen in the light of its internal conflicts, this all points to the moral that a higher integrating interest needs to be sought in representing the true needs of the productive sector, i.e. manufacturing , the extraction of minerals, agriculture and forestry. It is no good arguing that such an approach is "idealistic" or impractical, for our competitors have already succeeded in achieving such a higher interest.

It is most clearly manifested in the integrated purpose of the planning associations of Japan, and their common purpose with government and the financial institutions. If this were not so, then Japan would not be where it is today. But it is also hardly less clearly demonstrated by Germany and nearly all the countries of Western Europe. Of course any mention of "planning associations" raises hackles in British business circles because there is an inability to understand this term in any other light than old-style Socialist planning and nationalisation - all of which is justifiably

22-10

discredited. This is a reflection of the polarisation of thinking in modern Britain - the total inability to make any meaning out of the huge ground occupied between the two swings of the pendulum.

9   But there is also a third reason for the non-existence of any group promoting the objective needs of manufacturing. It touches on something we have not mentioned in this chapter, and would seem to finally endorse the unresolvability of British manufacturing's crisis, and put a lid on any further discussion of the topic. It lies in the fact that a vast and growing proportion of manufacturing in this country is no longer British owned.

Hence many corporate bodies no longer even have a moral obligation to concern themselves with the health of domestic manufacturing. Their attitude towards Britain is one of expediency for the purpose of maximising financial profits for the international conglomerate. Hence Britain is seen as an opportunity for exploiting low-skilled low-waged labour. This is already far advanced in the auto industry which has been transformed for mere assembly operation, but the progress of this tendency may also be seen throughout engineering as well as in the blue chip industry. Seen in this role Britain is taking on the status of an exploited Third world colonial territory.

This, of course, calls into question the entire function of international conglomerates which, of course, are not accountable to national states, and have no social or other obligations than the enrichment of themselves. Naturally a number of countries put restrictions on their activities, most commonly shareholding requirements for their own nationals, and the Scandinavian states have wisely raised effective barriers against these conglomerates in defending their low-population economies. Britain, on the contrary, because of her trading tradition, has put up no defences whatsoever.

All this explains why Britain is without any effective organisation to promote the disinterested aims of her manufacturing industries. Even if one chooses to appeal to the subjectivity of vested interest groups, it has now become difficult to identify those sectors that should be approached. It is no good approaching the largest manufacturing organisations to support British industry if their owners are sitting in Detroit, Tokyo or Frankfurt. Even if such a polite solicitation was to eventually reach their desks, they would merely smile at the naivety of the gesture before consigning the petition into the wastebin as an "irrelevance."

10   It is equally futile approaching the small or medium sized manufacturing plant, for although it may retain its individual loga and indicate the appearance of an independent enterprise, more often it will be part of a group the corporate office of

22-12

which is situated far away. The Chairmen, Managing Directors or Chief Executives of such firms - the title is irrelevant and meaningless, for in reality they are no more than factory managers - can say yea or nay to nothing outside their limited remit. They are a timid class of men, fearful of their future, and in matters touching the higher policies and finances of their conglomerates they are eunuchs. As for the idea of being called upon to support the cause of British industry, that would be far too "risky" to become involved in. Their foreign proprietors, quite simply, "might not like it."

As for the remaining manufacturing firms which are independent and actually managed by their owners, today they form so small a sector of British business, as to be ineffective as a lobby however admirable their attempts.

11   If British manufacturers cannot or are not prepared to promote the objective interests of their sector, then one is obliged to turn to established political institutions for help in that direction, but again there will be disappointment. This is because all political parties are no more than springboards for a wide assortment of vested interest groups, and the generalised ideologies they project act only as a veneer for the formulation and acceptance of public opinion. There does not exist any parliamentary lobby effectively representing the interests of domestic manufacturing. If there were then British industry would not have reached the nadir that it has today.

The reason for this failure is that those industrial lobbies and committees that do exist are totally dominated by orthodox financial interests which cannot be made consistent with the needs of domestic manufacturing. If the right and left broadly represent capital and labour, then the centre ground is even less helpful to industry. Whilst the Tories and Socialists at least have some interest in the topic, Liberal Democrats have none, since their thinking and membership is overwhelmingly swayed by middle class public sector requirements.

12   What action, then, needs to be taken in regenerating British industry ? Firstly, the cause of industry needs to be identified clearly as a public issue. It has to be impressed on the public consciousness what it is and what it is not. It is maximising profitable productivity, principally within the shores of our own country. It is not maximising pure money (or rentier) profits, since there comes a point when such profits entail the diminution of productivity and so loss of competitive edge. As it lies at the heart of economic activity, the responsibility for its success is with the community in total and not merely with those entrusted with its management.

Secondly, there is the need to sell the cause of industry to the public by underlining its social benefits. These entail full employment policies (witness the success in this area of those productive economies we have cited); the earning of

22-12

foreign currency and a healthy balance of payments; wealth creation circulating to the majority of our population due to the above factors; the greater democratisation of society; and a far higher standard of education for the majority in meeting the demands of a technologically advanced industrial society.

Thirdly, there needs to be established a non-party politico-industrial association aimed at attracting the membership of the general public in addition to industrialists, trade unionists and other decision-makers. Such an association would formulate its own thinking and policies in depth before imposing them through argument and appealing to the goodwill of decision-makers in all industrial, financial, political, trades union, and other bodies.

The need for such a disinterested industrial association promoting the higher purpose of social responsibility is made necessary by the fact that the decline of manufacturing is the sole reason for *all* our economic problems. Everybody is aware of this and yet, as shown in this chapter, all are impotent to effect necessary change, and ironically, government most of all, since administrations have always seen their role in this area merely restricted to adjusting fiscal policy.

It is especially necessary for businessmen and women to stand back and review the "rules of the game" and if they find them onerous or unfair in the light of industry's higher purpose, then to change them. This inevitably entails the call to promote national interests, and in the federalising world we live in, if this is followed by an outcry of "provincialism," this should give no grounds for embarrassment. If by the same rules of international business, the people of one country flourish whilst in another they are allowed to suffer economic oppression and unemployment, then somewhere there is injustice and the need for change. When we voluntarily surrender our autonomy, this does not mean that national problems evaporate, and even less does it mean that our right to refer to them is denied.

If we fail to take necessary action then Britain's economic decline will continue to worsen. And in that event we will have no option but to comfort ourselves with the illusion - as so often in the past - of having hit "the bottom" in anticipating a "rising" economy for the future. The truth is, is that there *is* no bottom. Is not now the time for some truly creative thought and action ? If what is proposed is a long-shot, then so be it. It is anyway preferable to sitting like a rabbit, paralysed by the headlights, to be crushed by the wheels of foreign trade in extirpating the last remnants of British manufacturing industry.

CHAPTER 23
Making The Financial Markets Work For Home-Based Industry

"Political power has been made responsible, but economic power has become irresponsible in society. The net result is that political power has been made more responsible to economic power."

Reinhold Niebuhr, *Moral Man And Immoral Society*, SCM Press, 1963, p. 15.

1 - Expertise not sufficient to reverse decline   2 - And neither are the exhortations of top industrialists   3 - Assessing the social ends of business   4 - The need for productive self-sufficiency   5 - So that financial problems are kept in control   6 - Dependence on international trade and the need for deficit funding   7 - Because equity funding has failed the Anglo-Saxon economies   8 - This is because of the dictatorship of the investor   9 - The unsocial outcome of our financial institutions   10 - The need to distinguish between and publicise different types of stock market investments

1   If, over a period of decades, leading businessmen and government efforts have failed to stem industrial decline, then the time has come for reassessing the foundations on which industry is believed to exist.

There is now one factor that has become quite clear: the regeneration of British industry is not simply dependent on applying conventional expertise, i.e. effective management in combination with the modernisation of methods and equipment. The "shake out," the "slimming down" or the "improvement" of the manufacturing sector over the past twelve years is sufficient demonstration of that. British industry's problems are very much more deep-seated.

The current emphasis on conventional expertise is not only to be found in political circles and business training centres. There are now not only more technical business books available in this country today than at any time before, but specialised bookshops on every aspect of business in all our major cities - and many of these bookshops did not exist much more than ten years ago. If the huge consumption of business literature was reflected in its intended purpose then the economy should be thriving as never before.

Unfortunately, this has not been the case. Instead, the proliferation of business manuals has been accompanied by the accelerating decline of British industry and the collapse of what is now described as the *real* economy. What this means in view of industry's crisis is that either there is something irrelevant about the business literature available, or else there is the need for the consideration of a higher priority before the application of conventional expertise.

23-3

2   Meanwhile, a number of leading industrialists have been particularly vocal over the last dozen or so years. Their message for the most part, has been that the only thing wrong with British industry is that businessmen should "get off their backsides," and get properly trained, and begin managing effectively. It may be questioned as to whether such complacently myopic industrialists are the most apt advisers in the present situation.

After all, of what real significance is their success if they are operating within a system judged to be failing overwhelmingly on a national scale ? All that we are really told of this success is that somehow they have proven to be the exception to the broad generalisation; that they are survivors, and that they have risen to the top within an industrial infrastructure that has woefully demonstrated its uncompetitiveness in world terms. Moreover, the doubtful value of their advice is reflected in the naivety of the cheery exhortations to get up off the pavement and put all hands to the wheel.

Not only has there been little realistic appreciation of underlying problems emanating from this quarter, but more significantly, no criticism of the system within which industry has been forced to operate. But then, it may be unfair to expect those who have succeeded within a failing system to criticise that system, as after all it has benefited *them*. It may also be that their great height has so exposed them to the rarefied atmosphere of passing clouds of nitrous oxide that they are unable to appreciate the hard realities of everyday business. Other advocates must therefore be found for presenting a sounder analysis and a better case for the future.

3   If age-old political conundrums of industrial ideology are to be avoided, then some very basic questions need to be asked. Little is to be gained by reducing the topic to a discussion of the usual partisan prejudices, for all such discussion becomes emotive ending inevitably in sterile stalemate. Such proposed basic questions that need to be asked fall into the "should" and "ought" categories. The answers to such questions will not necessarily provide immediate constructive suggestions, but they should act as pointers in identifying the underlying weaknesses of our own industrial system.

The first question might be: What should be the first priority of business ? The disinterested answer must surely be, Wealth creation for the community, so that it might pay for all its public needs that cannot be met from a self-wealth-generating source. This is an entirely non-political statement. It makes no attempt to discriminate as to whether needs should be funded via the public purse or the private sector. It only makes clear the point that wealth has to be generated as a first priority in maintaining the continuance of any community.

The question following on from this might be, How should wealth be distributed ? The answer is that it should be self-distributing through the business

23-4

process as widely as possible through the community. Again, in the world of the 21st century this may be taken as a non-political statement. Clearly it is undesirable that the process of wealth creation should be accumulated into too few hands since this amounts to withholding benefits from the majority - as well as reflecting a monopoly situation.

Furthermore, such accumulation tends to cause a coronary to the economic system, i.e. to the occurrence of crises despite that presence of great financial wealth, as has so often been experienced. The wider distribution of wealth is desired by all parliamentary factions: by the right because the maximising of successful privatisation is impossible without it, and by the left because of its inherent principles of justice.

The third question is: What kinds of business best contribute towards self-distributing wealth creation throughout the mass of the community ? The answer has to be (and it is currently demonstrated worldwide) those primal activities contributing to the survival of the community: i.e. the production and distribution of food, clothing, and all other marketable material needs and luxuries, including the construction of housing. Such activities not only fulfil essential needs and provide huge pools of employment, but are the primary source of all wealth creation, without which the service of financial industries could not successfully exist.

For example, the production of food by a primitive tribe, howsoever achieved (gathering and hunting) and the erection of huts, remain economic activities even when there is no medium of exchange. It has to be borne in mind, that in the final analysis, the economic end purpose of a primitive tribe is no different from that of an advanced industrial community. In both societies *Oikonomia* is no more than a call for good household management.

4   If, then, the primary (i.e. the planting and extraction industries), and manufacturing (secondary industries), are essential to self-distributing wealth creation, under what conditions are they best made to benefit any specific community ? Since we are discussing Economics or Household management, and the term household has to be understood as Nation, it follows that those industries must be self-contained within the controlling ownership of the community. Here we may touch on a political aspect of the matter, but hardly a party political aspect of any divisive ideological significance. The fact remains that if the economic mechanisms basic to a community's survival are considered, they cannot easily lend themselves to an international dimension, since the international factors are external and hence indeterminable.

The operation of such industries should therefore be home-based, and preferably, home-owned and controlled. With every foreign or internationally owned operation on home-based soil, there is not only a leakage of profits to foreign

23-5

parts, but the constant possibility that that operation may for any number of unpredictable reasons be transferred elsewhere.

Manufacturing enterprises therefore best benefit the community when they are: a) Wholly British-owned; b) Wholly operational in all their processes on British soil and so not lending themselves to low labour cost assembly only activities; c) Responding to the creative stimulus of a competitive system; and, d) Wholly independent of oligopolistic control. This fourth factor is very important, since it emphasises that if an enterprise is to remain competitive in the long-term, it must be managed primarily for its own internal productive purpose as opposed to those shorter-term compromises necessarily following on from serving the profitability of a conglomerate organisation.

5   The answer to these four questions gives the outline to any sound self-sufficient economy, to which all other problems become subordinate. For example, in a country that can produce and manufacture everything for its physical needs, and maintain productivity, financial questions become almost an irrelevance, and what in other countries might be perceived as crises are there almost passed-over unnoticed.

The exchange rate of the national currency, for example, takes on its own level without the need for comment, and even raging inflation over an extended period may occur (as happened in Japan in the 1970s) without the need for economists batting an eyelid. All this underlines the fact that the *real* economy is about tangible products as opposed to the availability of financial resources. When the discussion of a country's economy is concentrated solely on its finances, then something is amiss, and it becomes a good bet that the real underlying problems have been conveniently swept under the carpet.

The dangers and impoverishment of an economy that has become exclusively money-oriented were long ago pointed out by the great 19th century historian and parliamentarian, W.E.H. Lecky, when he wrote that, "the credit which a nation enjoys on the stock exchange is a deceptive test, for the finance of the market seldom looks beyond the prospects of a few years. A false security grows up, until the nation at last slowly finds that it has entered irretrievably on the path of decadence."[84]   More recently, Oswald Spengler interestingly wrote about the "Dictatorship of money" as a contributing factor in the downfall of cilivisations, due

---

[84]   W.E.H. Lecky, *Democracy & Liberty,* Longmans Green & Co., 1896, Vol. I, p. 50

23-6

to, "its want of solidity, which eventually leads to its losing its power and meaning."[85]   It cannot be over-emphasised, therefore, that the end of economics as with its beginning, has always to do with tangible products and not with any abstract medium of exchange.

6   Before reaching any final conclusions, two further questions have to be answered. Firstly, few countries, and certainly not our own, are self-sufficient. Britain is dependent on importing raw materials for feeding her factories, so that these materials may be converted into high value finished products   for profitable sale. It follows, naturally, that imports have to be paid for, and so a healthy export market has to be maintained. This, in turn, calls for a balanced exchange rate, so that our products may be attractively priced whilst retaining a sufficient level of profit. It is here that government involvement in the world of business cannot be evaded, or if it is, the lobbying pressures of business force its hand.

The other question, and it is the most crucial of all is, How is the financing of industrial investment to be best achieved ? Over the past decade, in the closed circles of industry, this has become an extremely emotive issue, although not one that has yet surfaced on the political scene. The financing of industry may at first appear an almost abstract question. The methods may seem generous in their wide alternatives: family lending, the clearing banks, 3i (Investment In Industry), venture capitalists, commercial banks, equity funding, or one of the innumerable schemes offered by other finance houses.

Unfortunately, none of the above have been of sufficient influence to reverse industrial decline. Their conditions have always been far too costly and short-term. If they have benefited certain sectors of service industry or pure trading concerns, they have never been able to stretch their facilities in properly serving the very heavy and long term investment needs of manufacturing.

The problem of financing industrial investment, however, is anything but abstract. If, over a period of time, we find our own industries in decline and those of our competitors progressing by leaps and bounds, it is only sensible we should look at their own systems of funding. The result is striking, for it everywhere shows a marked contrast from our own system of assisting industry.   Irrespective of whether we take Japan or Germany, or any of the other dynamic Far and South East Asian states, or almost any West European country, it will be found that debt-funding by industrial credit banks, or similar institutions, has accounted for the financing of the bulk of industry in these regions.

---

85 Oswald Spengler, *The Decline of The West*, Alfred Knopf, NY, 1928 ed., Vol. II, p. 98.

23-8

7   And it is the advocacy of debt-funding that has raised the hackles of so many bankers and financiers behind closed doors in high places in this country. Why ? If the post-War experience has clearly demonstrated that this is by far the most effective way of financing industry, then why the upset ? The failure of equity funding in promoting the manufacturing sector has not been confined to Britain alone. The failure has been made even more evident in America (in its sell-out to Japan with resultant mass job losses) as well as in other Anglo-Saxon economies, most notably Australia.

Clearly, very sensitive nerves are touched when raising the issue of debt-funding, and yet, what other alternative exists in the hope of reversing industrial decline ? Ideas cannot and should not be plucked out of the air. The commonsense approach must be to look at the success of our competitors. If we are to keep our feet on the ground, then only practical and proven ideas should be floated in the attempt to regenerate our own industries.

In overcoming the difficulty of these very sensitive nerves, three problems need to be considered. The first is the entrenchment of tradition going back at least 300 years. Britain's financial institutions, always more oriented towards international trade as opposed to home-based manufacturing, have an unbroken line of development from the last quarter of the 17th century. No other country in the world can trace such a sustained tradition of national financial culture based in its capital, and the success of this system over three centuries has engendered an intellectual rigidity on right and wrong modes of business practice that are almost immovable.

8   The overriding function of these institutions is, and always has been, service to the investor. In this lies the *raison d'être* and honour of the banker and financier. It is not his function to serve the interests of the manufacturer or any other business for which he has the responsibility of handling investments. In his eyes it is the function only of manufacturers or other traders to manage their businesses as best they may without help or interference from outside agents. In best serving the investor, the financier is necessarily neutral in his attitude towards funded enterprises, and if need arises, he will immediately sanction the withdrawal of funds from one concern into that of another, if thereby the investor profits.

The second problem touching these very sensitive nerves concerns vested interests. The banker and financier, separated as they are from the rest of the community, in a highly secretive profession, form a class apart. Although immense changes have taken place in the City of London over the past 30 years, with the Americanisation and streamlining of systems, and the introduction of a new type of "yuppie" executive, its institutions remain under the ultimate control of an exclusive and very old elite. Hence any apparent criticism of these institutions (however well

23-9

meant) or merely a pointing out of shortcomings, is rashly interpreted as an attack on the vested interests of a particular class.

The third problem touching these matters, concerns confronting bankers and financiers with proposals for the debt-funding of industry. A number of questions have to be raised in making such proposals a practicable proposition. Whilst recognising that present institutions do not have the expertise to introduce effectively a system of debt-funding, could not appropriate changes be made in making such a system possible ?

What objection could be laid against the proposition, for example, of extending the function of clearing banks by incorporating commercial departments comparable with those of German banks ? Since it has to be assumed that debt-funding, if it is offered, has to be profitable to the banks, then what is the objection against it ? Can any such objection be put down to anything more than intellectual stubbornness or myopia ?

Are there any circumstances in which bankers and financiers would be prepared to enter into an open dialogue on the question of debt-funding ? It may be that events will eventually force their hand, with the ever-changing development of the EU. It may be that the advent of European banks acting as European banks on British soil (and not merely as circumscribed by the regulations of the Bank of England, as at present) will bring chaos in its wake to the British banking community.

9   There are three lines of positive criticism which our bankers and financiers, as the stewards of our financial institutions, however, cannot escape. Firstly, they cannot escape the responsibility for the fact that financial trading has become so imbalanced in the size of its investments overseas and in its obsession in encouraging foreign deposits in this country, that our own home-based industries have suffered severely as a consequence. UK foreign investments already exceed those of all European countries north of the Alps put together.

The resulting damage to home-based industry arises from the following: a) The setting of the sterling exchange rate to favour this pattern of financial trading, as opposed to the interests of our own manufacturers (and it should be noted that both the Treasury and the Bank of England have *never* favoured the interests of the latter); b) Cash-starvation of British industry due to the unconscious bias of our financial institutions; and, c) The narrow conservatism of these institutions in failing to broaden their function, a deficiency following on from the huge degree of their success in serving the interests of investors worldwide.

The second line of criticism arises from the fact that this pattern of investment overseen by our financial institutions contributes to an excessive accumulation of wealth into too few hands. The same criticism applies, of course, to other Anglo-

23-10

Saxon economies whose manufacturing bases have been allowed to sink to dangerously low levels. If, on the contrary, investments were to be reallocated into the home-based productive sector, i.e. into the primary industries as well as manufacturing, this would result in a huge dispersal of wealth amongst the general population. This would be achieved through creating: a) Greater numbers of profit centres; b) More jobs; c) More spending power for the consumption of home-produced merchandise; and, d) Import substitution, greatly assisting our balance of payments and so lifting an oppressive tax burden.

The third line of criticism, following on from the above, is that our financial institutions, as presently operated in the interests of the investor, are not sufficiently self-wealth distributing to the wider community. In other words, investors themselves, form too small a class. It is certainly in the interests of those on the right, and of democracy generally, that the investing class should be broadened as much as possible - something that the late government, despite its credible efforts in this direction, never successfully succeeded in.

With the advent of employee share-ownership in conjunction with co-determination - tendencies that will certainly be pushed ahead by the EU - and added to this, the privatisation of ever more public utilities, the potential for increasing the investing class in the coming years is immense. But the investing class of the future will differ enormously in type from that of today, and cultural and structural changes will have to be made to existing institutions in meeting different needs.

10   In countering the above deficiencies, there is a proposition that may be put in making our institutions more accountable to, a) Home-based industry; b) The British people; and, c) The *real* economy. There is also a precedent for putting forward such a proposition. It concerns the need to distinguish stock market investments by type in serving the public interest. There already exists widespread publicity in the media against those investments allegedly offensive to the public conscience.

Of equal significance and of more profitable concern to the people of our own country would be the distinction between those stock market investments made in: a) Wholly UK-owned home-based productive enterprises; b) Foreign or internationally owned home-based productive enterprises; c) UK-owned home-based service sector enterprises; d) Non-UK owned home-based service sector enterprises; e) Passive assets in land or property in the UK; f) Passive assets elsewhere; g) UK overseas projects; and, h) Other overseas projects.

If, then, through the media, widespread publicity could be used in persuading the public to invest in the first of these categories, immense benefits would be won overnight in the struggle to reverse industrial decline. The ordinary investor would thereby be given the opportunity to either consciously place his assets with those concerns benefiting the real economy and the national interest; or else, to place those

23-10

assets, which in view of all their resulting knock-on effects, subtract from national wealth creation.

If leading industrialists are genuinely committed to promoting the interests of the *real* economy, and the best interests of manufacturing, I see no reason as to why they should express reservations in promoting the tentative proposals set out in this chapter. After all, the proposals are as disinterested as it is possible to make them. They transcend all the arguments of self-interest whilst promoting the self-interest of the community.

They amount to a critique of an older rentier capitalist system in favour of a newly evolving productive capitalist system that has already proven its worth in those countries more successful then ourselves. The *raison d'être* of each economic system stand at opposite poles of the spectrum: whilst in the first it is the Investor who is King; in the latter, it is Industry. Is it any wonder, then, that we cannot hope to match our toughest international competitors ?

Could not industrialists form themselves into a powerful lobby, entirely non-party political in nature, in promoting what can only be properly perceived as the national interest ? The ideas we are here concerned with are not the illusory myths of party faction, but the factual mechanisms of setting our economy aright by a series of down-to-earth practical measures.

It may be that such measures are incapable of stirring the public imagination but in that is to be found their laudable credibility. It is only the nebulous idea or the "fairy tale" that anyway inspires the public - never the practicality of economic mechanisms. Such proposals as here outlined are of course a challenge. They are also no more than a pencil sketch for our future prosperity. It is for our industrialists to colour in the picture indicating the way ahead.

***

Part IV

Action For Prosperity

"The British are not going to return to the old deferential world nor will they work well in jobs which give them no chance to express intelligent opinions. No real advance will be made which does not recognise this."

Charles Villiers, *Start Again Britain*, Quartet Books, 1984, p. 5.

When I first approached trade union leaders with the new concept of Advanced Industrial Action, some ten years ago, several General Secretaries of the smaller Northern industrial trade unions (long since absorbed by larger bodies) were taken aback by the proposals, as being far too militant and beyond the remit of trades union activity. Their predictable rationale, or excuse, was that "it is not the purpose of workers to interfere in the management process."

An aeon of time seems to have passed since then. The trade unions are no longer merely re-active organisations as reflected in the above quotation. Over the past twenty years they have changed out of all recognition. They are now intelligently pro-active in formulating ideas on every aspect of industrial management and organisation for the greater success of business - and of course, for the people they employ.

It is no exaggeration, perhaps, to hazard that today the relevant major unions are almost in competition with the Confederation of British Industry, the Institute of Directors, or the Institute of Management, with regard to both the quantity and quality of advice they are prepared to urge on government and other bodies for improving British industry. The bad old conviction that there exists an impassible divide between those at the work bench and those who manage is now happily gone forever.

Increasingly the trade unions are becoming interventionist in the business process in deciding what is acceptable or unacceptable in the organisation and management of industry in its widest context. Meanwhile, the strike weapon is becoming discredited as a futile mode of achieving the ends which working people seek to achieve.

A new industrial weapon is required in meeting the urgent needs of the future: Advanced Industrial Action. AIA can only be utilised successfully through the self-confidence and moral integrity of those employees comprising the Responsible. Society, who are fully informed about the business process and the economic system within which it operates. AIA is intended as the ultimate trades union weapon of educated employees in the new millennium, seeking a better future for themselves, their colleagues, their families, and the community at large.

***

Trades unionism in Britain is now at a cross roads. A huge question mark hangs over old attitudes and strategies. Are they any longer able to push forward the best interests of working people in meeting the needs of the new millennium ?

The strike weapon is almost defunct. Those national strikes in several major industries, now being considered as possible demonstrations against de-industrialisation and closures, are muted threats that may never be transferred into action. Has the strike weapon had its day as a significant force in promoting workers' interests ? There is no doubt that over the past decade the bark has become more fearsome than the bite, and this cannot entirely be explained away as the results of "union bashing" or Thatcherism.

But hidden from the surface activity of everyday politics, great undercurrents of volcanic strength are shifting the layers of society. But since the ground beneath our feet has not yet been shaken by the rumbling of the earth's crust, old attitudes remain steadfast and old remedies are being uselessly applied to changed conditions. The old lines of conflict no longer have any real meaning in promoting the best interests of working people. Slogans and attitudes that may have sounded "revolutionary" twenty years ago are today merely anachronistic, i.e. they no longer sound convincing and cannot be used for effective political action.

Since the old platforms have been cut away from the feet of organised working people as a unifying basis for action in the factory or on the street, and since industrial problems are MORE severe today than for several decades past, a confusing and frustrating situation has arisen. There is a void - and this has not been filled by a new Labour government. Where is the rationale for pointing out the way ahead and where the justification for convincing action ? Those who are exploiting national assets and enriching themselves at the cost of British jobs, enterprises - and even entire industries, can relax in ease at the indecision and apparent impotence of organised workers.

But not for much longer ! New Socialism has not only identified the new realities of our socio-economic situation but has drafted plans for the new era of industrial struggle against the ills which now confront us. Trade unionists must fight with the backing of the nation behind them, and not simply as narrow and separate interest groups, seemingly involved with "selfish" interests. They now need to be pro-active rather than re-active and recent developments have already revealed a shift in this direction.

The pre-eminent issues facing working people today are not wages and conditions of work, but the slaughter of jobs and industries. The greatest threat facing working people today are not "bosses" (in the ordinary sense) but de-industrialising rentier capitalism, and a financial system that destroys British-based jobs and industries. In the majority of businesses today, measured in terms of total industrial wealth, there is a clear distinction between Owners and Directors.

Working people today have an educational function to perform. They must bring their "Chief executives," "Managing directors," "Factory managers" - the title hardly matters as the function is the same - over to their side of the fence. These "bosses" are usually employees in the same sense as shop-floor workers, and both lose their jobs in identical economic circumstances, i.e. as pawns in a chess game played by a remote corporate body making quick profits through asset stripping and the skulduggery of international deals beyond the control of any government authority. All the ills of modern industry, including even poor training and incompetent management, stem solely from the hindrances of rentier capitalism.

Whilst New Socialism promotes profits, competition and free enterprise, it is in total opposition to rentier capitalism (the cancer of productivity) and is in no doubt that if working people fail to concentrate their energies in fighting this single and overwhelming evil, there will be no jobs, no firms, no industries and no associations to represent the dispossessed - irrespective of whether they belong to management or shop-floor.

The following ten chapters set out the practicalities for the industrial action of the new age. There has to be an end to the old talk of "Class struggle." That only deflects attention from the real issues to be fought against and is counter-productive in attracting public sympathy. If industrial action is to be truly effective then it must be seen to be carried out in the public interest as well as in the interests of working people.

24-2

CHAPTER 24
The Invisible Shift In Industrial Relationships

"Individuals and the Community exist for one another in the measure in
which they exist for themselves and the principles of unity and variety
mutually support one another as elements equally necessary and equally
real."

Otto von Gierke, *Genossenschaftsrecht*, 1913, Vol. II, p. 906.

1 - New grounds needed for industrial action   2 - As otherwise the interests of workers are not really promoted
3 - Outdated political doctrines benefit exploiters   4 - Demarcation between functions of managers and workers
unfavourable to the latter   5 - Cynical situation arising from this   6 - Invisible shift in industrial relationships
7 - Shop-floor workers no longer perceive themselves as proletarians   8 - Experiencing a closure   9 - Shop-floor
workers' heeding of inefficiency went unanswered   10 - Musings of a cost accountant.

1   Grounds of discontent for industrial unrest are changing. They need to. Old
doctrines are losing their credibility, and strangely, old models - once deemed heroic
- on which to base demonstrations of solidarity, no longer hold the conviction they
once did. Everywhere there is uncertainty. Today there is a reluctance in the labour
movement to take any kind of industrial action, whatever the path, in the stifling fear
that any step might possibly be counter-productive.

All this reflects an undercurrent of change - not so much in the labour
movement itself - as in the entire structure of society, and the revolutionary (even if
invisible) socio-economic causes that are bringing this about. The call to the so-
called "Workers" to fight for better wages and conditions against the so-called
"Bosses," no longer rings true with anyone who has followed, analysed and
understood the socio-economic changes of the past two decades. The idea of the
"Class war," as commonly understood, is even less convincing. The time has not
only come for a re-definition of terms, such as "Workers" and "Bosses," together
with all their often falsely emotive connotations, but for a radical re-drawing of the
battle lines, so that if the phrase "Class war" is to have any real or justified meaning
in the future, it will have a meaning that is very different from that in ordinary use
today.

2   These changes will come about because they need to, for if they don't, the
progress of working people towards a better future will be locked into a static or
worsening situation. In such a scenario when ancient prejudices and modes of
thinking are upheld in a greatly changed society, and such thinking has lost all
practical relevance, the rich are destined to become richer and the poor to become
poorer. This will simply be because the proverbial "working class" will have lost
its grip on political reality. In such circumstances, old-established radical ideals
become nothing more than illusions. In any real sense they are no longer radical,

24-5

since the proposed cures are both inapplicable and unattractive in the changed conditions of society, and they fail to arouse the imagination and sustain the enthusiasm of sufficient numbers of people. 86

3 There is a malaise in the labour movement today - almost an apathy in the face of a crisis situation, decimating jobs by the thousand, week by week, and undermining living standards by the million. When working people maintain outdated ideals or bolster up doctrines perceived as discredited - i.e. ideals and doctrines admittedly at one time of service to the working class - who are the gainers? The gainers are clearly the enemies of that class, for the reason that false perceptions or illusions are an invaluable distraction for furthering the interests of those who would exploit the majority. The new exploiters need to hide behind a screen of distraction and false hope, so that unseen, they might enrich themselves at the expense of the majority. Falsehood must be used in concealing the truth ! Political beliefs for a better future must be sustained for satisfying the hopes of the exploited majority, as otherwise there would be confusion, chaos and anarchy, and that would do no good to the stability of society. And preferably such beliefs should be ancient or well-established, since then they will be more distantly removed from satisfactorily answering the very changed conditions of the contemporary age.

4 Let us look at the changing attitudes of many trade unionists. Traditionally it has been held - and is still held firmly by some unions - that the function of Managers is to Manage, and of trade unionists to work within the narrowly defined limits of their occupation and to concentrate only on better wages and conditions of employment. How beautifully this traditional attitude serves the interests of the great manipulators and those who would exploit the majority for their own ulterior and grandiose objectives! With what benign expressions they will carefully endorse that it is "unfair" and "grossly unreasonable" that workers should be burdened with the concerns or responsibilities touching the internal management of the employing enterprise ! It is with devastating irony that shop stewards and other trades union leaders not only assent to this attitude of employers but bask in the satisfaction of mutual agreement and co-operation.

5 In this environment all the political skulduggery of pure rentier capitalism taking place in the boardroom is afforded full scope in the great game of monopoly. Without knowing what has struck him, or from whence it came or where to, the worker is wrapped up, packaged, sent bumping along the rollers on the production line, is hired-out, sold-off, and finally, dazed and hardly conscious of how he got there, pushed out at the final exit wrapped-round in a redundancy notice sticker,

---

86 See Appendix C.

24-8

marked, "Used-up and useless!" Despite two hundred years of trades union organisation, he remains as powerless over his fate as he ever was. Meanwhile, his employers make every endeavour to keep him in the dark until the moment before his next move on the chess board, and generally they succeed.

6   But things are changing. Mass redundancy is no longer an isolated event. And it no longer just effects shop-floor workers. It now also effects tens of thousands of middle and senior managers in many productive industries up and down the land. There is an invisible shift in industrial relationships. Industrial discontent is no longer the exclusive prerogative of so-called "Workers." Managers, and even top management, are equally involved in the decimation of jobs and industries - and many have more to lose in personal terms than shop-floor workers. But managers do not talk about the "tyranny of the bosses." They look for other underlying causes, identifying evils more analogous with the truth. In this kind of scenario old-style patterns of class warfare become a nonsense.

7   Meanwhile, over the decades, shop-floor workers are no longer what they once were. Many, even resent the term "Worker," preferring instead to be called "Employees." Their material demands and living standards bear little comparison with those of their forebears just two generations back. They run cars, own dish-washers and video machines, and live in wall-to-wall carpeted and centrally heated houses and flats - often perceiving themselves as "middle class." Of most significance, they are better informed and educated; and as shop-floor workers in the modern plant there is a greater demand on their skills and brainpower.

Consequently, not only do they exert a greater responsibility in the carrying out of their individual tasks, but they experience a greater confidence and sense of power in contributing to the total business process. Hence the old trades union philosophy of maintaining a clear distinction between the role of "Managers" and "Workers" is falling apart - certainly in theory if not yet in practice. The ideas of our more socially advanced European partners: of Co-determination (*Mitbesstimmung*) and employee share-ownership, etc., are at last beginning to make some headway in Britain. They need to !

8   Several years ago, as a recently recruited employee of a major manufacturing enterprise in the engineering industry - the last British company but one engaged in the production of its particular range of products - I was peremptorily summoned, one day, to attend an emergency meeting in the canteen. The reason was unknown but urgent ! Five minutes later I found myself amongst a crowd of two hundred bewildered and apprehensive employees, and since I had been with the company less than a month, I might have included myself as amongst the most bewildered and apprehensive of all. After several minutes, the Chairman, followed by other directors and top management, marched into the room. They remained no longer

24-10

than three minutes, before leaving the meeting in hasty retreat. Any further questions from employees were left to the Shop Steward to answer.

During those brief three minutes it was curtly announced that the plant would be closed in ninety days, with redundancy for all staff apart from a selected few key personnel who would be offered the option of employment in the northern factory. It was announced that the plant be cleared of employees within the next thirty minutes and that the factory gates be locked. The directors seemed to urge this in anticipation of the possibility of some kind of industrial demonstration. As soon as they had left, an angry murmur arose in the canteen. An angry young draughtsman, sitting opposite, exclaimed, "I bet you wished you'd never joined this firm !" I said nothing. His neighbour - still in his early twenties - resignedly drawled, "I'm used to this. It's the third time it's happened !"

9   The Shop Steward - more dazed and wearied than angry - who took over the meeting, said he had only known of the closure decision ten minutes before the present meeting had been convened. There was a short question and answer session. The Shop Steward explained how he, together with colleagues, had written to the American President of the financial holding company, six months earlier, listing complaints on the gross mismanagement of the company and the unnecessary wastage of costly resources. This had been followed up with the despatch of two copies of that letter. No reply had ever been received. Since senior management had never listened to what the engineers, planners and shop-floor technicians had had to say, the inevitable had happened: the company had been reduced to the verge of bankruptcy.

After twenty minutes the meeting broke up in an atmosphere of extreme gloom - only some of the older men smiling sardonically, muttering under their breath that they were anyway due for retirement in several weeks. The Shop Steward had stated there was nothing to be done. A decision had been reached and that was that! He cautioned (no doubt instigated by the directors) that those present were still in employment for the next ninety days, and that best behaviour should be maintained in avoiding the possibility of immediate sackings and loss of redundancy payments.

10   A week later, in the same factory, I found myself face-to-face with the Senior Cost Accountant. He had been left with the onerous task of calculating redundancy awards and informing the privileged few who were to be interviewed and offered the option of employment in the other factory two hundred miles to the north. With a furrowed brow, and pacing up and down his office like a caged animal, he came out with, "the City's to blame for this. If the City of London and its phony economy was blown-up sky high tomorrow, we could save these jobs and millions more ! If the City continues to have its way - I'm telling you - in five years time, there won't be a single job left in manufacturing industry !" Coming from an accountant, this

25-2
· was a revelation indeed ! He knew on which side of the industrial fence his true
interests were to be found.

CHAPTER 25
The Changing Priorities of Working People

"If a man seriously desires to live the best life open to him, he must learn
to be critical of the tribal customs and tribal beliefs that are generally
Accepted among his neighbours."

Bertrand Russell, *Authority & The Individual*, Allen & Unwin, 1949, p. 109.

1 - Triumph of the phony over the Real economy   2 - The skilled under the authority of the incompetent   3 -
Narrowing in the skills gap between workers and management   4 - A greater sharing of decision-making follows
from this   5 - Changing priorities of workers   6 - Top priority is company survival   7 - The insufficiency of
redundancy compensation

1   What conclusions are to be drawn from these short dramatic sketches ?
Firstly, the easy assumption that such scenes are in no way unique. They have been
- are - and will be - re-enacted up and down the country every day of the week.
Over the disastrous, de-industrialising Thatcherite years, they are scenes that may
have been re-enacted thousands of times over.

They are the inevitable consequences of the continuing erosion of the REAL
economy, as the PHONY economy of the get-rich-quick rentiers have a field day in
misdirecting the national financial resources that rightly belong to us all. This is
nothing less than a form of daylight robbery assented to by the establishment.
2   Secondly, it reflects the greater consciousness and sense of responsibility of
ordinary working people in their genuine commitment to the employing enterprise.
These particular trade unionists, under their shop steward, were not following the
narrow well-trod path of traditional trades union conformity, as might have been
obligatory, say, thirty years earlier. They were no longer being merely re-active but
pro-active. They were under no obligation to list their complaints of incompetence
against the management in writing to the Corporate Chief, even though it may be
argued it was their responsibility to do so. What was evident is that these workers
were badly led by technical management.

As shop-floor employees they had engineering skills giving rise to queries and
problems that were simply not understood by senior managers with limited
engineering knowledge and experience. As I was soon to learn, the amount of
engineering knowledge and skills in this particular company was almost in inverse
proportion to the status of decision-makers in the hierarchy of authority.
Consequently, the shop-floor workers not merely found their skills under-valued, but

25-5

instinctively and justifiably felt that they should somehow exert a discreet managerial power if the enterprise was to survive in the long term.

3   Thirdly, the administrative, sales and marketing side of the company, throughout all levels of management, felt at one with the shop-floor. This was made even more evident with the attitude of the Senior Cost Accountant, who blamed the company's troubles ultimately on the City, and its various machinations which filtered down to the different departments in influencing a company, resulting in its being stripped of skills, equipment and necessary investment for the quickest possible return in satisfying the avaricious investor. The moral of all this must surely be that there should be no grounds for conflict between shop-floor workers and management, or put another way, between "Workers" and "Bosses." What is evident today in the modern enterprise is that shop-floor workers not only have -

a) A greater absolute knowledge and control over skills than formerly in the more old-fashioned plant, but,

b) A greater relative knowledge in relation to managerial superiors.

4   This reflects a greater technical egalitarianism amongst employees, and necessarily leads to a greater democratisation in the style of management if efficiency is to be maintained. With egalitarianism and democratisation combined in running the industrial enterprise, this has led to a greater unity of purpose amongst all sectors of employees - including management. Having already accepted as a matter of course that wages and conditions of employment must meet a satisfactory level, what matters most of all is the long-term success of the industrial enterprise, and all must be committed to this single end. Irrespective of whether or not shop-floor workers are prepared to accept the greater responsibilities which go with Co-determination or employee Share-ownership - and such reluctance may remain entrenched - inevitably, conditions in the workplace are pushing them towards such a course.

A greater sharing of decision-making inescapably follows from the narrowing in the gap of skills and knowledge between the different layers in the hierarchy. When shop-floor workers can tell a "thing or two" to top management on the practicalities of engineering , the time has come for shop-floor workers to fully share in the management function of industrial enterprises.

5   Furthermore, over the past decade there has been a great shift in the minds of shop-floor workers as to their priorities. Wages and conditions of employment, although clearly important, are no longer pre-eminent. Most matters concerning the approach to wages and conditions of employment have been developed in fine detail over decades of negotiations between workers and employers. They have been routinised within an almost boringly complex bureaucratic system, and the Strike as an industrial weapon has become so predictable, even if nowadays a rarer event, as

25-7

to be hardly inspiring as a weapon of industrial revolt.

6   The modern Strike has almost become nothing more than an empty gesture of despair, simply because there seems to have been no other alternative in expressing pent-up feelings of intense injustice and discontent.   The top priority of workers today - in all levels of employment - are not wages or conditions of work, but the very survival of the industrial enterprise.   But the strike is not a suitable industrial weapon in fighting the new battles which now have to be fought.   The new battles of workers in the future will be against managerial inefficiency; financial or other decisions leading to the de-industrialisation of the enterprise; and the dangers of liquidation and bankruptcies.   These matters urgently call of a new industrial weapon.

7   The fourth conclusion to be drawn from the above sketches is that message to employees that Redundancy compensation is the bosses' only and ultimate weapon against the counter-measures of demonstrations against enforced redundancies and de-industrialising activity of any kind.   The Redundancy Payment is a message to workers which says: "It's our decision - we're in control.   Here's your compensation - now go away, and don't ask any more questions."   The Redundancy Payment has always been the successful "Keep Quiet Pill !"   The truth, however, as redundancy effects the vast majority of employees, is that no payment can be truly compensatory within a politico-economic system which is rapidly de-industrialising its manufacturing base.

Even if a worker immediately walks into another job with no intervening period of unemployment, an apparently "good" redundancy award may still be no satisfactory compensation in the long term.   Tens of thousands of workers have already discovered the truth of this at their cost.   This is because in a de-industrialising environment where the game of musical chairs is played as an on-going episode, fewer and fewer jobs become available.   Of course, for a time, the smartest and best qualified employees, will always be one step ahead of their colleagues in jumping into a vacancy to avoid an unemployment period. But even they will eventually be overtaken by events.   As the wheel of the jobs lottery is swung round and round, as average job periods become shorter and shorter, even the smartest employees will eventually be forced into the dole queue.   At first, maybe, such unemployment periods will be short and unworrying, but gradually they will not only become more frequent, but for increasingly long periods.   Eventually, the employee will be forced out of the industry, since the jobs are no longer there; his skills will be useless, and instead, he will be obliged to take up a quite different occupation at a much lower level of remuneration.

The fifth conclusion to be drawn from these dramatic sketches, is that they led me onto a train of thought that was to culminate in developing the concept of

26-2

Advanced Industrial Action, the subject of these chapters. What right had the incompetent, I thought, to ruin the livelihoods of the skilled and hard-working? Where lay the ultimate responsibility for the collapse of our manufacturing base ? What should working people do in countering threats of unemployment ? Is there the scope or the justification for a new kind of industrial revolt against the de-industrialising rentier capitalists in our midst ? How could such ideas be made a practical reality ? These are some of the questions we are attempting to answer in the following eight chapters.

CHAPTER 26
Workers And Bosses Against De-Industrialisation

> "The most insidious attack on the unity of mankind comes from those who insist on the relativity of all moral ideas and who deny the existence of universal principles binding on all men."

Morris Ginsberg, *Essays In Sociology & Social Philosophy*, Heinemann, 1947, Vol. II, p. 292.

1 - When dated politico-industrial attitudes become counter-productive 2 - Changes in business structures have devalued use of the Strike weapon 3 - Meanwhile, the MD of the smaller firm sees a truer friend in his employees than in his bank 4 - And a truer friend in his employees than in his government 5 - Better sense for owners and workers to unite in fighting rentier capitalism 6 - Time for workers to take stock of their best interests

1   As the structure of society changes, so must our perceptions change, if our understanding is to be matched with reality. Workers know this, but have not yet discovered a new direction for energising their industrial solidarity.

Every sensitive worker knows that the actions and thinking of industrial revolt of thirty years ago, simply makes him ridiculous in the eyes of the public when repeated or superimposed on today's conditions. It is Quixotic. It is not merely futile, but counter-productive. Great numbers of people witnessing anachronistic modes of industrial revolt merely mutter their exasperation about "bolshie" attitudes, and working people quickly lose their credibility and sympathy in the eyes of the majority. And it is simply not enough to explain away the public's attitude as having been duped by a "capitalist" press.

2   Nowadays with the close interdependence of our industrial infrastructure, it is important that all industrial demonstrations should be designed to win the sympathy , if not the active support, of the general public. In a society where the financial tentacles of industry are of Byzantine complexity, no firm should be regarded as a self-sufficient entity. Even the smallest back-shed enterprises are often (if not usually) part of giant and faceless conglomerates, and any conventional

26-3

demonstration confining its message to the employers of a single plant is often meaningless and ineffective if its cause is not associated with promoting wider issues.

Years ago, when the bosses of a factory were at the same time Directors AND Owners, and when factories were autonomous enterprises, they could reasonably be regarded as self-sufficient, and consequently, a more tangible relationship existed between all parties in a dispute. When there was discontent over wages or conditions, the Strike weapon was immediate and effective. This was because it struck at the pockets of directors and shareholders. Workers were in direct confrontation with necessary decision-makers. Negotiations in the factory board room was all that was needed, and all would be quickly resolved.

Those conditions no longer pertain. Bosses are often no longer owners. They are often, themselves, no more than employees, with no share capital in the company. As employed managers they have a bureaucratic approach to problems; no sense of urgency (since their authority is limited at every step); and no overriding threat to personal self-esteem or loss, since they are working on behalf of others. Possibly their sympathies may be closely allied with shop-floor workers against a remote ownership, especially if the cloud of de-industrialising capitalism is seen on the horizon. In such circumstances all kinds of games may be played by non-possessing bosses, and organised workers may find themselves sparring against shadows.

3 At the other end of the scale, in looking at the small business, managing directors have even greater reason to identify entirely with the interests of shop-floor employees. This especially applies to the engineering firm employing between five and ten persons, of which there are thousands up and down the country, engaged in pressing, stamping, die-casting and other specialised precision work. Several years ago I was engaged as a management consultant assisting manufacturing and engineering companies in eastern England. Part of my responsibility, in that capacity, was to examine closely the financial framework of companies including the personal financial status of directors. It transpired that the managing directors of some 70% of these newer and better run companies stood in a worse financial position than the humblest of their own employees.

In maintaining their competitive edge - in reducing job costs to customers - in enlarging their market share; these small firms were obliged - if they were forward-looking - to invest in machinery costing a quarter or half a million pounds, or more. Since reasonable, fair, or long-term borrowing facilities are unavailable from any source in Britain, by comparison with the encouraging and highly-favourable terms available throughout Continental Europe, these directors had to take the final plunge in trusting and risking all in their life's work.

23-5

Consequently, they came to own nothing - even the shirt on their backs being mortgaged to finance the firm. Their "friendly" high street lender, in implementing the usury of his bank (and currency inflation that goes with excessive interest), had not only seized their factories, but their machinery, warehouses, trucks, cars, vans, and even their life policies, stocks and shares, and private homes. They not only demanded their pound of flesh but their TWO pounds of flesh. One such managing director, I came to know over a period of years, had even been reduced to living in a small unheated caravan in the middle of a field, having lost the support of friends and relatives in his courageous attempt to maintain a valve manufacturing company - the consummation of his life's work and purpose - as he lived in the receding hope for a major contract from a prospective foreign client which never came.

4   Such managing directors, supported by their five or ten specialised workers, must have a vested interest in co-determination and employee share-ownership. If the financial burden could be spread and the collateral housing stock of half a dozen others be used for investment, this must surely be a blessed relief to the sole owners of companies. Or would it be ? The small firm is not only restrained by lack of investment but threatened by fluctuating exchange and interest rates, and until recently, by a callous Tory government that cared not a jot for the hard won efforts of entrepreneurs in building up the productive or REAL economy. In those circumstances, then, the invitation to employees to share in the burden of financial risk, would clearly be unfair.

Some years have passed since I last visited those small engineering concerns. Whilst loathing to foretell their present status I cannot refrain from contemplating their current situation. With interest rates greater than ever before, and bankruptcies lately at an all-time high, many of those firms must have now gone under. And their directors ? With their houses seized, and the bailiffs and their dogs having driven away their occupants, it is now a fair guess to predict that those same men - rejected by wives and children for their failure as breadwinners - are pacing the cold streets of some Midlands town, begging for employment or a warm meal.

5   Such is the fate of Britain's brave entrepreneurs ! In such a world, is it not justice as well as commonsense that managing directors, shop-floor workers, and all the intervening grades, should sink their common interests in fighting the real evils in our society ? It is unquestionably an absurdity - turning truth on its head - to label these Productive Capitalists as "exploiters" or "oppressors" of the working class. This is because such entrepreneurs are amongst the most exploited and oppressed class of all - exploited by the destructive evils of rentier capitalism under the control of our uniquely iniquitous financial institutions. 87

---

87 See Appendix D.

27-1

6   There is a crying need for industrial revolt, but revolt on new foundations against a new enemy. A close analysis of the greatest economic problems facing us today clearly points to the unnecessary futility of workers in revolt putting themselves beyond the pale of public sympathy - i.e. unnecessary if such revolt is to be both relevant and truly effective. There has to be a complete re-appraisal of values in the world of industrial relationships, so that new attitudes can be matched with new realities. This is not to suggest that there should be a dampening down or moderating of the spirit of industrial revolt, but on the contrary, that the embers should be stoked and fired up in preparation for a new era of mass demonstrations far more forceful than those in the past.

But such demonstrations would be placed within an entirely new ideological framework. They would be placed on a new track, with a new direction, aimed at combating and destroying the real and contemporary threats to the welfare of the community in total.

CHAPTER 27
New Battle Lines For Social Progress

> "All men are idealists and cannot help being idealists, provided we mean
> by idealism the striving for the satisfaction of needs which are specifi-
> cally human and transcend the physiological needs of the organism."

Erich Fromm, *The Sane Society*, Routledge & Kegan Paul, 1956, p. 29.

1 - Cynicism of "Class solidarity" today   2 - Separation of ownership and control has transformed class interests
3 - Transformation in the nature of capitalism   4 - Productive Capitalism differentiated   5 - The new battle lines:
The classless majority versus the Rentier Capitalists

1   How would this new ideological framework be achieved ? It can best be achieved by looking at the changed structure of society, and identifying a new pattern in the clash of vested interests. These may be cited as under:-

1. The growth of egalitarianism in terms of material expectations and technical knowledge in the workplace (although not in other spheres, e.g., class, culture, occupation, regional origin, etc.) has made the concept of the "Class struggle," repulsive to the majority of our population. Class war is seen as unnecessary and counter-productive in its divisiveness.

2. Stemming from the above is the up-ending of the ethic of the old radical ideal. When Marx, Engels, and others, called for class solidarity, there was a certain nobility and altruism in their thinking in view of the end to be attained, i.e., the classless society. Now all that has been soured. Partly because of the selfish introversion of each trades union in concentrating on its

27-2

own demands against other sectors in society; partly because of greater materialism and higher material expectations; partly because of the rat-race mentality penetrating all sectors of the community; and partly because of the socially divisive influences of pragmatism in the modern Anglo-Saxon world, those clinging to the old radical ideal tend towards a self-centred egoism that makes claims of "Class solidarity" a cynical obscenity.

3. The high technology and demand on brainpower in all spheres of modern industry, and the necessity for close co-operation resulting from this, brings workers and managers into a much closer relationship than formerly. There is no wish for enmity between the shop-floor and management, since it is now far more apparent that they are dependent on each other and working towards the same ends.

2

4. The direction and ownership of business is increasingly under separate spheres of influence. It is now increasingly evident that those who control the day-to-day business of manufacturing as Chief Executives, Managing Directors, or Factory Managers - the title is irrelevant - are in reality on the same side of the fence as shop-floor workers. There are several reasons for this:-

a) They are both employees ultimately under the same direction of the same employers.

b) Their fate is equally tied to the future of the enterprise, since the fully employed managing director cannot (and would not be allowed to) exert the freedom of the entrepreneur. Both are liable to the sack for negligence or mismanagement, and experience over the past years has suggested that the director is rather more vulnerable to job-loss than his employees.

c) Both the director and the shop-floor worker are subject to the unpredictable control of a remote employer, who might choose to asset-strip or sell-off the enterprise at a moment's notice with job losses for all.

d) Whilst the director and shop-floor worker (and of course employees in all intermediate levels) are committed to the production and marketing of a specific range of merchandise, and are psychologically united by all the necessary technicalities for achieving this, the remote rentier capitalist employer is only concerned with the game of monopoly in the buying and selling of enterprises, as and when they can bring him a quick profit. Safety pins and bulldozers are all the same to him since he only sees a product as a speculative opportunity.

e) Whilst the director and the shop-floor worker necessarily sink their interests in the long-term (as manufacturing is only viable on such a basis) the remote employer or rentier capitalist is only interested in the short-term in

27-5

enriching himself and his shareholders.

3   5. The industrial economic structure of society has been totally transformed over the past hundred years, so that to talk in 19th century terms of the "evils of capitalism" (as is still done by many today) is to talk nonsense. What has emerged today are two types of capitalism:-

a) Productive Capitalism, entailing those autonomous businesses involved in producing things or services within the free market; and,

b) Rentier Capitalism, entailing the "super-efficient" activities of high finance and the maximising of money profits for shareholders against all other interests.

Rentier capitalism is the cancer of productivity, since not only does it spread its tentacles throughout the entire economy in multifarious ways, but its usurious characteristics deprives manufacturing of essential investment for REAL wealth creation. Whilst Productive capitalism flourishes in a free market economy through competition and choice; Rentier capitalism destroys the free market through monopoly, inflation and the growth of huge bureaucratic structures.

4   6. In underlining the distinction between the two types of capitalism, and in defining the British financial system as Rentier capitalistic, it is useful to contrast this system with that of Japan and all the advanced West European countries. These latter are dominated by Productive capitalistic systems. These are defined according to the following criteria:-

a) That the overriding aim of industrial investment is to secure the long-term success of specific enterprises, and only secondarily to satisfy shareholders needs.

b) That banks and other financial institutions make capital available to secure the success of industrial enterprises as sources for national wealth creation.

c) That the political system be oriented towards *dirigisme* (i.e. directing and overseeing a privately owned economy) as opposed to *laissez-faire* (anything goes) as in a rentier economy.

d) That national interests be safeguarded against external (usually international) exploitation of financial assets: e.g., by putting limitations on foreign ownership, and controlling exchange and interest rates in the national interest as opposed to the priority of safeguarding incoming foreign investments.

e) That the state legislate for a socially democratic and classless society, so that all are trained to fully participate in the complexities of a modern industrialised community.

5   7. Consequently, the new boundaries for social division in the future, must

28-1

be between those who promote Social Wealth Creation (i.e. the participants and advocates of Productive capitalism); against those who promote Unsocial Wealth Creation (i.e. the Rentier capitalists). The criteria for identifying each category may be crudely defined as under:-

a) Productive Capitalists: Those engaged in the production of goods and services for their own immediate profit, as opposed to sacrificing the productive purpose as a source for usury or pure financial speculation.

b) Rentier Capitalists: Those engaged in exploiting the productive efforts of the economy; i.e. living off the periphery of the productive economy, so as to damage or reduce its effectiveness. Such activity may only be identified in specific instances (since benefit and harm is always a question of balance), but in general, rentier activity is promoted in great part by the following:- financiers; bankers; directors of building societies; venture capitalists; money-lenders; personal financial advisers; property developers; monopolists; great landowners (both rural and urban); speculators, and all those accountants and others directing - or forced to direct - productive enterprises on de-industrialising principles.

CHAPTER 28
The Struggle Against Rentier Capitalism

> "The first of all English games is making money. That is an all-absorbing
> game; and we knock each other down oftener in playing at that than at
> football, or any other roughest sport; and it is absolutely without purpose;
> no one who engages heartily in that game ever knows why."

John Ruskin, *The Crown of Wild Olive*, George Allen, 10th ed., 1897, p. 31.

1 - Necessary relevance of such a struggle   2 - Not so much a rentier "Class" as a rentier mentality   3 - And this must be fought against throughout all sectors of the community   4 - Ideological trauma of the political upheaval in Eastern Europe   5 - This, too, has left an ideological vacuum in the West   6 - Has the death knell been struck for the old radical ideal ?   7 - It is unresponsive to resuscitation   8 - It greatness should be appreciated within a historical context   9 - Working people today demand new kinds of freedom   10 - Towards the new kind of solidarity

1   Here, then, we have the basis for an up-to-date and relevant political doctrine, exactly matching contemporary economic needs. We also have the new battle lines for the conflict of the future.

Although we cannot claim to have drawn up divisions for a new Class struggle; we can nonetheless say we have drawn up lines for a battle that may be as intensely fought as any in the past. In this battle, shop-floor workers and company directors may unite as one, together with professional people, public servants, and

28-4

all those in the productive sector, against the might of the City of London, which together with its satraps, over the past decades, has wrought such devastation to jobs and industries in all parts of our country. These battle lines may be regarded as the last stage in the centuries-old struggle for attaining social and economic justice. It is not so much a distinctive class or social sector that now needs to be fought against, as a financial system and those implicated (either consciously or unconsciously) in its atrocious evils.

2   There is no clearly identifiable Rentier Class as such, in the sense of a Bourgeois class as conceived by Socialists, although there is a Rentier mentality that cuts across all sectors of society. This Rentier mentality is something that has to be fought against, since it is at variance with the values necessary for achieving a modern industrialised state. The Rentier mentality militates against the work ethic in its better form, and is especially derived from the pseudo-aristocratic values unique to the English upper middle classes, about which leading sociologists have written so much over the past four decades. The Rentier mentality was actively propagated amongst working people by political leaders in the 1960s and '70s with promises of "unlimited leisure" and an end to the "necessity of work."

3   This kind of utopianism held back the progress of the working class, not only through its demoralising influence in denigrating the positive psychological function of work, but in undermining the ambition of ordinary working people in climbing the ladder of the occupational hierarchy. Like other influences in the old radical politics, it achieved nothing in promoting the classless society, and it was counter-productive in its outcome. The evils of the rentier mentality, with its glorification of leisure and idle pursuits, is therefore to be found in some degree or form, in all sectors of society, and is to be fought against in the struggle for an egalitarian, free, and socially democratic society.

The rentier mentality saps the moral fibre of society, since it arouses the hope of material expectations for no return, and is in some degree responsible for all forms of crime arising from avarice. Again, the rentier mentality is part of the British disease - the symptom of a sick society divided by the internal contradictions of a class-ridden community. But such a society cannot be reformed by promoting class struggle (as may have been advocated in the past) but only by putting all energies into the destruction of the rentier capitalistic system.

4   Before outlining new principles for industrial revolt against the destruction of jobs and industries, it would first be useful to contemplate the world shattering events which took place towards the close of the 1980s, and how these have shaken - if not demolished - the old radical doctrines which maintained the hopes of ordinary working people for so long a period. This is not to suggest that the majority - or even substantial numbers - of British people, may have looked towards the East for

28-6

solace in solving their own very different problems at home; but it is nonetheless significant that the same political ideal, with the same theories as to the ultimate development of humankind, in its different forms, spread throughout the world, from its 19th century origins under the inspiration of its thinker of overwhelming influence. However contrasted the interpretation of those ideals may have been in Britain as compared with the East, the same pair of German thinkers have nevertheless been of enormous influence on all brands of radical thinking coming under the same general description.

5   However repugnant the political systems of the East may have been to great numbers of working people in this country, it remains a fact that the "Holy Grail" of the oppressed and downtrodden was perceived for seventy years as being in the guardianship of the Eastern half of Europe. It was there where the original fires were kept alight uncompromisingly in all their ideological purity and most intense form, and because of that, the East was seen as a scale by which all degrees of the "true faith" could be accurately measured according to its warmth or tepidity. Now all that has gone. A huge void remains. Whither now? Where is the measuring scale? Where are the thinkers for the New Millennium, and who shall lead ?

The events at the end of the past decade in the East bloc countries, were so sudden, so unexpected, and so inconceivable, that the advocates of the old doctrines in Britain and elsewhere are still stunned by their significance. As yet, there has hardly been time to get up from off the floor, let alone to reconsider the intellectual and practical implications of these events. All is uncertainty. There is no longer any true direction - only interim arrangements.

6   The most traumatic effect of the events of the last decade in Eastern Europe must surely be the instinctive question occurring in the minds of many millions of people: Is this symptomatic of the death knell of the radical ideal which in its many manifestations has so successfully led the working class to so many victories over the past hundred and fifty years ?

The question is so painful that many dare not hazard an answer, and yet the sight of so many idols - so firmly entrenched and sacrosanct - knocked to the ground in the High Temple of the East, must inevitably result in that ghastly question insistently raising its ugly head for an answer. With the turmoil of revolt and the struggle for freedom against innumerable restrictions in one country in Eastern Europe after another, the stubborn question simply will not go away. Lenin once claimed that a child nurtured by the state from the age of seven would by adulthood be ideologically committed to the Communist party for life. And yet since then seven times ten years have passed since the great radical ideal took over the reigns of power. Where has all the boasting gone ? Where is the benefit of that great propaganda ? What was its use, and what was its effectiveness when its own

28-9

· children coolly turned on their gods and destroyed them overnight?

7   There are some who will evade the question as to the future of the ideal, by simply arguing that it never had a proper opportunity in the first place to flourish. The soil had never been right. It had never been given a chance to work. It had never been put into practice. Unfortunately, these answers will not wash ! It is like blaming the faults of child nurture on the failures and viciousness of an old man on the point of death. They reflect an ignorance of relevant episodes of history over the past two hundred years. Sometime, somewhere, every permutation of the ideal has been tried and put into practice, either by self-governing states or by voluntary communities (often in the New World), with the result that for one cause or another, the different experiments either fell apart in a storm of acrimony, or evolved along lines of communal living that were originally unintended.

The truth and tragedy is that the old ideal is unresponsive to the best techniques of resuscitation. From the traditional perspective of the old industrialised capitalist Western world, only one thing is certain: the "Communist bogey" has disappeared forever into the mists of history. Little children and old women - and grown men too - may slumber in peace, confident that there are no longer any Reds under the beds. The very concept of the struggle between classical capitalism and Communism, and all the ideological clutter of both contestants for power, is now as dated as that between Cavaliers and Roundheads.

8   Whilst acknowledging the value of the ideal over the past two hundred years in pushing forward the material interests of oppressed peoples, and whilst recognising with respect within an objective historical context, the greatness of those leaders of the working class, the time has now come for a reassessment of radical political values. New conditions have created new problems that are not cured by the old medicines. Furthermore, working people today have new priorities and new demands if they are to be integrated into a classless society. For example, the concept of their solidarity as cloth-cap proletarians is not only anachronistic but contradicts almost all their attitudes and aspirations. The demands on brainpower of an increasingly technological society means that ordinary working people need to have a more competitive and acquisitive ethos than hitherto, and the consequences of this will be a more egalitarian society as the demand for skills diminishes differentials in the earnings' scale.

9   New freedoms occupy the minds of working people today: whilst in the past the emphasis was on freedom from specific causes of privation; today the emphasis is on freedom for the full development of the personality - intellectual freedom, and freedom to develop latent abilities. Such freedom calls for a balance between the conflicting demands of Collectivism and Individualism, whilst reviling them both when carried to their extremes. Certainly workers today exert a greater sense of

29-1

individualism than previously, and put a greater value on the concept of property. The majority are far more friendly towards the idea of business ownership, profits and competition, seeing these things as essential to maintaining a free society.

10 Of most significance is the need for a new kind of solidarity. Class solidarity should now be shovelled onto the dung heap. It is retrogressive and leads to negatively introverted attitudes. In its place should be put a more generous social solidarity - classless in its resolve - keen to embrace the community in total - only intent on confronting the evils of rentier activity. Under the influence of such a new kind of humane all-embracing social solidarity, ordinary working people would be leading the way towards the emergence of the truly classless society.

CHAPTER 29
Regenerating The Spirit of Trades Unionism

> "We need a system more safe, more flexible, more adaptable, and finally more life-sustaining than that constructed by our narrow and one-sided financial economy."
>
> Lewis Mumford, *Technics & Civilization*, Harcourt Brace & Co., NY, 1935, p. 390.

1 - What future for trades unionism ? 2 - Causes of its loss of strength 3 - Why New Socialism promotes the extension of trades union membership 4 - The key to regenerating trades union strength 5 - The need for doctrine in pursuing objective ends 6 - Working people as the leaders instead of the followers in society 7 - Trades unions must now become pro-active 8 - They must demand access to the "secrets" of the boardroom

1   Having reviewed the socio-political outlook of working people as they perceive their situation in the world today, and having concluded that for a number of reasons (already cited) that they may now be said to have reached a crossroads - even though there appears to be little urgency to take a chosen path - let us now return to the future of industrial relationships in the workplace.

What is to be the direction of industrial action in the future ? Already we have seen great changes in the attitude and use of the Strike weapon over the past decade. Trades unions are now muted organisations by comparison with their confidence two decades ago. Have trades unions reached the twilight of their existence ? Their bureaucratisation and intertwined connections with associations that might be seen as compromising their integrity (such as the CBI and employers federations), and a broadening perspective that tends to blunt their true and original purpose, all seems to suggest that they have now reached a "respectable" maturity, and of course, with maturity and age comes a loss of teeth and quick responsiveness.

After discussions with TUC officials and those of several major unions several

29-2

years ago, I could not escape the awful impression that trades union initiative is slipping imperceptibly into the arms of rentier capitalistic scheming. It seems as if organisations with the most militant intentions are not immune forever from the blandishments of the high and mighty. Meanwhile, of course, over the past decade, a multitude of obstacles have been placed before trades union militancy, but that does not entirely account for their gradual transformation into bodies which may almost be said to be part of the "Respectable Establishment."

2   It is the opinion of this author that many trade unions have dissipated their strength as industrial organisations over the past years by engaging in a wide variety of peripheral activities failing to reflect their true purpose. Unquestionably trade unions today lack the sharpness and determined sense of direction which they should have. Why ? It is partly because of their demoralisation through loss of membership from de-industrialisation, but it is also because of the great changes in society that have left the unions with out-dated attitudes and modes of industrial action. We have already identified these. To summarise, they are:-

1. The ideological unattractiveness of the Class war as a stimulus to industrial action.
2. The lesser effectiveness of the Strike weapon in confronting conglomerates and especially internationally or foreign-owned concerns.
3. The popular fear amongst the increasingly skilled sector of the work force that any strike action is liable to be counter-productive.
4. The difficulties of securing trades union membership and organising action when industrial plants are smaller and very much more widespread than previously.
5. The fact that in an increasingly technological and more informed society, it becomes difficult for shop-floor workers to perceive their interests as opposed to those of management.
6. The counter-productive effects in the long term of demonstrating against the modernisation of methods and machinery. (The Japanese experience has clearly demonstrated that the modernisation of methods and plant has not led to loss of jobs but to greater job creation. This, it should be noted, is the logical and practical outcome of implementing the most Productive economy in the world.)
7. The fact that the REAL enemies of working people are not all "bosses" or "employers," but only Rentier capitalists and those employers falling into the Rentier category.

All these factors apply throughout the trades union movement irrespective of the very different types of unions geared to serving the interests of varying groups.

3   The principles of New Socialism are moving towards a situation whereby

29-4

there would be an obligatory extension of trades union membership to cover all spheres of employment in all places of work, for only then can the trades union movement succeed in narrowing the psychological gap between shop-floor workers, office employees, management, and even chief executives holding an employment status. If the trades union movement is eventually to transfer its solidarity away from a "Class war" ideology to a total war against Rentier capitalism, then this can most effectively be achieved by increasing trades union membership to its maximum to include all personnel in the productive sector in the battle against rentier activity.

4   All the above factors point to the following conclusion: it is no longer of benefit to trades unions, or the interests of their members, to project the image of "Class solidarity" against the threat of an "immediate exploiting employer class." This is because such an attitude not only fails to reflect changed realities, but because it no longer carries conviction with the majority of working people. There is no longer any industrial muscle in using the "Class struggle" or "Class solidarity" as a rationale for organised action. What, then, should working people do in effectively promoting their interests ?

If they are to gain real power in securing the support of the majority of our population, and if they are to advance their long-term interests by yards instead of inches, then they need to objectify the nature of their social struggle. This means that industrial action needs to be promoted in the name of the public interest. How can this be achieved ? Only by setting sights on destroying the evils of Rentier capitalism. This social struggle on behalf of the public interest would be fought on the following grounds:-

1. In countering the effects of de-industrialisation.
2. To save jobs in British-based factories.
3. To save industries from extinction.
4. To assist local communities to maintain their existing patterns of population.
5. To promote the interests of national wealth creation, or those of the real economy.
6. To enlighten and assist management and employers as to their better long-term interests.
7. To unify all sectors of employees (from company chairmen downwards) committed to promoting the productive sector.
8. To demonstrate against the banks and other financial institutions for their failure to give support to manufacturing comparable with that found amongst our European competitors or Japan.
9. To fight against all aspects of rentier activity on the grounds of both the damage it inflicts on the real economy, and its injustice in maintaining a

29-7

class divided society: i.e. an economy based on rentiers versus workers. [88]

5   If the trades unions and working people are to objectify their struggle in the public interest, and to organise industrial demonstrations accordingly, it means that in winning and maintaining the necessary level of conviction and morale, great emphasis must be put on the doctrinal principles involved. There has to be a leadership of ideas, not of individuals; or rather, leading individuals have to be bound by the guiding principles of an effective doctrine. This is because ideas are more enduring and comprehensible than individuals, who change, or die, or even misinterpret the given word. Ideas have the function of uniting all members of an association to a single source of authority, and so to a common understanding and the most efficient basis for democratic representation and policy decision-making. Most of all, such ideas must be based on the highest ethical principles, so that they will not only have the widest popular appeal, but act as the most powerful motivation to those promoting them.

6   Ordinary working people armed with such a socio-economic doctrine, if organised on a sufficiently effective basis, will no longer be the followers in society but its leaders. This is because they will no longer be confining their activities within the narrow context of class interests, but instead, seeking to influence and lead the community in total as the truest representatives of that community. Their disinterestedness in pursuing such a path will inevitably place their social struggle on a higher ethical basis than earlier more self-centred efforts to allay inflicting ills.

Their responsibility will be for the total community and as the political representatives of that community, they will seek to identify their will with Absolute values as opposed to Class values. Inescapably they may need to enlighten those whose authority they serve. Senior managers, company chairmen, and even rentiers must be brought round to the true doctrine, and persuaded that in the long-term, their children and their existing extended family would better thrive in a freer and more just society under a Productive as opposed to a Rentier economy. Political, economic and moral arguments must be brought to bear in pushing forward the message. With such a doctrine for socio-economic reform, and under such a leadership, the classless society would emerge as a genuine reality.

7   Such industrial action as is now proposed is the logical - even inevitable - next step in the long history of progress in the workplace. If the Strike weapon is losing its effectiveness to achieve specific ends; if unemployment and declining union membership alone are weakening the power of trades union bodies, then other weapons have to be found in countering industrial ills. Although I suggested that

---

88 See Appendix E.

29-8

trades union strength, over recent years, was dissipated by too many peripheral activities, the opposite is also true. The concentration of each union on the immediate interests of its *current* membership only has led to insular and selfish attitudes towards the labour movement as a whole. Furthermore, such attitudes reflect an ostrich-like approach to urgent problems and have in fact been counter-productive. For example, the unions have done nothing to fight the ROOT causes of unemployment, this being the largest single problem today. The older type of trades union leader will naturally respond by saying that that's an unfair accusation - that it's not the job of trade unionists to turn round the economy. Quite so ! But things have to change. What if unemployment is to worsen at a much faster rate still - which is probable - and trades union membership is to be significantly decimated even further, and what if other forces are brought to bear (as yet unknown) and trades unionism is to be deprived of its last remaining teeth ? Is each union to remain aloof in glorious isolation - only concerned with its *current* membership until the final hour ? Clearly the time has now come for the trades unions to take stock and think pro-actively.

8   Trade unionists today are already deeply interested in the financial management of the firms employing them. Furthermore, they make every endeavour to follow the financial moves entailed in possible buyouts, senior management replacements, and other policy decisions. Although spoon-fed with updates from the corporate office, their lack of real information usually means they are left to merely reading the entrails. This is not good enough since shop-floor workers today not only hold the exclusive possession of a far higher percentage of skills in relation to management, but a far greater intelligence in understanding the financial background in running an enterprise. Nevertheless, such financial and management information is jealously guarded by employers. Shop-floor workers - as well as middle management - are still denied entry to the financial secrets of the board room.

New Socialism says that this is wrong. Workers have a right to such information since their livelihoods are dependent upon it. It is demeaning that shop-floor workers, managers and others, should be used as pawns in a chess game; and it is outrageous that entire industrial enterprises should likewise be used by remote corporate bodies as pawns for enriching remote shareholders. It is outrageous since the outcome is mass unemployment, closures, and even the economic demise of entire communities. [89]

---

89 See Appendix F.

30-1

CHAPTER 30
Promoting Advanced Industrial Action

"The most significant difference distinguishing different societies from each other are, in short, not different forms of constitution and government, but different types of economic and social structure."

R.H. Tawney, *Equality*, Allen & Unwin, 1952 ed., p. 75.

1 - The need for Advanced Industrial Action or the occupation of threatened plants   2 - This would be in serving the public interest   3 - No other group prepared to promote effectively the productive sector   4 - Criteria for justifying the occupation of a plant   5 - Necessary immediate circumstances   6 - Two sole purposes of Advanced Industrial Action

1   Since there is no other weapon in meeting the present and unique industrial problems of our time, New Socialism advocates the taking over of industrial enterprises, by employees and secondary demonstrators, in certain specific circumstances. We have called such occupations, Advanced Industrial Action (AIA).

The occupation of industrial plants facing closure, has been undertaken before by employees in isolated instances, either as an industrial demonstration or as a first step towards setting up a workers' co-operative; but what is now proposed is a far more systematic, decisive and high profile form of industrial solidarity. It is admittedly a form of industrial action requiring greater organisation and conviction than the implementing of the strike weapon, and because of the specialised skills needed in carrying through a successful occupation (as described below), e.g., detailed knowledge of financial practices in the running of a company, it would be necessary for a specialised unincorporated body, known as the Advanced Industrial Action Group (AIAG), to not only direct such occupations but take collective responsibility for their authority and outcome. The Advanced Industrial Action Group would be comprised of trained trades union activists, taken from different unions, with an in-depth knowledge of business, financial management, relevant aspects of law, and the desirable principles of Productive capitalism.

Since the prime purpose of any occupation would be to save the existence of a plant, the outcome of such authority is hardly likely to compromise the best productive interests of the company. Furthermore, the AIAG would wish to avoid encouraging trades unions to engage in any kind of activity that might be unusual or uncomfortable for them to implement. This consideration especially applies in the light of recent trades union legislation.

2   Having given due consideration to the reservations of trade unions, there can be no holds on the convincing rationale justifying the necessity for the occupation

30-4

of industrial plants. Such industrial demonstrations would amount to the most important altruistic action in which working people have ever engaged in. They would be demonstrations concerned with the the most important issue facing Britain today: viz., the need for taxable productive wealth creation, to pay for education; health care; housing; decent pensions and all the welfare benefits of a caring modern industrialised state. None of these benefits can be paid for in Britain without the regeneration of profitable manufacturing enterprises. Therefore, every occupation of an industrial plant would not only be carried out to save jobs and industries, but more significantly, to help create a prosperous and socially democratic society.

3   The ultimate reason justifying such a course of action would be that no other interest group is prepared to take serious or sufficient action for the regeneration of threatened industries. Talking-shops; pressure groups presenting petitions or proposals for legislation; and even parliamentary committees, are impotent in their efforts to move the granite resistance of rentier vested interests.   Meanwhile, manufacturers are locked into co-operating with a financial system (whether they like it or not) counter-productive to their efforts, and are fearful of offending their usurious lenders or be perceived as "knocking" the established "As is" situation.

In this they are hardly better than lemmings following a path of self-destruction, led as they are by a mixture of ignorance, hoping-against-hope, fear of more powerful vested interests, short-sightedness, myopic conservatism, and plain stupidity. Even enlightenment to the true facts often fails to motivate them towards pre-emptive action in saving their own enterprises from eventual and inevitable extinction. Hence it becomes the necessary and noble task of ordinary working people, not only to save jobs and industries, but to snatch their own "bosses" from the flames of destruction, and setting them on a new course for the regeneration of their broken companies. In this role, the interests of workers and "bosses" must be perceived as one, even if the judgement of the latter is clouded by the false consciousness of rentier sympathies or the empty hope of eventual salvation by our existing financial institutions.

4   An occupation would be carried out on behalf of any business or utility, threatened with closure or job losses, providing only that a sound case could be made for regenerating that enterprise on a profitable basis. It would be totally against the principles of New Socialism, and anyway, economically counter-productive in the long-term, to launch demonstrations on behalf of "lost leaders" or against redundancies due to the installation of new methods or machinery. But if, on the other hand, a business is to be closed on the grounds that it "No longer pays," and it is subsequently calculated that the costs of closure and the future maintenance of the site, is greater than continuing the operation of the plant (as indeed happened in the case of coal mines), then an argument will have been found for justifying an

30-6

occupation.

Advanced Industrial Action could be carried out on behalf of any kind of business, subject to the discretion of the AIAG; such discretion being guided by the possible publicity value of an occupation. The criteria for publicity value would depend not primarily on the size or location of the enterprise, but on the specific circumstances of the case as it illustrates the failure of rentier capitalism to successfully engage in profitable productivity. Therefore, department stores; mines; off-shore rigs; merchant ships; the larger agricultural estates; supply utilities; railways and construction sites, as well as factories, could apply to implement Advanced Industrial Action. These chapters, however, will confine themselves to describing those necessary steps in the occupation of a factory.

5   The occupation of a plant, or AIA, would be implemented in the following circumstances:-

1. After the threat of a large scale redundancy.
2. After the announcement of a questionable takeover.
3. In the event of liquidation or bankruptcy.
4. The closure of a plant for any other reason.
5. In the event of gross mismanagement threatening jobs or long-term profitability.

6   The sole purpose of Advanced Industrial Action would be:-

1. To save and regenerate industrial enterprises as autonomous profitable concerns answerable to their own productive purposes; and,
2. To seek maximum publicity in demonstrating to the general public the evils of de-industrialising employment-destroying rentier capitalism.

In view of the extreme measure in carrying out an occupation, such industrial action must put a strong emphasis on its benefit to the public interest. Workers would be demonstrating altruistically in saving wealth creating jobs, not only for their children but for their children's children. It would be a demonstration for a more effective and just economic system.

CHAPTER 31
Strategy For The Industrial Occupation

"It is not beside the mark to remind you, that the prosperity of industry depends not merely upon the improvement of manufacturing processes, not merely upon the ennobling of the individual character, but upon a third condition, namely, a clear understanding of the conditions of social life on the part of both the capitalist and the operative, and their agreement upon common principles of social action."

T.H. Huxley, *Science & Culture*, Macmillan, 1888, p. 22.

1 - Preparing the strategy for an occupation   2 - Steps required in initiating an occupation   3 - Not the purpose of the AIAG to supplement or supplant the function of trades unionism   4 - An occupation in collusion with employers   5 - Carrying out the occupation   6 - Authority relinquished to the AIAG   7 - First tasks of the Occupation Commander   8 - Preparations for the Industrial Efficiency Tribunal

1   Such occupations would need to be carried out after careful pre-planning, so as to minimise the risk of lost earnings or other benefits to employees, as well as minimising the risks of law-breaking. The strategy for each occupation would need to be judged according to many prevailing circumstances, e.g.:-

1. Timing of occupation in minimising employees' losses.
2. Layout of the plant, guarding of exits and entrances and the manning of look-out posts.
3. Personality of those controlling the plant in anticipating their response to the occupation.
4. Carefully planned steps, through confidential meetings and one-to-one discussions, in maximising the number of middle and senior managers as activists in promoting the occupation.
5. The acquisition and delivery into the plant of food and bedding (pillows and sleeping bags) in the event of a protracted siege.
6. The efficient maintenance of mains supplies, including telecommunications, and the installation of emergency utilities in the event of cut-off.
7. Sufficient medical supplies in the event of injuries or disease.
8. Locks, chains, bars, and other materials to prevent break-ins.
9. Loud hailers or a tannoy system in communicating with those outside the plant - especially in the event of an attack.
10. Preparedness to adapt the strategy in any way, at long or short notice, in meeting specific conditions, to maximise the success of the occupation.

2   Before a decision is taken to occupy a plant the following measures would

31-3

need to be taken:-

    1. That a meeting of employees be held and that a sufficient number vote, a) To occupy the plant; and, b) To participate in that occupation and to carry out tasks under the Occupation Commander. A vote of 50% of employees would normally be required.

    2. In the event of organised opposition against occupation, if this should reach the figure of 20% of employees, then the proposed occupation should not go ahead.

    3. A minimum of 5 employees organising the occupation must hold Individual membership of the AIAG. This would be for a small firm. Otherwise, 10% of those voting for an occupation should hold AIAG membership.

    4. That a written invitation be submitted by employees' organisers to the Central Office of the AIAG requesting an occupation, and that the two signatories to such a letter be AIAG members.

    5. That such a letter be accompanied by -

a) A statement on the company's present situation together with complaints of alleged mismanagement and threats to jobs and the plant;

b) A proposed strategy for the occupation of the plant, including numbers of persons to be appointed as guards, cooks, medical orderlies, etc., and,

c) Draft proposals for a desired solution to the problem.

    6. That an AIA Committee be set up with members separately responsible for the following functions:- 1) Chair person (Chief employees' representative); 2) Treasurer, to oversee expenses and possibly raise money for costs; 3) Press Officer; 4) Publicity Officer (in charge of producing leaflets, etc.); 5) Outside Activities Officer, for organising demonstrations in the locality for supporting the occupation; 6) Technical Officer, for maintaining all necessary equipment brought into the plant or already there; 7) Catering Officer, part of whose duties may entail organising workers' spouses for preparing dishes for buffet dinners; and, 8) Security Officer. Sub-Committees may be set up as required.

    7. That a negotiated fee be agreed for payment to the AIAG Central Office for directing the overall tasks throughout the occupation.

3   One thing should be made clear before initiating any AIA demonstration: there must be no negotiations or any kind of direct communication between officers of the AIAG and employers prior to completing the occupation of a plant. It is not the function of the AIAG to supplement or supplant the activity proper to trades union representatives. Advanced Industrial Action is only to be initiated in the following two circumstances:-

a) After the breakdown of trades union negotiations with employers, or,

31-5

b) In the event of no other alternative action being available by employees in the attempt to save jobs or enterprises.

If, on the contrary, AIAG officials were to become involved in negotiations alongside trades unionists with employers, an impossible situation would only become protracted. As discussions were drawn out *ad infinitum* by employers, any serious intention to cross the Rubicon by carrying out an occupation would inevitably become de-fused. It has to be noted that not only is a completed occupation a decisive action marking a point of no return; but it also symbolises a violent seizure of power, and as such, gives employees a clear advantage in a confrontational situation. AIA begins only when conventional trades union activity ceases. That is the perception as employers and the public should see the situation.

4   Employees embarking on Advanced Industrial Action might, in some circumstances, wish to carry out an occupation in collusion with the chief executives of a plant. This would most likely occur when the plant was under the overall direction of a Factory manager; but it could also occur when company directors are in charge of subsidiaries threatened with extinction by remote corporate bodies. In instances of collusion between workers and employers, the support of the latter may be expressed either overtly or covertly. When there is covert support from company directors, then, for publicity reasons, they may choose to present themselves as prisoners of the occupiers, confined to "cells" and voluntarily standing trial at the Industrial Efficiency Tribunal (see below), revealing evidence implicating the guilt of the controlling corporate body.

In other circumstances, when occupiers are facing popular and allegedly competent employers with whom they wish to have no quarrel or dispute, a situation will arise when the former must persuade the latter that the occupation is in the best interests of the enterprise in confronting the bank or government or other source of blame. In those circumstances every effort should be used in persuading employers to actively promote the occupation as a public demonstration against de-industrialisation.

5   As soon as agreement has been reached between employees' representatives and the AIAG Central Office for the occupation of a plant, the wheels of the system will be put into motion. On the agreed day at the exact hour - it could be any hour of the clock - the AIAG Central Office representative, as the Commander of the occupied plant, will arrive at the gates - or other venue - to be met by demonstrating employees. Whenever possible an occupation should be planned as a shock-surprise event, so that employers are put sufficiently off their guard to be confused, frightened and defensive over the following few days.

Three flags will be carried into the building, for flying in a prominent position on the roof or porch: the AIAG flag to be flanked by two Union Jacks. In addition,

31-8

huge cloth streamers with slogans, should be hung across the front of the factory and in other prominent positions. These streamers should carry the following slogans amongst others: "New Socialism Is Saving Britain;" "This Factory Is Under AIAG Occupation;" "The AIAG Creates Jobs For British People;" "Help Save This Factory And Support Our Cause;" "The AIAG Against De-Industrialisation."

6   As soon as the AIAG flag has been hoisted, the employees' representatives or the trade union (or unions) will cease to exert any official further responsibility or authority within the confines of the plant. They will have   relinquished their authority to the AIAG.   The AIAG, however, will only hold itself responsible for those acts it directly initiates. The occupation will be for minimum period of 48 hours, but may last for as long as desired by the occupying employees.

Throughout the occupation, every effort would be made to remain within the limits of the law. The act of occupation may be carried out without infringing the law. Here is not the place to explore into the technicalities as to how this is to be achieved. The Occupation Commander, for example, may justify his presence on the invitation of "authorised employees" to carry out on-site consultancy; or shop-floor workers may argue that "technical problems" oblige them to remain by their machines on a "round-the-clock" basis with rest periods on site.

7   The first task of the Occupation Commander will be to inspect security in preventing unathorised entry or exit from the plant at any time.   Only the Commander will issue such authorisation.   In practice, if the plant is still in operation, or part-operation, it may mean that employees continue to come and go according to their shift, but there would in any case need to be a hard core of occupying demonstrators, pledged to remaining at the plant over a 24-hour period. In many cases, however, the plant would not be in operation (e.g. in instances of liquidation or bankruptcy) and a total siege situation would pertain.

Having inspected the security of the plant, measures would then be taken for setting up a communications centre and a press office. The Commander, together with his aides or elected Committee (the original AIA Committee having been dissolved and reconstituted under his authority) would by this time have many documents at their disposal concerning the troubles of the company; covering its de-industrialising policies; internal management conflicts; incompetence; redundancy plans, etc. As the Committee sat in the boardroom, discussing different aspects of the company, and as witnesses were constantly called and questioned to lay out their complaints, recalling vivid stories of personal wrong-doing and the eccentricities of senior management in adversely effecting the running of the company; the files of the Committee would become thicker and thicker.

8   After many hours, the Committee would retire for refreshments, and following a night's sleep, the Commander would be at his desk at 5.0 am, preparing his papers

32-1

for the next stage of the operation. By 10.0 am, a meeting would be held in the press room. Journalists would be supplied with sensational material, well-spiced with interesting personal details, and after a question and answer session, plans would be announced for holding an Industrial Efficiency Tribunal.

Preparations would then be rapidly pushed ahead for holding the Tribunal. The Tribunal might be held in the canteen, or some other room, where tables and chairs would be placed at distance from each other on a dais, and where ample space is allowed for public spectators. The public would then be encouraged to participate in the occupation and to attend the subsequent Tribunal. In practice they would be secondary demonstrators, welcomed from any part of the country, but in gaining admittance to the plant, they would either need to show AIAG membership cards, or trades union credentials as part of a voluntary contingent sent to assist the occupation.

CHAPTER 32
The Industrial Efficiency Tribunal

> "Owners of industrial capital are normally somewhat dumb, and this is in itself socially significant; for it tends to show that as owners they have no group-mind and are passive in regard to social functions."

> C. Delisle Burns, *Industry & Civilization*, Allen & Unwin, 1925, p. 171.

1 - Purpose of the Tribunal: Every enterprise financially accountable as an autonomous unit   2 - Identifying and ridding rentier practices   3 - New Socialism's doctrines: the criteria for good and bad business practices   4 - Style of the Tribunals   5 - Other demonstrations during an occupation   6 - Opening of the Tribunal   7 - Its procedural structure   8 - The Chair person's Censorious Judgement   9 - The Constructive Judgement

1   The Industrial Efficiency Tribunal would perform a unique function. Its three purposes would be, a) To assess the efficiency of a plant as an instrument of Productive capitalism; b) To apportion blame, and when necessary, criminality according to the socio-economic criteria of the AIAG; and, c) To propose and attempt the enforcement of its measures for saving the enterprise.

In examining the costs of production, utilities, labour, other overheads, taxes, profits, etc., the plant would be judged on the grounds of its operating as an autonomous unit. If, in fact, that is not possible, i.e. if several plants at different locations co-operate in manufacturing the same item, then those factors would be taken into consideration. If, on the contrary, the plant is a wholly owned subsidiary within a group, the financial or accountancy implications entailing an indebtedness

32-2

to the corporate body or some part thereof, would be dismissed as irrelevant if that is the sole cause of indebtedness threatening closure.

Under a Productive capitalistic system, every plant must only be financially accountable to itself, and not be subjected to the use or misuse of detached third parties (i.e. speculators) only intent on the quick profit. If a plant cannot justify itself as a financially autonomous body, i.e. if after paying its employees and outgoings and selling its product, it is left without a profit and a sufficient margin for re-investment and shareholders, then in ordinary circumstances, it cannot justify its existence.

2   The Tribunal, however, is also concerned with *extraordinary* circumstances. That is, not only are enterprises ruined through rentier capitalistic games on the chess board, i.e. through the buying and selling of companies for a quick profit, and the asset-stripping that follows from this, including even, the acquisition and closure of companies merely to obtain the possession of building plots; but they are also ruined through internal rentier practices inevitable in the management of companies, due to the law and custom of our land. These are allegations that would simply not be understood by run-of-the-mill accountants, bankers and financial advisers, since they work within the narrow confines of their own claustrophobic disciplines. They cannot see anything wrong in the practices they have always followed and succeeded in.

The British exporting professional, on the other hand (like the present writer) has quite a different perspective of business practices. In view of the rentier handicaps of our financial practices and institutions, the experienced British exporter knows that any British company, irrespective of its skills, equipment, or existing financial resources, is in the long term like a minnow confronted by a shark when faced by a Japanese or European competitor. With our present financial institutions, there is no way in which any British company can secure its long-term existence.

There is a need, of course, to distinguish between internal or voluntary rentier practices (i.e. those that are blameworthy), from those that are external or imposed. Dick Taverne has most succinctly differentiated Rentier from Productive voluntary practices in the internal management of a company, when he wrote, "where British boards talk of profit and share price, their Continental and Japanese opposites talk products and market shares. ... British and American companies worry about making their assets sweat even if higher returns are won by surrendering market share, while their Continental and Japanese rivals are more concerned about the long-term benefits of increasing market share. The gradual loss of our share of a whole series of world markets is an all too evident consequence." 90   As far as imposed or

---

90 In *Economic Affairs*, October 1990.

32-4

external) rentier practices are concerned, most may be brought under the following headings: too-short accountancy periods; other accountancy practices in relation to taxation matters; the unavailability of long-term capital at low interest rates; unhelpful government policies on exchange and interest rates (all dictated by the demands of rentier capitalism), etc.

3   The criteria for efficiency and inefficiency, for good and bad management, for matters of right and wrong in all business decision-making, will be judged according to the rational economic doctrines carefully developed by New Socialism. Such doctrines derive their truth not from any intellectual constructs but from the empirical evidence of our competitors in Japan and Western Europe. It is only subsequent to this successful experience that the socio-economic doctrines of New Socialism have been carefully formulated.

Doubtlessly, managing directors, accountants, bankers, and others, who are called to account for their misdemeanours by the Industrial Efficiency Tribunal, accused of offences they had never before heard of, will at first be perplexed and anxious. They will gape in incomprehension and blank expressions. Their ignorance will be no defence. The greatest offences to humanity are unconscious acts. The worst crimes are unintended deeds. But the Chair person of the Tribunal will show leniency to the unwitting offenders. They will be afforded the opportunity to read the pamphlets of the AIAG and in this way, will discover for themselves their mistakes in the past.

4   The Tribunal would be headed by the Occupation Commander, assisted by two Vice-Chairmen. The Chair persons of such Tribunals would not only need to be knowledgeable in the socio-economic doctrines of New Socialism, but in the financial practices entailed in the management of different types of businesses. Initially, they would be mere amateurs - pushed into the office as AIAG activists - but with the passing of time, their function would jell in becoming professionalised.

The style and structure of the Tribunal would be reminiscent of impeachment proceedings, and since it will primarily be concerned with arousing public interest and support, its style of oratory would be Ciceronian, resembling that of those trials during the last century of the Roman Republic, when corrupt and powerful citizens were indicted for crimes against the public interest. 91 All those standing accused would conduct their own defence, although they might call and question witnesses, or ask a colleague to deliver a testimony of competence or good character. The notification to the accused to stand before the Tribunal would be a matter of hours rather than days, since every endeavour would be made to start proceedings within

---

91 The political speeches of Marcus Tullius Cicero may still be studied with benefit and used as a model by
   AIAG activists at Tribunal hearings.

32-5

24 hours of the occupation. In these courts, quick justice would be the rule ! However, the Tribunals might be adjourned at any time to allow the gathering of further evidence or the fetching of witnesses. If the occupiers were to suffer the humiliation of being violently ejected from the plant (only made likely in the event of insufficient defences being in place) then the Tribunal would be held in nearby premises hired for the purpose.

5   Meanwhile, as preparations were being made to hold the Tribunal, other activities would be initiated by the occupying forces for productive wealth creation. As secondary demonstrators from many parts of the country, flocked to the occupied plant, tasks would be found for all. Under the direction of the Commander, different groups would be formed, each with its leader and each with a specific purpose. Some groups would demonstrate outside banks, building societies, and other financial offices, with placards and petitions against the de-industrialising usury of our financial institutions.

In the event of the occupied plant having fallen foul of its own bank, that bank might be picketed - but in such a way as to avoid a confrontation with the law. Other groups would sell the publications of the AIAG, whilst others solicited for Individual membership in the town centre. Other groups would organise marches, or even impromtu meetings in town squares, pubs, or other suitable venues. Those participating in the occupation, and especially those engaged in activities outside the plant, would be urged to wear AIAG armbands.

During the day, in the plant, the office would hum with activity. Appointed occupiers would be engaged in telephoning relevant organisations, other firms, specialised bodies, etc., for support for the occupation. Both cash and personnel would be requested. In the evenings, de-briefing sessions would be held for the different groups, planning meetings for the following day, and discussion circles for those wishing to have a deeper understanding of the AIAG's socio-economic thinking. A 24-hour shift system would be in operation so that whilst the majority slept safely, the plant would be patrolled by security officers as others manned the look-outs.

6   At last, the moment would arrive for the Tribunal to open its first session. The only officials apart from the three Chair persons, would be the Clerk to call witnesses and keep order, and an unspecified number of stewards to watch over and control those called to give evidence. The press would be given full reporting rights, including permission to use cameras and recorders. The first Chair person of the Tribunal might, if he so chose, invite spectators to participate in the proceedings from time to time. He would do this either by calling out: "Any questions from the floor,?" or, after examining an accused person, crying out, "What comments does the floor have to that,?" or, "How far does this man's guilt extend ?" In this way the

32-7

decision-making of the Tribunal would be democratised, and the attending public be given a share as judges in the proceedings. Also, such participation would act as a reassurance to the Chair persons what might well be complex issues were understood by the spectators - and especially by the employees of the enterprise involved in the proceedings. All this would be reminiscent of Athenian legal proceedings.

7   The proceedings of the Tribunal would be structured as under:-

1. An opening address by the Chair person in which reasons giving rise to the occupation are put into perspective and the tone is set for the trial to follow. The Chair person would stand whilst giving this speech, as in a Roman trial, and the gist of his remarks would be addressed to the media.

2. The hearing of complaints against alleged inefficiency in the management and conduct of the company's business, and especially rentier malpractices in the financial management of the company; and/or the hearing of complaints against third parties that might have brought the company to a crisis situation, e.g. its bank, unfavourable legislation or government policy.

3. Inspection of the company's accounts, especially in regard to its share structure, and financial status within a group or international conglomerate. In the event of delays or refusal by the officers of the company to produce requested documents, this would be construed as showing contempt for the Tribunal, and consequently, hearsay evidence might be accepted as fact until such time as contrary documents are produced.

4. The presentation of a report on the financial exploitation of the Productive Purpose of the company. This would be prepared in strict accordance with the doctrinal principles of New Socialism.

5. The presentation of charges against the accused: i.e. directors and other specified officers of the company; or, responsible third parties, as bank managers, venture capitalists, stockbrokers, external accountants, etc., or, more remote sources of blame for the company's crisis, e.g. the government and its departments.

6. Calling the accused and their trial. In those cases where serious charges of de-industrialising rentier activity are to be heard, a Jury of 12 persons (preferably chosen from amongst employees of the company) may be requested to sit in judgement on the directors and/or responsible third parties. In the event of the non-appearance of the accused, or their refusal to plead, they may be judged guilty and denounced as Public Enemies. In assuring the non-contravention of the law, such a denunciation would not be pronounced by the Tribunal, but by a self-appointed body of 6 persons owing no recognition or allegiance to any other body, association, or individual. This

32-9

nebulous body of unnamed persons, hovering on the periphery of the proceedings amongst spectators, shouting occasional comments and slogans as a nice counterpoise to the legal finesse of the Tribunal, would act as a kind of Greek chorus in drawing attention of all present to the socio-economic principles of New Socialism and the necessity of their implementation.

8   7. The Chair person would deliver his Censorious Judgement on the accused, which may be as under:-

a) No adverse judgement on the officers of the company, or responsible third parties, since blame is put on remoter influences: e.g. the government or its departments for allowing invincible competition through unfavourable exchange or interest rates, etc.   The Tribunal may then censure the government or its departments.

b) The accused judged negligent and instructed to manage the company under the guidance of the AIAG.

c) The accused judged grossly incompetent and incapable of continuing to run the company.

d) The accused found guilty of serious rentier offices, and this may lead to their denunciation as Public Enemies.

9   8. The Chair person will deliver his Constructive Judgement in bringing the Tribunal to a close, comprising: a) An interim; and, b) A long-term plan for regenerating and sustaining the profitability of the productive purpose of the company. He may choose to dismiss or appoint new directors as he sees fit; create an employees' co-operative should this be judged practicable, or recommend other measures for the future of the enterprise. He may choose to negotiate behind the scenes with local authorities; favourable banks (which for obvious reasons shall not be named in this book); or other organisations or individuals to save the threatened enterprise. He may call for the temporary suspension of international trade agreements (for 18-month periods with the possibility of renewal), and the imposition of import duties to facilitate time for the regeneration of damaged industries. In fact, every conceivable helpful measure and recommendation would be taken to save the threatened company from extinction.

33-2

CHAPTER 33
The New International Struggle

"All people live in society for their mutual advantage; so that the good and happiness of the members, that is, of the majority of the members of any state, is the great standard by which everything relating to that state must finally be determined."

Joseph Priestley, *Essay On The First Principles of Government*, 2nd ed., 1771, p. 13.

1 - Value of the Tribunals as dramatic events   2 - But their main value will be in problem solving   3 - And in galvanising the hesitant towards positive action   4 - Familiarity with the Tribunals will engender their acceptance   5 - How rentier capitalism is devastating America   6 - And by different means the Third World   7 - AIA must be made to work in reversing de-industrialisation.

1   The immediate reaction of many to the above proposals - which even now may be set in motion without further ado - is that such Tribunals would be without a shred of legal authority. They would be perceived as dramatic events performed through a facade of imaginary legalities - mere assumptions of right and wrong. They would be dismissed as designed for creating a specific effect.

There would be a significant half-truth in all such perceptions, but that need not matter nor detract from the real value of their function. As dramatic events, their prime purpose must be seen in vividly revealing the root causes of our economic ills, and in clearly pointing to the practical measures needed in regenerating the manufacturing sector. These things need to be pointed out with such a simplicity of explanation and crystal clarity, that even the dullest wit may comprehend their true sense.   These economic lessons (which sometimes may entail considerable complexity) can only be taught effectively to the masses, and hold their attention, through the imagery of dramatic re-enactment, and its reporting through the media. The greatest value of these Tribunals as dramatic events should be seen as a moral force on the wider community. Their influence should be valued:-

a) Through demonstrating the evils of de-industrialising rentier capitalism, and,

b) In creating ever greater pressures for necessary legislation.

2   But their value as organs for the dissemination of enlightened political and economic thinking would be exceeded by their practical grasp of existing problems and attending to their solution.   The first purpose of any occupation and the subsequent Tribunal must be to find any viable path for sparing the enterprise from extinction. If the Tribunals fail in that function, they will have failed in all. They may draw up and finalise plans for regenerating broken companies on a profitable

33-4

basis, but if such plans are disallowed by a controlling group or by a financial institution demanding its two pounds of flesh, then the Tribunal cannot be said to have failed entirely in its office. It will then be for employees and secondary demonstrators to fight for the just and viable solution.

The Tribunal would not be in a position to dictate to usurers, but only to plead for more reasonable payment terms. Hopefully, most occupations would conclude after the achievement actual success, i.e. the saving of companies through agreement reached with all relevant controlling parties. With experience and time, such success rates should improve on a constant basis.

3   A further value of the style and speed of such Tribunals in saving the broken company, would be in their exercise of electro-shock therapy. The company in decline, or facing the immediate prospect of bankruptcy and closure, is in a tired depressed state, waiting only for what it believes is the inevitable. Its officers often lack imagination, energy and will, needed for taking those extraordinary decisions necessary for saving the enterprise. The industrial occupation and the hurried Tribunal that follows, is geared to galvanising all parties to implementing first emergency, and then interim, and finally, longer term measures for saving the company. It is also geared to shaking the full truth out of the most secretive and stubborn witnesses. The wide publicity of the Tribunal may also attract support from all kinds of unexpected quarters in saving the company.

4   Finally, over a period of time, the Tribunals would become more established in performing their proper function. They would seem less strange to the ordinary citizen, who was ignorant of the world of industry, and their image would become more acceptable to the majority. The sharpness of their inquisitorial style; their ferreting out of financial secrets; the unpredictability of their requests for new sources of evidence; and the populism entailed in spectator participation, would not only appear customary but even essential to achieving their ultimate objectives. They would convey a directness and integrity of purpose, contrasting markedly with the deviousness, slow pace, and hypocrisy of the ordinary court, that often appears to conceal rather than reveal striking pieces of evidence.

With the passing of time, what seemed outrageous or excessive in its demands, would become commonplace and accepted without question. As the Tribunals built up a system of precedent, based on earlier decisions and procedures, custom would become established both in the minds of the Industrial Efficiency Authority and the community at large, and eventually, custom would imperceptibly but inevitably mutate into regulation and law. Ultimately, the authority of the Tribunals would become an essential arm of the state in safeguarding the wealth creating productive sector, and all those social benefits and costs on the public purse deriving its support from the taxable income of such a sector.

33-6

5   Despite first impressions to the contrary, the philosophy of the AIAG and New Socialism, is international in its scope. It embraces the highest ethical ideals and the best interests of peoples throughout our world. Although amongst the advanced countries of the industrialised West, the evils of rentier capitalism are most acute in Britain, these evils are not unique to her. Due to the nature of the financial institutions themselves, i.e. the pre-eminence of *laissez-faire* and the Investor in capitalist activity, as opposed to the pre-eminence of those objects invested in, rentier activity is a severe problem throughout the Anglo-Saxon world. It is a problem most of all in America, the initiator of so many ingenious rentier practices (which have wrought considerable havoc on this side of the Atlantic over the past thirty years), but because of its huge size and massive internal resources, the evils of rentier capitalism may in the recent past not have been so apparent in that country. But now the birds have come home to roost. America's manufacturing base is possibly, in relative terms, far more devastated than our own. Suddenly Americans have awoken from a sweet dream to be confronted by the horror that everything they touch is from the Orient. Meanwhile, massive unemployment has been rising; banks have collapsed (190 in the first nine months of 1990); cities are facing bankruptcy; public welfare services and essential utilities are falling apart; and the country is saddled with a ruinous and worsening deficit.

Corporate debt (as of October 1990) amounted to 46% of the corporate sector's capital, an increase of 34% over the previous decade, and consumer debt after income tax was up 20% - far higher than during the previous recession. Robert Brusca, a senior economist at Nikko Securities in New York, bemoaned that, "everything we have learnt about economics has been turned upside down. Monetary policy cannot be used to help the economy and cutting government spending is the wrong thing to do at the wrong time." 92 Had he been better informed he would know that all these ills have arisen due solely to the activity of unrestrained rentier capitalism, which has destroyed the productive sector, or genuine wealth creation, or the REAL economy.

6   But rentier capitalism is also a major problem in the Third World, although there it takes on a different form from that in the industrialised West. In the Third World it is simply either, a) A matter of traditional rentiers living off the labour of the peasantry; or, b) A re-enactment of the socio-economic pressures of early 19th century capitalism, including child slave labour (of which the latest world figure has been calculated at 200,000,000), and the forced prostitution of women on a vast scale throughout South East Asia and Central and South America. The ills of the

---

92 Jonathan Confino, "Economic Gloom Grows Over America's Deficit," in *The Daily Telegraph*, 12th October 1990.

33-7

Third World call for different cures from those in the West. The Third World needs Intermediate Technology (and the more equal distribution in the ownership and control of the means of production that follows from this) but the great international rentier bankers are reluctant to assist with such a course of development. Their usurious profits cannot so easily be made when the means of production are so widely spread. Instead, their massive borrowing ends up in the pockets of drug merchants, proprietors of *Latifundia*, extortionists, gangsters and racketeers of all kinds.

Irrespective of whether we look at the searing economic problems in the Third World or those in the industrialised West, it is only New Socialism, with its formulated and proven principles for Productive capitalism, which can solve the major economic issues now facing our planet in satisfying both the needs of freedom and justice.

7   The magnitude of the problem faced by New Socialism in counteracting the heavy resistance of apathy, scepticism and entrenched pessimism, call for very special measures. It is because of this that Advanced Industrial Action and the successful occupation of threatened enterprises must be made to work in turning the tide of Britain's de-industrialisation. It embodies a call for a new direction in industrial solidarity, whereby working people (according to the broadest definition of that term), shall lead our country from the darkness of decline to the light of a new and more prosperous era.

****

PART V

The Human Priorities Of Politics

"The maxims of statecraft are still those that were in vogue in the eighteenth century. The slogans by which men win elections are just as foolish as they used to be. Short-sighted greed blinds communities to their long-term interests quite as much as it ever did. Skill without wisdom is the cause of our troubles."

Bertrand Russell, *Human Society In Ethics & Politics*, Allen & Unwin, 1954, pp. 211-212.

How can the philosophical approach of New Socialism be most concisely summarised ? With regard to human values, it is simply achieved through a synthesis between the demands of Collectivism and those of Individualism, as understood in both the individual's relationship with society and as a political stance in solving the major needs of the community.

For over two hundred years the problems of justice and injustice, of wealth and poverty, have circulated around the conflicting and seemingly insoluble demands of Collectivism and Individualism. These two concepts alone have any meaning in penetrating the core reality of political life. All else is mere illusion in which these two qualities are dressed up in a variety of political guises to do battle, as one era follows another. Here, for the first time, in the following chapters, is an attempt to lay the groundwork towards a common cause - by creating a synthesis between these hitherto ubiquitous and conflicting tendencies.

The human priorities of politics should be a question of moral choice and disinterested justice, and that is the basis for discussion in the following chapters. An objective approach to politics with regard to the best needs of the community, is at the same time the only viable intellectual and moral basis for such a study.

Only two lines of argument are opposed to such an approach, both stemming from the extremes of the political spectrum. Those on the right unselfconsciously proclaim that the only purpose of democratic political life is the pursuit of vested interests - howsoever narrow or selfish. Their argument is that democracy cannot be otherwise, and that morality has no business to intrude on the scene, and if it does so, it is in all probability hypocritical cant.

Those on the left proclaim the Marxist argument that we are all inescapably influenced by our own background and are therefore locked into the class war. There is no escaping from this. Historical materialism must run its predestined and inevitable course.

Both attitudes are closely similar. Not only do they both reflect a belief in the subjectivity of the individual, but they actually promote the idea of that subjectivity as a good in itself. Whilst the Marxist promotes the idea of class hatred as a necessary means towards a desired end in developing the logic of history; the Tory extremist excuses the excesses of selfishness and greed, as "the hidden hand" (to use Adam Smith's original phrase) which ultimately, and supposedly, contributes to the best material needs of the community.

Both attitudes are wildly wrong. They are also unreasonable and anti-intellectual. That is, they engender a mentality which revolts against the idea of questioning prejudice. Whilst Marxists (since the founder himself) have systematically resorted to abuse and ridicule in encountering difficult opposition; those on the right have simply turned a blind eye on the world in zealously pursuing their own egoistical ends. Their wealth and sense of comfortable security alone has deemed it unnecessary for them to even reply to their critics - let alone to indulge in the luxury of abuse.

Amongst thinking people in the contemporary industrialised West, such "traditional" political attitudes as described above, are no longer acceptable. Firstly, the world is a much more complex place than once imagined by the liberal thinkers of the last century, and whilst accepting that freedom is dependent on a competitive free enterprise economy, it has now become clear that the world needs but lacks an acceptable systematic philosophy circumscribing the limits of such an economy. We are now living in a world that has outgrown the ideas that originally brought it into being, and consequently, we are applying old and ineffective cures to problems of which we have little understanding.

Secondly, the intellectual subjectivism of the contemporary world, is not only responsible for all the immorality of political life but also for its short-sightedness and stupidity. The pessimism and fatalism we see today is traceable to such varied intellectual strands of thought as those of Hume, the evolutionists (in their different guises), Marx and Freud, and most of all, to the American philosophy of Pragmatism, which in its several manifestations (especially education) is threatening Western civilisation. These forces are a threat since they undermine the individual's belief in the validity of reason, in the value of scepticism, and in the need for constructive thought. In place of reason, it is argued, instinct and intuition is all that is needed in judging the right or wrong of any situation. It is unnecessary to elaborate on the immorality and massive destruction of life and property brought about by such strands of thought in the 20th century. Political philosophy has entered a watershed.

What is the answer ? If we are to emerge from the intellectual sterility of contemporary political life we must retrace our steps. If we are to unlock the creative power of thought in solving the very practical problems facing us today and in the near future, then we must re-establish Idealist philosophy to its former status. It is in *Ideas* where all creativity begins and ends, and it is only through *Ideas* and the perception of objectivity that the criteria for right or wrong can be found. It is in the failure of contemporary political systems, and in the disillusionment with political life, that grounds are finally given for the urgent need for a fresh intellectual approach to the world we live in. There is no other starting point to the solution of our most complex and urgent political problems than the pursuit of Idealist philosophy. All other paths lead inevitably to the hopelessness of cynicism and barren projects. 93

The following chapters are therefore based on the imperative for reason - the only civilised criterion in facing the problems of our age. If objectivity is not sought after in the discussion of any topic then such a topic is best left un-discussed. It is not only necessary to forego prejudice but to dismiss all the illusions promoted by political groupings of every hue. Only in this way can practical problems be discussed in their most practical context, i.e. through the development of the disinterested idea.

Politics is a huge subject. It is also the most important topic in public life. The following chapters are only concerned with the starting point of politics - the first human priorities.

---

93 It has to be said that it is the common opinion amongst contemporary British academics that philosophical Idealism was finally demolished by the logical criticism of G.E. Moore and Bertrand Russell at the start of the previous century. But as Mary Warnock, Melvin Richter, and others have rightly pointed out, even if the logic and metaphysics of the philosophical Idealists may be subjected to criticism, this is in no way a criticism of their purpose or the underlying truths they were trying to convey. In acknowledging the intellectual genius of Moore and Russell, they merely succeeded in criticising the *methods* of the philosophical Idealists but not the underlying validity of their truths. Melvin Richter observes of the Idealist philosopher, T.H. Green, that, "in his political philosophy, the whole is somehow superior to the sum of its parts; the conclusions are still alive in a way that their metaphysical and ethical 'foundations' are not." (Melvin Richter, *The Politics of Conscience*, Weidenfeld & Nicolson, 1964, p. 222.)

It would be truer to assert that the non-acceptability of Idealist philosophy amongst British academics today is not so much due to any criticism of Moore or Russell, or any of their "cul-de-sac" followers as A.J. Ayer and numerous others up until the present day, but rather simply to a change in fashion. The influences of fashion in philosophy (due to the subjective psychological environment of the day) is unfortunately, hardly less felt in the world of thinking than in the world of women's skirts. However, in the context of New Socialist Idealism, now under discussion, we acknowledge the conclusions of Moore and Russell in their refutation of the logical and metaphysical absurdities, or methodologies, of the 19th century Idealists.

34-2

CHAPTER 34
Expediency Versus Justice

"Many ... of the gravest ills flow from the acts of honest folk who fail to recognise genuine community interest with persons remote from or inferior to them, or to acknowledge these evils to be even the indirect but certain consequences of their own entirely legitimate and respectable if ill-designed acts."

George Catlin, *A Study of The Principles of Politics*, Allen & Unwin, 1930, p. 223.

1 - The dilemma of politics   2 - Immorality of political activity   3 - Nature of expediency   4 - All government entails assent and force 5 - Self-centredness of vested interest groups   6 - Knowledge leads to shared power in the community   7 - Meaning of disinterested justice   8 - Vested interest groups are the first cause of injustice

1   The tragedy of political life has always been the dichotomy found between the demands of expediency opposing those of disinterested justice. It has given rise to all the cross-purposes of argument, to all the confusion, and to all the conflict of political life, together with the shedding of countless millions of lives throughout history.

Worst of all, the dichotomy between expediency and justice has led humanity to lose faith in the possibility of achieving the just society. The endemic recurrence of apparently insoluble problems between different interest groups have led to the loss of belief in reason itself. Consequently, social conflict has led to the type of cynicism which argues that in political life there can be no eternal verities - no values to which we can all relate. Such an attitude - and it is universal amongst opinion-formers in the contemporary world - is dreadful to contemplate. It means, in fact, that there can be no meeting ground - no path of absolute reason - on which person to person may agree to believe and act in harmony. It is a cynicism which argues that group must confront group in uncompromising conflict, until the one subdues the other; or else allows for the botched decisions of unsatisfactory compromise.

2   If this remains the condition of political life in a world becoming increasingly conscious of its true nature and intrinsic faults, then in such circumstances, only the morally debased or the incorrigibly stupid, will be prepared to sink their commitment in political activity. In the past, on the contrary, in a world rife with false consciousness and greater self-delusion than exists today, there was always some semblance of excuse for self-righteousness amongst the wrong-headed, and this to some degree lessened the moral blame on the motivations of the misguided political activist. Today that can no longer be the case in a world where psychology not only reveals the feelings and underlying motivations of all, but is taking over even, as the prime pointer of morality from the authority of conventional religion. This is not to

34-5

suggest that the influence of psychology is taking over from that of true religion, but simply that religion will be forced to recognise the psychology of humanity if it is to maintain its moral authority in the future.

In a society foreseeing revolutionary changes in the excitement of a new millennium; in an age now coming to a close, that has witnessed the overturning of every privilege dividing the common purpose of humanity, there no longer remains any rationale for failing to appreciate the potential for or underlying equality of the human race. But of course the actualisation of that equality in practical terms is dependent on maximising equality of opportunity and measures to ensure that the full potential of the individual - irrespective of class origin - is fully developed.

3 The terms "Political Expediency" and "Disinterested Justice" need further elaboration in underlining their significance. Politics is a hard practical activity entailing the use of force between different groups in the community, and ultimately, it means coercion in the business of government. Expediency is a compromising rough shod process, thrown up by groups in conflict with one another, often trampling on feelings, principles, best solutions and ordinary commonsense; and invariably, great numbers are offended and angered by the outcome of its unsatisfactory decision-making. Nevertheless, it is accepted as inevitable, made necessary by the force of conflicting interests over which none seem to exert any final controlling authority. Hence expediency is a kind of blind force, used as an instrument of power for attaining specific ends, but something hardly appreciated for its own sake - often least of all by those resorting to its use. Expediency is the kind of force used by groups and government in countering the embarrassment of blocked paths, and yet it is a force that rarely fails to succeed. It is responsible for actions and decisions that none forethought or anticipated, and none called consciously into existence. When not used hypocritically as a stratagem for crushing an opponent (which it often is) expediency is always the outcome of second choice, or as the inevitable alternative replacing the ideal line of action. As a contemporary thinker has observed on the nature of the politician, "although (he) uses the technical knowledge of the expert, his exercise of power ultimately rests on rationally and unjustifiable decisions among competing values and interests and on the will to carry them out." [94]

4 It has often been said that any government - even the most disliked and authoritarian - cannot survive without the co-operative assent of the majority, but it is the unique purpose of democracies to make that assent far more apparent and real and acceptable to the majority. Nevertheless, the governmental power of

---

[94] Thomas McCarthy, *The Critical theory of Jügen Habermas.* Polity Press, 1984, p. 9

34-5

democracies is no less determinative or authoritarian for that as a ruling force, than are dictatorships or unjust tyrannies. Taxes are paid and laws are obeyed no less conscientiously in democracies than in totalitarian societies, irrespective of the unpopularity of those taxes or laws. If the use of force has a different style in one society as compared with the other, in the final analysis, in both it is force that ensures the payment of taxation and subservience to the rule of law. 95

5 Political expediency describes those forces interacting between social and economic vested interest groups. Such interest groups, having specific purposes of their own, often narrow or selfish, are always found to clash and be in opposition with others, having opposite or different ends in the community. The nature of this social and economic conflict of interests need not be overtly expressed nor even be a conscious phenomenon to those in its midst, but may be covert or unbeknown. Most institutions blithely assume their beneficence - cannot bear to think otherwise, even though they may act against the better interest of large sectors in the community. The wealthy rentier who has never paid his way by real work, may have the most benevolent disposition towards humanity, and may genuinely feel he has not a latent or potential foe in the world. Protected as he may be by an affluent reassuring environment, and by the comforting consolation of a satisfying ethic, he may nonetheless be totally unaware that in fact he stands in a conflict situation with an underclass. His wealth not merely holds him in thrall, but reflects a situation whereby a great proportion of the community may be withheld from experiencing the full development of their potential.

This situation is reflected not merely in economics but in culture. The fact that this underclass may experience a total satisfaction with its condition, and be free of envy or want, merely compounds the evil, for whilst it serves to salve the conscience of the rentier, it does so in the latter's knowledge of the unfulfilled potential of the greater part of humanity. Is contentment with a humble lot, therefore, sufficient justification against the argument for the need for social change? Most certainly it is not. Even pigs may feel contentment in the filth and darkness of the dirtiest sty, but they nonetheless remain unenlightened creatures. This argument may be best appreciated by the following comparison: a hundred and fifty

---

95 T.H. Grren, amongst others, has argued that Will and not Force is the basis of the state. See his lecture on this topic in his, *Lectures On The Principles of Political Obligation*, Longmans, Green & Co., 1927. I would not disagree with his argument which was principally intended to oppose the Hobbesian social contract theory of anarchy, fear and force giving rise to the necessity of the protective state. I would not choose to quarrel with Green's line of thinking which would seem to aptly agree with what we have said about the dependence of all government on the "co-operative assent of the vast majority," for that "assent" constitutes, in a sense, the will of the people.

32-7

years ago the unhealthy, undergrown physical monstrosities, comprising the majority of our people, represented an acceptable standard to the unthinking majority of the time. But those standards would not be acceptable today to any sector of society. Hopefully, a hundred years hence, the intellectual and educationally under-privileged standards of the majority in contemporary society will be totally unacceptable in that unknown future. Factors of contentment cannot be allowed to enter into the structure of this argument (which is a purely political discussion) since they are not qualities giving the individual the potential of shared power in the community.

6   Knowledge gives value to the individual in integrating him within the shared assets of the community. It gives him dignity and self-respect - it is his right as a human being. The individual should have the right to the full development and extension of his mental powers through education in all its aspects, technical, cultural, spiritual, and moral; in the same way that he should have the right to food, shelter, and warmth. Eudemonistic principles cannot be used as the cornerstone for the ethical society, for the simple reason that feelings of contentment are so often and so easily induced through the creation of myth or delusion, or what has been called the creation of a false consciousness. In the history of the world *Panem et circenses* (bread and circuses) have not been exclusively the instrument of the Roman ruling class. They are more significant, perhaps, in the world of today.

Something must be done to satisfy the discontent of the unemployed masses - to ensure that they make no demands for a fairer share in the control or ownership of available wealth ! Those are the interests of today's ruling elite ! TV soap opera, the soft porn of the popular press, the glorification and scandals of High Society, and mass spectacular sporting events, are the "bread and circuses" of the present era, for it is these things which induce a sense of amnesia or numbed contentment in facing the harder realities of the world. These are the socially acceptable opiates of the community - although in the eyes of the more enlightened, they are condemned as morally enervating time-wasting trivia or *Kitsch*. The unacceptable opiates (but hardly less harmful as social solvents in the community) are hashish, marijuana and heroin, and all their derivatives. But soap operas, soft porn, and heroin, all have the same design and end purpose in the community: the erasing of reality through illusion, and the inducement of forgetfulness, so that the power-wielders and financially strong in society, might have a freer hand in manipulating the rest of the community.

7   This immediately leads us into the consideration of disinterested justice. This means justice from an objective standpoint, when the interests of vested groups are set aside or excluded as factors in causing injustice. Disinterested justice has a philosophical base and is rooted in *reality*. It is to be contrasted with conventional justice which is rooted in law and custom. The latter is man-made and imposed by

34-8

those with economic power in the community, seemingly as a substantive thing
bearing an equal relationship on all, but in fact clearly showing a bias in favour of
those with power. Its fallibility is due to the factor of expediency, i.e. that kind of
expediency which argues that the status quo is in itself the right justification for the
order of things. It is the expediency which argues that the "As is" situation should
always predominate over the moral "Ought."

The question of the individual's relationship with the community in terms of
disinterested justice is a vast subject, and cannot be discussed in all its aspects in a
book of this restricted length. The topic has been most thoroughly considered by
John Rawls (unquestionably the major moral philosopher of our time) in his book,
A Theory of Justice. The core of his philosophy, as elaborated in depth in his social
contract theory, may be summed up in the words, "do unto others as you would have
done unto yourself," and it is hard to envisage a sounder starting point for any
practical theory of ethics. The ethical system of the American, John Rawls, exposes
all the naivety and falsity of Utilitarian ethics (i.e. the clumsy populism of "the
greatest happiness of the greatest number") which have dominated the Western
liberal world for the past hundred and fifty years. The question of disinterested
justice will become increasingly important on the political agenda as changes are
forced on society by the momentous developments of the present millennium, and
hence as a discussion, topic, it has an urgent appeal.

Disinterested justice entails a sensible maximising of equality of opportunity,
and justice perceived as fairness. It also requires that the demands of liberty be
respected. In the words of Rawls, "the force of justice as fairness would appear to
arise from two things: the requirement that all inequalities be justified to the least
advantaged, and the priority of liberty. This pair of constraints distinguishes it from
intuitionism and teleological theories."[96] Rawls is explicit in his condemnation of
expediency, and implicit in his criticism of faulty democracy, when he states, "that
the rights secured by justice are not subject to political bargaining or to the calculus
of social interests." [97] But at the same time, "the theory of justice assumes a definite
limit on the strength of social and altruistic motivation. It supposes that individuals
and groups put forward competing claims, and while they are willing to act justly,
they are not prepared to abandon interests. There is no need to elaborate further that
this presumption does not imply that men are selfish in the ordinary sense. Rather
a society in which all can achieve their complete good, or in which there are no
conflicting demands and the wants of all fit together without coercion into a

---

96 *A Theory of Justice*, OUP, 1972, p. 250.

97 Ibid., p. 4.

35-1

harmonious plan of activity, is a society in a certain sense beyond justice. It has eliminated the occasions when the appeal to the principles of right and justice is necessary." 98 The purpose of these chapters is to define how justice may be maximised within the political dimensions of society.

8   The first step towards this is to turn our attention to the nature of vested interest groups, since it is in them that is to be found the seminal cause of political injustice. The positive aspects of justice - the development of hopes and aspirations - cannot be considered until after we have looked at the negative factors and evils of injustice. All vested interest groups purport to be in harmony with the cause of fairness and justice, and when they fail in this, then they project themselves as warlike bodies, fighting against evil and sin. Ultimately, all groups - even the most wicked - are forced to project themselves as promoting Goodness and Justice howsoever these may be perceived. They are forced to do this in appealing for the co-operation and support of those whom they address, for the only attraction of any cause lies in its apparent goodness.

The reason for this is that the most powerful (and generally, the only) force in influencing humanity, both individually and collectively, is the *idea* of Goodness and Justice, since all actions and thoughts, from the most commonplace to the most sublime, may be subjected to the criteria of "goodness" or "badness." The act of pouring tea into a cup is no less subject to the criterion of "good" or "bad" as to how it is performed, than are the underlying principles guiding the acts of a government. In the real world there is no such thing as the intentional pursuit of evil. The Devil only exists in myth - often as a convenient whip with which to beat an opposing group.

---

98 Ibid., p. 281.

35-2

CHAPTER 35
The Self-Justifying Cynicism of Vested Interests

"All virtues are really social, or more properly, the distinction between social and self-regarding virtues is a false one. Every virtue is self-regarding in the sense that it is a disposition, or habit of will, directed to an end which the man presents to himself as his good; every virtue is social in the sense that unless the good to which the will is directed is one in which the well-being of society in some form or other is involved, the will is not virtuous at all."

T.H. Greeen, *Lectures On The Principles of Political Obligation,* Longmans Green, 1927, p. 244.

1 - How the idea of their "goodness" is perverted into self-delusion   2 - But this is complemented by pragmatism that sees unfairness as inevitable   3 - But this expediency does not resolve substantive issues   4 - Falsity of all vested interest groups   5 - Hope for the future   6 - Way out of the dilemma   7 - The pragmatist's argument for vested interests   8 - And the consequent short-termism of their outlook   9 - The dangers of superficial populism 10 - Human priorities in politics cannot be identified by analysing party programmes   11 - Proper criteria in assessing what the individual really wants

1   There has to be a rationale for all actions, and ultimately, that rationale has to be based on the idea of "goodness." In a world that all know is imperfect, because all things are imperfect and transient, and in a world of conflict when all social conflict is bad, there is resulting from this a greater intensity in the struggle for goodness and justice. Without such a struggle the world would simply fall apart.

Therefore vested interest groups are at all times dominated and inspired by the idea of their own goodness, but the idea is subjective being fully meaningful only to themselves. But their increasing egocentricity is soon superimposed by self-delusion and all manner of things assisting them in the belief in their own goodness. Eventually they are impervious to rational argument for they see their own groups as ends in themselves. This is applicable, for example, to all political parties and pressure groups that perceive the world from their own narrow perspective alone.

2   This, however, is complemented by a pragmatism in all groups that appreciates that expediency is inescapable. The argument is then projected, with some complacency, that universal fairness is unrealistic because of this same expediency. It is argued that in the cause of free action or free enterprise, for example, that a few must be sacrificed to being pushed against the wall for the "many." The truth, however, is that the "many" may be the "few" and the "few" the "many," for the sense of number conveniently becomes an illusory perception. For example, when many are forced into unemployment or dispossession through the ideals of laissez-faire projected to the many, it is the many who suffer. In this

35-5

situation, false Principle is made to be triumphant over Practical benefit. Other groups may argue that in the cause of a more egalitarian society, a minority must be restricted in its economic, occupational or other activities. This minority, however, may eventually be transferred into a majority, and increasingly oppressive measures may be taken to restrict those said activities.

3   In this way society becomes increasingly polarised and unfair, and further grounds are created for conflict. At the same time substantive political issues are not resolved, i.e. on a fair or disinterested basis; but instead, there is a great juggling for favours amongst different groups in the community. The entire process leaves a feeling of dissatisfaction, as if nothing of significance had been achieved. This pragmatism or "trimming" of vested interest groups is accompanied by hypocrisy, for it calls into being a kind of half-justice. Despite loud claims to the contrary, or the alleged inner convictions of their representatives, vested interest groups are hardly if ever concerned with disinterested justice, which ultimately is the only true justice. This, anyway, is the tendency of political groupings in a democratic environment.

4   There exist, however, vested interest groups, far more blatant in their demands, and these are relatively free from this mild self-induced form of hypocrisy. They set out to be "absolute" or "universal" in their appeal, but they culminate in becoming ruthless and authoritarian, and invariably undemocratic. They base their premise on the belief that their particular group is entitled to justice as against others in society on grounds of class, colour, race, sex, language, or religion, etc. There is hence a duality between their universalistic appeal and the fact of their exclusivity, e.g., the universalism of Communism requiring the liquidation of the bourgeoisie, and the hecatombs of human bones and flesh that this brought about in the previous century. In reality, therefore, such groupings are neither absolute nor universal. In all instances, such groupings base their moral and scientific beliefs on unsocial principles, and usually, the falsity of their beliefs is simple to demonstrate.

Hence whilst vested interest groups in democratic communities defend their privileges with arguments of hypocrisy and expediency on the grounds that society is impervious to sufficiently desirable change; authoritarian communities raise privilege (of one kind or another) to a pedestal, on the grounds that the proletarian, or the Nordic, etc., is more deserving than those not falling into such categories.

5   Fortunately, all that may change. We are now reaching an evolutionary stage in our development when all the old delusions and injustices of the past may be thrown over forever. Certainly, for the first time in history, the intellectual knowledge is available for a great leap forward into a better future. Already we live in an age that strives towards disinterested (or real) justice to a greater degree than in any previous era. This is not to suggest that the way ahead is free of powerful

35-7

forces to be broken down, but that new reforming groups are less encumbered by blinding illusion than hitherto.

Nevertheless, the achievement of true justice often seems as far distant as ever. This is not because of the way unorganised individuals (or the silent majority) perceive the world we live in, but because the older, more powerful, established organisations have failed to progress in their moral perception of humanity's rightful place in the community. In other words, the inertia of the group has been responsible for hindering the mental development of its individual members. This is especially true in Britain, in an increasingly divided society, where political issues are sharply polarised. It means, of course, that Britain's hope for the future lies in her silent majority shaking off its lethargy and throwing over the established institutions that are resistant to change.

6   What then is the way out of this wretched dichotomy between the interests of expediency, the so-called needs of impersonal political forces, and disinterested justice, representing the best needs of the individual in society ? The only way out is to match the demands of technological progress in its transforming society, with the best needs of the individual in meeting that challenge. Fortunately, the progress of technology, when contributing to the everyday needs of the majority, will put an increasing demand on the skills and brainpower of that majority to such an extent that it is unlikely that calls for extending the franchise for higher educational standards would be necessary. Accompanying those standards should be a higher political awareness and scepticism of imposed patterns of authority, so creating a more egalitarian and just society than existed in any previous age. In this way a higher morality would be achieved in society, not through the teachings of prophets or preachers, but simply through the widening application of advanced technology. Such a view of our future, after the horrors of the late century, might seem a reversion to the optimism of 19th century liberalism, but the receding threat of war between the major powers and a genuine will towards lasting world peace in the face of an impossible alternative, does seem to justify a return to that earlier spirit of hope and optimism.

7   Before investigating the actual priorities of politics, it has to be pointed out that there are many in our democratic society who argue that disinterested justice is not the concern of politics - and should not and cannot be so. These people - the pragmatists in our midst - the advocates of expediency - will argue passionately that the true and only purpose of representative democracy is the pursuit of private and individual and vested interests - howsoever selfish, narrow, or vicious these might be. These people will argue that anything contrary to that would be contrary to the interests of representative democracy. In a certain sense these people would be correct, but only when concerned with *representative* democracy as a thing in itself

35-9

if divorced from the *purpose* of democracy. The *mechanism* of democracy, when raised on a pedestal, can and has often been used in recent history as a stepping stone to the greatest crimes against humanity. With the aid of a half-measure of truth and an equal half-measure of hypocrisy, the democratic system is used against the democratic purpose.

8   These same pragmatists or advocates of expediency will go on to argue that there is no such thing as objectivity; that every man and woman is a selfish end in him- and herself; and that immediate desires should be the sole criteria for political decision-making. All these arguments are an apology for ignorance, and all promote the tendency towards a self-delusion and irresponsible hedonism. If there is no such thing as objectivity then no individual can be expected to successfully relate with another, since there is no criteria for this and criteria is dependent on transcending subjectivity. If the individual is not more than a selfish end in him- or herself, then he can have no purpose or sense or purpose within the community, since he becomes isolated and unsocial. If immediate desire is to be the criterion for decision-making, then not only does self-centredness become so intense that the community is divided by intolerable dissent, but short-termism would bring political chaos in its wake.

Furthermore, these same people will argue that democracy is not concerned with values or eternal verities but solely with the mechanism of deciding popular choice, and that *that* choice must have overriding precedence over all other considerations. Lastly, they will argue that anyone attempting to intercept any of the above forces is acting against the interests of democracy. In summary, it is argued by many in Britain today, and particularly by the privileged, that politics is and should be solely about questions of popular choice, and as to *What the people want.* For many this is the starting point in politics: find out what the people want, and then act on those conclusions.

9   It is the firm conviction of the present author that such a starting point *on its face value* is not merely false but mischievous. The ultimate purpose of politics should naturally be to give the people what they want, but not if interpreted as merely satisfying the immediate demands of unthinking superficial populism. The outcome of unthinking reactions of the moment, should anyway not be perceived as "what the people want." There is always a gap between short- and long-term considerations and interests, and the man who wants to hang his neighbour today because of some petty annoyance, is not the same man tomorrow after the cooling of passion and time for disinterested reflection. Wrong judgement by the individual in the sphere of public life particularly occurs in those fields where he is less well-informed, and consequently, because he has fewer facts to weigh both sides of the argument, he is more easily swayed by impulse and irrationality. In situations where the emotions are allowed to run rip, ignorance is always bliss! The secrecy in the

35-11

way in which we are governed in contemporary Britain has created fertile soil for political demagogues of all parties, so that misinformation is mischievously used by powerful vested interest groups pulling the strings of the commonweal. In this way all sectors of the population are at some time used as puppets by cunning elites controlling financial power - and financial power is the basis of all power in the community.

10   In this environment of publicly contrived delusion and misinformation, it therefore becomes very difficult - if not impossible - for the lone individual to think through what he really wants for himself or herself in the name of the community. The problem is compounded by the realisation that there is a gap which has to be filled in linking the best needs of the individual with the best needs of the community, and it is the political abstraction so created in uniting these interests, that is so often used for unscrupulous purposes. It is for this reason that political truth in the sense of identifying the best needs of the individual or the community can hardly, if ever, be found through analysing the stated aims of political groups. Priorities in politics can only be identified through the broader philosophical approach of analysing sociological phenomena that attempts to cut through all the cultural clutter that is thrown up to deceive and divert from the true path to social betterment.

11   Hence the following questions need to be answered: How does the individual know what he *really* wants,? and, How are the collective wishes of the community to be known ? The answer to these questions will be the prime purpose of the present chapters. A perception of the human condition clearly indicates that intuitional and teleological approaches tend usually to conceal ulterior or unconscious motives, often resulting in a mischievous outcome. The remaining alternative is the simple approach of considering the individual as a purely physical being with natural desires and tendencies. In this light he is regarded as a mechanistic object that needs to be kept in optimum condition and good working order. Not only do his body and limbs need to be kept physically fit, but his most vital organ, the brain, needs to be intellectually stretched. As a social being, totally integrated into the community, he needs access to information on all aspects of the society in which he develops, and particularly with regard to political and financial power bases, for without such knowledge, he cannot exert sensible choice or be a full and meaningful member of the community. Without such knowledge he remains merely a pawn - albeit may be a contented one. Of course, he has a psyche, and in this lies his greatest complexity, but this is looked after by avoiding frustration and by fulfilling so-called spiritual needs.

In answering the first question of the previous paragraph, it has to be said that the individual only knows what he really wants when, a) He has a sufficient

36-1

knowledge of *him-* or *herself*; and, b) He has a sufficient knowledge of the world in which he lives, but it has to be remembered that neither of these spheres of knowledge can exist without the other if this self-knowing condition is to be met No person in the sphere of reality can be purely a being within him- or herself, for that only belongs to the realm of insanity. The individual only takes on reality and meaning as a social being, and this is partly reflected in the fact that the greatest number of good individuals flourish best in the best communities, whilst the greatest number of bad , or under-utilised, or under-privileged individuals are found in the worst communities.

The answer to the second question of the previous paragraph will occupy the following eight chapters. 99

CHAPTER 36
Political Realism In The Just Society

"Pragmatism encourages us to believe whatever we wish to believe, and denies that truth has any other meaning than what suits us."

Dean Inge, *The End of An Age*, Putnam, 1948, pp. 12-13.

1 - The purpose of politics   2 - The political activist typified   3 - Required qualities of the political activist   4 - Illusion in personal and political life   5 - Political illusion historically perceived   6 - The starting point in politics has to be an examination of economic causes   7 - But this must entail a disinterested consideration   8 - A re-active approach to issues apportions blame to the wrong causes   9 - Unacceptability of Old Socialism because of its re-active causes approach

1   The purpose of politics should be the need to resolve substantive issues and deep-seated problems within the structure of society, and to relate these to the best needs of the individual, assuming that equality of opportunity should be maximised in real terms without sacrificing the fabric of the community. The above needs elaboration before it is grasped in concrete and intelligible terms, and that will be the prime task of the present chapter.

---

99 In the Anglo-Saxon countries it has customarily been thought amongst "ordinary opinion" an insolence to cast doubt on the *rightness* of "expressed" or "popular" ideas and decisions. After all, they are the outcome of democracy. Such doubts are too often used as tools by authoritarian forces in making their own will prevail. Prospective dictators have too often said, "it is not this that you as an individual *really* desires, but this, and it is only because of unenlightenment that you cannot grasp the nature of your own real wishes." Trust in the " popular will," however, because of the misuse of 20th century democracy, is not accepted with the openness that it once was. T.H. Green, the greatest Liberal philosopher (and a Hegelian) during the closing decades of the last century, addressed this problem in a forthright way in his lecture, *On The Different Senses of "Freedom" As Applied To Will & to The Moral Progress of Man*, op. Cit.

36-2

2   But first something more must be said in dismissing the populist starting point in politics. Those who enter active politics with the populist viewpoint (and in my experience they are many) are sources of mischief and confusion. As Prof. Joad has so rightly remarked, "the world is full of well-meaning people who are desperately anxious to do right, yet only too often because of bad judgement do wrong. Indeed, there is considerable ground for the view that most of the world's ills are due not to the harshness of men's hearts, but to the thickness of their heads."100 The attitude of such people is peculiarly English in that a vague desire to do good, or be "useful," in a decidedly amateurish or meddling fashion is too often the motivation towards local and national politics. They take their choice from three or four alternatives - "Maybe a winner, maybe a loser !" (as it was once expressed to me) - and their feelings are rarely raised above that of lukewarm enthusiasm or annoyance, except in instances of petty breaches of procedure or internal wrangling and rivalry amongst colleagues. Their satisfaction is derived chiefly from the ritual of endless formalities and committee procedures, and on only the rare occasion are they called upon to express a political opinion - let alone to string together a series of ideas. Although they view themselves as individualistic (and may appear so on the exterior or in a gathering) they are in fact highly disciplined and conformist. If they are uncritical of the leadership or the party, it is not so much because of any inherent wish to conform but rather because of their general acceptance of "what is" and an apparent inability to formulate intelligent critical attitudes.

Once having chosen their political grouping, all thinking seems to stop, or become frozen in the moment of conversion, for from that time onwards their trust is put in the ultimate wisdom of the party. When they are asked to cast a vote on issues, those issues are only perceived within the limiting narrow vision of the party. Thenceforward, their real thinking and political energies descend from the consideration of substantive issues to the sordid everyday bickering of petty intrigue. That is the reason why far more commonsense and breadth of vision in the discussion of politics may be heard amongst ordinary people - often with little education - than discussion amongst the politically committed. The latter are too often intellectually constrained by party doctrine (however loose this may be) or by party discipline. They are literally stupefied by their membership of a political organisation. All this is compounded by the fact, as pointed out by James Burnham, that, "the distinguishing quality of Anglo-Saxon politics has always been hypocrisy and hypocrisy must always be at pains to shy away from the truth." 101 These

---

100   C.E.M. Joad, *Guide To The Philosophy of Morals & Politics*, Gollancz, 1938, p. 214.

101   James Burnham, *The Machiavellians: Defenders of Freedom*, Gateway Books, Chicago, 1963 ed., p. 86.

36-5

generalisations may not apply to the majority of political activists, but they do recur on a sufficient level of frequency to be significant.

3   It is our argument that the vocation of politics demands a high degree of social and moral responsibility, and that the business of politics cannot be responsibly entered into without a sound knowledge of comparative economics and the social sciences, together with a sufficiently critical understanding that only comes with life experience. Mere "intuition" or "commonsense" are by no means sufficient qualities to justify an entry into the occupation of politics. Too many such "intuitive" souls are made the instruments of vested interest forces of which they often never become aware. The rank and file political activist is more usually a cog in a machine - a humble private in an army marching he knows not where - an automaton, manipulated by sinister forces of which his leader in turn is but an instrument.

4   The world in which we live is far more complex than most are prepared to admit. Because of the many layers of illusion in the everyday world of sensory perception, reality and truth is difficult to identify. In the sphere of interpersonal relationships, maturity during the course of life succeeds in stripping off many of these layers of self-delusion; but in the sphere of political life, only rarely are these layers stripped off down to reveal the bare reality of existence. This is simply because the majority are deprived (or deprive themselves) of the essential knowledge and/or experience needed to understand the fantasies standing between them and reality. These comfortable and luxuriant mirages are created by sinister forces, so manipulators might more easily exert power, unseen, uncriticised and out of reach. As each layer of illusion, is removed, the bonds of oppression, confining the understanding, are unlocked, until at last the core of reality is finally brought into the realm of experience.

5   It is our purpose in this book to strip off these layers of illusion until the hard core of reality is reached. That we live in a world of political illusion is beyond all doubt. The ordinary, unthinking, satisfied mortal in his daily life may find this contention of an "unreal" world difficult to grasp. This is because he lives in what he feels is at the apex of the world's progress - that all has been unfolding towards this present point in time - that he stands somehow on a summit - but has no idea, and cannot contemplate an unknown future, or a higher state of existence for himself or his fellow beings. If, however, this ordinary mortal looks historically at the world, from the earliest times until yesterday, he will clearly perceive there has been a growing consciousness, as one layer of illusion has been stripped down to the next. Both man (or woman) as an individual and man as a unit in society has experienced and benefited from a developing consciousness. As George Catlin has aptly observed, "our civilisation has ceased to grow unconsciously, and is becoming, as a world-wide civilisation, self-conscious and in need of intelligent control over its

36-6

least extent." 102

Man no longer walks fearfully in the forest, eager to propitiate at every turn the tree spirits; and neither does he fear the magic spells of pagan priests; or contradicting the dogmas of a thousand theologians over the past two millennia; or cower before the threats of noblemen and gentry; and neither does he give credence (if he has any sense) to the doctrines of Tories, Old Socialists or Liberal Democrats, as the media for eternal verities. These things already represent illusions that have been contemptuously stripped off and cast aside as rotten matter. Nevertheless, in a world as complex and fraught as ours there still exist many more layers of illusion to strip off and cast aside. That will be our task, and in pursuing it, we shall seek to uncover the real forces oppressing humankind and society.

6   Where, then, should be the starting point in politics ? Our answer is that it should entail a disinterested consideration of the most urgent economic issues of our time. We insist that these should be economic issues, since economics is the source of all political power in the community as well as the source of all cultural attitudes. These facts are indisputable. 103 Those, for example, who trace back first causes in society to cultural factors cannot find a lever of interpretation for necessary political change. Their political outlook remains, therefore, in our view, sterile, unrealistic and naive.

For example, the argument that Britain's industrial decline is due purely to cultural factors, howsoever widely examined, can never give a pointer to the future. Sermons on "British decadence," "lack of will," etc., may convey a grand impression of moralising and, may indeed lead to the most interesting sociological debates, but when the last word has been spoken, there is still no indicator for the future. All that remains is a sad sense of fatalism - that history has progressed along its inevitable and senseless course.   Historiography that conveys a cultural explanation for events in history is merely half written. Facts - the most significantly

---

102   George E.G. Catlin, *A Study of The Principles of Politics*, Allen & Unwin, 1930, p. 54.

103   Hence, we agree wholly with Marx, that in any interpretation of our political problems, or indeed, with those of history, economic factors must be sought as first causes. However, we cannot agree wholly with the development and tendency of dialectical-materialism as elaborated by Marx and Engels and their later followers. There are several grounds for our objection: firstly, and obviously, because their predictions have been proven wrong; secondly, because of the naivety of their sociological approach; thirdly, because there are secondary and cultural factors of overwhelming significance in influencing human thought and action, and these are wrongly pushed aside by Marxists as irrelevant; and fourthly, because of the philosophical reason that we cannot accept the dated 19th century materialist conception of man's place in the universe.

There are clearly psychological or "spiritual" qualities inherent in humanity which cannot possibly lend themselves to the stark or rigid materialistic interpretations of Marxism. Time and the experience of history has made this amply clear. Furthermore, we feel that the search for *reality* is to be found on the firmer ground of philosophical Idealism. One of the best and most readable refutations of economic forces seen as the exclusive influence of human motivation may be found in Bertrand Russell's excellent book, *Power, A New Social Analysis*, *Allen & Unwin, 1938*.

36-8

deciding facts - illustrating underlying economic forces in society, have simply been omitted, sometimes intentionally but more often out of ignorance.

7　　In stating that we should seek a disinterested consideration of economic issues, we mean that a *re-active* approach should be avoided. By a re-active approach we mean an intuitive seizing on solutions in the face of urgent and highly-charged issues, for although such solutions may seem relevant in the short-term, they are too often proven to be counter-productive in the long-term. Most bad policies are brought about by a re-active approach to urgent issues. It is the emotive content alone of such issues which is responsible for a less considered or rational approach, for such issues are tackled merely on their superficial face value. History, and indeed, contemporary political life, is full of such examples. The following supposedly benign measures may be cited as examples of the re-active approach in tackling the question of unemployment:-

1. Increasing public sector employment;
2. Retaining labour intensive as opposed to capital intensive (or automotive) methods in industry;
3. Extending work-sharing patterns in industry;
4. Organising voluntary unpaid work schemes in different sectors of the community; and,
5. Paying a minimum wage to all irrespective of employment or unemployment status.

As a superficial alleviation of present ills, the above may be advocated as "wonder cures," but in the long- and even medium-term, their effects would be economically disastrous. They would inevitably result in:-

1. Falling living standards;
2. Greatly increased taxation;
3. De-industrialisation and loss of further jobs;
4. Intense balance of payments problems;
5. A lower status in all occupational spheres;
6. De-skilling of employment; and,
7. A general social malaise due to the loss of a sense of purpose in the community in the wake of industrial regression.

8　　A re-active approach to political issues also means the tendency to cast blame falsely on the wrong causes of social ills. For example, when jobs are being decimated in industry, it is easy for workers and managers to blame unfairly the immediate "bosses" for unemployment - and especially to blame those persons who actually carry out the sackings - when in fact blame may lie in a remoter quarter, e.g. in de-industrialising rentier capitalism. Most conflict in political life is based on arguing at cross-purposes and to misunderstanding underlying issues that are

36-9

accountable for the social and economic evils in society.

The starting point in politics must be concerned with *urgent issues*, for only then will political life remain immediately relevant to the present, as it should be. The concentration on urgent issues ensures that political life is empirical and practical, as opposed to its being motivated by remote or utopian influences. The identification of *urgent issues* means identifying the most important underlying problems in a society, so that the majority might benefit from the solution of those problems. It also calls for a realistic appreciation of those problems within the context of that society's technological and economic development. For example: if in the face of a planetary environmental threat, it was advocated that an industrially advanced society should revert to the subsistence economy of a primitive or pre-industrial peasant community, such a political stance would be utopian and unrealistic.

A more thoughtful and sounder approach would be legislation to utilise the exhaustion of fuels from the industrial and domestic sectors for further energy purposes, or at least, the filtering out of harmful chemicals. Unfortunately, the emotive strength of ecological issues is at present so strong, that utopian answers may have a stronger appeal than the more scientific alternative which meets the retrenched opposition of financial forces on the grounds of cost. In the poorer areas of the world, by our criteria, urgent issues should be solved not by supplying the useless and costly technology of the developed West, but by heavy investment in intermediate technology, so that the peoples in those areas may be aided by their own efforts to help themselves towards types of wealth creation more within their reach. In contemporary Britain, the most urgent issue is not wealth distribution but wealth creation - but more of this anon.

9   It has to be said at this point, that our criticism of the re-active approach in politics clearly implies our non-acceptability of Old Socialist methods which consciously operated within a subjective environment. Old Socialist subjectivism tried to justify its stance through historical-materialism. All the hatred and class warfare of Old Socialism could only find its moral justification through the beliefs that Old Socialists were acting out the inevitable course of history: that they as a Class were destined to overthrow the bourgeoisie which in its turn had overthrown the older feudal order. The enthronement of proletarians, in theory the achievement of the ultimately just society, in practice merely replaced one privileged elite with another. Even the mildest and later forms of Old Socialism could not escape this sharp confrontational approach which advocated the necessity of class conflict. Through the existence of this conflict, or re-active approach, Old Socialism became inescapably locked into the eternal lie of half-truth. Consequently, although it could fulfill the superficial desires of the majority, it could never resolve the underlying

37-1

substantive issues of society. Therefore, Old Socialism was doomed to compound political problems, until eventually it destroyed itself by this very process.

In summary, therefore, the starting point in politics should be:-

1. Disinterested, in ensuring that the best interests of the community in total are served as opposed to promoting the aims of vested interest groups;
2. That *urgent* issues be addressed, in ensuring that solutions are found to the most pressing problems in society; and,
3. That those issues be investigated in sufficient depth until their underlying basic economic causes are clearly uncovered.

CHAPTER 37
Maximising The Individual's Potential In The Free Society

"As all individuality comes to fruition in society, so all individuality must in some way give itself up to society."

R.M. MacIver, *Community*, Macmillan, 1936 ed., p. 96.

1 - The community exists for the individual to the same degree that the individual exists for the community   2-Laissez-faire's threat to the just community   3 - Basic rights of the individual   4 - The individual's right to the fulfilment of his potential   5 - Why the teaching of citizen rights is of limited value   6 - Enlightenment should be an obligatory part of education   7 - The right to spiritual fulfilment means the right to free choice   8 - And to cultural facilities strengthening the bonds of the community   9 - The problem of Meritocracy   10 - Definition of justice is constrained within its historical context

1   Before elaborating on the above, it is first necessary to define justice in the sense of the individual's place in the community, since the community exists for the individual to the same degree that the individual exists for the community. This latter supposition may sound strange if not alarming to the conventionally thinking Western liberal. It is more common to argue that the community (or state) exists for the individual, and has no more meaning than that.

We shall clearly demonstrate that such an attitude is not merely a nonsense, but if logically pursued, is mischievous and damaging to the individual's own best interests. Concurrently, of course, we also repudiate the argument that the individual only exists for the state. The truth of the situation can only be realised by understanding that the Individual in isolation can have no more meaning in reality than can the idea of the community in isolation. A community without individuals is unthinkable in the same way as the development and full potentiality of the individual could not be imagined without the aid of the community. Even a Robinson Crusoe, and all that he thought and meant in relation to the external world, could never have been without the consciousness of his own past in a living community. The individual cannot exist as an isolated end in himself, for all that he

37-3

thinks and does bears a relationship to the community and the world around him.

2   Those who promote the idea, or actually believe, that the community has no function beyond that of existing for the individual, are the extreme advocates of laissez-faire and by implication are led to forfeit the constraints of social responsibility. "By letting things be," they allow the bully to have full rein to his impulse in the name of freedom. The community is not seen as the source of co-operation, creativeness and constructive social interaction, but as an opportunity for exploitation, manipulation and underhand dealing, irrespective of the consequences. The community is seen as a barrier to freedom (as it was in the eyes of Mrs. Thatcher) - as a necessary nuisance - an object for opposition rather than integration. The selfishness or egoism of the individual in trampling on others, inevitably sets the individual apart from the community, and in a deeper sense, it even sets him apart from himself. The individual who fails to appreciate the needs of his fellow beings, or puts a higher value on himself than on others (and there are a thousand unconscious ways in which this may be politically manifested) is dividing himself from the interests of the community. More significantly, he is also acting against his better self, for in subjecting others to things he would not have done to himself, he is distancing himself from the opportunity and benefits of social interaction as a fully integrated member of the community. Hence he is denying himself the natural role of a successfully integrated social human being. Consequently he necessarily remains an incomplete human being. He becomes instead an object of increasing isolation, ridicule or dislike, ultimately taking on all the horrid characteristics of Dostoevsky's hero in, *Notes From The Underground.*

3   The idea of justice for the individual is therefore meaningless unless it is understood in the sense of total integration within the community. The logic of this will soon be comprehended. In defining justice, we must turn to the needs of the individual. These are divided into, a) Matters pertaining to basic material want (often the only concern of governments); and, b) The development of individual potential (too often only the concern of the better parent or guardian).

In taking category, a) Firstly, every person should be free of those basic material wants necessary for survival and good health, viz.: nourishment, sufficient and appetising; clothing of quality and acceptable appearance to the community; well-built housing, and enough warmth in cold seasons. Secondly, every person should be entitled to a good parenthood, to include protection against deprivation, cruelty and isolation from social interaction. Thirdly, every person should be entitled to an effective full-time education in preparation for adulthood, and especially in preparation for a life of remunerative work. Fourthly, every person should be entitled to the full development of his or her individual potential in the service of the community. This means that the individual is entitled to continuous training or

37-5

education throughout life, so that he might, a) Progress in an upwardly mobile direction until retirement age, and , b) Never be allowed to fall into a de-skilled status. Fifthly, every person should be entitled to work until retirement age, and to all the benefits and protection of work. All these things not only entail the positive and constant intervention of the state, but necessitate that the state should have ultimate power in all matters in promoting the better interests of the individual. For example, parenthood should be regarded as a stewardship for the state, for if that is not the situation, the parent might in theory be allowed unmolested to abuse, batter or even murder his own child. That, of course, was the situation that actually existed in the worst proletarian areas of early Victorian and laissez-faire England.

4   The above are basic freedoms in the sense that they ensure the individual's economic success in the community. In summary, they are concerned with freedom from material want. Freedom in its fullest sense, however, is concerned with much more than that. The fourth of the above conditions, viz. The development of the individual's potential therefore needs further elaboration. This, entailing category b), is dependent on two factors: firstly, the right to Information, and secondly, the right to spiritual fulfilment.

The individual cannot be self-fulfilled, or give his best to the community, unless he has free access to information on the nature of the world he lives in. If he is denied this (for any reason or circumstances), he will inevitably be used as an unknowing pawn for the vested interests of others, and those others will create an attractive veil of illusion to ensure that he succumbs to their power. Knowledge alone can break down those barriers of illusion, so that the individual may clearly see his true place in society - may recognise those areas of exploitation and injustice and see where he is led by false or mischievous prophets. On the most obvious level, there must be no secrecy in the way we are governed.

5   Freedom without knowledge is meaningless, and this truth was illustrated with stark clarity in the famous parable at the opening of the Seventh Book of Plato's *Republic*. If the individual is to be educated to know the world in which he lives, then there has to be a radical extension of our educational system. It is not sufficient (as at present) to teach people to know their rights, for mere legal knowledge is only superficial, and although it may serve to arouse resentment and reactivate the individual to seek redress for wrongs done, it does not enlighten him on his sociological status in society. Worse still, an exclusive obsession with teaching people their citizen rights often does little more than push people into political groupings wherein they are exploited for other ulterior motives. The outcome of a society free of false consciousness, where all had a disinterested appreciation of their true place in society, and where all had the freedom to reorganise into new meaningfully significant groupings, would therefore mutate into a genuinely

37-7

democratic community.

The sociological status of the individual in the community is hence the only *reality* he possesses as a social being. His legal status, his membership of church or club, his occupation, his house, clothes and other possessions, are merely superficial or meaningless definitions of the individual's *real* status in the community, unless all these things are at the same time related to the criteria of a sociological perspective. That perspective, of course, needs to be taken from two viewpoints: firstly, with regard to the institution or object in view as to its collective image in the eyes of the community; and secondly, with regard to the psychology of the individual in his relationship with that institution or object. For example, the membership of a church congregation may either be because of the social status it happens to convey, or because of Christian conviction. The two motives, of course, may be poles apart. The above outward possessions are merely symbols, important to the individual on the conscious level, but having little significance within themselves in reflecting full intellectual or spiritual development. These symbols (as we all know) too often divert the individual from his true purpose or self; and worse, and more significantly, they are used by powerful vested interest groups as weapons of seduction in manipulating great sectors of the community.

6   Without the right of the individual to freedom of information, and this has to imply the need for an obligatory course of instruction on the same grounds that reading and writing are obligatory in the curriculum, the individual can neither be self-fulfilled in serving his own most personal interests or those of the community. All of us must have occasionally experienced those sad situations of encountering highly-intelligent but ill-educated individuals unjustly tied to menial occupations. All of us must have sometime sighed to ourselves, "if only he (or she) had been given a rightful opportunity in life, then what advances he'ld have made in the world !" Only deprivation or privilege - and in a just world both terms are interchangeable and identical - prevents the development of the individual's full potential. An individual barred from the full development of his potential not only suffers injustice against himself, but the community in total incurs the same injustice. This is because the worth of an individual, in terms of character and ability, is a gift to the community; in the same way that ignorance or criminality is a deprivation of the community. In the real world, material and moral standards, peace and contentment, are ultimately dependent on a satisfactory level of information disseminated to all throughout the community.

7   The right of the individual to spiritual fulfilment means the right to free choice in all matters affecting the individual in relationship to both his inner self and the community. However, spiritual fulfilment cannot be satisfactorily achieved without the pre-condition of access to information as elaborated in the above paragraphs.

37-8

On the most obvious level, the free choice of a career cannot be achieved without the following conditions:-

1. Awareness and knowledge of the career itself;
2. An objective knowledge of one's own potential, to include strengths and weaknesses;
3. An awareness of other major categories of careers;
4. Access to the knowledge for entry into that career; and,
5. The actual and economic possibility of entering such a career.

Naturally, in a complex society, there are other intervening factors that decide the outcome of choice, e.g. fluctuations in demand for specialised skills in addition to pressures for entry into specific occupations.

This must inevitably lead to competition and disappointment, and it should therefore be the function of educational and employment bodies to sensitively assess and direct future and current job-seekers into correct occupational channels. Correct occupational channels are those best suited to the intrinsic personality and ability of the individual, and no serious attempt has yet been made in this country towards total occupational guidance along such lines. Instead, the choice of occupation tends still to be dictated by the influences of family background, regional employment patterns, and cultural or "image" factors putting their own mark on every occupation. Nevertheless, the primary task of the community in this respect must be to ensure the maximising of equality of opportunity.

8 The right of the individual to the spiritual fulfilment of his inner self, clearly means the right to believe and worship as he chooses, but it also means much more than that. In an age when established religion is increasingly losing it appeal, but men and women have no lesser spiritual needs for that, spiritual fulfilment tends instead to depend more on a balanced upbringing in a socially fortuitous environment so that the individual might develop as a mature and morally developed personality within the body of the community. This achieved, he will then more easily be facilitated to embrace those values and ideals of benefit to both himself and the community. But to ensure that the individual might more fully develop the spiritual side of his character, it is important that the community makes available those cultural facilities which assist in improving and strengthening both character and general attitudes to life and existence.

But in facilitating this development, education, too, must play a vital role, so that the individual might enjoy the best music, books, philosophy and works of art that are available to the society in which he lives. It is essential that these spiritual or cultural assets should be so broadly disseminated within the community that they are universalised and so not appropriated or comprehended on an exclusively class-pattern basis. As Tawney has so rightly remarked, "what a community requires, as

37-9

.   the world itself suggests, is a common culture, because, without it, it is not a community at all." 104 The value of art - indeed, of all spiritual values - is to act as a socially cohesive force, or focal point or attention, so that all are brought to the realisation of the essence and underlying unity of humanity. The greatest art in all civilisations, and unquestionably, all folk art, is not simply a private matter for the isolated individual. Art should not be esoteric or elitist as it so often appears today. Art is a social phenomenon, and if it is not to be appreciated in a group environment, it should certainly lend itself to appreciative discussion within the group. Unquestionably, the cultural assets of a community have a social role to play in both integrating the community and stimulating the spiritual and creative attributes of its members.

9   The theoretical apportioning of rights of the individual in the just society, as described above, however, is not sufficient in ensuring the realisation of such an ideally just society. Even the most optimistic hopes for maximising the egalitarian nature of our society in an increasingly social democratic environment cannot hope to achieve what is ultimately required. The advances already made towards the democratisation of society are considerable but they are not sufficient. It can now be assumed, for example, that there is an overwhelming consensus amongst the reasonable majority on the following:-

1. That taxes should be paid in proportion to, a) the level of income, and, b) total available wealth. The reasons for this are purely practical in maintaining a viable national economy. It is merely a secondary consideration that it is morally wrong to impose taxation irrespective of ability to pay. That taxes should be levied on a proportional basis may seem an obvious necessity in our own age, but this was certainly not so in a previous era.

2. That there can no longer be any ethical rationale for maintaining hereditary privileges or wealth conferred by the state, i.e. for maintaining a hereditary aristocracy. The reasons for this are moral, since firstly, there is no evidence that those born into the aristocracy are intrinsically superior, biologically, intellectually or morally than those born into other sectors of society; and secondly, privileges or status stemming from birth are in themselves morally wrong. There is, additionally, a second practical consideration as to why the maintenance of a hereditary aristocracy is wrong: viz. in such societies there is a tendency for subordinate sectors in the community to form their own imitative privileged groupings and closed vested interest groups, and such exclusivity undermines the sense of community and the opportunity for social

---

104   R.H. Tawney, *Equality*, Allen & Unwin, 1952 ed., p. 31.

37-9

mobility in both an upward and downward direction. This is particularly true in 20th century Britain.

3. That there is a level of material deprivation below which no person should be allowed to fall, i.e. no person should be starved to the extent of immobility or the need for hospitalisation, or should be deprived of the right to shelter under a bridge and the protection of cardboard covering. In the medieval period such equivalent protection was dependent on charity and the church. In the modern era such protection falls to the responsibility of the state.

In the more traditionally liberal countries of the Western world it is still popularly held that a person is entitled to unlimited wealth providing he has achieved this legally through his own efforts, i.e. through work or speculative share dealing. In the more socially democratic countries of the world, however, there exists the conviction that no person has the right to unlimited wealth, since, a) He or she must inevitably appropriate a disproportionate share from others in the community, and, b) An excessive proportion of economic and accompanying political power must result from such an excess of wealth. History has anyway never succeeded in demonstrating the contrary.

In view of the above consensus on justice and the basis of distribution held by the reasonable majority in the industrialised West, there still remains the threatening cloud of the emergence of the unjust Meritocratic society. This important topic has been most incisively examined by my friend, Michael Young, in his book, *The Rise of The Meritocracy*.[105] The problem of the future simply lies in the possibility of the more intelligent forming a natural hereditary elite that might unconsciously oppress the less fortunate mortals in their midst. In our own time, for example, there exists a situation not pertaining before, viz. marriage (or sexual partnership) between individuals both of whom are highly qualified equals in a particular profession. It is the opinion of this author, however, that this entails a lesser threat than might at first be thought. For example, those in the medical and legal professions, both in this country and in Scandinavia, falling into the above category, known to the author, are more liberal and generous in their sympathies towards the poor and downtrodden, than those of the same professions with spouses of inferior intelligence. The pointer is clear: it is primarily the stupid or mentally deficient who anticipate a threat to their own status and hence tend to raise defensive barriers of class privilege in safeguarding the future of their heirs.

---

105   *The Rise of The Meritocracy*, Penguin, 1968, by Lord Young of Dartington, author of the Labour Party's 1945 election manifesto, originator of the Consumers' Association and the Open University, and the first Chairman of the Tawney Society, the Think-tank of the former SDP.

38-1
The prospect of the unjust meritocratic society can only be countered by the following:-
1. By raising minimum material living standards;
2. By maximising the ownership and control of property in its different forms throughout the general population; and,
3. By imposing just and acceptable sumptuary laws on the life-style of the *very* richest members of our society.

10   In defining justice for the individual within the constraints of the community, we can progress no further than the above at this stage in our investigation. Next we must investigate the nature of our modern industrialised society, particularly in view of the impending changes of the new millennium. Justice as a political concept cannot be discussed as an abstraction. It cannot exist within a vacuum. It only takes on meaning within an historical context. For example, justice as defined by the elders of a primitive tribe would be very different from any definition given in our own era. Likewise, in every historical epoch, the wise men of their own age would (and have) defined political justice from very different viewpoints, and consequently, have reached very varied conclusions.

CHAPTER 38
The Moral Bankruptcy of Our Financial System

> "The perfecting of an adequate system of rights and duties for the modern exchange economy requires a degree of technical discrimination and expertness that no representative assembly can hope to possess."

Walter Lippmann, *The Good Society*, Allen & Unwin, 1938, p. 301.

1 - Two threats to social progress: vested interests and war   2 - Environmentalists' opposition to progress   3 - But it arises out of their misinterpretation of the term "progress"   4 - Industry of the future will be environmentally safe   5 - But only if labour and capital cease to oppose necessary investment   6 - It is laissez-faire and not progress that threatens the environment   7 - Rentier capitalism contributes towards both de-industrialisation and pollution   8 - Disillusion with contemporary political conditions 9 - Reasons for this as they apply to Britain   10 - Limitations of popular pressure groups

1   Let us define, then, the exciting conditions of the new era into which we are now moving. If our hopes are to be fulfilled, it will be an age of unprecedented technological progress, calling for skills and brainpower from the broad base of the community on a scale never before demanded. If political circumstances allow human and natural resources to be organised as desired, then not only will living standards be increased to higher levels than heretofore, but equality of opportunity will be so maximised as to create a comparatively egalitarian community.

38-4

Two things only threaten to block the achievement of such a society: the vested interests of selfish elites who thrive on the profits of an "As is" situation and are against all change; and the occurrence and draining expenditure of war. Both are interrelated, for it is only the selfish elites who thrive on the profits of destruction. Undoubtedly, technological progress in the future in all its socially desirable forms will be of greatest relative benefit to those at the base of society, just as in the past such benefits have percolated down from the apex of society to benefit an ever-broadening strata of the community.

2   The covert (and never explicit) opposition to technological progress of privileged elites in a desperate struggle to preserve the status quo and the accompanying vested interests of an "As is" situation, is not only the direction from which such opposition to progress is found. More obvious is the fear in Western industrialised countries of threats to the environment, of pollution, and the erosion of the protective ozone layer due to the excessive burning of mineral fuels, and the creation of acid rain, resulting in the global "greenhouse effect." Already the latter has begun to be manifested in changing climatic conditions, such as the conversion of large grain land areas in the mid-Western American States into arid dust bowls, excessive rain in other areas, and the melting of the polar ice caps. Because of this ecological damage and greater threats in the future, the popular imagination has been seized by prejudiced interest groups that would cast an undiscriminating blame on "industry" and "progress" for all that has happened.

3   Such an undiscriminating condemnatory attitude arises from a biased analysis, giving a false impression of what is truly at stake. Firstly, if these groups and individuals blame "technological progress" for the ecological threats that are facing us, they are stating a contradiction, for any measures, conscious or unintentional, that damage the long-term interests of humankind and the environment cannot by any definition be described as "progress." They should rather be described as a "regression," or alternatively, as the "perversion of progress." Secondly, it is anyway questionable as to whether the industrial sector (when at its worst) should take the first blame for damaging the environment. The responsibility for acid rain over Western Europe by Britain, for example, is with far more justice likely to fall on the domestic sector, i.e. on the burning of natural gas by millions of householders in poorly insulated dwellings. The answer to such an accusation, if well-founded, might be that town dwellers be obliged to reside in vast apartment blocks, well insulated and heated by sophisticated systems of low-output energy sources.

4   Thirdly, there is a totally false view in the popular mind as to the true nature of modern industry. To many, industry still conjures up a picture of huge smoke stack factories billowing out black clouds of pollution and any amount of noxious chemicals, employing thousands of labourers engaged in soul-destroying repetitive

38-5

tasks. In every respect this is a dated picture - relevant thirty years ago - but today, hardly more meaningful than describing modern industry in terms of the mill with steam driven machinery. Today smoke-stack industries represent a minuscule proportion of the manufacturing sector, as indeed does the manufacturing plant employing its thousands. Only in the bulk production of chemicals, and steel rolling and smelting, do smoke stack industries have any remaining significance, and even in these, the application of modern processes should shortly remove the emission of harmful gases or recycle them for other energy purposes.

Manufacturing processes are increasingly undertaken on a much smaller scale for a wide variety of reasons, e.g.:-

1. Because of the development of robotic and information technology;
2. Decrease in labour intensive methods;
3. Power sources as electricity and oil, ensuring that the location of industry is not dictated by geographical factors;
4. Increasing specialisation of processes by manufacturing concerns as opposed to costly diversification; and,
5. New technologies allowing manufacturers to produce low-cost or individually tailored runs - something that was impossible just ten years ago.

Not only is the entire structure of industry changing but also its sociology. The typical operative of the future will not be a low-paid semi-skilled proletarian, as in the past, but a highly-paid university trained technician or engineer. He will certainly see himself as "middle class," and the skills, training and intelligence required of him will eventually give him a higher status than the bank clerk or other office worker. His responsibility for the efficient maintenance of equipment valued at millions of pounds, will inevitably ensure that such trust is proportionally rewarded in the salary scale.

5   All the above is progress, but as to whether such progress will be allowed to go ahead unhindered, is another question. The resistance to progress by powerful vested interests on both sides of the political spectrum in Britain has in great part been responsible for our relative decline and the relative fall in living standards by comparison with our leading competitors. Much has been said in the past about the wrecking activities of many of our trades unions in opposing the installation of automated machinery in maintaining old-established manning levels or in maintaining inefficient working practices, but little has been said about the nefarious activities of vested financial interests that (often unbeknown to themselves) have equally been responsible for withholding progress. These financial interests, in wrecking the hopes for industrial progress, have been manifested through a wide variety of practices, as:- 1. Asset-stripping; 2. Undesirable accountancy practices; 3. Contrived distortion of share valuations; 4. The pursuit of financial profits as opposed to

38-7

productive profits; 5. Crafty speculative activity; and, 6. The re-direction of financial resources away from productivity into the passive assets of land and property. All these activities that have held back industrial progress, entail the making of money out of money as opposed to making money out of *things* and socially desirable services; or expressed another way, it entails the promotion of harmful rentier capitalism as opposed to beneficial productive capitalism.

6   Clearly implied in industrial progress in its true sense is due consideration for the protection of the environment. As we have said, industrial progress damaging the environment is a contradiction in terms, since the objective purpose of industry is long-term benefit to the community, and if it fails to measure up to that criterion, then the social benefit of industry is negated.

Such an interpretation of the purpose of industry, however, is not that of laissez-faire or classical capitalism. The laissez-faire (and especially the American) rationale for industry - and indeed, for business in general - is that its prime (if not sole) purpose, is to maximise pure financial profits for shareholders. This ultimately translates, of course, into the purpose of making money out of money; and is quite separate from the purpose of pursuing business for its own productive sake or for the community. Consequently, in America we have seen greater ecological damage than elsewhere in the world, with all except one of the Great Lakes so poisoned as to be denuded of plant and animal life; entire forests decimated of their foliage, and trees stunted to dwarf-like size. This has been accompanied by massive corruption by large conglomerates, in their attempt to suppress information on such damage, or to cast blame in other directions, such as on the Soviets or on natural disasters as the volcanic eruption of St. Helens.

7   The rape of the environment by industry in America, as elsewhere in the world, occurs primarily through pursuing pure money profits to the sacrifice of all other interests. In the process, the interests of industry itself are sacrificed. Not only are old methods retained on the grounds of their continuing "profitability," but those methods are expanded, and any evidence as to their harming the atmosphere or lakes and rivers, is rigorously suppressed, since exposure would damage shareholders' profits. Likewise in America, in recent times, when industry is found to damage the health of employees, the international conglomerates have merely transferred their manufacturing plants to India (e.g. Union Carbide moved to Bhopal), or to Mexico, or elsewhere in the Third world, where health and safety regulations have a lower priority or where officials may be corrupted by bribes.

But at the same time that the environment is damaged by repudiating the required costs of investment in cleaner manufacturing processes, so too in the name of greater profit margins, investment is withheld from modernising technology. There is a great irony in the fact that whilst on the one hand America is perceived

38-8

as the most advanced industrialised nation in the Western world, on the other, her factories have long been decrepit and antiquated. One of the surprising findings of British managers visiting partner companies in the US is the realisation that their manufacturing plants are no better and often far worse than our own. All this is definitive evidence of the moral and material bankruptcy of classical capitalism. Hence in the contemporary world where there exists a clear separation between the owners and managers of larger scale industry - and of smaller industry too when such enterprises are encompassed within a group - it is not industrialists (in the true meaning of the word) who are responsible for sacrificing the interests of industry or the environment, but financiers. It is not industrialists (i.e. the production managers, engineers, marketeers and sales personnel) who have been responsible for decimating manufacturing or polluting the environment, but financiers and bankers in league with unimaginative accountants - i.e. those holding the purse strings of industry - who have brought about the ills we see today.

8   Having defined the nature of true justice and identified the original cause of injustice, and having concluded that the starting point in politics should be a consideration of factors that are Economic, Disinterested, and Urgent, we can now move over with confidence from the general and theoretical to the practical and specific.

All the disillusion with political conditions in the contemporary world arises from the fact that technology and material progress have moved faster than the ability of ordinary people to adapt their thinking and attitudes to changed conditions. Inevitably, therefore, the majority feel confused, frustrated, isolated, angered, or sceptical about the world in which they live. Their upbringing and education has not fitted them for contemporary conditions. Their attitude is purely a problem of philosophical outlook, compounded, of course, by insufficient knowledge of the changes that have occurred and their significance to the community. They become anachronistic, cynical or reactionary, in a world to which they cannot relate and in which they become increasingly alienated. Progress and its benefits have left them far behind.

Those who have failed to move with the times cannot be properly fitted into any class category. They are found across the entire spectrum of society. What they have all had in common, however, is the failure to digest the *relevant* knowledge of their time, and knowledge in this sense is not purely technical or intellectual, but moral and philosophical. They are the most wretched victims of progress, ranging from the cloth-capped proletarian of the North with his great-grandfather's brass watch and chain, to the myopic upper-class couple in the Home counties, musing tearfully over happier days in India in a distant past. All have fallen victims to ignorance through the inertia of lazy minds and an inherent complacency of almost

38-10

genetic stubbornness.

The occurrence of these regressive characteristics is especially particular to Britain, and the reason stems from five factors: the polarisation of our society; the secrecy by which we are governed; an exaggerated individualism; faults in the educational system, and, the outcome of laissez-faire. All these factors not only contribute towards dividing society into mutually exclusive interest groups but tend to widen the differences between those groups - especially in the political sphere. Furthermore, such exclusivity tends towards promoting egocentricity, and an insensitive self-satisfaction that deadens curiosity in things beyond the self. These conclusions can be best understood by any comparison with the societies of our northern neighbours. In the industrially advanced societies of the Baltic or the North Sea coast, not only is there to be found a greater sense of common purpose, but a greater awareness of the need for perfecting the just society, and an infinitely greater curiosity in the world around us. Consequently, it is rare in these societies to encounter individuals who pine for the past or fail to appreciate the benefits of the present. The peoples of the North are more integrated into the progressive purpose of their own societies, and consequently, they have prospered whilst Britain, in relative terms, has withered. [106]

10   The consequences of political cynicism in Britain, irrespective of whether it has arisen out of the individual's failure to adapt to changing circumstances, or contrariwise, his disgust that political institutions in their turn have failed to adapt, has resulted in the alternative phenomenon of popular pressure groups. As people have become increasingly disillusioned with politicians and political parties, they have turned to supporting single issue causes. Admirable as many of these groups may be, resort to pressure groups is a poor substitute for allegiance to broadly-based political movements. The reason for this is significant: for although it is the specific end of a pressure group that first attracts its members, after the passing of time, those members begin to perceive the world and all its problems through the eyes of that single group. Inevitably, through an advanced form of subjectivism, those long-term members are drawn to adopting a one-sided view of the world. Most pressure groups are concerned with peripheral issues, and no broad-based political philosophy can be developed out of a peripheral issue. It also has to be said, of course, that pressure groups can never represent more than one half of the truth, since they are

---

[106] During ten years residence in Scandinavia, I can recollect only one occasion of an individual's pining for the past - apart from the occasional sentimental yearnings of White Russian emigrès. On that occasion it was a middle aged Finnish countess who pined for the "good old days" of Tsar Alexander II. It should be noted, however, that she was drunk at the time.

39-1

usually established to counter abnormal or unbalanced forces in society. The setting of opposites against opposites, therefore, merely compounds rather than solves problems.

All these factors underline the urgent need for considering the human priorities of politics.

CHAPTER 39
Social Prosperity Only Achievable Through Autonomy

"Economic struggle is not waged by applying force to subdue the enemy but (always thinking in structural terms) by utilising to the fullest degree all opportunities afforded by a given situation, and by taking advantage unhesitatingly of the calculated negative chances inherent in the situation of the opponent."

Karl Mannheim, *Essays On The Sociology of Knowledge*, Routledge & Kegan Paul, 1952, p. 259.

1 - Definition of Social Prosperity   2 - Need for an objective political doctrine   3 - Bankruptcy of historical-materialism and political individualism   4 - National economic autonomy necessary for the just community   5 - Concept of Nationality contrasted with Nationalism   6 - Contemporary Internationalism the vested interest of the far right   7 - How economic crises are exacerbated by international interests   8 - But this is not an argument against the greater need for international co-operation   9 - Contemporary international institutions bureaucratic rather than democratic   10 - Forces of international finance not answerable to any political authority and hence the principle of Nationality is of overriding importance

1   It is necessary to define our use of the term Social Prosperity. There is a hint that the words might suggest a contradiction. Prosperity refers to material well-being and our use of the term clearly infers the pursuit of this. Social, however, suggests the harmonising or equalising of conditions in society to the individuals of which it is composed, and Prosperity would be seen only as an indirect outcome of this. It is common to talk of "Individual prosperity," but not of "Social prosperity." By using the term Social Prosperity, we mean it in the special sense of creating politico-economic conditions within the community in enabling the individual to maximise his potential and earning power whilst at the same time ensuring that his interests are not sacrificed to vested interest groups. In effect, this means the socialising of all those dynamic wealth-creating forces in the community, so that those forces may in no way be diminished. It means giving free scope to the individual within the constraints of a competitive but socially conflict-free community.

2   There is a need today for the foundation of a political economy transcending the vested interests of particular groups in the community. Because of the evolutionary stage we have reached in the democratisation of society in both East

39-4

and West, and despite the existence of powerful reactionary forces in all parts of the world, the time has never been riper for the acceptance of an objective political doctrine in guiding us through the maze of problems threatening us today.

Most thinking people have long come to the realisation that any political system involving the pursuit of vested interests in the attempt to solve substantive issues, leads merely to a running round in circles, or to a see-saw motion between conflicting groups in the community. In this way political emotions are allowed free play as a revanchist comeuppance is enjoyed alternately by one group and then another, but real issues remain unsatisfactorily resolved. As Will Durant has observed, "it is the simplest thing in the world to construct a philosophy out of our wishes and our interests. We must be on our guard against being Communists, because we are poor, or Conservatives because our ship has come in." 107 All the political cynicism we see today stems from the pitiful sight of this dog chasing its tail.

3   Contemporary dialectical-materialists, on the other hand, view this process as inevitable, believing that ultimately it will lead to the promised millennium, but both their historical-materialism and the receding promise have made them at the same time stupid and complacent. History has long proven that it is not going to move along the rails laid down for it by any doctrinaire philosopher in the distant past, and meanwhile, the economic dimension of historical-materialism has been totally discredited in all its aspects. Reading the entrails of the future can be a legitimate task in political science but only if pursued circumspectly by utilising and integrating all branches of relevant knowledge.

If, therefore, in looking to our political future, we cannot place trust in the individual's pursuit of vested interests, or in the collectivist's trust in historical-materialism, we are thrown back on the necessity to think through our situation from an entirely new perspective. We are forced, once again, to become objective rationalists - or at least, to attempt that achievement. Objectivity can only be sought and maintained by concentrating on a moral "ought" situation as opposed to an expedient "As is" situation, and of course, any sound system of morality can only be based on exactly that approach. But first there has to be a firm grasp of the socio-economic forces in society, and of the basic economic necessities facilitating the existence of a modern industrialised community.

4   Furthermore, such consideration can only be examined within the total economic activities of a community or nation. In other words, it is useless to discuss the "oughts" in a community if that community is anyway not fully autonomous.

107   Will Durant. *The Mansions of Philosophy*. Garden City Publishing Co.. NY. 1941 ed.. p. 47.

39-7

These remarks are made primarily in the light of two factors: firstly, with regard to communities that are units in a larger economic or defensive federation; and secondly, to communities economically dominated by the powerful forces of international conglomerates. The status of nationality is therefore of crucial importance in discussing the question of justice in the community, for unbeknown to itself, over a period of time, a community can almost invisibly relinquish its economic independence, awaking one morning to find it no longer has the political wherewithal to amend social injustice within its own system.

5 We shall use the term Nationality as opposed to the term Nationalism for the reason that the latter is often used in the context of promoting narrow or selfish interests, usually with assumptions of cultural or racial superiority used as instruments for dominating over other national groupings. Our use of the concept of Nationality is meant in quite a different meaning: i.e. in the sense of solving internal political problems by counteracting external factors preventing the solution of those problems. If an Idealist or Realistic approach is to be attempted in solving the greatest social and economic problems within Britain (or anywhere else) - and it has to be noted that philosophical Idealism equals Realism in its ultimate meaning - then the principle of Nationality has to be pursued. In the industrialised West this principle is actually promoted by all the Scandinavian countries, most notably through their guarded attitude towards international conglomerates and the ruthless tide of international capital. In Britain, on the other hand, the more usual attitude is that our economic system is so inextricably bound up with the wider implications of international capital that there is nothing that can be done about the situation anyway.

6 This is a noxious attitude to our present situation. It is used as an excuse for tolerating all the economic ills under which we linger today. It not merely kills off discussion but even thought. The fact that our economy is dominated by international conglomerates more powerful than national governments seems to make any consideration of substantive economic issues with regard to the possibility of radical change a sterile area for discussion. Consequently, the greatest advocates of internationalism in the contemporary world are not the Socialists of the far left (as in the 19th century) but politicians of the right who are the mouthpiece of the banking fraternity and big business. The external forces of international finance are such that every time a radical solution to our greatest economic problems is pinned to the mast, it is shot down as a "non-starter," without the opportunity for discussion.

7 The ills to which international finance has lent itself in conjunction with the incompetence of international political institutions which have unwittingly become their tool, may be witnessed worldwide: from the food mountains in Europe to the famines in Eastern Africa, and from the promotion of wars between impoverished

39-8

peoples by arms merchants, to the destruction of the planet's lung through the wholesale felling of the rain forests in Brazil, Africa and the Far East. All these social and ecological evils have only been made possible because of the huge financial profits accrued by their heartless promoters. How else is it possible to explain that countries reduced to the direst poverty are still able to maintain the most destructive wars, both civil and against their neighbours, using the most modern and expensive conventional weaponry ? It is certainly not to the benefit of their diseased and famine ridden peoples. By no criterion can these struggles be described as wars for "National liberation." They are self-destructive in every sense. Their sole beneficiaries are the international bankers, credit brokers and arms merchants who are too eager to exploit any political situation in stuffing their own pockets. How is such a crazy situation made possible ? In the words of G.D.H. Cole, "as the world is, the less advanced countries do not so much borrow money from the more advanced as have loans thrust upon them even against their will."[108]

How else is it possible to explain the senseless felling and burning of the rain forests, so that four harvests are sown and reaped before the topsoil in its turn is washed away and the ground made useless for further planting, in a world that currently produces food in excess to feed the planet's population ? It is only explained through the short-term demands of international creditors for the payment of long-term debts that can anyway never be paid. None of these crazy policies are pursued for national interests, but merely as desperate measures to satisfy the neat bookkeeping methods of the international banking fraternity in its greedy career. These are some of the reasons why the principle of nationality should be pursued.

8   None of this is to be used as an argument against international co-operation, for clearly, international co-operation and the wise instruments thereof have become more important today than at any previous time in our history. But so too, the principle of nationality has become of overriding importance as a way towards solving our most urgent social and economic issues. There are several reasons for this. Firstly, there is no such thing (at the present time) as a Political World Community. There are political world institutions of various sorts, but none that are directly representative of the peoples of the world, i.e. none that are sensitive to an electoral process. There do not (as yet) exist in the true meaning of the term "Political world leaders," for the cultural, economic and political differences between peoples remain so great, that there is not the opportunity for the development and emergence of such leaders. In addition, of course, there do not yet exist any political institutions to act as a medium for such leadership.

---

108   G.D.H. Cole, *The Intelligent Man's Guide Through World Chaos*, Gollancz, 1932, p. 124.

39-10

Secondly, there is a principle that still remains in force (and first formulated by the Greeks) that there is a natural limit to the size of a political community. Although we can no longer go along with the Greeks in maintaining that no successful community (or *Polis*) should exceed those few thousands that could be assembled into the *Agora* of their City-state, it still remains true that the most successful and most democratic societies are situated in the smaller geographical regions of the world where communications are easier and whose peoples tend towards greater homogeneity. In this category must be included the peoples of the Benelux and Scandinavian states, Switzerland, Singapore, Taiwan, New Zealand and the coastal nation of Australia. The future, however, may see the emergence of a truly international ideology and if institutions are formed to serve as an effective medium for this, these in turn may coalesce to serve the foundation for a genuine political world community.

9   The present situation, however, is very far from that. The great political international institutions existing today are not democratic but bureaucratic, and those purporting to have some democratic representation are so far removed from the consciousness of their electorates as to be nothing more than Ghost assemblies, more answerable to their contiguous bureaucracies than to their more distant constituencies. Such international institutions as exist today, irrespective of whether or not they may have a tenuous regard for regional interests, are easily and shamelessly manipulated by the forces of international finance. There is nothing surprising in this sinister reality. Such institutions are not geared to respond to democratic forces, even though some may have nominally in-built democratic functions. Practical democracy in the contemporary world ends at national frontiers. This means that international institutions exist in a political vacuum they should never have been confronted with, and this vacuum has been filled by the only other power that can exist: viz. by the forces of international finance.

10   This does not merely include the international banking fraternity, but of increasing significance, the great international trading conglomerates, that move billions of currency values from one country to another free of any significant controls, for the simple reason that they are far more powerful than any national government. It is these forces that threaten, undermine or even destroy the autonomy of national states, and render national governments impotent in the face of their greatest economic crises. The principle of nationality should therefore be actively pursued on the following four grounds:-

1. So that countries might exert their full autonomy in freely implementing policies best for their own peoples without the need of having to bow to the demands of bald "expediency" - i.e. the adamantine power of international finance;

40-1

2. So that peoples might reserve for themselves the democratic right to block the power and activities of international finance and trading conglomerates, on the grounds that such power is unrepresentative.

3. That countries might defend their interests against forces that appropriate for themselves the national wealth of peoples; and,

4. So that each country might independently seek to perfect its socio-economic system, so serving as a model for the rest. It has to be assumed, in general, that the more industrially advanced countries will reach this state of relative perfection prior to developing states which may be hampered by far more serious economic or cultural hindrances.

In the contemporary industrialised West, the destruction of wealth and national economic institutions is less endangered by the threat of war than by international bankers and trading corporations. If social progress is to be advanced, then the influence of these forces must be pushed aside, so that the pure political power of national institutions may exert its full pressure through the unhindered democratic process. The principle of national autonomy, seen in this light, therefore, does not conflict with the humane spirit of internationalism, but rather, is complementary with it.

CHAPTER 40
The True Foundations For Disinterested Politics

"Individuals, indeed, and still more frequently classes do constantly support laws or institutions which they deem beneficial to themselves, but which certainly are in fact injurious to the rest of the world."

A.V. Dicey, *Law & Public Opinion In England*, Macmillan, 1905, p. 14.

1 - Factors on which the social good of the autonomous community is dependent   2 - Achilles heel of liberalism has been its concern with Means rather than Ends   3 - Its philosophical hedonism has been its undoing   4 - Foundations of disinterested politics   5 - How the Socialist conception of Distribution may lead to the slave society   6 - Powerful financiers alone would be the beneficiaries of the "Leisure" or "Unemployed" society   7 - Distribution in itself fails to reflect a change in power relationships   8 - This is because it fails to take account of the forms and uses of wealth   9 - Wealth creation alone is the primary principle of disinterested politics

1   In integrating the different sectors of an autonomous community towards the social good, so implementing disinterested authority, it is necessary to assess and balance three elements in society: firstly, social needs and values; secondly, the circumscribing of centralised economic power, through decentralisation and the spreading and equalisation of ownership; and thirdly, the need to guarantee the rights of the individual to ensure his full development and the opportunity to "knock" the

40-3

system of constituted authority if he so desires.

2   Because of the need to balance these three elements, we question the entire philosophy of conventional liberalism. This is because liberalism has only traditionally been concerned with the way in which authority is executed, and has seemed to be oblivious to the fact that all authority is equally determinate (as we have earlier remarked) irrespective of the basis, origin or style of that authority. A pauper is no more better off under a democratic than under an authoritarian regime, and if the former may seem to offer him more "rights" these merely remain a cynical mirage in the light of his helplessness. In the modern era, in the industrialised world, liberal regimes have given rise to greater examples of social injustice as well as to extremer forms of poverty, than have authoritarian regimes of the older model. Herbert Spencer, one of the greatest liberal thinkers at the end of the last century, for example, was totally opposed to any legislation restricting the sale of dangerous goods as an outrageous infringement on the liberties of the entrepreneur. He believed, as with others of the liberal persuasion, that the weak and the poor should be left to perish as they were trampled on by the strong, as an inevitable and evolutionary law of nature, and that any interference by the state amounted to unwarranted tyranny. Such intellectual myopia took no cognisance of the fact that the assumed "law of nature" might undiscriminatingly destroy both good and bad alike. Such thinking is now again very much in the fore in contemporary Britain which continues to be haunted by the ghost of Thatcherism.

3   The obsession of liberalism with the nature of governmental power and the need to curb arbitrary authority, and its philosophical hedonism or populism, has dulled its sense - if not killed off its interest - in solving substantive issues. 109 Far more important than questions of authority or the gauging of alleged wants, are the

---

109 The politics of contemporary liberalism is still cursed by this philosophical hedonism which undermines its ability to act as a determined unified force. This hedonism has an atomistic effect on its organisational structure: firstly, through excessive decentralisation; secondly, through a proliferation of vested interest groups; and thirdly, through a fudging and blurring of national policy as an inevitable consequence of the first two factors. The crisis of the British political centre, for which there were such high hopes in the early 1980s, was seemingly resolved in 1987 with its ruin. This resulted in the break-up of the SDP Liberal Alliance into two separate parties: the dominating SLD and the continuing SDP rump. However, the larger grouping has been swamped by the hedonism of the old Liberals. The dynamism and organisational efficiency of the old SDP was sacrificed on the altar of this merger, and the result has been the electoral contraction of the political centre to its pre-1981 level.

T.H. Green was the one great political liberal who identified the weakness of this philosophical hedonism in contemporary Utilitarian thinking and sought to remedy the fault in several series of academic lectures towards the close of the last century. In the words of T.H. Green, "Utilitarianism proper ... requires no vocation of man but the attainment of pleasure and avoidance of pain. ... They do not seek the ground of actual rights in a proper natural rights, but in an end to which the maintenance of the rights contributes." (*Lectures On The Principles Of Political Obligation*, Longmans, Green, 1927 ed., p. 43) It is ironic that this damning criticism of liberalism (more relevant today than when originally spoken) should have come from the lips of a man who was himself a politically active Liberal.

40-5

actual needs of the community as objectively appreciated. Liberals may respond to our call for a more disinterested approach with the charge of implied arrogance; but our reply to such an answer would be that mainstream liberalism has not succeeded in creating just and socially egalitarian societies measuring up to the standards enjoyed by our competitors elsewhere. In basing its decision-making policy and ideology on a shifting and superficial appreciation of immediate wants, mainstream liberalism has taken no account of the factor of false consciousness, and hence it has lacked a firm groundwork for lasting principles.

4   It is our purpose to formulate principles for the good of the community that not merely transcend the narrow perspective of vested interests but also transcend the shifting sands of popular opinion. What should be our starting point, bearing in mind that our discussion should be based on the Disinterested, the Urgent and the Economic ? First principles dictate that we should not primarily look at the distribution of wealth (which is a vested interest issue and so contrary to our principle of Disinterestedness) but rather at the creation of wealth, which is not merely a basic principle of economics but basic to existence itself.

Obsession with the principle of distribution as a *primary* issue in politics or morality (notwithstanding that it remains the most important issue) has led political thinkers and philosophers to sound off tangentially in a variety of wrong directions. These wrong directions have simply been pursued due to an insufficiency of sociological knowledge and ignorance of hidden economic forces. They have invariably been pursued due to a misunderstanding of the nature of humanity in its totality. In addition to seizing on secondary instead of primary political issues in solving major social questions, high emotions have been allowed to intervene in colouring the perception of such issues and this in turn has led to the dogma of rigid prejudice. Consequently, new and sometimes worse abuses are allowed to substitute those of an earlier era. History is packed with such examples.

5   The conviction that the question of distribution is the *primary* political issue soon hardens into the belief that is the only political issue, and in the politics of the left, this conviction is currently leading to one of the greatest misconceptions of our time. It is leading to the false optimism of the Leisure Society theorists, whereby an excess of "alleged wealth" will comfortably fulfil the needs of a vast unemployed population. Under the umbrella of this theory, long-term unemployment need carry no fears, for the new information technologies will simply create such an excess of wealth that through the skill of re-distribution none need ever be deprived. The real truth, as we demonstrate below, leads to a very different scenario. The Leisure society when transferred from the theoretical to the practical sphere would inevitably lead to the slave society as we already noted in Chapter 8. Such re-distribution would amount to nothing more than the "dole." Irrespective of the name it is given,

40-8

and irrespective of the level of the re-distribution itself, such a society would be based on charity, and the recipients never could nor would enjoy the full rights or privileges of the donors, i.e. the remaining working population.

6   By the law of nature, the recipients would be perceived as the drones or parasites of the community and there would be no rebuttal to the charge. But far worse than this perceived status would be the economic fact that the beneficiaries of this Leisure society would not have a legal, or what is more important, an actual stake in the economic control of society. It would inescapably be a two-class society with all the ills of a class-torn community. The ultimate beneficiaries of such a Leisure society would not be the petitioning recipients but the small financial class in lining their own pockets. This is just one example of the misconception in regarding the question of distribution as the primary issue in politics.

7   It should also be understood that the question of distribution in itself gives no answer to power relationships within the community, but merely assumes that the simple fact of greater distribution of wealth inevitably leads to a wider distribution of power. But often, this is very far from the case. Socialist policies in post-War Britain, for example, did not succeed in granting greater political power to the majority of the population other than that exclusive power exerted by trades union organisations. The centre in British politics is now very aware of this former deficiency of the political left, and is foremost in attempting to amend the fault by encouraging decentralisation in the regions; by co-determination in the workplace; and by share-ownership schemes. Post-War taxation policies have most notably been total in their failure in democratising the structure of society, and it is only the general raising of living standards of majorities in all post-War industrialised societies which has succeeded in masking this fact. Most significantly, and of greatest irony, the worst and most exploitative aspects of rentier capitalism developed in Britain under the very noses of Labour party administrations with the reorganisation of the City after 1945.

8   Distribution considered as a first principle in politics is doomed to failure since it fails to take account of the origin and uses of wealth in its different forms as a dynamic or living force in the community. The distributionists tend to have a static view of wealth. They see it in terms of *money*, as a measurable quantity existing *per se*, which may be moved about whilst still retaining a constant value. This fallacy usually arises from a misunderstanding of the business process, for they see business not as a creative individual force defying all the rules of the collective mind, but as something lending itself to a bureaucratic framework. This, indeed, is the greatest fallacy of Socialism, and has been proven so by the 20th century experience. It has led to all the failures of nationalisation, both in this country and in the East bloc.

It should be noted, however, that the popular Socialist ideal of Distribution as

40-9

an end in itself, and the Socialist failure to appreciate the economics of wealth creation, has been helped by the historical perspective of feudal and the post-feudal society of landed gentry and aristocracy almost up to our own time. Here we see the formation and relative permanence of passive wealth - of a gloriously leisured and idle class, which sits on the land whilst collecting in the rents of a huge labouring population. These are the original of the Rentiers we have written so much about in the present book. They have been aped by the manufacturing class of the previous century and British industry has suffered from the result. It is hoped that they are not now to be aped by the Leisured or Unemployed classes of the future - or at least, that their idleness is not to be held up as a tolerable alternative to gainful employment. Such an alternative would be very far from tolerable for the reasons given above. In any case, in the modern democratic industrial community, intent on a sound wealth creating base, there can be no room for those who fail to make a *positive* contribution through *work* to the good of the commonweal.

If by some strange hypothetical possibility all the wealth of the nation were to be equally re-distributed on a per capita basis, then within a very short period, the same inequalities would again appear in society, for the equalisation of wealth is not dependent on the simple act of re-distribution but solely on the methods by which wealth is constantly renewed. Spendthrifts (and a majority of us may fall into the category of unintentional spendthrifts) will always lose more than they gain, i.e. their spending ability will always gain on their earning ability. The great Austrian economist and sociologist, Ludwig von Mises, has carried the thesis a step further by arguing that, "our whole civilisation rests on the fact that men have always succeeded in beating off the attack of the re-distributors." [110]

9   Therefore the process of wealth creation and its structure in the community must be considered as the primary principle in politics. The survival of the community is dependent on wealth creation and on no other factor. It is a nonsense to discuss distribution without first fully appreciating the workings of wealth creation, for an obsessive or conscientious determination to distribute available wealth may (and has often) led to destroying the goose which lays the golden eggs. Wealth creation is the most basic of all social activities, having priority over all others. It entails ploughing, sowing the corn seed, reaping, milling, manufacturing the shoes for our feet and the shirts for our backs. Almost all that we touch and feel is the outcome of wealth creation.

All that is necessary in the material world is the result of wealth creation, and wealth creation is all that is necessary for material existence. Wealth creation is

---

110   Ludwig von Mises, *Socialism*, Jonathan Cape, 1953 ed., p. 51.

41-2

hence the primary and most disinterested issue in political life since its object effects us all in equal measure.

CHAPTER 41

The Underlying Grounds of Conflict In The Contemporary World

> "I think the spirit of Reasonableness as the highest and sanest ideal of human culture, and the reasonable man as the highest type of cultivated human being. ... The Reasonable Age, if that should ever come about, will be the Age of Peace. It will be the age in which the spirit of Reasonableness prevails."
>
> Lin Yutang, *The Importance of Living*, Heinemann, 1938, p. 433.

1 - The free society is dependent on maximising the individual's control of wealth   2 - Conditions necessary to achieve this   3 - Need for decentralisation and competition   4 - And co-determination   5 - But these things are dependent on fortuitous cultural and educational conditions   6 - Need for a renewed individualistic spirit amongst working people   7 - Underlying conflict in the modern world is between the demands of Individualism and Collectivism   8 - Proletarian Collectivism is anachronistic 9 - But Conservatism is no less anachronistic   10 - Forces of Individualism and Collectivism should not be matched with the conventional political divide   11 - Giant capitalist conglomerates no less Collectivist than left wing organisations   12 - But Collectivism, too, embodies social values

1   If, therefore, a society is to be truly democratic, i.e. if power is to be more equally distributed so that exploitation - or alleged exploitation - of human resources is reduced to the minimum, then this is not to be achieved by the superficial means of simply ensuring a more equal distribution of available wealth, but rather by involving the majority in those processes entailing the *control* of wealth. This is because wealth in a living or working community is not a stagnant factor like muddy water in an enclosed pool, but is fluid, like the clear water in a running stream. Hence the most significant aspect of the enjoyment of wealth is not so much its ownership as its control, i.e. its creation and use, before its inevitable diminution through consumption or devaluation. This is because the most important aspect of nearly all wealth, irrespective of its form - it may be buildings no less than money - is the need for its constant renewal.

2   In political terms, extending wealth (or economic distribution) to the majority can only be achieved by the following:-

    1. In changing the structures through which wealth is created;

    2. In extending financial and economic education; and,

    3. In extending rights, so that all might enjoy the free availability of owning and at the same time controlling wealth - not merely the means of production.

However, it should be noted that the last condition, viz. Rights, is very much subservient to the first two. The granting of Rights in themselves, as we have earlier

41-6

noted, is a meaningless gesture, for legal status without the back-up of more powerful sociological factors (e.g. education or money) amounts to nothing more than empty theory.

3   The change of structures through which wealth is created calls for two lines of action: firstly, the decentralisation of business activity and the encouragement of competition, so maximising the proportion of owners or entrepreneurs within the community; and secondly, radical changes to the status of those remaining business organisation that cannot, for one reason or another, be broken down into smaller units. Fortunately, as we have earlier noted, manufacturing plants in the future (if evolutionary progress is not to be halted) will for the most part exist on a much reduced scale. Retail and other service industries direct to the public may easily be broken down into smaller units without any sacrifice to their overall efficiency simply through their sale as franchises so that their central distribution organisation, and if necessary, their corporate character, may be retained intact.

4   As for those giant organisations that cannot be desirably broken down into smaller units, e.g. those engaged in the manufacture of steel or chemicals, their radical change may be achieved through the following three lines of action: firstly, co-determination or effective industrial democracy; secondly, a share-ownership in the company; and thirdly, a change in the legal status of the enterprise so that employees are incorporated as part-owners and managers alongside directors and shareholders - but having preference over external shareholders. Co-determination must include the following three facilities and rights: firstly, to examine all aspects of the enterprise; secondly, to criticise; and thirdly, the power to amend.

5   The successful introduction of the above conditions, however, is dependent on the effective education of the majority. There has to be the will to own and the will to control, and these characteristics are dependent on a complex of cultural factors, but such factors are useless if not accompanied by the knowledge and the intellectual ability to understand the financial and economic aspects of managing a business enterprise. Without such relevant knowledge, which in the future, in a genuinely democratic society, should form part of the core curriculum in secondary education, it would not be possible to stimulate that sense of ownership and control in the majority population, or the will towards it. The existence of such a Will, however, is vitally dependent on a highly developed sense of individualism, and the repudiation of the Collective spirit and everything associated with the resentment of the proletarian ethos.

6   The Collective spirit, or the sense of solidarity, is admittedly apt and necessary in maintaining trades union rights, i.e. in protecting employees against the abuses of employers, and trades unionism will have an increasing role to play in the future; but in the employees' co-determinational activity in Managing the enterprise,

41-8

such a spirit of Collectivism may be inapt. This is because co-determination, if it is to be effective, concerns the individual's immediate relationship with his function in the enterprise, and his critical or constructive sense is not dependent on feelings of Collectivism, but on the contrary, on the initiative which arises from within his own individualism. It is only through the knowledge of his function within the company that he can make an intelligent contribution to that company, and it is only through the development of a critical and creative ability, and the use of those skills, that he becomes a fully integrated individual within the company. In this way, and through developing a reciprocal understanding of the will of the company, he becomes one with the company, totally identifying with its purpose.

7   This brings us to the crux of the argument set forth in these chapters. The real conflicts of interest being fought out today in any modern industrialised community, are not between Conservatism or Socialism or the compromising middle ground of some form of Liberalism (for these are historical myths having little bearing on contemporary problems) but the conflict between the attitudinal interests of Individualism and Collectivism. Old Socialist theory has been totally discredited, and Old Socialist practice the world over is in shreds of confusion, emerging only towards success through the discreet adoption of capitalistic ideas. Likewise, the Conservative theory of laissez-faire defies the experience of the late 20th century, and most notably so in America its ideological homeland.[111] Meanwhile, the practice of Conservatism has done nothing to solve the major problems of social injustice or the mal-distribution of wealth. Likewise also, the middle ground in politics has not succeeded in formulating a satisfactory alternative needed to embody a set of radically new concepts. It has merely fallen between two stools through a love of compromise which has exceeded its ability for creative thought and invention, and consequently, has called upon its head the contempt of those on both sides of the political spectrum.

8   Again, progress or the world of reality, has moved far ahead of the world of perception. Applying solutions to the problems of today or tomorrow, derived from ideological thought processes of forty or a hundred years back, is not merely to misunderstand the true nature of the world we live in today but to compound problems. The factories of tomorrow will not need "proletarians" in any sense of the term, and so what is the use of a Socialism which puts the proletarian at the centre of its doctrine ? Not merely is the economics of Old Socialism wrong, but even more so the resentful spirit of its proletarian Collectivism. In the modern

---

111   It should be noted in this context, that contemporary America, the home of laissez-faire, is far more bureaucratic, protectionist, interventionist and regulatory, in its control over business than present day Britain.

41-10

industrialised society, men and women doing useful highly-paid work do not want to be resentful. It is only those in the ailing, retarded, unmechanized industries with their low rates of pay that can afford to be resentful, and the answer there is rapid mechanisation.

9   Likewise, where taxation is inevitably creating an economically more egalitarian community amongst the average majority, leaving aside the increasing poverty of the long-term unemployed or the increasing riches of the new Yuppy class, what sense is there in calling for the privileges of a Conservative society, when such privileges are perceived by the vast majority in the modern world as having no foundations in morality ? When the spirit of Conservatism amounts to nothing more than the cry of selfishness or a blind appeal to hold back the wind of change, what reason can it have to justify its existence? Of course, in the real or practical world, Conservatism - and Socialism too - can justify themselves by their own contradictions - by defying their own logic, but that is no consolation to the ordinary voter who wants to exert his democratic right and can only do so by clinging onto the abstractions of ideology in forming sensible judgements. It is only through the medium of the presentation of ideas, and often nebulous promises, by our political representatives, that democracy can be said to operate in any meaningful sense in embracing the rule of the majority.

10   Hence, the business of politics necessitates linking relevant abstractions and ideals to the reality of existing conditions and power groups. The ideas behind Conservatism and Old Socialism fail totally in this purpose, as also do those behind the parties of the British centre. The concepts of Collectivism and Individualism, however, have a vital relevance for our time. Collectivism is commonly associated with the left and Individualism with the right, but these simplistic associations do not meet up with the true reality. It is correct to associate Collectivism with the idea of equality, and Individualism with that of liberty, but beyond that comparison the terms call for careful analysis. Classical Socialism is all out Collectivist in spirit, but modern forms of Socialism are desperate to incorporate qualities of Individualism in emphasising the need for individual rights and self-expression, as well as bowing to the psychological demands enabling a more efficiently productive society. Conservatism has always (and still) emphasises the value of Individualism, linking this with the qualities of laissez-faire and the entrepreneur, but big business, on the other hand, is by necessity strongly Collectivist and is increasingly so. There is very little room for individualism in the contemporary giant corporation, and the giant multi-national of today has no lesser claim to be described as a Collectivist organisation than a British trades union of the far left. More than fifty years ago Walter Lippman observed that, "though great corporate capitalists continued to invoke the shibboleths of Liberalism when confronted by the collective demands of

41-12

the workers or the hostile power of popular majorities, yet they were thoroughly imbued with the Collectivist spirit through their attachment to protection and to the concentration of control." [112]

11   Both the multi-national and the old-style trades union demand a commitment entailing an authoritarian obedience, which although ideologically at variance with each other, is very similar in form. Both lay down their conditions from on-high and both are ruthless in their dealing with deviants from the given rule.   Both are antipathetic to the forms if not to the spirit of democracy. In a world of vast institutions - irrespective of their purpose - the individual is increasingly absorbed and crushed by their Collectivism and demands to conform. It does not matter if that institution is an employing industry; a trades union; or, a government department, the freedom of the individual is increasingly diminished by the standardisation and stereotyping of functions, and greater restrictions are laid on his freedom of expression through work.

By this means, work processes and economic functions may appear to move towards greater efficiency, but ultimately, if men and women are not allowed a due regard for their self-expression through performing their work function, the psychological results may be damaging to the cause of efficiency. Such resulting inefficiency may (and does) result in frustration, absenteeism, sickness and simply failure to perform to the optimum.

12   The quality of Individualism, therefore, should not be seen as the exclusive preserve of the right, for in reality, it transcends the narrow possession of any political ideology. But what of the values of Collectivism, for we have only glanced at this in a critical light ? Despite the criticism to which Collectivism has been exposed from all directions during the past few years it nevertheless carries inherent values for the good of society. When C.V. Dicey traced the development of law and public opinion in England in the modern era, he saw the first half of the 19th century as the age of Individualism and the latter half as that of Collectivism, and historians see the last hundred and thirty year period of our social history as an age of increasing Collectivism, and have generally regarded this factor as a subject of concern - albeit inevitable. But the social values implied in Collectivism are no less valuable than Individualism to any successful community. These values include the sense of community itself and the will to co-operation; a realisation of the oneness of humanity and the obligation to assist and serve our fellow beings irrespective of their relevance to our interests.

The spirit of Collectivism demands that we consider the needs of strangers no less than neighbours and friends, and it transcends all functional and   class interests.

---

112   Walter Lippmann, *The Good Society*, Allen & Unwin, 1938, p. 47.

42-2

This is the positive concept of Collectivism as it should ideally flourish in the community. Hence both Individualism and Collectivism in their positive aspects are not merely complementary values within the community but are applicable and universal to all, transcending the narrowing differences of any specific political outlook. 113

CHAPTER 42
The Meaning of New Socialism

"Collective achievements are utterly sterile and illusory if they do not incorporate the deepest needs of the individual flesh-and-blood human being."

L.T. Hobhouse, *Social Development*, Allen & Unwin, 1924, p. 245.

1 - Need for integrating Collectivism and Individualism   2 - New Socialism would entail the emergence of a new moral outlook   3 - Those in the future would view the present with horror and dismay   4 - Possible examples of this   5 - Inevitable democratisation of society   6 - Achieved through the General Will   7 - Those opposing the concept of the General Will by implication support Might as Right   8 - The General Will is integral to the philosophy of New Socialism   9 - Since it subordinates the place of vested interests

1   As we advocate freedom in its broadest sense and argue that this freedom should be enjoyed by all, this in turn can only be facilitated by introducing broad spheres of legislation as we have put forward in earlier chapters. We have also observed that such a universal freedom can only be facilitated by ensuring that there is a radical change in the mental attitude of the majority.

There has to be a greater acquisitive sense in terms of education, wealth and cultural attributes, linking in with a complementary benevolent collective sense for the community in total. Such a sense would defy the current political sense of Tories, Old Socialists or compromising Liberal Democrats. It would appreciate the creative dynamism necessary in maintaining the economic and industrial foundations of the community, whilst at the same time appreciating the need for co-operation and social unity. These values would be embodied in New Socialism.

2   But New Socialism would amount to more than just a fusion between Individualism and Collectivism, or competition and co-operation, or howsoever these opposites and often opposing qualities may be viewed. The combination of such a formula would inevitably give rise to an entirely new quality, differing in aspect from

---

113   For a further discussion on the problems of Collectivism and Individualism, see the following: Ludwig von Mises, *Socialism*, (J. Cape, 1953 ed.) pp. 63-68; Oswald Spengler, *Preussentum und Sozialismus* (Munich, 1920) p. 14; Pribram, *Die Enstehung der individualistischen Sozialphilosophie* (Leipzig, 1921), p. 3 onwards; and Dietzel's article, *Individualismus* in the *Handwörterbuch der Staatswissenschaften*, 3rd ed., Vol. V, p. 590.

42-5

. both original ingredients. A synthesis would need to be formed. New Socialism would entail the emergence of a new attitude towards society. A new moral outlook would be created leading to changed practical relationships between individuals and groups. Its acceptance would undoubtedly reflect a marked progress in human relationships, and would be seen no less as a logical progression of society than that comparison between English society of today and that, say, of the time of Dickens. Human relationships and the sense of justice and obligation to and between individuals and groups has unquestionably advanced in moral and practical terms since the first half of the last century. But there are still further steps to be climbed until the summit is reached - if indeed, the summit is yet in view. New Socialism in terms of improved moral and social conditions, would entail a measured progression no less than that existing between our own time and the start of the last century. It would mark the ultimate preparation for the new millennium.

3   The concept of New Socialism embraces the needs of the dynamic business community of the new age with all the considerations of social justice. It brings into being the integrated community - far more purposeful in the world of work and yet far more conscious of the need for social harmony. Once the New Socialist community has been achieved, men and women will look back in dismay at their own historic past: not simply in surprise at the injustice of former ages, but more markedly, perhaps at the crass stupidity and wanton waste of an age of senseless conflict. They will view the present much as we today view the wars of religion and oppression of the post-Reformation era - as so much nonsense and destruction in the cause of illusory values.

4   What tomorrow will be those illusory values of today ? They will be the actual (but unspoken) Authority of management Against workers; they will be the resentful self-glorification of the "working class" against the power of the "bosses;" they will be the conviction of financiers and all those employed in the money markets, that finance need not be primarily used for enriching the community through home-based industrial investment; they will be the prejudice that shareholders profits must have priority over company profits; they will be the belief that any one sector in the community has rights over, or is better than, any other minority or majority group; and they will be all those privileges of trades and professions that act as barriers to the freedom of the layman or act as an unwarranted taxation on his purse.

5   Accompanying or fast following such changes in attitude would be deeply felt moral changes in the life of the community. A more egalitarian community that is neither proletarian nor privileged nor bourgeois (in the old sense), but is at once competitive and co-operative in its social interaction would inevitably give rise to a sense of greater humanity and communal understanding. This is because such a society would not feel threatened or hemmed-in by either an oppressive privileged

42-7

class or by the precipitous fear of the bottomless pit of proletarianism. The absence of these threats or the need for guarding defensive class barriers would engender a greater mutual trust between persons of all occupations and skills. A greater egalitarianism and more standardised system of education would result in a culturally more homogeneous society. Easier, more open, spontaneous and honest relationships would emerge between such occupationally disparate sets as the hospital consultant and the plumber; the bank official and the office cleaner; the lawyer and the electrician's mate; the teacher and the refuse collector; or, the professor and the long distance truck driver. Each would more easily appreciate the common humanity and functional value of the other in a world that is dependent on a multiplicity of qualities and aptitudes. If the achievement of such an ideal community seems remote, we might remark that it is already coming into fruition in the greater part of northern Europe, and particularly in the democratic Scandinavian countries, or in the Far East, as in Singapore, to whom we should look for a model.

6   The progress towards such an integrated community forms part of the inevitable logic of our civilisation. This is because there is no other direction in which we may hazard civilisation can progress. All other routes would be retrogression or reaction. Such a community would be brought about by the realisation of the General Will. We define the General Will (in the absence of any fully satisfactory previous definition of this concept) as the ever latent tendency of a community Willing towards its moral and material good and the outcome of this. But this does not mean that progress itself is constant and uninterrupted. The general will cannot be easily defined through analysing the ideals of party conflict - the swinging pendulum of the extremes - but only through the socially beneficent outcome of the democratic process - those values, both moral and material, that emerge in society almost unconsciously. They are values that are suddenly there, established and unquestioned, likes votes for women or racial equality, or the ever-widening recognition of rights for the majority or those of multifarious minority groups.

7   Many who are covertly opposed to the realisation of progress (and there are social scientists amongst their number) have been opposed to the very concept of the general will, either denying its existence or maintaining that it defies clear identification. Their main ground for philosophical opposition to the concept has stemmed from faith in the beneficent outcome of class-based party strife as the democratic medium for progress. Their trust in the status quo, in the existing structure of political decision-making, has obliged them to see an intrinsic goodness in the representation of vested interests and in a polarised governmental system. Such intrinsic goodness does not in fact exist since it too often deflects from the actualisation of the general will. Such people repudiate the existence of such a

42-9

disinterested process as an underlying general will existing in society. Consequently, they favour a more subjective viewpoint, recognising the total unpredictability of class and party strife. Economic groupings, so their argument goes, are justified by their own Might alone. The concept of Right has no place here, and might is justified in the eyes of the majority, purely through the ballot box and the Queensbury rules of the democratic game. There is no place here for the thread of an underlying goodness running through society transcending the petty vested interests of class or party, for such belief is dismissed as "abstract" or "metaphysical," or just not relevant to day-to-day politics.

8   The idea of the general will is so often absurdly dismissed because it cannot be properly understood or "demonstrated," so inferring that that which confounds the comprehension cannot be said to exist. Such a stance is no less ridiculous than an attempt to call on the ordinary person to deny the wonders of contemporary science, or even the workings of his or her own body, simply because they are beyond the understanding of the ordinary layman. All scientific discoveries begin first with unsupported conviction only later followed on by demonstrable proof, and of all sciences, the social sciences are young, still awaiting demonstration in many spheres of activity.

If, on the other hand, the concept of the General Will should be subjected to philosophical as opposed to scientific criteria, then in the words of Prof. Joad, "the difference between the conclusions of science and of philosophy is, in a word, not one of truth but of verifiability." 114 The greatest truths are often those that longest defy the demonstration of proof. But the existence of the general will (as here defined) is beyond doubt most clearly demonstrated by the outcome of over two hundred years of European history. The importance of the concept of the general will and the philosophy of New Socialism, will be found in the following:-

1. Belief in the unitary purpose of humanity;
2. The right to equality of opportunity;
3. The repudiation of vested interest groups as ends in themselves;
4. The repudiation of class privilege; and,
5. That individuals are ends in themselves within the purposes of the integrated community.

9   By promoting the concept of the general will, divisive political groupings and vested interests are subordinated to their proper role in the community, so that they might be seen in their true perspective as narrow and selfish entities only unconsciously acting as a medium for the good of society. 115

---

114 C.E.M. Joad, *Return To Philosophy*, Faber & Faber, 1935, p. 172.

115 Despite the whining of many social thinkers in regretting that they cannot accept the concept of the General

43-1

CHAPTER 43
Freedom Within The Integrated Community

"No one ... dares today to survey life in its entirety; analysis leaps and synthesis lags. We fear the experts in every field, and keep ourselves, for safety's sake, lashed to our narrow specialities. Everyone knows his part, but is ignorant of its meaning in the play. Life itself grows meaningless, and becomes empty just when it seemed most full."

Will Durant, *The Mansions of Philosophy*, Garden City Publishing Co., NY, 1941 ed., pp. viii-ix.

1 - Every community has its own character and will   2 - This is demonstrated by statistical research   3 - The "Integrated" as contrasted with the "Organic" community   4 - Unacceptability of the concept of the organic community   5 - Limitations of Hegelianism   6 - But recent research has underlined the contemporary significance of Hegel as a social thinker   7 - Importance of the Hegelian system lies in the emphasis placed on the emergence of the integrated or classless society   8 - Demonstration that the Whole is greater than its constituent parts   9 - Freedom can only finally be maintained by the power of the state   10 - Theory of the Integrated community can stand the rigours of scientific criticism   11 - The representation of functional interests

1   This immediately brings us to the question of the Integrated community. If we accept the existence of the general will, it follows that a community must have a will and personality belonging to itself. This is simple to accept. In the case of the nation that personality may be expressed in terms of its national character. The true personality of a community, however, may be unclear to itself for several reasons: either because it is in a state of rapid change; or because it is politically divided into a patchwork without an organised centre for expressing opinion; or because it is defined in terms of a small area or district, or merely a street, and there is no media for expressing its personality or general will.

Again, there have been social scientists and thinkers who have been keen to deny that a community has a will or personality of its own, by advancing the atomised concept of the community, in suggesting it is only composed of separate individuals that have wills or personalities that do not lend themselves to a generalised description. Such a particularistic view of society is clearly a nonsense,

---

Will, I believe that Rousseau's original definition, as elucidated in several sections of the *Social Contract*, still embraces the essence of the argument. He distinguishes between the "Will of all," i.e. the sum of wills of individuals, as expressed through any democratic action irrespective of its good to the community - and sometimes it may bring about the worst of social evils; and the "General Will," that looks to the common interests (Book II, Cap. 3). This is emphasised by his statement that, "that which generalises the will is not so much the number of voices as the common interest which unites them (Book II, Cap. 4). Rousseau identifies the *volunté générale* with the "law of reason," maintaining that, "it is always right, but the judgement which guides it is not always enlightened. ... Individuals see the good which they reject; the public will the good which it does not see" Book II, Cap. 6).

43-4

and it is difficult to understand why such thinkers are loathed to concede the real existence of general or collective entities. It is my belief that the fear of such thinkers stems from an entrenched belief in a laissez-faire society, and an unthinking trust in the beneficence of exaggerated individualism.

2   If one turns, however, from these often abstract thinkers to any up-to-date marketing organisation, or to the research arm of any major advertising agency, the assurance will soon be forthcoming from these quarters that not merely every region but every district and sub-district and street has its distinctive will and personality. This will and personality is not demonstrated by the vagaries of mere intuition, but by hard statistical facts painstakingly compiled by an army of professional interviewing researchers. Such marketing and advertising organisations will, of course, know very much more about the will (or desires) and personality (or views and economic status) of a community, than will that community often know about itself, even if only because research areas are broken down into such small units. This, then, is the factual or statistical proof that there exists in society a General Will, and its existence is the basis for the evidence of the coming into being of the Integrated community.

3   The term *Integrated* community is chosen in preference to the term *Organic* community for significant reasons. The term Organic community has been applied to such social contract theories as those of Hobbes' *Leviathan*, in describing the body, limbs and mind of the state, and subsequently, to Hegelian and Neo-Hegelian descriptions of the state, the community, or, the nation, when these terms have become interchangeable or identical. The ultimate absurdity of the concept of the Organic community in comparing it with a living or biological organism was made most evident in the first quarter of this century by Oswald Spengler in his book, *The Decline of The West,* in which he attempted to demonstrate that all cultures have a natural life-span and are doomed to an inevitable death through a "natural" almost biological-like process. The genius and learning of Spengler won over the minds of many in the earlier part of the century, but more serious critical historians have subsequently found irreparable faults in his analysis, and his thesis can no longer be a subject for serious positive study in any academic institution.

4   Furthermore, the pessimism of such a predestined view of the world is unacceptable to New Socialists. If our community is doomed to perish due to internal factors that are impervious to any conscious effort to reverse the process, what sense is there in devoting our energies to the good of society as we experience it ? No person can think beyond his own age and its knowledge base in putting his mind to the practical purpose of politics. He can only think and act within the constraints of his own culture - howsoever strong his attacks on the existing system and howsoever radical his appeal for reform. Belief in the organic theory of the

43-7

community, when carried to its extreme form by Spengler and others, is therefore intellectually malign, since it not only undermines trust in reason but also in the will to do good for humanity, since any good works will be felt to be of little avail in the long term.

5   Nevertheless, for many reasons, as elaborated in this and earlier chapters, we are obliged to follow the intellectual stream of Hegelian thought, but this does not imply we can necessarily be held as apologists for any specific concepts promoted by the Hegelian or Neo-Hegelian schools of philosophy. This is because we have advanced beyond their own time and by a dialectical process, circumstances and patterns of thought have also changed, and new critical modes of thinking are needed in looking to the future. Such a stance would not have been taken amiss by the Hegelians themselves. Because some of the aspects and arguments on the concept of the organic nature of the community as formulated by G.W.F. Hegel, and others, and particularly by the British Neo-Hegelian philosopher, Bernard Bosanquet, have been exposed to such intensive criticism in this country and elsewhere, we shall avoid the term organic in favour of the term Integrated community This is not to suggest that these philosophers were wrong in their conclusions, but merely that they may have been faulty in the presentation of their arguments or in the clarity of their exposition.

6   The major criticisms aimed at Hegel and Dr. Bosanquet have not so much been that they were intrinsically wrong in their moral or intellectual views of the world order, but that the complexity of their arguments seemed confusing and unclear. On these grounds they must stand the test of semantic criticism, but we have to maintain that their underlying intuition in the final analysis is to be aligned with the truth. The methodological fallacies of Hegel, I believe, in constraining the fulfilment of his purpose, may be brought under three headings: firstly, the over-ambitious vastness of his vision in attempting to explain the nature of existence; secondly, the attempt to embrace, historically, all the main trends of Western thought within the synthesis of his own philosophy, and thirdly, the limitations of language in expounding that philosophy with clarity. However, it is our contention that those limitations should not be an invitation to the impatience of contemptuous dismissal, but rather, to further exploration and research. And such research over the past thirty years by leading scholars worldwide has indeed been fruitful in its outcome in contributing towards a more positive appreciation of Hegel as a social thinker and his relevance for our time.

7   Nevertheless, it has to be pointed out that the discrediting of Hegelian views has too often originated not from the writings of the master himself but from those minor spheres orbiting the greater star. In the popularising of Hegel's philosophy, his concepts have perhaps been falsified, and most notably, the concept of the

43-8

Organic nature of the state might fall into this category. To identify Spengler's view of the rise and fall of cultures, for example, with those of Hegel, is clearly wrong, but so too we would not accept a literal interpretation of Hegel's own *Philosophy of History*. Every thinker of the past has to be studied with critical discrimination for none have succeeded in formulating a faultless intellectual system.

The importance of the Hegelian system, in our view, lies in the stress it places on the need for, or underlying existence of, the coming into being of the free and unitary society. The unitary or Integrated community is as yet unrealised, but as we have already demonstrated above, it is a great potential of our time - a gradual but inevitable realisation. In upholding the concept of the Integrated community, we are not announcing a final situation for humanity, for that can never be in a world of never-ending change and progress; but we are predicting an end to vicious class conflict and the narrow aims of selfish party conflict, as we know these things today. It implies a heartfelt call for industrial harmony and social peace in a classless community ruled according to the principles of reason and justice.

The recurring theme throughout this book has been the need for the diminution of class-based political conflict and this can only be achieved through the realisation of the Integrated community. This is not merely a truth in which it is necessary to believe for the moral welfare of our future, but fortunately, a truth which can now be demonstrated in fact through sophisticated systems of statistical sociological research. If such research and its outcome could be utilised in the form of political power, not only could it lead to the abolition of all political parties but at the same time to the creation of the most democratically managed society.

8   The Integrated community, however, has a will and personality greater than the constituent parts of which it is composed. In the past, this was an argument that has again been difficult to grasp, and accordingly it has been met by retrenched opposition. Again, it entails a concept which is a moral imperative (for reasons given below) and its existence as a reality, in terms of functional purpose, is simple to demonstrate. That the Whole is greater than the Parts of which it is composed is best illustrated by taking the analogy of the business enterprise. The rationale for the existence of any business is the function of its Purpose, i.e. its product or service.

A number of people with varying abilities and backgrounds are brought together to perform different functions in promoting the purpose of the enterprise. Every one of those persons is there to achieve the single and unified purpose of the enterprise, each in his different way, and although some may foolishly argue amongst themselves as to which group or individuals are more important in achieving that single purpose, the truth is that no group and no individual alone could achieve that purpose without the complementary skills and co-operation of all those others comprising the personnel of the enterprise. An enterprise of all chiefs and no Indians

43-10

would be no more useful than an enterprise with a production department, but lacking quality control, planning, marketing, selling, accounts, administration and personnel departments. Such an enterprise would be crippled, and eventually bankrupted. The integration and smooth running of the enterprise is not merely in the interests of all committed to its purpose; it is crucial to the livelihoods of all those individuals committed to the enterprise. The failure of that Purpose not merely reflects on the reputation of those committed to the enterprise, it actually damages their material interests. Hence the *purpose* of the company must necessarily override, or have a higher priority, over those individuals of which it is comprised, irrespective of the status of the individuals concerned.

If the purpose of the enterprise is to be upheld as a principle contributing to the good of all, then all must stand in equality before that purpose, and the salesman or accounts clerk are no less important in fulfilling their functions than is the managing director. This means that when the effectiveness of the company's purpose is threatened, it is those who endanger that purpose who sacrifice the benefit of the remaining employees and the greater benefit of the purpose itself. At all times the purpose of the enterprise remains paramount and sacrosanct, for without it, all would be doomed to lose the means of their livelihood.

9   This analogy is drawn since the business enterprise is a microcosm of the community in total. Whilst the purpose of the enterprise is the success of its product or service in the marketplace; the purpose of the community or nation is the success of the state in integrating the departments of administration in ensuring the highest material and moral welfare for the totality of the people. In every country, the state has - and should have - despite misleading theories to the contrary, ultimate authority on all economic and social matters effecting the community; and if this is not exerted through positive injunction, then it exists through default. Freedom in all its aspects, for example, is enabled, and afterwards maintained, solely through the power of the state. It has to be noted, though, that the argument that the Whole is greater than the Parts, does not imply that the state can do no wrong or is above the law; or what is equally valid in principle, that sovereignty and liability are not mutually exclusive.

10   In defining the nature of the Integrated community we are avoiding the use of all abstract or abstruse argument. Hence by distancing ourselves from the concept of the organic community, we are avoiding all the intellectual pitfalls of Hegelian philosophy of an earlier era. Therefore the concept of the Integrated community, as defined here, may lend itself to the rigours of scientific examination. This is because it is not based on a mere intellectual construct. To recapitulate: the definition of the Integrated community is the coming into being of the General Will towards the creation of a freer, more homogeneous and harmonious society. To a degree it is an unconscious process, gradual but inevitable. Its presence may be demonstrated both

43-11

historically in terms of time, and through sociological research in terms of space. If the concept, despite the clarity of its presentation, is met by opposition, this is only because of the threat it offers to the status quo of our existing divisive system of representative government now undermining the industrial infrastructure.

11 The democratisation and the bringing into being of such a classless and homogeneous society, at once competitive and co-operative, can only be realised on a secure and permanent basis through radical changes to the structure of government itself. This would be achieved through the representation of functional interests. On the most basic level, employees would have a share ownership and co-determinational stake in their employing enterprises. These enterprises (i.e. their purpose) would each be represented by an elected delegate to sit in the assembly of a relevant trade federation. That delegate might be a shop-floor worker, a director, or a clerk in the company - his status as an employee would be irrelevant in representing the totality of the company's interests. The trade federations and other bodies representing occupational spheres of employment, self-employment and the retired, would elect from amongst their own number, delegates to a National Assembly of Occupations.

Meanwhile, on a parallel basis, in conjunction with the unionisation of all occupations, delegates would be elected to a National Assembly of Earnings. Whilst the former body would be concerned with industrial, commercial and professional efficiency and governmental assistance enabling this, the latter would be concerned with earnings and employees' rights and protection. These two assemblies would act as an advisory body to a third National assembly of constituency delegates representing the interests of localities. These latter delegates would offer themselves for election on purely local issues of expenditure or planning.

A higher, or Governing Assembly, would be formed out of these three subsidiary bodies. This would be a National Assembly For Economic and International Co-operation. As differences on specific technical issues arose in the lower assemblies, delegates with varying viewpoints would be nominated by their peers to the higher assembly, but their seats in that assembly would only be confirmed through a system of proportional representation to the national electorate. As the issues at stake would entail specific technical matters, and as opposing viewpoints would be addressed to the electorate, such candidates would not only be Delegates rather than Representatives, but the entire electoral system would entail a Referenda on issues rather than a choice of competing personalities. Through such a system, the entire emphasis of politics would be laid on the choice of technical alternatives in achieving specific socio-economic ends, rather than on the appointment of fluid human material as the mouthpiece of abstruse and unreliable promises. In this way not only would political life become far more realistic in its concentration on solving substantive problems, but it would also become more democratic in the sense of direct people power.

The cabinet of such a government would be composed of members from all four such assemblies. The interests of the ordinary elector would thus be represented in four directions: firstly, from the perspective of his occupation; secondly, from that of his earnings and employee rights; thirdly, from that of his locality; and fourthly, from that of general economic and international interests. This bare and incomplete description of the proposed re-structuring of the instruments of government (drawn up in the light of a comparative study of democratic institutions worldwide) might convey a dry-as-dust picture of political life, but it should be remembered that in the real world new problems will arise in the public mind to replace the old, and these will fall naturally into the moulds provided for them.

In this way, it may be assured, the attempt to de-personalise political life in concentrating on the reality of basic issues is carried to its furthest limits. It may likewise be asserted that in this way the three priorities of politics will be pushed to the forefront: i.e. that Disinterestedness, Urgency and the Economic Dimension will together and at all times predominate in the discussion and solution of our greatest issues.

*****

PART VI

Conclusions

"The more unequal the income distribution, as Keynes, Galbraith, Myrdal, Kalecki and Malthus all recognised, the more likely it is that the economy will suffer from periodic crises of underconsumption."

Will Hutton, *The State We're In*, J.Cape, 1995, p. 180.

44-1

CHAPTER 44
The Responsible Society

"Persons with feeble and untrained intellects may live according to their conscience, but the conscience itself will be defective. To cultivate the intellect is therefore a religious duty; and when this duty is fairly recognised by men, the religion which teaches that the intellect should be distrusted, and that it should be subservient to faith, will inevitably fall."

Winwood Reade, *The Martyrdom of Man*, (1872), Watts & Co., p. 434.

1 - Confronting the threats ahead   2 - Need to develop the business instinct   3 - Ethical development of humanity   4 - Egalitarianism in practice   5 - Wealth for welfare   6 - Changing values   7 - Future of the trade unions   8 - Education for citizenship   9 - Importance of the family

1   The Responsible Society, as defined in the opening remarks to Part II of this book, i.e. a society whose workforce is committed to part-owning and managing the means of production and distribution, is even now coming into being in subtle and unexpected ways. The powers of Rentier capital find it difficult to oppose the principle of co-determination for a technologically highly-educated workforce is anyway psychologically unsuited to the resentful herd-like instinct of the older proletariat. It finds it even more difficult to oppose the principle of employee share ownership in a society which is supposedly becoming ever-more responsible for its self-determination.

None of this, however, need be seen as in any way diminishing the intensity of the struggle which lies ahead between the conflicting interests of Rentier capitalism and the Humane interests of society in its totality. As we have noted throughout this book, the future of social struggle will not take the form of a class war, but rather of productive workers and those at all levels in most occupations against a particular capitalistic system, which is constantly self-destructive in terms of jobs; industries in specific locations; the structure of communities; the human proportions for desirable living; and the ecology of the environment. We have noted that the system to be fought against is not merely irrational, or non-responsible to any nation state or other democratic authority, but more ominously, exerts a force over which its own directors have no control, irrespective of industrial or collective will.

This has arisen through the overpowering might of international financial market forces, reacting to a sophisticated worldwide computer network, and moving capital at such a speed, that no account is taken - or could be taken - of the desirability of the consequences. The beneficiaries, supposedly of this unpredictable

44-2

and exciting system, are ordinary investors but the scale and repercussions of this uncontrollable process are so far-reaching, that even they are threatened with the ground from being cut from beneath their feet. In the longer term, therefore, no one really benefits from corporate or global capitalism, apart from that minority operating the system, and most of that minority, when they reflect on the mechanics and consequences of the system, may regard it as working to the adverse interests of humanity. In the shorter or medium term global capitalism may be said to benefit the peoples of those newly industrialising countries with a natural business instinct - but painfully, as appalling conditions are experienced in factories or dormitories where their workers are obliged to live.

As we have argued in this book, globalisation need not be accepted as an inevitable evolutionary outcome of earlier forms of capitalism. It should rather be seen as a disease or cancer of the Productive economy, and since it may be described as a loose cannon on the stage of the world economy, it needs to be confronted and fought against for the evil that it is. Globalisation is not amenable to controls or regulation, and it is contrary to the interests of the vast majority since it directs and is not directed by the human will. We have said there can be no class war in the future in resolving socio-economic issues since there are no identifiable classes in the battles which lie ahead. This is because all levels of society are confronted in the same way, in facing the same dangers, from the juggernaut of Rentier capitalism. We shall therefore use the generalised term, the Humane class, in describing those opposed to Rentier or corporate capitalism. The term may be interchangeable with that of the Responsible society.

2   In earlier chapters we have also seen that whilst society is becoming increasingly polarised in terms of haves and have-nots, a classless society is also emerging. The reasons for this are two-fold: firstly, as we have said, the economic threat of Rentier capitalism endangers society in its totality; and secondly, the social democratic ideals of the modern era are centred around the classless middle-middle majority. The extravagance of the very rich is today of far lesser significance as a social ill to the structural balance of society than it was sixty or a hundred years ago. That is, their values have a diminishing influence on those of the majority. Also, they are a small enough minority for clear identification for purposes of taxation or other forms of appropriation. Of most significance, perhaps, is the factor that this wealthy minority is despised by the middle-middle majority, since the latter is educationally and culturally equal to or superior to the former. The very rich, therefore, can no longer exert a mystique through the power of money alone.

The very poor and the remnants of the old proletariat are likewise of diminishing political significance, again, because of their limited numbers relative to the larger population. The very poor are usually alienated from any political

44-2

motivation, but a minority (particularly amongst the young) are drawn to the defunct ideology of Old Socialism. The Quixotic appeal of the far left for "class warfare" is motivated more out of desperation for an enemy to thump and knock down, than out of a desire to resolve substantive issues in society. The capitalism portrayed by the far left is an image of 19th century socio-economic conditions, having little relevance for our own time. The far left represent a diverse number of colourful Marxist and Anarchist rebel groups, concentrated in inner cities, with fluid memberships, which are effective in student circles and organising street demonstrations, but little else. They are regarded as a major nuisance by main line political parties, not so much because of their influence on parliamentary groups, but because of the stereotyped image they portray to an ill-informed general public as to all movements left of centre.

The middle-middle majority, or the Humane class, or the Responsible society, therefore has immense potential for political power, as mainstream values from all sectors of the community coalesce towards this classless centre. What are - or should be the values of this class in creating the New Socialism? If the majority are to be empowered economically (and this is the only significant form of political power), then the business instinct needs to be developed to a high degree. It is not sufficient that the rising generation should be taught the facts of business and how to handle money wisely and creatively, but that they should be taught to love money as amongst the first of virtues. This is because the survival, health, and welfare of the individual and his or her dependents, is reliant on business acumen, or the skilled handling of the means of exchange. The response to such a call may be that money "corrupts," or that the "love of money is the root of all evil." [116] But this is not to be the situation in the context of a Socialist society. The purpose of Socialism must be to construct a framework within society to prevent excessive accumulation or abuses in the use of money. A greater truth is anyway to be found in the amendment to the above quotation, attributed to both Mark Twain and Bernard Shaw, viz., the far more meaningful statement that, "Lack of money is the root of all evil."

It is necessary to engender a love of money in the majority in creating both an egalitarian society and in empowering the individual as a unit in the community. It is not sufficient that the development of the business instinct should be left to secondary school level. If the right psychological attitudes are to be imprinted on the mind, then the business instinct must be developed through games and play at primary school level. Business acumen should naturally be taught in conjunction with other complementary values, such as honesty, co-operation, generosity,

---

116 I *Timothy*, vi, 10.

44-3

benevolence, and love for humankind and the environment. These values should be taught through example; developing healthy relationships in study and play; and only lastly in middle, upper or secondary school, through introducing Ethics as a new study in the curriculum. But ethics should not be taught as a philosophical discipline (which would be too advanced for schoolchildren) but through entertaining selections from the Roman moralists as Cicero, Seneca, or Marcus Aurelius, or in the worldly wisdom of Bacon's Essays which are encyclopaedic in their sound advice.

3   Developing the business instinct does not mean, of course, that all will become successful in business. Many may grow to loathe business (in the same way they may grow to loathe mathematics or history, or any other topic) but developing business acumen must nevertheless remain a foremost priority in a democratic Socialist society. There will remain many occupations for which a good business instinct may not be essential, e.g. in teaching, medicine, science, and many skilled positions in larger types of business, but even for these categories of employees, a sound business instinct would still be invaluable, firstly, in managing household accounts, and secondly, in participating as active buying and selling shareholders within a financial framework designed to serve majority interests.

Glancing at the other side of the coin, in a Socialist society, it also has to be recognised that there are many spheres of activity where the profit motive or market forces are either inapt or become a social evil. An example of the latter would be in the high pressure selling of financial services, or in medicine and dentistry. Examples of the former would be, a) Those services which cannot be fully sustained through the market, as bus and railway services; and, b) Those essential utilities, which in the public interest should be restrained within low price brackets, as water, gas, electricity, telecommunications, etc. It is not suggested that any of the above should be nationalised, but that they should be offered under licence to competing enterprises, subject to state regulation and inspection.

The Humane class would be an apt description for this classless-type society of the future which is even now coming into being. There is an evolutionary development in ethical standards as may be witnessed by anyone taking the trouble to study the social history of Europe during the past two hundred and fifty years. In mid-18th century London, for example, it was quite acceptable for a group of young blades of aristocratic lineage to laughingly place bets, as they sat in an ale house, as to whether a starving beggar would drop dead in the street within the next ten minutes. Such a scene was actually recorded in one of the letters of Horace Walpole. Such a scene would have been impossible, a hundred years later, in the mid-Victorian era.

44-4

But the standards of the early and mid-Victorian era were atrocious by comparison with those of our own time. Dickens was not merely a social reformer, but a writer of stories with an ethical message, more poignant and more influential, in the modern epoch, in changing human behaviour than the entire corpus of the Bible. A hundred and thirty years after his death, in our own time, the idea of drunken magistrates; of savage cane-waving schoolmasters; of filthy orphanages filled with ragged half-starved urchins; of gin-soaked nurses sitting impatiently by the bedside, waiting for the death of their charges; of criminally deceitful and ravenously greedy lawyers concocting spurious accusations against their innocent victims, are as inconceivable today as the idea of those aristocrats awaiting the death of a beggar would have been to the Victorians a century before their own time.

There is therefore an evolution of ethical development in the same way that there is of technological development, and furthermore, it should be noted that there is an interconnection between the two. This is because increasing technology makes greater demands on brainpower, necessitating higher standards of education throughout the community, and this in turn contributes to both equalising status in the community and to raising the sense of social consciousness. The ownership and control of property in the private sphere by the individual, in addition to that of business or public life, all contributes to the weight of responsibility and obligation in creating the just and egalitarian society. The future may therefore witness changes as dramatic as those which divide us from the Victorian era.

4   Egalitarianism does not mean equality in value of material possessions, but rather equality in outcome in terms of satisfying the healthy psychological needs of the individual. Equality in terms of the first definition would be destructive of individual liberty. There are some of considerable wealth who have few possessions out of choice - preferring usually to be investors in the activities of others, and this is an entirely laudable and social attitude; and there are others, of modest means, who surround themselves with a great quantity of valued (if not valuable) possessions, such as clothing, furniture, bric-à-brac, and books. Some hate the idea of the responsibility which accompanies possession, and consequently choose to rent rather than buy a property; whilst others crave for possession since they find in its a sense of security. None of these attitudes necessarily have anything to do with the acquisition of wealth, or the ability for acquisition, or the business instinct, since they are psychological states of mind usually traceable to earliest childhood. To take an extreme example, an emperor may choose to spend his days in a Wendy house, where the ceilings are so low that he cannot even stand upright, as occurred with Peter I of Russia. 117

---

117   He suffered, of course, from agoraphobia, a psychological disease in all likelihood brought on by the

44-4

All this illustrates the diversity of human nature, and democratic Socialism in appreciating the need for freedom, has to grant that people choose to live in a wide variety of conditions. The principle of egalitarianism therefore has to take into consideration these important psychological factors. Egalitarianism as a practical reality, therefore, means - and can only mean - a common understanding as to fairness or unfairness with regard to excess or absence in the ownership of wealth or possessions. It is rather an attitude of mind setting the acceptable parameters of ownership, which may differ between one individual and another according to differing needs.

Clearly, extreme wealth, defined as superfluity; or poverty, defined as material want, are both social ills within the body politic, since the one is a symptom of waste, and the other a symptom of human suffering. But just as the very highly skilled or sought-after, as scientists, brain surgeons, and inventors, are deserving of rewards well above the average, so also are they deserving of valuable paintings, beautiful gardens, and mansions, in enriching their spiritual lives and in complementing the superiority of their minds. So, also, more humble people, with a strong aesthetic sense are deserving of elegant objects in decorating their homes, for the absence of these things would deny a need. In a world where all are free to choose, subject only to the limitations of their purse, the diversity in conspicuous affluence should give no rise to natural envy.

In describing the egalitarian society, there is no need to discuss in terms of abstract generalities. Examples may be cited of existing societies which are as classless and egalitarian as is likely to be achieved. The Scandinavian and Benelux countries have long been upheld as examples for inspiration, and more recently, the societies of Japan, South Korea, Taiwan, Singapore, and Hong Kong, are well deserving of study for their meritocratic values and egalitarian conditions of life, which are free from envy and resentment so pernicious in the West.

As someone who lived for a decade in Scandinavia in the 1960s, I can say that even then these societies were socially far in advance of those to their south. The following illustrative factors may be cited: there was far lesser differentiation in dress between different economic or occupational groupings; those from the highest professional grades often resided in the same apartment blocks as those engaged in lowly or manual work; and dance halls, night clubs, and other gathering places were usually frequented by those from every milieu; and whilst pride in class status was almost non-existent (apart from that amongst a minuscule and unofficially recognised

---

terrible childhood experience resulting from the Revolt of the Streltsy Guard, when he, his elder brother, and mother, were threatened with being torn to pieces, during the butchery in the Kremlin.

44-6

nobility), pride in occupational status through the award of rings (signifying diplomas and degrees), top hats, swords, and orders worn on the breast, was universal amongst all sections of society, and helped to promote the welfare of their economies.

5 A humane society requires that none should feel it tolerable that there is poverty, disease, and suffering in its midst, and that the public social conscience calls for a proper preparation for life (as described above with regard to developing the business instinct), and failing this, the safety net of a free and comprehensive welfare service. But a good welfare service and an effective educational system entail costly expenditure, and so the top priority of any country must be social wealth creation through the Productive sector.

The present situation in Britain is most unsatisfactory, due to the decline of wealth creating industry and the consequent lack of readily distributable financial resources from taxation and full employment policies. Tertiary education should be free (as otherwise the families of the poor are discriminated against), and meanwhile, the NHS is failing in many directions. It is disgraceful, for example, that Britain incurs the highest percentage of deaths through cancer (59,000 annually) than any of her EU partners, and that this is simply due to the refusal, due to budgetary constraints, of available drugs. And every family in Britain stands in the mortal shadow of such a threat. The present Welfare Reform Bill, for example, is nothing more nor less than a euphemism for further NHS cuts. Is this to be the Socialism of the future? Not only should prescription charges be substantially reduced, but alternative remedy medical services should be freely available, as they are in Germany and elsewhere.

The present financial structure of the NHS is possibly unsuited to bear the costs of further extending its existing arrangements. A better (and proven) alternative may be the creation of competing health insurance companies, all operating under the *dirigiste* authority of the state, and covering compulsorily every sector of the population. By this means, and through flexibility an element of choice, all branches of medicine could be brought freely within the reach of all. Pension arrangements in Britain are also a disgrace by comparison with those in Continental Europe. The Personal Pension Plans, of our Rentier capitalistic system, have recently been revealed for the swindle that they are. In ensuring that our elderly population do not live out their final years in deprivation, pensions should be equivalent to two-thirds of final (or highest salary), and financed as they are on the Continent under the auspices of the state.

6 What ideally should be the mental attitude of the leaders of the New Socialism? Apart from commitment to the economic principles of the Productive economy, in a fast changing world, they should be independent and sceptical in

44-6

outlook. A balanced personality and a sound ethical approach to issues calls also for a religious sense, but this does not mean attachment to the superstitions or myths of any specific church. The value of a religious sense is displayed more clearly by its absence, for the personality of the declared atheist is too often marked by an underlying bitterness, or emptiness, or unimaginativeness in the grasp and development of ideas. There is a lack of spirit or purpose, and seemingly, a sterility in the sphere of creativity. The psychological value of the religious sense is to be found in its underpinning ethical ideas, and in its encouraging the promotion of good works, for the goodness of the state is ultimately dependent on the goodness of the individuals of which it is comprised.

Out of such a religious sense may come a belief in God, not as a being but rather as an abstraction, representing the Absolute good towards which we all might strive. In repudiating the fallacies of revealed religion, this would mean a return to deism, and all the good which springs from a rational approach to life and cosmology. The words of Tom Paine, a committed deist, should be borne in mind when he wrote that, "all national institutions of churches, whether Jewish, Christian, or Turkish, appear to me no other than human inventions, set up to terrify and enslave mankind, and monopolise power and profit." [118] As new Socialists should strive towards the truth, always concerned with concrete or worldly values, they should hold the great monotheistic religions in quiet disdain because of the mischief and erroneous values they have propagated over the past millennia. But the prejudices of those adhering to organised religion should be respected, and there is no reason why serious Socialists should not enjoy the aesthetic experience of church services, in the same way that educated citizens in ancient Athens or Rome enjoyed the pagan temple rites whilst disbelieving in their meaning or truth. It also has to be borne in mind that despite the falsity of organised religion, the churches nevertheless perform a valuable function as bonding agents in the community (as we noted in Chapter 6) - often for those with personality problems. Furthermore, at a time when the churches are encountering more apathy than in any previous period, their clergy are beginning to reassess their role, and most are genuine in their will for a better society on *earth*. For these reasons the clergy should be befriended and brought into the Socialist fold.

Because of the deep concern for the ecology of the environment, over the past two decades, there has been a gradual return to nature worship and a revived interest in the pagan cults of the past. This is because the monotheistic religions are so people-centred *vis-à-vis* the omnipotence of God, that the natural world has been

---

118   Tom Paine, *The Age of Reason*, Carol Publishing Group, 1995 ed., p. 50.

44-7

excluded from the religious dimension. In other words, the natural world is disdained from the religious viewpoint. It is too often perceived as merely existing for the casual use or wanton misuse of humankind. This perception of the relationship between humanity, the physical world, and God, is no longer acceptable to the thinking members of the younger generation. Buddhism with its respect for all creatures and the environment is becoming widely popular in the age of ecological consciousness, and when this is not capturing the imagination, then primitive beliefs that all trees, plants, mountains, and rivers, have their own spirits, seem apt in the struggle to preserve the living treasures of nature against the depredations of the large corporations. Meanwhile, in the realm of *Realpolitik*, respect for nature is no longer merely a question of sentiment, for it has become an essential component in preserving the planet and humankind.

7   As indicated throughout this book, the role of the trade unions will be of overwhelming importance in bringing into being the New Socialist society, but in the next decade, the unions will need to accelerate the speed of change even beyond that of the previous years. Pro-action with regard to the way business should be organised and managed will not be sufficient. If the middle and senior levels of employees are to be drawn into the trades union movement in significant numbers - and we believe this is necessary in achieving desired change - then there has to be a transformation in attitude as well as of image in ensuring such success. There will need to be a spirited militancy in the determination for reform, but this would be very different from the resentment-driven proletarian militancy of the past. The militancy of the future may still be anger-driven, but with a joyfulness and self-assurance which proclaims that, "We are more knowing and skilled than the stooges who ruin good business and industry."

Bernard Shaw once wrote a short book giving a Socialist interpretation - still very much valid today - of Wagner's tetralogy, *The Ring of The Nibelung.* [119] It might be suggested that Wagner's joyful music drama, *The Mastersingers of Nuremberg*, be made the official opera of the trades union movement, since it embodies the essential values of modern trade unionism: viz., the importance of innovation; impatience with petty rules restricting the individual in the striving for greater creativity; the need to reward merit; the spirit of pride and co-operation amongst trades people; a strong sense of community within a classless environment; and a great collective solidarity. The mean-minded Sixtus Beckmesser, the town clerk and figure of fun, would represent the futile and rigid dogmas of the past,

---

119 *The Perfect Wagnerite: A Commentary On The Nibelung's Ring*, published by Constable in 1898 and often reprinted.

44-8

which have obstructed the advance of Socialism in facing the changes of the new age; Hans Sachs, the much-loved highly-respected poet and shoemaker, would represent the reforming and generous spirit of the new trades unionism; whilst Walther von Stolzing would represent the new and essential constituency of middle and senior management - often entrepreneurial in temperament - to be drawn into the extended membership of the labour movement. The story and grandiose leitmotifs of Wagner's music drama, culminating in a joyous festival of banner-carrying trades people parading in a field beyond the city limits of 16th century Nuremberg, could serve as a spiritually uplifting experience in unifying all trades unionists towards a sense of common purpose. If the trades union movement is to fully exploit the opportunities which lie ahead, then much thought and time must be given to practical planning.

8   The Responsible society cannot be brought into full fruition without an effective educational system, and unfortunately, the British system is amongst the most wanting in the industrialised world. There are many reasons for this, quite apart from cut-backs in the educational budget, and the added administrative burden which has been piled onto teaching staff. The main failing is the inability of the school system to prepare pupils for the life of work or vocational study in tertiary education. A career path should be prepared for children at an early age and the relevant skills embarked upon. Those not progressing to university should be led into proper 3-year apprenticeship schemes, as in Continental Europe, where they are given a sense of status and direction. The majority of those entering university should already have a career path, since there is a vast wastage of public funds on generalised courses with no proper aim or outcome. Consequently, many are obliged to take up vocational or more specific studies after graduating in subjects which prove of little further use.

The study of citizenship in our schools is already being envisaged by the present government, and this should include not only instruction on the departments and mechanics of government, but on the purpose of democracy and how it will impinge on the lives of pupils themselves. Citizenship studies should demonstrate how a pluralistic society may be held together by democratic Socialist values, and as to the parameters of political doctrine with regard to what is acceptable or non-acceptable for the health of a democracy. Naturally, a generous proportion of time should be allowed for free discussion, but the teacher should be sufficiently knowledgeable in the social sciences to guide pupils away from malign tendencies such as support for totalitarianism or theocratic authority.

Full citizen rights and obligations cannot be undertaken by the individual in defending and promoting the democratic state without knowledge linked to a good reasoning ability, and these are not possible without a firm grasp of language. The

44-9

teaching of English in our schools has possibly never been poorer than it is today, not merely in spelling and the use of grammar, but in vocabulary and comprehension. If English is to be taught effectively, then children must be guided into loving literature so they are motivated towards a lifelong pleasure in reading worthwhile books. The parallel benefits of this would not simply lead to a higher appreciation of cultural values, but a greater awareness and sensitivity to social issues. Unfortunately, the Oxbridge establishment, through a particular form of elitism, has designed a curriculum in the teaching of literature, totally unsuited to secondary education. The first priority in the teaching of literature should be the absorption of the *meaningful* in terms of rational comprehension as opposed to intuitional feeling, since the former is the essential instrument for universal communication as opposed to the latter which rises no higher than the expression of the aesthetic. Such teaching should be aimed at maximising understanding in the mind of the majority, and lighting the spark of enthusiasm for literature in the mind of that majority.

In pursuing this purpose, Shakespeare, for example, could be dropped from the school curriculum (to be reserved for the pleasures of the university student), since the perceived ambiguity of the text outbalances the benefits to be derived from the grasp of rational meaning. There is a moronic school of thought which argues that literature is primarily of value through the beauty of its cadences and the music of its structure, and that meaning is merely of secondary importance, or need not be comprehended in the fullness of its intention. Such an approach to literature, which is typical often of the ill-educated parvenu snob intent on projecting a facade of culture, is to be repudiated entirely. In responding to the needs and anticipated level of secondary pupils, quality books should be chosen for study which are both thought-provoking and entertaining, and yet represent the highest standards of English prose and poetry, such as the major works of Bunyan, Defoe, Swift (unbowlderised), Fielding, and other writers of the past three hundred years; and in poetry, Dryden, Pope, Wordsworth, or Tennyson. In the sphere of drama, the plays of Shaw, Wilde, Sheridan, or Goldsmith could be performed in preference to Shakespeare - or even the comedies of the classicist, Ben Jonson, since his characters, situations, and plots, may be more easily appreciated by the ordinary modern person of today. It should be appreciated by those who teach literature, that if a book, poem, or essay, fails to convey an immediate sense of meaning and relevance to its intended readers, then it is failing in its purpose.

9   A book on the values of New Socialism cannot be completed without some remarks on the status of family life in contemporary society. The stable upbringing of children is more dependent on the family than on any other institution, and it must be the function of the state, in so far as it is possible, to protect the interests of the family during an era of its rapid change. Due to the emergence of women's rights

44-9

and the rise of feminism, which have to be respected, the institution of marriage is being transformed throughout the industrial world. There may always have been power conflict, to a greater or lesser degree, between married couples in all cultural environments, but the equalisation of rights has led to the intensification of open conflict and the breakdown of relationships on a scale never before witnessed.

There was a time, earlier in the century, when the plays of Strindberg were regarded as the fantasies of a sick mind - partly because he was cruel and unstable in his personal relationships - but today, his dramas of married life, such as *The Father* and *The Dance of Death*, are regarded as realistic in-depth studies of the breakdown of marriage in all its torment. The only enduring feature in family life is the love of parents for their children, which indeed is the primary purpose of marriage seen as a social institution. The future of marriage is unknown, and it is probable that family life may only be improved by legislating for benefits to the extended family. This is because the isolation of the unitary family contributes to tension and conflict on the first appearance of "serious" differences. When several generations live in the same household, on the other hand, there are balancing factors which diminish differences: e.g., the distraction of other problems; the opportunity for a "shoulder to cry on;" a sense of humour which comes from many individuals being thrown together; and a greater sociableness which distracts from the pain of personal anxiety.

Few marriages are perfect in any society, and in a civilised community, it is better that bad marriages should be *made* to last for the overriding interests of children, than that they should be dissolved through the acrimony of divorce. This is because research seems to have concluded that children suffer more through the consequences of divorce than through the consequences of unhappy marriage. This should not be taken as an argument that husbands and wives should be obliged to endure unhappy lives, for society should enable them in the light of day to take lovers and mistresses, who in their turn should be accepted into the fraternal embrace of the extended family.

Legislation in benefiting the extended family could be effected through tax concessions for several generations living together as a single household, and such legislation could include unmarried or widowed aunts and uncles, or second cousins, etc. The social benefits of extended family households would be considerable, in addition to acting as a cohesive influence in preventing the breakup of marriage: e.g., in countering the racketeering of those involved in the sheltered housing industry; in reducing the occurrence of loneliness amongst the elderly; in exposing the rising generation to the experience of a broader social environment; and lastly, in reducing the pressures for greater housing stock.

44-9

In a democratic society where the rights of both men and women are fully realised and equal, none can claim the prerogative to "own" another in any exclusive sense, and therefore jealousy must be seen not only as symptomatic of immaturity, but as the sin of unjustified possessiveness, contradicting the basic principle of human freedom. If disputes over power are not the cause of marital breakdown, then the latter almost invariably degenerate into quarrelling over the division of property. To lessen such bitterness, and the resultant suffering inflicted on children and others closely related, and in anticipating the breakup of any such partnership, it might be useful if legislation was introduced forbidding any union until a marriage settlement had been drawn up for the division of property in the event of marital failure.

Such a marriage settlement would take into consideration the occupational status and earnings of both partners, so that in the event of divorce neither would feel that gender discrimination had been imposed by the law. Shared bank accounts need anyway to be outlawed, since they are sources of major friction. Such marriage settlements would need to be re-drawn at 5-yearly intervals, but their prime value would be seen as delineating clear lines of demarcation as to the ownership rights on all items of property of each partner. It would seem that there are few other viable options open to the state in upholding the institution of marriage.

What we have described as New Socialism and the values which it embodies throughout this book, is not simply an intellectual construct, but a logical deduction from the consequences of the present development of society. It is not a prediction of the future, for history cannot be predicted, for unanticipated events, disasters, or the might of opposing vested interests can always overturn the best plans for society. It is no more than a description of the best turn of events, if humankind is allowed to exert its will in the happy light of reason and justice.

******

APPENDIX A

(From Chapter 13, Section 5.)

A Terminology For New Socialism

If New Socialism is to be realised as an everyday activity, then this can only be achieved by using the vocabulary of New Socialism in a meaningful way. Therefore, in trades union negotiations, or in any general discussions on the meaning or promotion of Socialism, the following terms should be used in presenting arguments. The index will be useful as a guide to more detailed illumination of most terms listed below.

Economic Concepts

Productive Capitalism or the Productive economy (designated the Rhine mode of capitalism by Michel Albert). The *Real* economy which is job-creating and geared to maximising market share, and circulates wealth throughout the majority population. Modelled on the systems of Continental Europe and the dynamic economies of the Far East.

Rentier Capitalism or the Rentier economy (designated Neo-American capitalism by Michel Albert). The *Phony* economy which concentrates wealth into fewer hands through monopolistic or highly speculative modes of activity. Modelled on the Anglo-Saxon systems of business, but found widely throughout the impoverished Third world.

Productive Profitability profits achieved through maximising market share and the intense concentration on productive activity.

Rentier Profitability profits achieved primarily through *rente*, or the passive assets of land or property, or accrued through investments, or by adding extra or excess margins onto a restricted output of goods or services, and otherwise concentrating on money profits.

Social Wealth Creation derived from business activity which circulates wealth and maximises job opportunities. Any wealth creation which is beneficial to the wider community.

Unsocial Wealth Creation derived from business activity which concentrates wealth into fewer hands and diminishes job opportunities. Any wealth creation which is malign to the community - including all criminal activity.

Productive purpose that which should be the sole purpose of a business enterprise in a free competitive environment, i.e., the objective purpose of a company in maintaining its long-term aims.

Rentier purpose   the corrupting or short-term purposes of an enterprise, usually pursued by corporate shareholders, which sacrifice reinvestment for improvement and competitiveness in maximising rewards for investors.

Creative intervention   state initiatives in co-operation with business in promoting directly the productivity of UK-based enterprises.

Dirigiste authority   state direction or on-going intervention into the private sector or public bodies, in promoting welfare or wealth-creation or industrial planning associations, whilst remaining separate from the organisations so directed.

Economic interest sectors   economic interests which cannot be defined as class-based interests.

Economic sector struggle   reflecting social conflict of the majority against existing economic forces, but that majority cannot be distinguished as a specific class.

National Enterprises   independent businesses, but refers especially to those liberated from corporate control.

Independent Enterprise Boards   responsible to the DTI (or equivalent bodies in other countries) to encourage and oversee the smooth transfer of industrial plants and other businesses from the financial control of corporations to that of the newly founded industrial investment credit banks.

Social Prosperity   those socio-economic conditions enabling the individual to maximise his career potentiality and earning power, whilst not sacrificing his interests to those of vested interest groups.

Advanced Industrial Action (AIA)   co-operation between workers and managers in the struggle against corporate interests to save productive enterprise; often culminating in the occupation of industrial plants.

Advanced Industrial Action Group (AIAG)   an unincorporated body comprising activists from different trade unions for pursuing AIA, and undertaking the occupation of industrial plants on their own responsibility.

Industrial Efficiency Tribunal   for the trial of de-industrialising corporate directors and others by the management and workforce of a subsidiary, conducted under the auspices of the AIAG.

Profitability Inspection Committee   trades union bodies for inspecting the level and mode of profitability within individual enterprises.

Other Political Concepts

Responsible Society   that committed to the ownership and control of the means of production, distribution, and exchange, especially through employee share-ownership and co-determination.

Humane Society alternative term to the Responsible Society, but laying emphasis on the greater understanding between differing individuals in a varied society.

Principle of Nationality the democratic right of a people to overcome unrepresented international financial or corporate power in protecting the interests of the majority.

Disinterested Justice justice as fairness: that which is uninfluenced by subjective vested interests and entails equality before the law.

Vested Interests those of any individual or group of any kind.

Subjective Vested Interests those which conflict for any reason (but usually economic) with any individual or other group in the community; so giving rise to social struggle damaging to the totality of a community's interests. (In the economic sphere Jeremy Bentham has designated these as Sinister Interests.)

Substantive Issues those underlying often concealed problems of society, having a separate and independent existence, as distinguished from the surface, more superficial, or populist issues of political life.

Reactive Attitudes those false subjective views which apportion blame on wrong or superficial causes for social ills, or lead to the superficial and unsatisfactory solution of substantive problems.

Integrated Community a description, based on empirical evidence, of the politically homogeneous (although pluralistic) society emerging, or brought into existence, for the equal benefit of all. The term is used in preference to the older and fallacious concept of the "Organic" community.

New Idealism an intellectual tool, which whilst repudiating the methodologies of the older schools of philosophical idealism, demonstrates the reality of ideas as a necessary step in unlocking the unwarranted constraints on constructive thought. It has also been formulated in view of the intellectual failures of materialistic thinking in the spheres of both criticism and synthesis.

APPENDIX B
(From Chapter 17, Section 23.)
Economic Failure of The UK's Rentier Capitalistic System

as demonstrated through our international trading record and poor manufacturing expressed through export figures.

a) *The UK's Imbalance of payments based on January-December 1998 figures:-*

Value of imports in excess over exports in £m by country

1 - Japan	6338		38-Faroe Isles	82
2 - Germany	4848		39-Hungary	58
3 - USA	4263		40-Botswana	57
4 - China	2091		41-Peru	53
5 - Switzerland	2051		42-Guyana	49
6 - Hong Kong	1918		43-Jamaica	47
7 - South Korea	1624		44-Papua New Guinea	47
8 - Taiwan	1452		45-Zimbabwe	45
9 - France	1345		46-Swaziland	37
10-Malaysia	1308		47-Lithuania	30
11-Italy	1147		48-Ivory Coast	25
12-Bel/Lux.	1131		49-St. Lucia	24
13-Finland	948		50-Macao	23
14-Thailand	940		51-Belize	22
15-Norway	902		52-Sweden	22
16-Singapore	851		53-Bahamas	21
17-Netherlands	624		54-Cambodia	18
18-Philippines	595		55-Madagascar	15
19-Indonesia	588		56-Liechtenstein	14
20-El Salvador	535		57-Morocco	13
21-Russia	529		58-St. Vincent	13
22-Canada	427		59-Namibia	11
23-Mauritius	260		60-Brazil	9
24-Latvia	209		61-Bolivia	8
25-India	204		62-Cameroon	6
26-New Zealand	198		63-Niger	6
27-Austria	190		64-Honduras	5
28-Vietnam	176		65-Burma	4
29-Chile	173		66-Surinam	4
30-Bangladesh	166		67-Dominica	4
31-Sri Lanka	159		68-Laos	3
32-Costa Rica	136		69-Mongolia	2
33-Denmark	130		70-Cape Verde	1
34-Pakistan	125		71-Fiji	1
35-Iceland	100			
36-Estonia	91		Grand total of import imbalances:- £ 39,641,000,000	
37-Portugal	90			

b) *Those countries with whom the UK has an excess balance of payments based on January-December 1998, figures in £m:-*

The following list gives a pitiful impression of Britain's international trade. The countries over which Britain has an excess balance of exports fall predominantly into the two following categories: a) those which are entirely dependent on imports, since their manufacturing bases are negligible, e.g.,the oil-rich Gulf states, and, b) poor Third world countries, many of which are politically unstable, are unreliable payers, and often forfeit on their debts. No major industrialised countries will be found in the following list. It leaves the impression as if Britain is only content to gather up the crumbs of world trade.

1 - Saudi Arabia	1791	41-US Virgin Isles	52	81-Kenya	9
2 - Ireland	1673	42-Azerbaijan	48	82-Guinea	9
3 - Greece	670	43-Benin	41	83-Grenada	8
4 - Poland	522	44-Paraguay	41	84-Haiti	8
5 - Dubai	476	45-Bermuda	36	85-Afghanistan	8
6 - Turkey	441	46-Angola	34	86-New Caledonia	8
7 - Sharjah	388	47-Curaçao	34	87-Mozambique	7
8 - Nigeria	328	48-Congo	32	88-St. Kitts	7
9 - Iran	295	49-Slovenia	32	89-British Virgin Isles	6
10-Qatar	263	50-Algeria	31	90-Liberia	6
11-Argentina	261	51-Antigua	30	91-Albania	6
12-Egypt	219	52-Ethiopia	30	92-Anguilla	6
13-Puerto Rico	200	53-Slovakia	30	93-St. Helena	6
14-Oman	193	54-Uganda	30	94-Nepal	5
15-Israel	172	55-Falkland Isles	29	95-Iraq	5
16-Lebanon	158	56-Uzbekistan	29	96-Maldova	5
17-Kuwait	148	57-Tunisia	24	97-US Oceania	5
18-Mexico	146	58-Dominican Republic	19	98-French Polynesia	5
19-Abu Dhabi	140	59-Cuba	18	99-Armenia	4
20-Czech Republic	138	60-Senegal	18	100-Burkia	4
21-Venezuela	122	61-Georgia	18	101-Ceuta & Melilla	4
22-Ukraine	118	62-Sierra Leone	18	102-Marshal Isle	3
23-South Africa	115	63-Djibouti	17	103-Mayotte	3
24-Malta	106	64-Gabon	17	104-Romania	3
25-Jordan	98	65-Togo	17	105-Burundi	2
26-Cyprus	90	66-Uruguay	16	106-Malawi	2
27-Libya	88	67-Andorra	15	107-Montserrat	2
28-Tanzania	83	68-Gautemala	15	108-Rwanda	2
29-Bahrain	77	69-Mali	15	109-Turks & Caicos	2
30-Panama	77	70-Barbados	14	110-Austr. Oceania	1
31-Yemen	75	71-Belarus	13	111-Bhutan	1
32-Brunei	73	72-Yugoslavia	12	112-Br. Ind. Oc. Terr.	1
33-Gibralter	71	73-Bosnia	11	113-Equat. Guinea	1
34-Ghana	67	74-Gambia	11	114-Lesotho	1
35-Croatia	63	75-Cayman Isles	10	115-Sao Tome-Prince	1
36-Sudan	61	76-Macedonia	10	116-Somalia	1
37-Syria	57	77-North Korea	10	117-Tonga	1
38-Kazakhstan	56	78-Zambia	10		
39-Aruba	55	79-Turkmenistan	9		
40-Trinidad	55	80-Eritrea	9		

APPENDICES

Grand total of import imbalances (71 territories):-   £ 39,641,000,000
Grand total of export balances   (117 territories):-   £ 11,292,000,000
Total imbalances in excess of export balances:-   £ 28,349,000,000

(Source for the above figures: *Export Times*, May 1999)

APPENDIX C

(From Chapter 24, Section 2.)

Job Losses In The Productive Sector

It has not been easy compiling the following figures due to changes of definition and omissions by the Central Statistical Office. It is apparent that this has partly been due to government attempts to "doctor" the statistics. Consequently, for the sake of greater accuracy and completion several tables have been used as indicated below. The situation has been further complicated by the change in 1992 to the Standard Industrial Classification with regard to the Analysis by industry of employees in employment.

JOBS LOST BETWEEN 1977 - 1988/1998

Figures in '000s	1977	1988	1998	Actual jobs lost	% down
Agriculture, forestry & fishing:	388	313	255[1]	133,000	34 %
Coal extraction & solid fuels GB*:	350	121	43[2]	307,000	88 %
Food, drink & tobacco:	711	570	429	282,000	40 %
Chemical/man-made fibres:	436	324	309[3]	127,000	29 %
Metal manufacture & extraction of metal ores & minerals:	483	177	-	306,000	63 %
Mechanical engineering:	925	765	-	160,000	17 %
Instrument engineering:	150	104	-	46,000	31 %
Electrical & electronic engineering:	753	561	-	192,000	25 %
Ship building & repairing:	182	53	-	129,000	71 %
Motor vehicles & parts:	750	269	-	481,000	64 %

---

1   & hunting
2   Mining & quarrying of energy producing materials.
3   Manufacturers of textiles & textile products.
*   GB = figure for Great Britain, otherwise for the UK.

Figures in '000s	1977	1988	1998	Actual jobs lost	% down
Metal goods not elsewhere specified:	535	137	-	398,000	74 %
Textiles:	512	242	173	339,000	66 %
Clothing & footwear:	388	314	265[4]	123,000	32 %
Timber, furniture, etc.:	258	240	-	18,000	7 %
Paper, printing & publishing:	537	483	466[5]	71,000	13 %
Other manufacturing industries:	331	76	-	255,000	77 %
Construction:	1,270	1,043	975	295,000	23 %
Transport & communications:	1,468	1,324	-	144,000	10 %
Retail distribution:	2,753	2,152	-	601,000	22 %
Leather goods & fur:	41	29 (1982)	13[6]	28,000	68 %
Bricks, pottery, glass, cement, etc.	264	207 (1982)	-	57,000	22 %

4 Clothing, footwear & leather goods.
5 Manufacture of pulp, paper & paper products, publishing & printing.
6 Of leather & leather goods.

TOTAL JOBS LOST IN ABOVE SECTORS BETWEEN 1977 - 1982/1988/1998:- 4,492,000

Sources: Annual Abstract of Statistics (CSO) for 1983, 1984, 1990 & 1999.

JOBS LOST BETWEEN 1983 & 1988

Figures in '000s	1983	1988	Actual jobs lost	% down
Index of production & construction industries:	7,217	6,745	472,000	7 %
Index of production industries:	6,173	5,702	471,000	8 %
Of which manufacturing industries:	5,525	5,215	310,000	6 %
Agriculture & horticulture:	331	295	36,000	11 %
Energy & water supply:	648	487	161,000	25 %
Electricity (GB):	155	143	12,000	7 %
Gas (GB):	95	82	17,000	17 %

APPENDICES

Figures in '000s	1983	1988	Actual jobs lost	% down
Other mineral & ore extraction	817	687	130,000	16 %
Metal manufacturing & extraction of metal ores & minerals:	253	168	85,000	34 %
Non-metallic mineral products	215	196	19,000	9 %
Basic industrial chemicals (GB):	125	115	10,000	8 %
Other chemical products & preparations:	220	205	15,000	7 %
Metal goods, engineering & vehicles:	2,549	2,364	185,000	7 %
Hand tools & finished metal goods inc. doors & windows (GB):	205	197	8,000	4 %
Other metal goods (GB):	140	137	3,000	2 %
Machinery for agriculture, metal working, textile, food & printing industries, etc.:	211	192	19,000	9 %
Mining & construction machinery, etc. (GB):	86	73	13,000	15 %
Aerospace & other transport equipment (GB):	209	180	29,000	14 %
Alcoholic, soft drink & tobacco manufacture (GB):	183	97	86,000	47 %
All other food & drink manufacture (GB):	243	218	25,000	10 %
Clothing, hats, gloves & fur goods (GB):	207	204	3,000	1 %

Sources: Annual Abstract of Statistics, 1990 & 1998 eds., pp. 110-111.

APPENDIX D

(From Chapter 26, Section 5.)

The growth of Corporate Bankruptcy

Company liquidations (all types notified) in England & Wales:-

1971	1972	1973	1974	1975	1976	1977	1978	1979	1980	1981	1982
7,956	7,743	6,872	7,466	9,315	10,112	9,481	8,701	8,567	10,860	12,234	15,975

1991	1992	1993	1997
21,827	24,425	20,708	12,610

In Scotland for the same periods as indicated above:-

456	472	368	419	480	528	49	504	452	621	686	756
616	670	551	477								

In Northern Ireland for the same periods as indicated above:-

77	52	46	42	54	87	74	89	71	113	138	162
183	156	158	113								

Total UK company liquidations:-

8,489	8,267	7,286	7,927	9,849	10,727	9,604	9,294	9,090	11,594	13,058	16,893
22,626	25,251	21,417	13,200								

(Sources: Annual Abstract of Statistics (CSO), 1983, 1984, 1990 & 1999 eds.)

Company insolvencies:-

	1983	1984	1985	1986	1987	1988	1991
England & Wales: Compulsory liquidations	4,807	5,260	5,761	5,204	4,116	3,667	8,368
Creditors voluntary liquidations	8,599	8,461	9,137	9,201	7,323	5,760	13,459
Scotland: Compulsory liquidations -	263	272	306	299	253	228	304
Creditors voluntary liquidations -	258	251	231	212	203	168	312
N. Ireland: Compulsory liquidations -	15	19	36	56	5	60	112
Creditors voluntary liquidations -	96	64	75	108	91	63	71
Total UK company insolvencies -	14,038	14,327	15,546	15,080	12,045	9,946	22,626

Continued from the above -	1992	1993	1997
	9,734	8,244	4,735
	14,691	12,464	7,875
	310	286	254
	360	265	223
	79	73	60
	77	85	53
	25,251	21,417	13,200

(Sources: Annual Abstract of Statistics (CSO), 1990 & 1999 eds., p. 307.)

APPENDIX E
(From Chapter 24, Section 9.)

Figures Illustrating Britain's Dependence On The Productive Sector
i.e. manufacturing & the primary industries of farming, horticulture, forestry, fishing & the extraction of ores and minerals.

Visible balance of trade (£ million) between exports & imports (fob value):-

1978	1979	1980	1981	1982	1983	1984	1985	1986	1987	1988
-1,593	-3,344	+1,355	+3,250	+1,908	-1,509	-5,169	-3,132	- 9,364	-11,698	-21,553

Invisible trade balances (£ million) illustrating the increasing insufficiency of the service sector (including rentier activity) to maintain the national economy when compared with the above figures:-

| 2,529 | 2,794 | 1,465 | 3,378 | 2,679 | 5,267 | 7,054 | 6,335 | 9,430 | 7,258 | 6,209 |

(Sources: Annual Abstract of Statistics (CSO), 1990 & 1999 eds.)

APPENDIX F

(From Chapter 29, Section 8.)

Illustration of A Major Cause of Cash-Starvation of UK-Based Industry Through Excessive Investments & Lending Abroad

Total UK investment overseas (£ million) -

1978	1979	1980	1981	1982	1983	1984	1985	1986	1987	1988
4,593	6,776	8,175	10,474	11,656	12,612	15,903	28,234	34,379	15,913	24,937

Sterling lending abroad by UK banks (£ million) -

| 1,030 | 210 | 2,778 | 3,019 | 4,019 | 2,232 | 4,933 | 1,635 | 5,955 | 4,638 | 4,569 |

Deposits with & lending to banks abroad by the UK non-bank private sector -

| 280 | 1,138 | 2,502 | 1,864 | 598 | 863 | 3,239 | 1,253 | 2,782 | 5,311 | 3,035 |

(Source: Annual Abstract of Statistics, Transactions in External Assets & Liabilities, 1990 ed.)

Select Bibliography
and quoted texts

The following bibliography, divided into sectors as listed below, is necessarily limited by space due to the breadth and subject matter of the book, and so consequently, is mainly concentrated on quoted sources:-

1 - On The Foundations of Justice   2 - Economics For a Stable Society   3 - Economics For Prosperity   4 - Co-determination & Industrial Harmony   5 - On The Productive Economies   6 - The Problem of Rentier Capitalism   7 - The Failure of Rentier Capitalism   8 - Industrial Funding Comparisons Between Rentier & Productive Capitalism   9 - Historical Factors   10 - Other Socio-Political Issues   11 - Other Philosophical Issues

1 - ON THE FOUNDATIONS OF JUSTICE

Catlin, George, *A Study of The Principles of Politics*, Allen & Unwin, 1930.
Green, T.H., *Lectures On The Principles of Political Obligation,* Longmans Green, 1927 ed.
Harrison, Fed; Hudson, M.; Miller, G.J.; &, Feder,K., *A Philosophy For A Fair Society*, Shepheard-Walwyn, 1994.
Joad, C.E.M., *Guide To The Philosophy of Morals & Politics*, Gollancz, 1938.
Lippmann, Walter, *The Good Society,* Allen & Unwin, 1938.
MacIver, R.M., *Community*, Macmillan, 1936 ed.
Rawls, John, *A Theory of Justice*, OUP, 1972.
Richter, Melvin, *The Politics of Conscience*, Weidenfeld & Nicolson, 1964.
Russell, Bertrand, *Human Society In Ethics & Politics*, Allen & Unwin, 1954.
Warnock, Mary, *Ethics Since 1900*, OUP, 1962.

2 - ECONOMICS FOR A STABLE SOCIETY

Capra, Fritjof, *The Turning Point,* Wildwood House, 1982.
Chossudovsky, Michel, *The Globalisation of Poverty*, Zed Books, 1998.
Dore, Ronald, *Corporatism & Accountability: Organized Interests In British Public Life*, Clarendon Press, 1990.
Drucker, Peter F., *The Age of Discontinuity*, Heinemann, 1969.
Douthwaite, Richard, *Short Circuit*, Resurgence, 1996.
Douthwaite, Richard, *The Growth Illusion,* The Lilliput Press, Dublin, 1992.
Galbraith, J.K., *Economics & The Public Purpose*, André Deutsch, 1974.
Gray, John, *False Dawn: The Delusions of Global Capitalism*, Granta Books, 1998.
Karliner, Joshua, *The Corporate Planet,* Sierra Club Books, San Francisco, 1997.
Korten, David C., *When Corporations Rule The World*, Earthscan, 1996.
Martin, Hans-Peter & Schumann, Harald, *The Global Trap,* Zed Books, 1997.
Rowbotham, Michael, *The Grip of Death*, Ian Carpenter, 1998.

3 - ECONOMICS FOR PROSPERITY

Drucker, Peter, *The New Realities,* Heinemann Professional Publishing, 1989.
Kennedy, Paul, *Preparing For The Twenty-First Century*, Harper Collins, 1993.
Parker, Peter, *For Starters*, J. Cape, 1989.
Villiers, Charles, *Start Again Britain*, Quartet Books, 1984.

Woods, Frank, *Business Accounting*, Pitman, 5ᵗʰ ed., 1989.
Woolf, Emile, *Auditing Today*, Prentice Hall, 4ᵗʰ ed., 1990.

4 - CO-DETERMINATION & INDUSTRIAL HARMONY

Dore, Ronald, "The Confucian Remedy For Industrial Success," *Government & Opposition*, Vol. 20, No. 2, Spring 1985.
Dore, Ronald, *The Japanese Firm*, OUP, 1996.
Dore, Ronald, *How The Japanese Learn To Work*, Routledge, 1998.
Jenkins, Clive & Sherman, Barry, *The Leisure Shock*, Eyre & Methuen, 1981.
Rifkin, Jeremy, *The End of Work*, G.P. Putnam, NY, 1995.
Sherman, Barry, *The State of The Unions*, John Wiley, 1986.
Taylor, Robert, *The Future of The Trade Unions*, André Deutsch, 1994.

5 - ON THE PRODUCTIVE ECONOMIES

Clapham, J.H., *Economic Development of France & Germany*, Cambridge UP, 1923.
Dawson, W.H., *Industrial Germany*, Collins, 1912.
Dore, Ronald, *British Factory - Japanese Factory: The Origins of National Diversity In Industrial Relations*, Univ. Of Calif. Press, 1973.
Dore, Ronald, *The Japanese Firm: Sources of Competitive Strength*, Clarendon Press, 1994.
Dore, Ronald, *Taking Japan Seriously*, Athlone Press, 1987.
Emmott, Bill, *Japan's Global Reach*, Century, 1992.
Johnson, Chalmers, *MITI*, Berkeley, Univ. Of California Press, 1982.
Henderson, W.O., *The State & The Industrial Revolution In Prussia*, Liverpool UP, 1958.
Knowles, L.C.A., *Economic Development In The 19ᵗʰ Century*, Routledge, 1932.
Levy, H., *Industrial Germany*, Cambridge UP, 1935.

6 - THE PROBLEM OF RENTIER CAPITALISM

Albert, Michel, *Capitalism Against Capitalism*, Whurr Publications, 1993.
Carr, Albert Z., *Business As A Game*, J.M. Dent, 1971.
Chomsky, Noam, *World Orders, Old & New*, Pluto Press, 1997.
Frieden, Jeffrey A., *Banking On The World*, Hutchinson Radius, 1987.
Gray, John, *Endgames*, Polity Presss, 1997.
Harrison, Fred, *The Power In The Land*, Shepheard-Walwyn, 1983.
Hutton, Will, *The State To Come*, Vintage, 1997.
Hutton, Will, *The State We're In*, J. Cape, 1995.
Pollard, Sidney, *The Neglect of Industry: A Critique of British Economic Policy Since 1870*, Erasmus Univesitet, 1984.
Qualey, Carlton C. (Ed.), *Thorstein Veblen*, Columbia UP, NY, 1968.
Raw, Charles; Hodgson, G.; & Page, B., *Do You Sincerely Want To Be Rich,?* André Deutsch, 1971.
Raw, Charles, *Slater Walker*, André Deutsch, 1977.
Smith, Keith, *The British Economic Crisis*, Penguin, 1986.
Tawney, R.H., *The Acquisitive Society*, G. Bell, 1925.
Tawney, R.H., *Religion & The Rise of Capitalism*, Penguin, 1938.
Veblen, Thorstein, *Absentee Ownership*, Viking, NY, 1935 ed.
Veblen, Thorstein, *The Theory of Business Enterprise*, Scribner's, NY, 1904.
Veblen, Thorstein, *The Theory of The Leisure Class*, Allen & Unwin, 1924 ed.
Weber, Max, *The Protestant Ethic & The Spirit of Capitalism*, Routledge, 1985 ed.

7 - THE FAILURE OF RENTIER CAPITALISM

Bacon, R., & Eltis, W., *Britain's Economic Problem: Too Few Producers*, Macmillan, 1978.

Barnett, Corelli, *The Collapse of British Power*, Methuen, 1972.

Bellini, J., *Rule Britannia*, J. Cape, 1981.

Benn, Ernest J.P., *The Confessions of A Capitalist*, Hutchinson, 1925.

Boltho, Andrea, "Growth," in *The European Economy: Growth & Crisis*, Oxford, 1982.

Burns, C. Delisle, *Industry & Civilization*, Allen & Unwin, 1925.

Buxton, Neil K., "The Role of The 'New' Industries In Britain During The 1930s: A Reinterpretation," *Business History Review*, 49, 205-22, 1975.

Central Policy Review Staff, *The Future of The Car Industry*, HMSO, 1975.

Feinstein, Charles, *The Managed Economy*, OUP, 1983.

Gamble, Andrew, *Britain In Decline*, Papermac, 1981.

Hannah, Leslie, "Mangerial Innovation & The Rise of The Large-Scale Company In Interwar Britain," *Economic History Review*, 2nd ser., 27, 252-70, 1974.

Hannah, Leslie, *The Rise of The Corporate Economy*, Methuen, 1976.

Harley, C.K., "Skilled Labour & The Choice of Technique In Edwardian Industry," *Explorations In Economic History*, 11, 391-414, 1974.

Katzenstein, Peter, *Between Power & Plenty*, Madison, Univ. Of Wisconsin Press, 1978.

Kilpatrick, A. & Lawson, T., "On The Nature of Industrial Decline In The UK," *Cambridge Journal of Economic*, 4(1), 85-100, 1980.

Leggatt, T., *The Evolution of Industrial Systems*, Croom Helm, 1985.

Longstreth, F., "The City, Industry & The State," in *State & Economy In Contemporary Capitalism*, C. Crouch (ed.), Croom Helm, 1979.

Maddison, Angus, "Phases of Capitalist Development," *Banca Nazionale del Laboro Quarterly Review*, 1977.

Moggridge, D.E., *British Monetary Policy 1924-31*, Cambridge UP, 1972.

Minns, R., *Take Over The City*, Pluto Press, 1982.

Pollard, Sidney, *Development of The British Economy*, E. Arnold, 1981.

Pollard, Sidney, *Britain's Prime & Britain's Decline*, E. Arnold, 1989.

Pollard, Sidney, *The Wasting of The British Economy*, Crrom Helm, 1984.

Pressnell, L.S., "1925: The Burden of Sterling," *Economic History Review*, 2nd ser., 31, 67-88, 1978.

Rothschild, Michael L., *Bionomics*, Futura, 1992.

Stamp, J., "The Report of The Macmillan Committee," *Economic Quarterly*, 41, 424-35, 1931.

Supple, Barry, *Essays In British Business History*, OUP, 1977.

Wiener, Martin J., *English Culture & The Decline of The Industrial Spirit*, Cambridge UP, 1980.

8 - INDUSTRIAL FUNDING COMPARISONS BETWEEN RENTIER & PRODUCTIVE CAPITALISM

Cairncross, A.K., *Home & Foreign Investment 1870-1913*, Cambridge UP, 1935.

Cameron, R.E., *Banking In The Early Stages of Industrialisation*, OUP, NY, 1967.

Carrington, J.C. & Edwards, G.T., *Financing Industrial Investment*, Macmillan, 1979.

Carrington, J.C. & Edwards, G.T., *Reversing Industrial Decline*, Macmillan, 1981.

Cole, G.D.H.(ed.), *Studies In Capital & Investment*, New Fabian Research Bureau, 1935.

Cottrell, P.L., *Industrial Finance 1830-1914*, Methuen, 1983.

Edwards, G.T., *How Economic Growth & Inflation Happen*, Macmillan, 1984.

Edwards, G.T., *The Role of The Banks In Economic Development: The Economics of Industrial*

Resurgence, Macmillan, 1988.
Mathias, P., *The First Industrial Revolution*, Methuen, 1983.
Pressnell, L.S., *Country Banking In The Industrial Revolution*, OUP, 1956.
Saville, J., "Some Retarding Factors In The British Economy Before 1914," *Yorkshire Bulletin of Economic & Social Research*, 13(1), 51-60, 1961.

9 - HISTORICAL FACTORS

Beer, M., *History of British Socialism*, Allen & Unwin, 1948 ed.
Braudel, Fernand, *Civilization & Capitalism*, Collins, 3 vols., 1985.
Churchill, Winston, *History of The English Speaking Peoples*, Dodd Mead & Co., NY, 4 vols., 1966 ed.
Coulton, G.G., *Medieval Panorama*, Cambridge UP, 1938.
Dore, Ronald, *Land Reform In Japan*, Athlone Press, 1984.
Fletcher, Ronald, *The Making of Sociology*, Nelson, 2 vols., 1972.
Haver, George H., *The Age of Ideas*, P. Owen, 1957.
Johnson, Paul, *A History of The Modern World*, Weidenfeld & Nicolson, 1991 ed.
Keegan, William, *The Spectre of Capitalism*, Vintage, 1993.
Mommsen, Theodor, *History of Rome*, Bentley, 5 vols., 1894 ed.
Pollard, A.F., *Factors In Modern History*, Constable, 1910.
Rogers, Thorold, *Six Centuries of Work & Wages*, Swan, Sonnenschein & Co., 1909 ed.
Reade, Winwood, *The Martyrdom of Man*, (1872), Watts & Co.
Skidelsky, Robert, *The World After Communism*, Macmillan, 1995.
Spiegel, H.W., *The Growth of Economic Thought*, Duke Univ. Press, Durham & London, 1991, 3rd ed.
Thomas, Hugh, *An Unfinished History of The World*, Hamish Hamilton, 1979.
Zeldin, Theodore, *An Intimate History of Humanity*, Sinclair-Stevenson, 1994.

10 - OTHER SOCIO-POLITICAL ISSUES

Acton, H.B., *The Illusion of The Epoch, Marxism-Leninism As A Philosophical Creed*, Cohen & West, 1955.
Burnham, James, *The Machiavellians: Defenders of Freedom*, Gateway Books, Chicago, 1963.
Camilleri, Joseph A., *Civilization In Crisis*, Cambridge UP, 1976.
Cole, G.D.H., *The Intelligent Man's Guide Through World Chaos*, Gollancz, 1932.
Dicey, A.V., *Law & Public Opinion In England*, Macmillan, 1905.
Fromm, Erich, *The Sane Society*, Routledge & Kegan Paul, 1956.
George, Henry, *Social Problems*, Kegan Paul, Trench & Co., 1889.
Ginsberg, Morris, *Essays In Sociology & Social Philosophy*, Heinemann, 3 vols., 1947.
Hailsham, Lord, *The Dilemma of Democracy*, Collins, 1978.
Heren, Louis, *Alas, Alas For England*, Hamish Hamilton, 1981.
Hobhouse, L.T., *Social Development*, Allen & Unwin, 1924.
Huxley, T.H., *Science & Culture*, Macmillan, 1888.
Johnson, Paul, *Enemies of Society*, Weidenfeld & Nicolson, 1977.
Kuusinen, O. (Ed.), *Fundamentals of Marxism-Leninism*, Lawrence & Wishart, 1961.
Mannheim, Karl, *Essays On The Sociology of Knowledge*, Routledge & Kegan Paul, 1952.
Marquand, David, *The Unprincipled Society*, J. Cape, 1988.
Mises, Ludwig von, *Socialism, An Economic & Social Analysis*, J. Cape, 1951 ed.
Mumford, Lewis, *Technics & Civilization*, Harcourt Brace & Co., NY, 1935.
Nisbet, Robert, *Twilight of Authority*, Heinemann, 1976.
Russell, Bertrand, *Authority & The Individual*, Allen & Unwin, 1949.
Ruskin, John, *The Crown of Wild Olive*, George Allen, 10th ed., 1897.

Taylor, Gordon Rattray, *Rethink: A Paraprimitive Solution*, Secker & Warburg, 1972.
Tawney, R.H., *Equality*, Allen & Unwin, 1952.
Young, Michael, *The Rise of The Meritocracy*, Penguin, 1968.

11 - OTHER PHILOSOPHICAL ISSUES

Bacon, Francis, *The Advancement of Learning*, Clarendon Press, 1920 ed.
Camhis, Marios, *Planning Theory & Philosophy*, Tavistock Publications, 1979.
Durant, Will, *The Mansions of Philosophy*, Garden City Publishing Co., NY, 1941 ed.
Honderich, Ted, *The Oxford Companion To Philosophy*, OUP, 1995.
Inge, Dean, *The End of An Age*, Putnam, 1948.
Niebuhr, Reinhold, *Moral Man & Immoral Society*, SCM Press, 1963.
Paine, Tom, *The Age of Reason*, Carol Publishing Group, 1995 ed.
Roubiczek, Paul, *The Misinterpretation of Man*, Routlege & Kegan Paul, 1949.
Russell, Bertrand, *Autobiography*, Allen & Unwin, 3 vols., 1967/1969.
Russell, Bertrand, *In Praise of Idleness*, Allen & Unwin, 1935.
Shaw, Bernard, *The Perfect Wagnerite: A Commentary On The Nibelung's Ring*, Constable, 1898.
Whitehead, A.N., *Process & Reality*, Free Press, NY, 1978
Yutang, Lin, *The Importance of Living*, Heinemann, 1938.

***

Index
References are to Chapters and Chapter Sub-Sections

ARENA BOOKS - Political Science titles

Foundations of New Socialism *a vision for the New Millennium*
by Robert Corfe

How can sincere support be given wholly to a political party unless it has clear principles underpinning its base? Such a question is of particular relevance when asked of the Labour party in view of the events which have shattered the foundations of Socialism worldwide over the past decade. The author, who has considerable practical experience as a Labour party activist, sets out to re-establish the concept of *Socialism* as a vision for the future. But the forward-looking view of New Socialism needs to be very different from the old. The transformation of society over the past sixty years means that old doctrines have to be replaced by new if Socialism is it to be made attractive to the modern man or woman. At the same time the author appreciates the traditions of the past, and through his sound knowledge of the "science" or theories of the movement, he is able to trace an evolutionary thread which may also satisfy the demands of Old Socialist stalwarts. What emerges is a framework for motivating the enthusiasm of existing party workers, and for bringing many millions of politically uncommitted people into the movement.

The following themes are examined in depth in major sections of the book -

CULTURE & EGALITARIANISM
Six chapters in which class and elitism are discussed in relationship to high culture. The author shows how culture, stripped of its class associations, would be purified in the process, so alleviating the fears of those who anticipate that standards might be threatened.

THE POLITICS OF PROPERTY
The psychological aspects of property as they effect the individual and society open up new vistas for Socialist thinking on the function of property. False notions are exposed and the acquisitive instinct is recognised as a natural trait to be channelled rather than repressed. Eleven chapters.

DEMOCRACY: REAL & ILLUSORY
Democracy as a form of government and way of life is discussed from many viewpoints, and erroneous beliefs taken for granted in the UK are exploded as myths. It is argued that people power should be maximised in many spheres of activity in ensuring real democracy. Seven chapters.

THE ROAD TO CONSTRUCTIVE POLITICS
After examining those intellectual forces of the 20th century responsible for blocking constructive thought, the author identifies the paramountcy of Ideas, and sets out the framework for a new idealistic philosophy as an effective dialectical tool. Twelve chapters.

ISBN 0-9538460-2-4

Price:- £14.99

ARENA BOOKS - mass market titles

Death In Riyadh dark secrets in hidden Arabia
by Geoff Carter

This is not only a travel book but a thought-provoking documentary on inter-cultural relationships between the different races and nationalities comprising the huge expatriate population and native Arab residents of the oil-rich peninsula.

The many characters portrayed, presented in a variety of authentic stories encountered by the author on his travels, are centred around the horrific event of a public stoning in Saudi Arabia. Some of the stories have a humorous flavour, but all are concerned with the human problems - many of them poignant - of expatriates and Arabs alike, living cheek by jowl in a society of gaping contrasts.

It would be simplistic to interpret the book as merely a critique of the harsher aspects of Arab life from a Western perspective, for in the cause of future concord, the author calls for a dialogue between the cultures of the Middle East and the West in the name of social justice and modernisation. The present strains, in what has become a multi-cultural society following the influx of millions, mostly from the Third World, anticipates the possibility of trouble in the future.

The status of women is highlighted and discussed in several dramatic episodes, and a compassionate view is taken of Asian guest workers in the light of their widespread mistreatment in the Gulf.

The rigidity of tradition would seem not merely to prevent the development of a modern mind-set, but in the perceived threat of Westernisation, to trigger an even more regressive attitude, as is shown clearly in this book. But note is also taken of the Arab outlook on the Western world, together with their horror of Western liberal values, and their passionate arguments for resisting change are recorded in detail.

An element of suspense and mystery is maintained throughout the book as the execution of the condemned victim progresses through the narrative, only interrupted by recollections of other personalities and the stories surrounding them. Is the condemned person male or female? And what was the offence? No prior information is posted by the authorities on the public punishment or execution of offenders. The attitude of many readers to the horrific episode may change considerably as the facts leading up to the execution are revealed towards the end of the book.

The prolific travel writer, **Peter Biddlecombe**, writes -

"Brilliant ! Read *Death In Riyadh* and you'll never want to buy another gallon of Saudi oil again. Anyone with any sense of decency, let alone half-a-litre of justice, should buy two copies: one to read and the other to throw at Robin Cook's ethical foreign policy ! A book of adventure and true compassion, and an un-put-downable read."

ISBN 0-9538460-1-6   Price:- £14.99

ARENA BOOKS - mass market titles

My Conflict With a Soviet Spy
The story of the Ron Evans spy case

by Eddie Miller

Ron Evans was probably the most notorious Soviet spy of British nationality working out of Scandinavia in the post-War period. Here, for the first time, the full story of the Ron Evans spy case is told in all its drama and excitement as it occurred in the mid-1960s.

Whilst on the one hand Ron Evans was a leading radio engineer with a brilliant intellect, working on sensitive defence contracts; on the other, he was a determined and deft conspirator, manipulating a wide circle of oddly assorted people to achieve his illicit ends. KGB and MI6 agents play a prominent part in this story of seething conflict, an assassination attempt, and death; and only now, in deference to the spirit of the Thirty Year rule, is it possible to reveal the true facts behind this Cold War drama.

Many nationalities and colourful individuals, including diplomats and an eccentric Finnish aristocrat, were involved in the complex intrigue surrounding Ron Evans underhand activities. The author, who unwittingly found himself in conflict with the Soviet agent, was by a curious set of circumstances led into the role of spy-hunter, which eventually led to the arrest and conviction of Ron Evans.

But that was not the end of the story. Worse was to follow. Due to an unfortunate turn of events, an MI6 agent who was implicated in a counter-plot, found that his cover was blown, and following his capture and arrest by the authorities of a neutral power, Britain's entire Scandinavian intelligence network came crashing down.

The book is illustrated with press photographs taken at the time of the events

ISBN   0-9538460-4-0   Price:- £14.99